Judicial Dialogue

Judicial Dialogue

Martin Belov (Ed.)

eleven
international publishing

Published, sold and distributed by Eleven International Publishing
P.O. Box 85576
2508 CG The Hague
The Netherlands
Tel.: +31 70 33 070 33
Fax: +31 70 33 070 30
e-mail: sales@elevenpub.nl
www.elevenpub.com

Sold and distributed in USA and Canada
Independent Publishers Group
814 N. Franklin Street
Chicago, IL 60610
USA
Order Placement: (800) 888-4741
Fax: (312) 337-5985
orders@ipgbook.com
www.ipgbook.com

Eleven International Publishing is an imprint of Boom uitgevers Den Haag.

ISBN 978-94-6236-963-4
ISBN 978-94-6274-364-9 (E-book)

Table of Contents

Introduction

The book *Judicial Dialogue* is the result of the joint effort of 13 scholars coming from leading European universities working predominantly in the fields of Constitutional Law, Comparative Constitutional Law and EU Law, and also in the spheres of Financial Law, International Public Law and International Private Law. Many of them have already published prestigious and highly visible books, book chapters or scientific papers related to judicial dialogue. The book is defined by its multidisciplinary character addressing a wide range of problems related to judicial dialogue and the role of courts in contemporary legal orders. The current volume is the result of the III Sofia Legal Science Week. This is an annual international scientific conference held at the University of Sofia 'St. Kliment Ohridski', Faculty of Law.[1]

The book provides multilayered and multifaceted analysis of judicial dialogue as a phenomenon with increasing importance in contemporary law – domestic, comparative, international and European. It provides for a critical analysis of the role of courts in multilevel constitutional games and in the context of an increasingly pluralist structure of the legal order at the beginning of the XXI century. The book combines the analysis of fundamental and conceptual issues with comparative research and topical case studies. Moreover, it explores some of the most profound implications of judicial dialogue in the EU in financial matters and in private international law and international dispute settlement. The theoretical conceptualizations of judicial dialogue are paralleled by analysis of the case law of several national courts of key importance and the jurisprudence of the Court of Justice of the European Union (CJEU) and by socio-legal and sociological research of the explored phenomenon.

Judicial dialogue is still a hot topic in the field of constitutional law, comparative constitutional law and EU constitutional law. The enhanced role of supranational expert players has triggered waves of concern among the scholars and the politicians. We are witnessing trends towards supranational technocracy. In this regard, the privileged position of international and supranational courts in determining fundamental issues with huge constitutional importance related to human rights, financial, taxation, budgetary and economic matters, environmental issues etc. is an important part of the scientific discourses on the future of democracy, the role of technocracy in our societies and constitutional systems, and the influence of this enhanced judicial standing on fundamental constitutional principles such as sovereignty, democracy and separation of powers.

1 If you are interested in receiving more information about this event, please contact Prof. Martin Belov at his e-mail: martinbelov@yahoo.com.

Moreover, we are witnessing political and judicial revolts against the decisions and the overall standing of international and supranational courts. All these factors enhance the status of domestic constitutional and supreme courts as arbiters and guardians on the point of intersection between domestic, international and supranational law. The international and supranational courts, most notably the Court of Justice of the EU, as well as the national constitutional courts, quite visibly in the case of the German Federal Constitutional Court and the Italian Constitutional Court, are becoming ultimate players in multilevel constitutional games.

The tipping point of the academic interest is not just the jurisprudence of a specific court, but rather the exchange of case law between domestic, international and supranational courts. In that regard, judicial dialogue is considered as an indicator of existing problems, as a solution to problems or as a problem itself. The visible shift towards legal realism in the last decades is reflecting and also contributing to the increasing importance of judicial dialogue.

This book will address some of the most important theoretical and practical issues of judicial dialogue conceptualized as one of the main manifestations of the role of courts in contemporary legal orders. It will start with discourses on the constitutional dimension of the problem (Part I). It will critically assess key issues in judicial dialogue on financial matters (Part II) and in the sphere of private international law and international investment (Part III). With regard to the judicial dialogue on financial matters the book will be allocated on the crossroads of two of the most important discourses in the current European academic debate. These are the discussions on judicial dialogue as the key phenomenon of supranational constitutionalism and the debates on financial constitutionalism and the role of courts in financial crisis management. Finally (Part IV), some important case studies of the engagement of the Italian and Dutch courts in judicial dialogue with the international and supranational courts and especially with the CJEU will be offered to the reader. This will allow for an insightful analysis of the judicial dialogue between some of the most important and activist domestic, international and supranational courts.

The first part of the book is devoted to the constitutional issues arising out of the judicial dialogue as a phenomenon of the constitutional, comparative constitutional and European constitutional law. It includes four contributions. These are my chapter 'Judicial Dialogue – Westphalian or Post-Westphalian Constitutional Phenomenon?' which is Chapter 1, and Chapter 2, by Patricia Popelier and Catherine Van De Heyning 'Constitutional Dialogue as an Expression of Trust and Distrust in Multilevel Governance', Chapter 3 by Ivan Ingravallo 'The Court of Justice of the EU as an EU Constitutional Court: Is It Lawful (and Desirable)?' and Chapter 4 by Aleksandra Kustra-Rogatka 'Constitutional Courts, Fundamental Rights and Judicial Dialogue with the Court of Justice of the European Union'.

Chapter 1 of the book is structured around one central research question: Is the judicial dialogue a Westphalian or post-Westphalian constitutional concept? The main assumption underlying the analysis is that we are experiencing a clash between Westphalian and post-Westphalian constitutionalism which are two phases of modern constitutional development providing for different organizing and explanatory schemes for the constitutional order. The chapter claims that judicial dialogue is among the few post-Westphalian constitutional concepts which might help us to better understand and structure the constitutional (dis)order in the age of constitutional pluralism.

Proving the post-Westphalian nature of judicial dialogue is accomplished in several analytical steps. Initially, the concepts of Westphalian and post-Westphalian constitutionalism are presented. This is done by outlining the main elements of these two concepts which are consequently compared with each other. Furthermore, judicial dialogue is presented as a transformative device for the role of courts in the course of transition from Westphalian to early post-Westphalian constitutionalism. Finally, the relationship between the judicial dialogue and key Westphalian and post-Westphalian concepts is exposed. The tension between judicial dialogue and sovereignty and constitutional supremacy as central organizing elements of the Westphalian constitutionalism and also with democracy and separation of powers is used as the central argument for its post-Westphalian nature.

Chapter 2 by Patricia Popelier and Catherine Van De Heyning proposes original conceptualization of the constitutional character of the dialogue between the CJEU and the national constitutional courts. It compares the theoretical assumptions on the aims, role and structure of judicial dialogue with the practical incentives of the national constitutional courts to engage with it and to use it for the achievement of strategic and tactical goals with constitutional importance. Indeed, the theoretical concept provided by the authors is exemplified with regard to the referencing practice of the Belgian Constitutional Court. However, this chapter is not a case study. It provides for a theoretical model tested against the judicial dialogue between the CJEU and the Belgian Constitutional Court. In the words of the authors, "aim of this chapter is to develop these propositions as a theoretical model for future research on institutional dialogues".

The authors suggest that, from the CJEU's viewpoint, the judicial dialogue aims at harmonizing the application of the EU law and at safeguarding the fundamental principles of the EU law, including those developed by the CJEU itself. However, according to them,

> over time, nationalist counter-reactions have started to transform the identity of the European Union. With clauses such as Art. 4.2 of the Treaty on the European Union (TEU), which demands respect for the national identities of Member States, and Art. 5.3 on subsidiarity, the core value of the EU legal system, centered on the internal market, is put into perspective by the dynamics between integration goals and national sovereignty claims. This gives national courts an opportunity to shift the purpose of the formal dialogue by

> arguing for national identity considerations in order to tone down the prevalence of EU law, or by questioning EU laws in light of the subsidiarity principle. These types of arguments are more easily included in constitutional narratives developed by constitutional courts. Constitutional courts have in effect opened dialogues on constitutional matters such as fundamental rights, constitutional limits to the European mandate and constitutional identity. Forcing the CJEU in such conversation, however, would make it drift away from the mechanism's initial purpose to ensure the uniform application as a precondition for an internal market.

In order to propose a feasible conceptual model for constitutional dialogues, Patricia Popelier and Catherine Van De Heyning have provided an analysis of the actors in the preliminary references dialogue. In their account, a proper analysis would take into account not only the actors directly engaged in judicial dialogue, for example, the CJEU and the national constitutional courts, but also the other actors, triggering, influencing, or otherwise involved in it. Consequently, they have outlined the role of actors that have influenced the engagement of the CJEU and the Belgian Constitutional Court in judicial dialogue.

The central role for the analytical concept of constitutional dialogue proposed by Popelier and Van De Heyning is played by the concept of trust. This is why they have suggested a multilevel concept of trust and distrust and have outlined the mechanisms to build trust at the European level based on a system of institutional and substantive controls and informal mechanisms. Furthermore, the authors have researched the incentives for the constitutional court to trust. Finally, they have provided for a case study on the trust and distrust in the formal dialogue between the Belgian Constitutional Court and the CJEU. In this case, they have outlined several types of constitutional conversations.

Popelier and Van De Heyning have come to several conclusions. In their account, the "concepts of trust and distrust are helpful to understand the complexity of institutionalized constitutional conversations". Their analysis proves that judicial dialogue is not an isolated phenomenon limited to exchange of case law between courts. The authors have emphasized the fact that

> circles of participants in the conversation are included at both levels, each with their own interests, with varying relationships of trust and distrust, and with different purposes for joining the conversation.

Another very important conclusion of the authors is

> that it is utopian to expect constitutional courts to enter into a conversation with the CJEU with the sole purpose of furthering the uniform application of the treaties in general and of the internal market in particular.

In Chapter 3, Ivan Ingravallo is focused on the way the CJEU gradually acquired the position of a constitutional court of the EU. The engagement of the CJEU in judicial dialogue with the national constitutional courts via preliminary rulings is analyzed in most of the chapters of this volume. However, the focus on the role of the CJEU as a constitutional court of the EU is especially emphasized in Chapters 3 and 4.

Chapter 3 starts with systematization of the main case law of the CJEU by virtue of which the Court emancipated itself from the Member States and upgraded its institutional standing in order to become a genuine constitutional court of the EU. According to Ingravallo, this process is intrinsically intertwined with the emancipation of the EU legal order from both the national and international law. The author believes that the establishment of a jurisprudential web of case law devoted to a system of interrelated questions legitimated the self-ascertainment of the CJEU as a constitutional court and made impossible the successful challenging of this institutional position by the Member States. In other words, the principles of primacy of EU law and autonomy of the EU legal order were both the result of the functioning of the CJEU as a constitutional court and safeguards for its status as such.

Chapter 3 outlines the main features of the CJEU as a constitutional court of the EU. The author does that by tracing the historical development of its role as the constitutional court of the European Communities and later on of the EU. Ingravallo stresses the importance of the preliminary ruling procedure combined with extensive teleological interpretation of the EU law by the CJEU for the strengthening of its constitutional position. In that regard, he outlines the emergence of an increasingly hierarchical relationship between the CJEU and the domestic courts of the EU Member States which, in his account, contributes to the standing of the CJEU as a constitutional court of the EU. The author's main claim is that the teleological interpretation of the EU law, especially the one stemming out of preliminary rulings and addressing the primacy of the EU law over the domestic law of the Member States and the autonomy of the EU legal order, is the key to understanding the way the Court has gained the key status of a constitutional court of the EU.

The author renders a critical assessment of what he calls "self-proclaimed 'constitutional' character of the CJEU". The functioning of the CJEU as a constitutional court of the EU is exposed with regard to its role in shaping and promoting key doctrines and principles of the EU law such as the primacy and direct effect of the EU law, the autonomy of the EU legal order, the principle of loyal cooperation, the human rights protection and so on. On the basis of a case law based analysis, the author comes to the conclusion that "from the viewpoint of the EU legal system there is no doubt that the Court is and considers itself as the Constitutional Court of the EU".

Furthermore, Ingravallo explores how the EU Member States accepted the standing and role of the CJEU as a constitutional court of the EU. According to him, this stance of the Member States has been reaffirmed by their acceptance of the doctrines developed by the CJEU visible also in most of the subsequent treaty reforms. The disagreements of the Member States, sometimes in the form of political or judicial revolts, are according to Ingravallo exceptional. Thus, they are actually reaffirming the CJEU's standing as a constitutional court of the EU.

Nevertheless, the relationship between the CJEU and the national constitutional courts is not always one of harmonious coexistence and mutual recognition. There are important instances of jurisprudential constitutional conflicts which foster the need for judicial dialogue. This is the special contribution of Ingravallo to the problem of judicial dialogue which he analyses from the perspective of the role of the CJEU as a constitutional court of the EU. The author outlines two main factors which, according to him, trigger concerns of the national constitutional courts related to the prointegration constitutional jurisprudence of the CJEU. These are the "progressive growth of the competences attributed to the EEC/EC/EU combined with the increasing number of its Member States". Ingravallo defines as central elements of judicial discontent the federalist trends in the jurisprudence of the CJEU and its attempts at furthering its hierarchical standing with regard to the national constitutional and supreme courts.

Finally, Ingravallo also devotes special attention to the CJEU's approach as a constitutional court in relation to international agreements concluded by the EU. He demonstrates the similarity between the approach of the CJEU and the national constitutional courts to the international treaties and uses it as a further example of the nature and role of the CJEU as a constitutional court of the EU.

Chapter 4 by Aleksandra Kustra-Rogatka focuses on the role of the multilevel system of fundamental rights protection as the key factor for triggering, influencing and shaping the dialogue between national constitutional courts and the CJEU. It explores some of the main strings and cornerstones of the judicial constitutional politics and the subsequent power constellation between the CJEU and the national constitutional courts. Kustra-Rogatka presents, through the lenses of the concept of judicial dialogue and in the light of cases with great importance, the strategies of the CJEU to enhance its standing within the emerging international and supranational judicial network and the strategies of the domestic constitutional courts to resist such power expansion. More precisely, the chapter focuses on the judicial dialogue between the CJEU and the national constitutional courts via recourse to preliminary references. In that regard, Chapters 3 and 4 have similar analytical goals.

The main object of analysis in Chapter 4 is the Melloni and the Tarricco II cases, which are important examples of judicial dialogue between the Spanish and the Italian Constitutional Courts and the CJEU. Thus, the chapter can be conceived as part of the discussion on constitutional nationalism and constitutional globalism shaped through judicial dialogue between constitutional jurisdictions – national and supranational.

Kustra-Rogatka duly notices the departure from the "strategy of splendid isolation" limiting the role of constitutional courts to domestic constitutional law towards a more activist judicial engagement in European constitutional politics. According to her, the recognition of the pluralist nature of the material constitution in the context of the EU integration is one of the main reasons for the increasing engagement of constitutional courts in multilevel judicial dialogues through preliminary references as a "proceduralized form of discourse". In this regard, Chapters 1, 3 and 4 of this volume are attempts at analyzing the judicial dialogue through the lenses of broader theoretical paradigms such as constitutional pluralism and multilevel constitutionalism.

Kustra-Rogatka problematizes the constitutional protectionism of national human rights standards by the constitutional courts of the EU Member States. This is achieved through an analysis of two very important cases – the Melloni case and the Tarricco II case. The author uses these two cases to demonstrate different approaches of the national constitutional courts with regard to the relationship between the EU law and the national constitution. Kustra-Rogatka emphasizes "the constitutional court's autonomous reasoning for a decision to lower (Melloni) or maintain (Taricco II) the constitutional standard of protection" as two strategies for engagement in multilevel constitutional politics through judicial dialogue between the national constitutional courts and the CJEU.

The author makes an interesting observation. She uses the Melloni case and the subsequent response by the Spanish Constitutional Court as an example of her finding that the engagement in judicial dialogue via preliminary references is not always the result of the desire of the national constitutional courts to escape isolationism in the sphere of domestic constitutional law. Kustra-Rogatka suggests that "despite submitting questions for preliminary ruling, they [the national constitutional courts] wish to mark their autonomy and maintain their position as the ultimate player in multilevel constitutional games".

Moreover, the author has studied the so-called "threatening references of appeal".[2] She compares and presents the Tarricco II and the Gauweiler cases as examples of resurgent constitutional nationalism, as instruments for reaffirmation of the standing of the national constitutional courts as ultimate players in multilevel constitutional games using the threat of reactivation of constitutional control with regard to the EU law and as occasions for setting 'counter limits'.

Nevertheless, according to Kustra-Rogatka:

---

2 *See* D. Paris as cited in Chapter 4.

> contrary to the FCC's order for reference in the Gauweiler case, the Constitutional Court's decision to initiate the preliminary ruling procedure in the so-called Taricco II case should, however, be seen rather as an expression of common sense, compromise and willingness to cooperate, as the Constitutional Court rejected two extreme alternatives: 1) the application of the controlimiti doctrine without initiating the preliminary ruling procedure 2) the full acceptance of the application of the Taricco test in the Italian legal system.

Kustra-Rogatka also emphasizes the novel approach of the CJEU in Tarricco II regarding the relative primacy of the EU law over the domestic constitutional orders. She highlights the use of the common constitutional traditions as alternative limitation of the primacy of the EU law existing in parallel with the national constitutional identity. Thus, the author explicitly shares the thesis launched by Marco Bassini and Oreste Pollicino and suggests that "the CJEU accepted in Taricco II Constitutional Court's suggestion to identify common constitutional traditions (but not constitutional identity) as a lingua franca of co-operative constitutionalism in Europe".[3]

Kustra-Rogatka finally comes to the conclusion that the current system of multilevel constitutional protection of human rights "means that constitutional courts are forced to reevaluate their role as national guardians of respecting human rights". She criticizes the unwillingness of the Italian Constitutional Court to cope with the conciliatory approach of the CJEU in Tarricco II and its preference to stick to controlimiti and constitutional identity rather than to multilevel European cooperative constitutionalism based on primacy of EU law tempered by common constitutional traditions.

Chapter 4 by Aleksandra Kustra-Rogatka and Chapter 11 by Silvia Marino are engaged in an interesting intellectual dialogue. This is due to the fact that they both devote special attention to the Tarricco II case as the cornerstone of the contemporary judicial dialogue between the CJEU and the Italian Constitutional Court.

The second part of the book also comprises four chapters devoted to the judicial dialogue on financial issues. Chapter 5 titled 'Are Courts Engaged in a "Dialogue" on Financial Matters?' is the contribution of Cesare Pinelli, Chapter 6 called 'The Role of Courts in the Eurozone' is by Gavin Barrett, Chapter 7 by Joan Solanes Mullor is labeled 'What Goes Up Must Go Up: Raising Judicial Scrutiny over the European Central Bank through Judicial Dialogue' and Stefano Dorigo's Chapter 8 is designated as 'Taxpayer Protection in the European Legal Context: A Dialogue of the Deaf between National and Supranational Courts?'

Chapter 5 by Cesare Pinelli aims at exploring the courts' contribution to the resolution of the Eurozone crisis by virtue of judicial dialogue. The principle aim of the author

---

3 *See* M. Bassini and O. Pollicino as well as M. Bonelli as cited in Chapter 4.

is to present the broader repercussions of the courts' involvement in the financial crisis management. According to Pinelli,

> scholars have extensively treated the question of whether this case law changed the relationship between courts and the political branches, while minor attention was devoted to the issue whether courts continued to interact among themselves when it comes to financial matters, and eventually to the problem how such interaction may take place.

Hence, this chapter aims at filling in this gap in the scientific discourse. Pinelli exposes the huge divergence of opinions in the scientific literature on the role of courts during the financial crisis. He points out that

> going from the 'dramatic increase' of the judicial power to the system's 'dejudicialization', these assumptions cover the whole spectrum of possibilities regarding the well-known dichotomy between judicial activism and judicial self-restraint.

The analysis is accomplished in several steps. Initially, Pinelli reflects on whether and how courts interact on financial matters. Then he engages in the debate on the courts' reaction to the financial crisis and the responses given by the courts to alleged breaches of fundamental rights and to the legality of measures adopted during the Eurozone crisis. The next analytical step is the discussion of the procedural limits to judicial review. The author then presents the French Constitutional Council's ruling and the Irish Supreme Court's preliminary reference to CJEU. He devotes a lot of attention to the case law of the German Federal Constitutional Court taken not in isolation but in the course of an intense judicial dialogue with the CJEU that led to important practical and conceptual results. Pinelli engages in exploration of the concrete parameters of the judicial dialogue on financial matters between the CJEU and the German Federal Constitutional Court. Thus, he provides detailed analysis of the relevant case law, for example, OMT, Gauweiler, Weiss and Lisbon. Pinelli includes as part of his analysis of the judicial dialogue on financial matters cases such as Pringle which originate from other jurisdictions. Finally, the author compares the German Federal Constitutional Court approach with that of the CJEU and arrives at important conclusions.

Gavin Barrett's Chapter 6 is devoted to the role of the courts in the Eurozone as "the epicenter of much of the European Union's constitutional evolution in recent times". The main aim of Chapter 6 is to expose the engagement of both the CJEU and the national courts in dealing with Eurozone and financial crisis management matters and thus also with the further development of the financial constitutionalism in the EU.

Both Gavin Barrett and Cesare Pinelli observe the reluctance of the CJEU to engage in the financial crisis management. Nevertheless, according to both the authors, the CJEU played an important role in promoting the capacity and competence of the EU level political players in coping with the crisis. Thus, judicial self-restraint was not detrimental to the functioning of the CJEU as a partner of the European Central Bank (ECB), the Council, the European Commission and the European Parliament in coping with the financial crisis management. The main contribution of the CJEU according to both Barrett and Pinelli was the support for the crisis management measures, especially those of the ECB, paralleled by reasonable restraint for activist engagement in sensitive political issues. This has been done to an extent through a judicial dialogue with a concerned German Federal Constitutional Court and to a lesser extent, through other national constitutional courts. In this regard, Chapters 5 and 6 critically assess cornerstone decisions of the CJEU adopted in the course of vertical judicial dialogue with national constitutional courts, for example, the Gauweiler and Pringle cases.

Barrett classifies the case law of the CJEU into "pre-crisis era case law, crisis-era rulings and post-crisis era jurisprudence". He points out the fact that the role of the CJEU in the Economic and Monetary Union or the EMU was far less visible than in the construction and further development of the European communities and later on of the EU outside of the realm of financial constitutionalism. Nevertheless, he provides an insightful research on the precrisis case law of the CJEU in the domain of the EMU, for example, *Commission v. European Central Bank* and *Commission v. Council.*

Both Barrett and Pinelli appeal for a moderate and well-founded scientific evaluation of the degree of activism and involvement of the CJEU and the national constitutional courts in the financial crisis management. They both agree that the degree of involvement of courts in financial matters has visibly increased during the crisis period. However, they also point to the fact that CJEU and most of the national constitutional courts (with the exception of the German Federal Constitutional Court or the GFCC) were adhering to judicial self-restraint and leaving the financial crisis management to the political institutions.

Moreover, both Barrett and Ingravallo in Chapters 6 and 3, bring to the fore the fact that the CJEU was very active in the formative decades of the European integration when a decisive push was needed in order to pave the way for intense integration resulting in the EU. However, they both suggest that during the last decades, the self-restraint of the CJEU prevails. In the words of Gavin Barrett:

> What it is perhaps key to recall is that Van Gend en Loos, Costa and the like were decided at a time when judicial activism was needed to advance the cause of European integration. In contrast, the major euro-crisis cases were decided when the safeguarding of European integration needed something quite differ-

> ent viz., that the law not become an obstacle. Thanks to the case law of the Court of Justice, this need was met.

Barrett delimits three types of crisis-era case law of the CJEU: First, rulings concerning the legality of general developments or reforms altering the structure or underpinnings of EMU; second, rulings linked to the fallout of rescue packages and the conditionality imposed on Member States as a result; third, sticking to Fabbrini terms, cases "reviewing regulatory or legislative measures pushing for greater financial integration against the opposition of a single member state".[4]

Barrett provides an insightful analysis of the first group of cases focusing on Pringle, Gauweiler and Weiss. He suggests a very interesting interpretation of the Pringle case. According to Barrett, Pringle is the continuation of two types of case law of the CJEU. First, it demonstrates continuity with the "'Court's teleological approach' in 'questions like supremacy and direct effect in earlier cases like Costa v ENEL and Van Gend en Loos'". Second, in Barrett's account, Pringle

> also continued a stance of deference to the political decision-making apparatus in a highly politically controversial area which is also reminiscent of its approach in Commission v. Council – a case that effectively ushered in the economic crisis by allowing the Council to paralyze the operation of the original Stability and Growth Pact. The 2004 case involved judicial deference in the face of political misbehavior. The 2012 case involved deference in the face of political action necessary to safeguard the Eurozone's very existence.

Barrett comes to very important conclusions regarding the key trends in the jurisprudential development of the EMU. They stem out of the analysis of the Pringle and Gauweiler cases. According to Barrett,

> Gauweiler marks another step along the route first traced by Pringle away from the original rule-based EMU to a more policy-based approach. Put another way, EMU seems to have been moving away from what might be termed its original 'blind watchmaker' form of governance (in which simple adherence to rules is expected to produce by itself the necessary elements of a functioning economic and monetary union) towards a model involving a much more discretionary and interventionist role for institutions like the ECB and for the European Stability Mechanism. Ultimately, what is most significant about Pringle and Gauweiler is that both are permissive judgments allowing the putting in

4 *See* F. Fabbrini as cited in Chapter 6.

> place and operation of what Fabbrini terms 'key components of the new architecture of EMU'.

Barrett also stipulates that "further contribution to this permissive process" has been made by a subsequent CJEU decision in that context, namely Weiss. According to the author "the case can be regarded as Gauweiler II". Moreover, Barrett suggests that in Weiss "the Court expressly confirmed its Pringle-Gauweiler approach". Barrett comes to the important conclusion that

> overall, Gauweiler and Weiss have all seen the Court of Justice decline to see the law frustrate what, if it is not a revolution in economic and monetary union is at least a major evolution – a shift away from the original rule-based EMU to a more policy-based approach involving a much more discretionary and interventionist role for institutions like the ECB and for the European Stability Mechanism and less trust in the efficacy of a rigidly literal approach to rules to safeguard the continued existence of the Eurozone.

The author also poses another very important question:

> why national courts have been involved in adjudicating on EMU-related issues in the first place, given the European nature of the issues involved, which would seem to make adjudication by a European-level jurisdiction the more natural place to which to have recourse.

Another central concern for Barrett is not only why the national courts engaged extensively in EMU matters but also whether such involvement is desirable. The author gives several answers to these questions which are of crucial importance for understanding the courts' involvement in EMU issues. Barrett outlines three arguments in favor and seven arguments against the involvement of national courts in EMU issues. Such a systematic approach to the advantages and disadvantages of this type of engagement is original and constitutes a major theoretical contribution.

Moreover, Barrett systematizes the main issues "upon which national courts have been called upon to adjudicate". He differentiates between "architecture vs. bailout-related cases", *ex ante* challenges, *ex post* challenges and indirect challenges to European norms by reference to European standards and challenges to the substance of measures or alleged procedural infringements.

Finally, the author arrives at several conclusions. He outlines, in a very systematic and convincing way, eight generalizable lessons that can be learned from such national cases related to the involvement of national courts in EMU issues. The general conclusion drawn by Gavin Barrett is that

> one of the most prominent features of judicial approach to the Eurozone at both national and supranational level, has been to stand aside to let the other branches of Government or governance forge ahead.

He believes that this reluctance and self-restraint had one major positive outcome. It allowed the political institutions to do their job and save the Eurozone.

Chapter 7 by Joan Solanes Mullor addresses one fundamental issue which is the problem of the legitimacy and accountability of supranational expert institutions in general and the ECB in particular. The chapter assesses the contribution of the CJEU and the national courts in promoting such legitimacy and accountability of the ECB through vertical judicial dialogue.

Joan Solanes Mullor's Chapter 7, similar to the contributions of Cesare Pinelli, Gavin Barrett and Ivan Ingravallo, provides an analysis of the most important CJEU decisions in the sphere of financial constitutionalism, for example, Gauweiler and Weiss. However, the approach and the ultimate aim of the research of these contributors differ according to the specific object of exploration underlying their respective chapters.

Chapter 7 commences with a report on putting the issue of judicial control of the decisions of the ECB via judicial dialogue in context. This is the context of agencification – a process that has gained momentum in recent decades and was in the center of the debates on the rise of supranational technocratic government. In Solanes Mullor's text, the ECB is considered to be paramount and paradigmatic example of agencification.

Solanes Mullor presents the conceptual logic underlying the agencification as part of the theory and practice of the 'regulatory state'. He differentiates the issues of legitimacy and accountability of the EU agencies, the ECB in particular. The author outlines the different tools for holding the EU agencies, including the ECB, accountable and shows the secondary role initially played by judicial scrutiny of their activity which has been pushed aside in favor of administrative control.

Similar to the papers of Gavin Barrett and Cesare Pinelli, Joan Solanes Mullor provides an analysis of the famous Gauweiler and Weiss cases. However, he does that from a particular perspective – the judicial dialogue between the GFCC and the CJEU underlined by the conceptual problems of accountability and especially of the (lack of) sufficient democratic legitimacy of the ECB.

Joan Solanes Mullor differentiates between substantive and procedural judicial control over the decisions of the ECB. In his account, the CJEU activated via preliminary ruling of the GFCC, accomplished a combined review, thus setting a new mixed standard of judicial review with procedural and substantive components. According to the author

> just as the preliminary request for procedural review by the BVerfG pointed to deeper issues regarding the legitimacy of the ECB's decision-making, ultra vires

> control of the ECB would provide, at a deeper level, a means for ultra vires control of the general powers of the EU.

Here Solanes Mullor makes an important claim. He believes that

> in this context, oversight of ECB's actions is instrumental to the primary objective of the BVerfG, which is not concerned about establishing the specific standard of judicial review of policymaking decisions of the ECB per se. Although defining the standard is an internal affair of the EU, the repercussions the standard has on the relationship between Member States and the EU essentially transforms the question into a challenge of the legitimacy of EU integration from the national perspective.

Solanes Mullor outlines the strategy and main features of the judicial dialogue between the CJEU and the GFCC in Gauweiler and Weiss. According to him, the GFCC was aiming at a broader review of the activity of the ECB touching upon the principle issue of the democratic legitimacy of the EU institutions whereas CJEU avoided it by reducing the control to ultra vires review. Solanes Mullor comes to the intermediate conclusion that "despite the restraint of the CJEU, Gauwelier and Weiss led to a new standard of judicial review for EU agencies". He defines this new standard as a "mixed standard in that it contains both procedural and substantive components".

The author provides for an original analysis of the procedural and substantial elements of the review. He suggests that although CJEU left large discretion to the ECB – at least larger than the GFCC wanted – it anyway set a precedent which opened the way for imposing further limitations of the competences of the ECB by virtue of substantive review based on the implementation of a proportionality test of its activities. According to Solanes Mullor, the "mixed standard of judicial review" of the activities of the ECB which have been triggered by the Member States, more precisely by the GFCC, in the course of judicial dialogue with the CJEU "is stricter than those traditionally applied to EU agencies". One of the main claims of the author is

> that Gauwelier and Weiss add a substantive component to the proportionality test which, combined with the already well-known procedural elements, establishes clear limits on the policymaking power of the ECB. This mixed standard of judicial review is stricter than the long-standing and highly deferential standard that had been developed over the last decades by the CJEU to review EU agency actions.

Joan Solanes Mullor comes to the conclusion that

> the EU agencification process and the questions over the role and boundaries of judicial review had largely remained an internal affair of EU institutions with minimal involvement of national organs. The CJEU's approach in Gauwelier and Weiss substantially breaks with this long-standing pattern regarding the judicial standard of review developed during the EU agencification process, especially with regards the substantive review introduced under the proportionality test. In this new approach, the initiative at the national level has been determinant, and the raising of a stricter standard of judicial review resulted from dialogical interaction between the national and EU levels.

The author also emphasizes the fact that the judicial dialogue between the CJEU and the GFCC

> led, for the first time, to discussions over the legitimacy of the EU agencification process at the EU judicial level and reformulated the hitherto limited proportionality test into a more powerful judicial tool for EU agency oversight.

Another important conclusion by Joan Solanes Mullor is that

> successful recourse to the preliminary ruling not only bolsters the involvement of national organs because it was activated by a national court. Citizens now have an easier avenue to challenge EU agency actions by going through their national courts rather than being forced to follow the path of the action for annulment procedure with its restrictive standing doctrine for individuals.

The author also highlights the fact front that "substantive and strict scrutiny based on fundamental rights represent an unexplored avenue for oversight of the EU agencification process. Here again, judicial dialogue may prove determinant as a trigger mechanism".

Chapter 8 by Stefano Dorigo opens a discussion on the rights of the individual in his capacity as a taxpayer. The author emphasizes two types of asymmetries which are detrimental to the taxpayer's rights. First, while the human person in his capacity as an individual is subject to a plethora of human rights in his capacity as a taxpayer is rather subjected to the discretion of the state. In other words, the taxpayer's rights and his overall standing towards the state is definitely limited in comparison to the general human rights protection of the individual. This is explained by Dorigo with the still predominant understanding that taxation belongs to the 'hard core' of state sovereignty and thus enjoys special protection as a device for securing the public interest.

The second asymmetry detected by Dorigo is the increased protection of the taxpayer in international and EU law in comparison to national law. Dorigo underlines that this increased protection does not stem from the international or EU law itself but is actually granted by an extensive human rights interpretation by the international and supranational courts and especially by the CJEU. According to him "supranational courts afford the taxpayers rights well beyond the strictly textual interpretation of the international norms in which they are embodied". In this regard, Dorigo devotes special attention to the case law of both the CJEU and the European Court of Human Rights addressing the protection of the person in its capacity as taxpayer and thus providing for taxpayer's rights.

Furthermore, Dorigo exposes the difficulties in transposing of supranational case law and its achievements in the domain of taxpayer's rights in the national systems. This is done by virtue of research of three rights of crucial importance for the protection of the taxpayer. These are the taxpayer's right to be heard, the *ne bis in idem* principle concerning tax claims and the prohibition of self-incrimination. The author demonstrates that while the Italian courts in principle accept the need to comply with the decisions of the CJEU and the European Court of Human Rights (ECtHR), in practice they actually deviate from them trying to avoid the granting of the taxpayer's rights provided by the jurisprudence of the international and supranational courts.

This situation is symbolically defined by Stefano Dorigo as a "dialogue between deaf". He outlines the main features of this phenomenon and critically assesses its most problematic aspects.

Stefano Dorigo suggests that there is a huge mismatch between the protection of the taxpayer's rights on international and EU level and at the domestic level. He outlines two main reasons for this situation – the broad and vague formulation of human rights in international and supranational law and the adherence of the domestic constitutions to the prevalence of the interests of the state to human rights in the sphere of taxation.

One of the main claims Stefano Dorigo makes is that nationalism in the domain of taxation must be moderated and tempered by virtue of the application of international and supranational standards related to the taxpayer's rights. The author believes that this can be achieved only through an open and sincere judicial dialogue between the national, international and supranational courts. According to Dorigo, the objective precondition for the success of such enterprise, for example, the gradual harmonization of domestic taxation principles and standards with international and supranational ones, must be paralleled by a paradigmatic shift from legal nationalism in taxation towards a more transnational and supranational tax order superseding the egoisms and particularities of the distinct national tax orders. In his opinion, this also implies change of attitude and the legal culture of the judges.

Finally, Dorigo makes several proposals for strengthening the dialogue between the courts in the tax area. They are a logical result of his main thesis that judicial dialogue on tax matters and especially the dialogue focused on taxpayer's rights must be fostered as a tool for achievement of less nationalistic and more human rights oriented approach towards taxation. This claim is grounded not so much on functional needs for tax harmonization but rather on the transformation of the functions of taxation from a mere device for securing public revenues aiming at the assurance of a financially stable statehood into an instrument for wealth redistribution for broader social purposes.

Dorigo believes that formal judicial dialogue, based on preliminary rulings, is important but also deficient to an extent. Its main problem, according to the author, consists in its publicity which makes this form of dialogue prone to populism which is why Stefano Dorigo suggests that the engagement should also include alternative forms of judicial dialogue. In his account, such forms may be, for example, mutual training initiatives and informal joint deliberative bodies that should produce increased knowledge and awareness of the national judges of the emergent international and supranational standards in the field of tax law in general and in the domain of taxpayer's rights protection in particular.

The third part of the book is devoted to judicial dialogue in private international law and international dispute settlement. It comprises Chapter 9 by Florian Heindler, 'Judicial Dialogue and the Pluralist Structure of the Legal Order at the Beginning of the XXI Century' and Chapter 10 by François Andia 'The CJEU's Extensive Conception of the EU Legal Order – An Impediment to Judicial Dialogue. CJEU's Achmea Case, a just Judicial War?'

Florian Heindler starts with a distinction between 'domestic' and 'foreign' from the viewpoint of private international law. He highlights the different perspectives on what 'foreign law' really is. Heindler researches the concept of 'foreign law' from an institutional perspective as well as from the viewpoint of the individual judge. Furthermore, he outlines the advantages of the pluralist approach in comparison to the dualist approach to foreign law. More precisely, Heindler criticizes the fact that the dualist approach ignores the supranational and international dimensions of the *lex fori* since the foreign law nowadays usually comprises the foreign domestic legal order and also the EU law and the international law to which the foreign state is bound. Thus, he engages in the broader discussion on legal pluralism from the particular perspective of private international law.

Heindler explores the different approaches to foreign law used by the courts. He critically analyses the different methods used by the courts for determining the content of foreign law. In this regard, he devotes special attention to the formal and informal judicial networking. The author engages in the discussion on judicial dialogue exactly from the viewpoint of the capacity of judicial networks to improve the knowledge on foreign law.

Florian Heindler provides an analysis of the issues stemming out of the predominant approach which clearly distinguishes between domestic and foreign law thus drawing clear demarcation lines in a dualist way. In this regard, he indirectly engages in the debate on the future of dualism and pluralism as ordering paradigms for legal orders and as platforms for judicial dialogue. The author focuses on the deficiencies of the use of foreign judicial decisions by domestic courts. He critically assesses the problems stemming from the use of foreign judicial decisions and also the issues produced by self-restraint from engagement in horizontal judicial dialogue.

Finally, Heindler concludes that

> the use of contemporary communication technology and formal and informal networks coincides with a more flexible approach to the concepts of foreign and domestic. The judicial dialogue in a pluralist system of legal order affects civil courts dealing with cross-border cases as well.

In Chapter 10, François Andia analyses the impact of a recent CJEU case, the 'Achmea' case, on the future of the bilateral investment treaties in the EU. This is done from the viewpoint of the concept of judicial dialogue. According to the author, although the dialogue has been initiated by the arbitration tribunal it has been actually prevented by the CJEU. Andia compares the CJEU's judgment in the Achmea' case to a "political murder". This is due to the fact that the decision could have a potentially heavy negative impact on "the intra-EU investment arbitration motivated by political ulterior reasons".

Andia stipulates that "CJEU declared this Tribunal's arbitration clause a threat to the EU legal order's autonomy". In this regard, he raises the question: "To what extent was the CJEU's decision necessary to protect the EU legal order autonomy from this 'outside' arbitrator?" Another issue, brought to the fore by Andia and described by the author as "political assassination" is whether such an attitude by the CJEU, is just and necessary.

The fourth part of the book is devoted to the engagement of national courts in judicial dialogue. It provides for an insightful research into the discourses on judicial dialogue in Italy and the Netherlands. The fourth part comprises two chapters which critically assess the involvement of the Italian Constitutional Court and the Dutch courts in judicial dialogue with the CJEU. Chapter 11 by Silvia Marino is titled 'The Dialogue between the Italian Constitutional Court and the Court of Justice of the European Union' and Chapter 12 by Michiel Duchateau is called 'Are Dutch Judges in Search of a Dialogue?'

Chapter 11 by Silvia Marino is devoted to the judicial dialogue between the Italian Constitutional Court and the CJEU. It traces the hallmarks of the history of this dialogue by outlining the cases with structural importance for the development of both the EU law and the domestic constitutional law of Italy. The analysis of the case law allows the exposure of the emergence of key paradigms of the EU constitutional law such as the primacy, direct effect and the respect for the national constitutional identity as well as of fundamental paradigms of the integration of the Italian constitutional order into the EU order, for example, the uneasy recognition of the just mentioned judicially shaped doctrines of the EU law and the concept of 'controlimiti' established by the Italian Constitutional Court in response to the EU constitutional expansion. An important feature of the analysis provided by Marino is that it reflects not only the judicial dialogue between the CJEU and the Italian Constitutional Court, but also the responses to similar problems given by the constitutional courts of other EU Member States.

What is particularly interesting is that Marino clearly demonstrates the shifts in the attitude of the Italian Constitutional Court towards the EC and later – the EU, which produced periods of EU skepticism and restraint and EU friendliness. The author outlines the initial launch of the doctrine of 'controlimiti' as a possible shield or even a sword against excessive expansion of the EU law in 'sacred domains' of domestic constitutionalism. She analyses the phase of disuse of this concept due to enhanced permissive consensus of EU integration and the subsequent and recent rebirth of constitutional nationalism in the case law of the Italian Constitutional Court.

A very interesting part of the analysis provided by Marino concerns the different solutions given by the Italian Constitutional Court with regard to the issue of how the Italian courts should proceed in case of alleged potential simultaneous infringement of both the EU law and the Italian Constitution. Here the author critically assesses the changes in the procedure and more precisely the sequence of approaching the CJEU and the Italian Constitutional Court. She also analyses the relatively recent shift in the self-perception by the Italian Constitutional Court allowing for its involvement in direct judicial dialogue with the CJEU via preliminary references.

Particularly important is the analysis provided by the author devoted to the Italian Constitutional Court standing with regard to international law and more precisely to the legal effect and hierarchical standing of international human rights law (case law of the ECtHR included) in the Italian legal order.

Similar to several chapters in this volume, Silvia Marino devotes special attention to the "Tarricco saga". She has a particular approach to it in the context of highlighting the main trends of the judicial dialogue in which the Italian Constitutional Court is involved. In that context, Marino defines it as "the last chapter of this judicial dialogue".

It should be mentioned that the unexpected conflict-oriented response of the Italian Constitutional Court to the decision of the CJEU in Tarricco II is critically assessed by two of the contributors to this volume – Aleksandra Kustra-Rogatka and Silvia Marino. Both authors highlight this phenomenon as an indicator of the changing, less conciliatory and less EU friendly, mood in the relationship between the Italian Constitutional Court and the CJEU. Silvia Marino gives three possible explanations for this novel attitude of the Italian Constitutional Court which can be read in Chapter 11.

Chapter 12 by Michiel Duchateau provides a provocative and insightful analysis of the novel tendencies of slowly emerging judicial constitutional protectionism accomplished by the Dutch administrative courts. These courts are known to be rather EU-friendly and to avoid engaging in any form of national constitutional protectionism or constitutional nationalism. Dutch constitutionalism is an advanced example of sincere and extensive application of open statehood where EU law and international law have clear predominance over domestic law. Furthermore, as Duchateau explicitly explains, sovereignty is not an extensively applied concept in Dutch constitutionalism.

However, the rejection of the Treaty on the Constitution for Europe in 2005, the subsequent theoretical and political debates, the rise of extreme right parties and the recent developments in the case law of the Dutch administrative courts lead Michiel Duchateau to pose the question: "Is all quiet on the Dutch front?" One of the claims of the chapter is that the analyzed decisions of the Dutch courts may be signaling a novel tendency which is largely underresearched and remains unnoticed while it may be indicative of a new turn in the attitude of the courts towards the EU integration in the Netherlands.

In this regard, Chapter 12 is devoted to the emergent trends for increased activism of Dutch courts on the issue of the relationship between the Dutch Constitution and the EU law with regard to their recent case law. Michiel Duchateau's aim is "to assess their potential as the start of a judicial dialogue on the fundamental issue of the Europeanization of core constitutional values". In his account, these recent judicial decisions adopted by the three most important Dutch administrative courts

> has raised the question whether following the German example of (in)direct judicial dialogues with the CJEU, as the Netherlands Scientific Council for Government Policy (WRR) suggested in 2007, would be the best way forward.

The author puts forward an intriguing and challenging question: "Invoking the Constitution: What is it good for?" In order to answer that question and to highlight the possible future developments of the Dutch case law on the issue of the primacy of the EU law and the necessary safeguards for the supremacy of the domestic constitution, Duchateau invokes the standing of the UK Supreme Court and the German Federal Constitutional Court on this issue stemming out of their jurisprudence. He proposes arguments for the advantages of following the standing of the UK Supreme Court instead of that of the German Federal Constitutional Court in the Dutch constitutional context.

Duchateau formulated his main arguments on why following the German approach is inadequate in the case of the Netherlands as follows:

> The Dutch constitution hardly contains any provisions that clearly cannot be deviated from by EU law and there still is no Dutch constitutional court. More importantly, this approach does not seem to sit well with the Dutch traditionally open approach to international law and the clear choice of the constitutional legislator in 1983 to stick to this open approach in principle.

That is why the author prefers the UK approach to the issue of the relationship between the EU law and the domestic constitution as provided in the Miller and HS2 cases of the UK Supreme Court. He suggests that

> such a line of case law could stress that Europeanisation is an exercise of sovereignty rather than a limitation of it, while still assuring the unrestrained application of the EU law in the Dutch legal order. Like the (UK) European Communities Act 1972, this could serve as a good and insightful evidence of the clear choice that the Dutch constitutional legislator made in 1983.

Part I
Constitutional Aspects of Judicial Dialogue

1 Judicial Dialogue – Westphalian or Post-Westphalian Constitutional Phenomenon?

*Martin Belov**

1.1 Introduction

This chapter is based on the general assumption that we are undergoing transition from one phase of constitutional development to another. It consists in the shift from Westphalian to post-Westphalian constitutionalism[1] which is to a great extent predetermined by several coinciding factors. The most important among them are the information and technology revolution, the globalization, the structural transformation of capitalism and the increasing complexity of the socio-political orders. These are phenomena of great importance which are profoundly transforming the socio-legal conditions of our constitutional orders. However, they are not paralleled by sufficient advance of the legal and constitutional orders producing adequate adjustment to the changing social and technological context. We are witnessing the questioning and pressures for redefinition of paradigms, principles and concepts with fundamental importance for constitutional law. The principles of sovereignty, democracy and welfare state, the concepts of jurisdiction and territoriality of power, the hierarchy as universal explanatory and ordering model of the constitutional order and as key structure of constitutional semiotics are put under increasing pressure for adjustment by the phenomena mentioned in this paragraph.

The crisis of Westphalian constitutionalism has become evident during the last decades. It produced a crisis of territoriality[2] and territorial constitutional politics, a crisis of sovereignty and hierarchy and a crisis of parliamentarism and representative democracy. Moreover, we are witnessing the emergence of relatively novel phenomena such as con-

---

* The author is grateful to Emanuel Castellarin and Giuseppe Martinico for their extremely helpful comments on this chapter.

1 For more about the concept of Westphalian constitutionalism, *see* N. Walker, 'The Idea of Constitutional Pluralism', *Modern Law Review*, Vol. 65, No. 3, 2002, pp. 317-359, M. Belov, 'The Challenges to Westphalian Constitutional Geometry in the Age of Supranational Constitutionalism, Global Governance and Information Revolution', *in* Belov M (Ed.), *Global Constitutionalism and Its Challenges to Westphalian Constitutional Law*, Oxford, Hart Publishing, 2018, pp. 13-81 and the contribution of N. Walker in Avbelj M, Komárek J (Eds.), Four Visions of Constitutional Pluralism, *EUI Working Paper Law*, No. 21, 2008, p. 8.

2 *See* M. Antonsich, 'On territory, the nation-state and the crisis of the hyphen', *Progress in Human Geography*, Vol. 33, No. 6, 2009, pp. 789-806.

stitutional identity, judicial dialogue, post-territorial and aterritorial forms of power, fragmentation of sovereignty, financial constitutionalism and so on.

In that context, the increasing importance of the courts both within and outside of statehood is remarkable. The emergence of a 'global judicial empire'[3] is triggered by the rising prominence and political role of international and supranational courts and especially by their engagement in judicially produced networked constitutional politics.

However, in recent years the fragile and still emerging shapes of post-Westphalian constitutionalism are also put under huge pressure. Their *raison d'etre*, their future and desirability are increasingly contested. Neo-nationalism, illiberal democracies,[4] populist constitutionalism,[5] anti-global constitutionalism and global anti-constitutionalism[6] are questioning and even denying the need for structural reshaping of the constitutional order and for reform of Westphalian constitutionalism aiming at the construction and development of supranational and global constitutionalism. They are proposing alternative visions for constitutional reform which are actually meant to lead to reconstruction and reestablishment of conservative and nationalist versions of Westphalian constitutionalism. The 'back to the roots of Westphalian statehood' movements which are currently gaining momentum are focusing and trying to build on authoritarian, illiberal or revolutionary trends in the constitutional history of the XIX and the XX centuries presented as another version of 'true constitutionalism'. In fact, they are to a certain extent an 'invented tradition'.[7]

Hence, currently we are witnessing a double crisis of both Westphalian and post-Westphalian constitutionalism. However, the crisis is at times also an opportunity. A double crisis may constitute even a double opportunity. My general suggestion is that we need to rethink and reconsider the paradigms, principles, concepts and normative ideologies of traditional or Westphalian constitutionalism in order to reassess their adequateness to the contemporary socio-legal and technological conditions. We will defi-

3 *See* M. Belov, 'Global Rule of Law instead of Global Democracy? Legitimacy of Global Judicial Empire on the Edge of Westphalian and post-Westphalian Constitutionalism', *in* Belov, M (Ed.) *The Role of Courts in Contemporary Legal Orders*, Eleven, The Hague (forthcoming). For comparable concepts framing the global system of increasingly networked courts, *see also* A. Wiener & Ph. Liste, 'Lost Without Translation? Cross-Referencing and a New Global Community of Courts', *Indiana Journal of Global Legal Studies*, Vol. 21, No. 1, 2014, pp. 263-296 and A.-M. Slaughter, 'A Global Community of Courts', *Harvard International Law Journal*, Vol. 44, No. 1, 2003, p. 191 and the following.

4 *See* F. Zakaria, *The Future of Freedom: Illiberal Democracy at Home and Abroad*, W.W. Norton & Company, New York, 2007, pp. 22-43, F. Zakaria, 'The Rise of Illiberal Democracy', *Foreign Affairs*, Vol. 76, No. 6, 2007 and A. Pap, *Democratic Decline in Hungary: Law and Society in an Illiberal Democracy*, Oxford, Routledge, 2019.

5 *See* P. Blokker, 'Populist Constitutionalism', available at: *Verfassungsblog.de*, 2017, p. 1-5 and L. Corrias, 'Populism in a Constitutional Key: Constituent Power, Popular Sovereignty and Constitutional Identity', *European Constitutional Law Review*, Vol. 12, No. 1, 2016, pp. 6-26.

6 *See* K. Lachmayer, 'Counter-Developments to Global Constitutionalism' *in* M. Belov (Ed.) *Global Constitutionalism and Its Challenges to Westphalian Constitutional Law*, Oxford, Hart publishing, 2018, pp. 89-99.

7 *See* E. Hobsbaum & T. Ranger, The Invention of Traditions, Cambridge, Cambridge University Press, 1983.

nitely live in a civilization which will be profoundly different from the one we have known for the last couple of centuries. This process seems to be to an extent inevitable and objective. The reason is that the information, technology and AI revolution will bring us very soon to a novel level of social order which will also require novel constitutional responses. Hence, we are in great need of new constitutional paradigms, concepts, principles and ideologies that will allow us to master the complexity of the incoming world.

In that regard, this chapter aims to address the question of whether judicial dialogue is a Westphalian or post-Westphalian constitutional concept or both. Indeed, judicial dialogue emerged as early as the second half of the XX century. This means that judicial dialogue is not an entirely a new concept. It is partially rooted in the late Westphalian constitutional modernity. However, the first signs of transition towards post-Westphalian constitutionalism were evident since the end of the XX century. In addition, judicial dialogue is not comfortable with many key postulates of Westphalian constitutionalism. It is hardly reconcilable with parliamentocentrism, legicentrism and the idea of the purely apolitical role of the courts. It is incompatible with Westphalian constitutional and international law based on exclusive sovereignty, absolute constitutional supremacy, executive and legislative power driven international relations and *pacta sunt servanda* and state consent principles.[8]

Judicial dialogue puts the courts, especially the constitutional and supreme courts as well as the international and supranational courts, in the position of ultimate players in multilevel and pluralist constitutional and constituent power games.[9] It suggests the existence of post-sovereign judicial networks mastering the complexity of the constitutional web of meanings, interests and claims for authority, validity and legitimacy. Thus, judicial dialogue goes beyond national and popular sovereignty, hierarchy[10] and even democracy and separation of powers providing for a rather novel model of rule of law based and dispersed 'judicial sovereignty'. Whether such a trend is desirable or not, which are the factors for its emergence, how can it be fostered or prevented are questions that go beyond the scope of this chapter. It should be noted, however, that judicial dialogue, with all

8 According to P. Lindseth, "We must thus dispense with an idealized understanding of a 'Westphalian' principal with unbridled control over administrative agents or power to direct regulatory outcomes within a particular territory. This is an ahistoric reading of state sovereignty if there ever was one ... as well as a caricature of the principal-agent relationship that is far from the actual historical reality." *See* P. Lindseth, 'Reflections on the "Administrative, Not Constitutional" Character of EU Law in Times of Crisis', *Perspectives on Federalism*, Vol. 9, No. 2, 2017. For the increasing dysfunctionality of the *pacta sunt servanda* and state consent principles, *see also* J. Weiler, 'The Geology of International Law – Governance, Democracy and Legitimacy', *Zeitschrift für ausländisches öffentliches Recht und Völkerrecht*, Vol. 64, 2004, pp. 547-562 and N. Grossman, 'The Normative Legitimacy of International Courts', *Temple Law Review*, Vol. 86, 2013, p. 62 and the following.

9 *See* M. Belov, 'Constitutional Courts as Ultimate Players in Multilevel Constituent Power Games: the Bulgarian Case', *in* Belov, M (Ed.) *Courts, Politics and Constitutional Law*, Oxford, Routledge, 2020 (forthcoming).

10 For more about the transition from hierarchy to pluralism, *see* A. Torrez-Perez, *Conflicts of Rights in the European Union*, Oxford, Oxford University Press, 2009, p. 41 and the following.

its pros and cons, is a theoretical concept, a legal and empirical phenomenon which exceeds the conceptual, institutional and legitimacy framework of traditional or Westphalian constitutionalism.

This chapter will start with a brief presentation of the concepts of Westphalian and post-Westphalian constitutionalism. Furthermore, the different status, roles and conceptualizations of the courts in Westphalian and post-Westphalian context will be outlined. The adequacy of judicial dialogue with regard to the main principles of Westphalian and post-Westphalian constitutionalism will be assessed. Furthermore, judicial dialogue will be put in context by virtue of comparison with several key post-Westphalian concepts. Finally, a conclusion will be made with regard to the status of judicial dialogue as a Westphalian or post-Westphalian constitutional phenomenon.

The main thesis of this chapter is that judicial dialogue is among the few post-Westphalian constitutional concepts which may allow us to reorganize our understanding of constitutional law and to restructure and organize in a novel way the emerging early post-Westphalian constitutional order. I have provided elsewhere an analysis of other post-Westphalian concepts such as constitutional identity,[11] space of flows and post-territoriality.[12] I have also devoted special attention to the transition from Westphalian to post-Westphalian constitutionalism from the perspective of constitutional semiotics.[13] The revolutionary character of the clash between Westphalian and post-Westphalian constitutionalism has also been analyzed.[14] Consequently, this chapter is to be understood as a continuation of my efforts to outline a theory of post-Westphalian constitutionalism. Here I am presenting judicial dialogue from the particular perspective of the counter position between Westphalian and post-Westphalian constitutionalism.

1.2 THE CONCEPT OF WESTPHALIAN AND POST-WESTPHALIAN CONSTITUTIONALISM

Westphalian constitutionalism is the predominant constitutional system of governance which has emerged in early modernity in Western Europe and the USA. The key organization code of Westphalian statehood had been established with the Westphalian peace treaties of 1648. It consists in the recognition of formal equality of the states, non-intervention in internal affairs and ultimate sovereignty within a territorial jurisdiction of authority and power. Another important feature of Westphalian order, which emerged

11 *See* M. Belov, 'The Functions of Constitutional Identity Performed in the Context of Constitutionalization of the EU Order and Europeanization of the Legal Orders of EU Member States', *Perspectives on Federalism*, Vol. 9, No. 2, 2017 and M. Belov, *Bulgarian Constitutional Identity*, Sofia, Sibi, 2017 (in Bulgarian).

12 *See* M. Belov, 'Revolution, Contestation and Transition: Towards a New Global Constitutional Order?' *The Global. Rethinking Global Governance from Geneva*, 2019, available at: https://theglobal.blog/2019/01/14/revolution-contestation-and-transition-towards-a-new-global-constitutional-order/?fbclid=IwAR2Pt0esqACdhHjS4869XOb7K57hseq3LBJm8yN-XfRrLGlK7GsYfxVtVVE, p. 97-141.

13 *See* M. Belov, The Challenges to Westphalian Constitutional Geometry.

14 *See* M. Belov, Revolution, Contestation and Transition.

at a later stage, was secularism. It additionally reinforced the absolute claim of political authority by the modern state.

The Westphalian order was conceptually based on the theories of absolute and ultimate state sovereignty that took the concrete form of monarchical sovereignty.[15] Thus, both Westphalian international order and Westphalian political theory contributed to the establishment of territorial statehood and absolute monarchy. Their merger and amalgamation with nationalism produced the modern Westphalian statehood. Later on, in the late XVIII century and the beginning of the XIX century, Westphalian statehood was transformed and upgraded into a Westphalian constitutional statehood with the emergence of the Western constitutional civilization. During the XIX and the XX centuries, it has spread, at least formally, to the whole world.

It is important to underline the fact that Westphalian constitutionalism has been built upon Westphalian statehood which initially emerged in the form of absolute monarchy. Indeed, constitutionalism and absolutism are antipodes from the viewpoint of political philosophy. Constitutionalism is a denial of absolutism. It is a political philosophy, normative ideology, constitutional model and socio-political movement for replacement of absolute monarchy with limited statehood based on rule of law and separation of powers.

However, there are two pillars of Westphalian statehood which are characteristic and fundamental to both its absolutist and constitutionalist phases. These are sovereignty and hierarchy. Another fundamental manifestation of hierarchy – the supremacy of the constitution – has been added with the emergence of the constitutional civilization and especially with the rise of legal positivism. Absolute monarchy borrowed the hierarchy from the church – especially from political Catholicism. Then it gradually secularized it making it an ordering scheme for the state. Indeed, there were absolute monarchies such as France under the *Ancien Régime* which were far from clearly structured hierarchical orders. However, hierarchy has already been seeded as a pillar of the emerging nation state. Later on, legal positivism and especially the Kelsenian legal normativism finally made hierarchy a universal matrix for ordering the constitutional order and the legal system. They also ultimately detached hierarchy from religion.

Hence, hierarchy is intrinsically modern and typical for all phases of the Westphalian statehood, and also characteristic for the 'mature phase' of the development of Westphalian constitutionalism during the XX century when legal positivism and Kelsenian normativism prevailed. In that regard, hierarchy was a modernizing strategy used during the whole Westphalian period. Absolutism used it to pave the way for and to consolidate the modern nation state. Legal positivism brought the hierarchy to the front as a device for organizing the system of sources of law and the system of the state institutions.

---

15 The theories of Jean Bodin and Thomas Hobbes are the most representative ones for the early Westphalian political order. *See* J. Bodin, *The Six Books of a Commonwealth*, Forgotten Books, 2018, pp. 1-816 and T. Hobbes, *Leviathan*, London, Penguin classics, 2017, pp. 1-688.

Westphalian constitutionalism became the underlying legal, philosophical and political paradigm for the 'constitutionalism within statehood'. All substantial variants of constitutionalism – liberal, democratic or revolutionary, republican or monarchic and so on, have been framed by Westphalian constitutionalism as an overarching concept of the modern constitutional statehood. This means that all variants of modern constitutionalism based on different constitutional ideology, constitutional axiology and institutional design have been unfolding within the ideal and legal confines of Westphalian constitutionalism as underlying fundamental constitutional paradigm.

Westphalian constitutionalism is preconditioned upon specific constitutional ideology, constitutional axiology and institutional design. Constitutional ideology is the system of normative beliefs which forms the durable patterns of behavior of the constitutional actors – the citizens and the office holders. Constitutional axiology comprises the system of constitutional values and constitutional principles. The institutional design encompasses the constitutional model of state institutions, institutions of the public sphere and civil society, human rights, citizenship and sector-specific constitutions, for example, the economic and financial constitution.

The constitutional ideology of Westphalian constitutionalism is structured around a mixture of nationalism, state-centrism, humanism and rationalism. Westphalian statehood emerged and developed within the confines of the nation state. The nation state was a reformist project which aimed at radically replacing the fragmentation and particularities of the late medieval order. Although rooted in absolute monarchy, the nation state was triumphant under the socio-political conditions of the XIX and early XX centuries. However, the link with absolute monarchy should not be underestimated because it is of crucial importance for the understanding of sovereignty as one of the key principles of Westphalian statehood with structural importance for the constitutional order of both absolutism and nationalist constitutionalism. It is the principle of holistic and absolute state sovereignty which constitutes one of the central points of departure from Westphalian to post-Westphalian constitutionalism.

Sovereignty, the presumption of national distinctiveness and the subsequent constitutional nationalism,[16] national solidarity and prevalence of national interest form a complex of phenomena which lies at the core of Westphalian constitutionalism. Initially, the Westphalian constitutional orders were conceived as self-enclosed political orders powered by an existential and self-referential political community – the nation.[17] Westpha-

16 Constitutional nationalism is a phenomenon describing the system of constitutional provisions which aim at preservation of the national distinctiveness of the constitutional order. Constitutional nationalism puts the emphasis on the peculiarities of the socio-political community framed by a constitution adopted especially to reflect the history, interests and needs of a particular nation. It is also a device for preservation of the self-sufficiency of the domestic constitutional order protecting it from uncontrollable penetration by international and supranational legal standards especially the ones promoting globalism, multiculturalism, pluralism and open statehood and society.

17 *See, e.g.*, A. Smith, Nationalism, Cambridge, Polity Press, 2010.

lian constitutionalism is a state-centered phenomenon. This conclusion is related not only to the prevalence of the *raison d'Etat*, but it also stems out of the human rights and citizenship ontology related to the fact that in Westphalian constitutionalism human rights are both provided by the state and directed towards the state. Under the Westphalian constitutional logic, human rights are supposed to offer protection from the state, inclusion in the state or aid from the state.[18]

This state-centrism of the human rights design can be traced to the very roots of Westphalian statehood. The full dependence of the human rights from the state is evident in the theory of Thomas Hobbes as one of the intellectual cornerstones of the early Westphalian statehood. However, it is also characteristic of the later phases of development of Westphalian statehood. For example, the simultaneous rise of legal positivism and welfare state at the end of the XIX and the beginning of the XX centuries was an important factor for the establishment of the state-centric conceptualization of human rights.

In that regard, human rights related judicial dialogue as a phenomenon of the late XX and the beginning of the XXI centuries plays a dual function. It is an escape from the traditional restriction of the human rights to the confines of the statehood. At the same time, it is also a device for negotiation of meaning of central elements of the human rights such as core, periphery, permissible limitations, proportionality and balancing and so on at the edge and at the point of intersection between different national, international and supranational legal orders.

Westphalian constitutional orders are not only self-enclosed and supposedly self-sufficient they are also extremely hierarchical. The pyramid is the main ordering device of the Westphalian constitutional geometry.[19] It is the matrix for ordering and explaining key concepts of Westphalian constitutionalism. The most important among them are the system of sources of law, the institutional order and the relationship between the citizen, the society and the state. The principle and concept of absolute constitutional supremacy is the climax of the hierarchical ordering of the Westphalian constitutional order.

The legal supremacy of the constitution is paralleled by the concept and principle of sovereignty as the ultimate criterion for political, authoritative and power supremacy. The supremacy of the constitution is safeguarded and is a symbol of the political prevalence of the sovereign. And vice versa, the constitutional supremacy is the result of the political omnipotence of the sovereign power.

Indeed, constitutional supremacy and sovereignty are currently mutually supportive. However, there were periods in history when they were mutually contradictory and existed in a situation of political and conceptual tension. In theory and during the years of at least formal global spread of democracy, namely from the fall of the Berlin wall until the end of the first decade of the XXI century, sovereignty and constitutional supremacy

---

18 *See* I. Berlin, *Liberty*, Oxford, Oxford University Press, 2002 p. 166 and the following.

19 *See* M. Belov, The Challenges to Westphalian Constitutional Geometry, p. 13 and the following.

were mutually reconciled. And they were both challenged by the emerging supranational and global constitutionalism.

However, in previous periods of authoritarianism, sovereignty clearly dominated over constitutional supremacy. Clear examples are the Nazi rule in Germany, the communist rule in the countries belonging to the former Soviet bloc or the authoritarian regimes in the European South such as Mussolini's dictatorship in Italy, Franco's regime in Spain, Salazar's regime in Portugal and the military dictatorship in Greece. In such cases, unrestrained or loosely restrained political power had definite prevalence over rule of law in general and supremacy of the constitution in particular.

Moreover, sovereignty and constitutional supremacy are climaxes of the political and legal aspects of the constitutional order which has been developed since the 'long XIX century'.[20] However, sovereignty had emerged much earlier with the rise of absolute monarchy. It preceded not only the constitutional supremacy but the very concepts of modern or Westphalian constitution and constitutionalism. And it was legal positivism and especially the Kelsenian normativism which brought the legal aspects of the constitution and constitutionalism to the front. The constitutional supremacy was one of the most important instruments for emancipation of the constitution and constitutional law from the total grip of the ultimate political power. Constitutional supremacy enabled the emergence of constitutional institutions such as the constitutional court and the other forms of constitutional control and the primacy of the constitutional rights which later served as counter-majoritarian devices for safeguarding the rule of law against the totality of state power. In that regard, the supremacy of the constitution, or more precisely the competition of claims of national and supranational constitutional standards for primacy in the composite constitutional orders of the emerging supranational and global constitutionalism were also the triggers of judicial dialogue as a phenomenon unfolding on the edge between Westphalian and post-Westphalian constitutionalism.

In fact, both sovereignty and constitutional supremacy were tools for promotion of constitutional modernity. Sovereignty justified the claim for unification of the modern state, for its internal hierarchical organization and for its recognition as coequal partner in the international relations. Constitutional supremacy was a device for safeguarding the ultimate control over the validity of the sources of constitutional law by the domestic sovereign power. Both sovereignty and constitutional supremacy were preconditioned upon hierarchy, closed statehood and constitutional nationalism which is why sovereignty and constitutional supremacy are typical elements of Westphalian constitutionalism. They are the two main manifestations of hierarchy as the universal ordering code of the Westphalian constitutional geometry. They are the projections of the hierarchy in the political and legal systems constituting the two main aspects of the Westphalian statehood.

---

20 For the 'long XIX Century', *see* E. Hobsbawm, *The Age of Revolution: 1789-1848*, New York, First Vintage Books, 1996 and E. Hobsbawm, *The Age of Capital: 1848-1875*, New York, First Vintage Books, 1996.

Furthermore, Westphalian constitutionalism is a territorially entrenched phenomenon. It is preconditioned upon fixed 'container-like' territoriality.[21] Key concepts and principles of Westphalian constitutionalism, such as sovereignty, jurisdiction, welfare state and to a great extent democracy, are presupposing the existence of territorial statehood. Thus, they are territorially entrenched phenomena.

Westphalian constitutionalism is paralleled and coexists with a Westphalian international legal order. It is based on the principles of state consent and *pacta sunt servanda*[22] and is compatible with unilateralism, bilateralism and intergovernmentalism in international law. The international aspect of the Westphalian legal order is structured around a system of fully independent states freely joining or withdrawing from international organizations. The states are always in the position of the 'masters of the treaties'. The international organizations are simple devices for mastering joint policy goals stemming out of the increasing complexity of the modern society and its subsystems.

Unanimity of decision-making in the international organizations is safeguard for sovereignty and indirectly is supposed to be guarantee also for constitutional supremacy. Indeed, majority voting is not that rare in international organizations. Nevertheless, it is usually conceived as a potential threat to state sovereignty since the states can be outvoted and thus their interests may not be sufficiently taken into account or may even be disregarded. In that regard, the decision taken by the French Conceil Constitutionel in 1978 that majority voting in the IMF is not incompatible with constitutional supremacy even if France is in the minority is an example of the gradual departure of some of the West European states from Westphalian constitutionalism. It should be mentioned that the end of the 1970s was the initial phase of the neo-liberalism and globalization.

Westphalian constitutionalism puts the national governments, ministers and heads of states in the center of the international relations and the external power of the states. In other words, the institutions of the executive power are settling the coordination tasks of the Westphalian international community. The parliaments and the peoples are supposed to be ultimate internal safeguards of sovereignty and 'guardians of the values and interests of the national constitutional fortress'.

Post-Westphalian constitutionalism is gradually emerging since the end of the XX and the beginning of the XXI centuries. It is ideological, axiological and institutional order which challenges, but also coexists with and upgrades the Westphalian constitutionalism. It is not sure whether it is possible or even desirable that Westphalian constitutionalism should be replaced by post-Westphalian constitutionalism. What is visible, however, is that there is a new discourse in constitutionalism which is developing on the basis, in parallel and sometimes in contrast to traditional – Westphalian – constitutionalism. Hence, post-Westphalian constitutionalism is a powerful phenomenon which has huge

21 *See* N. Brenner, 'Beyond state-centrism? Space, Territoriality and Geographical Scale in Globalization Studies', *Theory and Society*, Vol. 28, No. 1, 1999, p. 55.

22 *See* J. Weiler, Op. cit. and P. Lindseth, Op. cit.

structural impact on the traditional constitutional orders based on the principles of sovereignty, territorial constitutionalism and national representative democracy in the course of rising supranational and global constitutionalism.

Post-Westphalian constitutionalism has constitutional ideology, constitutional axiology and constitutional design which are demonstrating important differences from Westphalian constitutionalism. Universalism and cosmopolitanism are confronting nationalism and statism as central elements of the post-Westphalian constitutional ideology.

Humanism is being challenged by the post-modern deconstruction of the human identity and the rise of AI challenging the concepts of humanity, identity and personality and their reflection in constitutional law. However, it is also reinforced by the spread of a global human rights' civilization and the development of intense human rights' regimes.

Rationalism is promoted to its highest level by the claim to Universalist rationality by constitutional and international law and the impact of new technologies. However, it is also impeded by the rise of the importance of collective emotions and constitutional mythologies[23] fostering irrational political and social behavior and the return to pre-modern collective identities with metaphysical or historical legitimation. Thus, the rationalism of Westphalian constitutionalism is challenged by both pre-modern and post-modern emotional constitutionalism in the context of the early post-Westphalian situation.

Post-Westphalian constitutionalism is based much more on rule of law than on sovereignty and democracy. The claims of constitutional pluralism[24] are much more easily reconcilable with the concept of global rule of law or at least 'rule of law beyond statehood' than with sovereignty and post-national and supranational democracy. In a system without a single power center, where sovereignty is increasingly challenged and hierarchy is partially dismantled as universal explanatory and ordering code, there are tremendous problems which should be solved or at least met with constitutionalist response. The need for legitimation of the post-Westphalian constitutional (dis)order and especially for coordination of the co-existing national, international, supranational and global legal orders produces massive challenge to the coherence of the constitutionalism within and beyond statehood. The traditional principles for structuring of the legal orders, for example, sovereignty and hierarchy, and the coordination and management of the international legal

---

23 *See* A. Marciano (Ed.), *Constitutional Mythologies. New Perspectives on Controlling the State*, New York, Springer, 2011.

24 *See* N. MacCormick, 'Beyond the Sovereign State', *Modern Law Review*, Vol. 56, No. 1, 1993, N. MacCormick, *Questioning Sovereignty: Law, State, and Nation in the European Commonwealth*, Oxford, Oxford University Press, 1999, N. Walker, 'The Idea of Constitutional Pluralism', *Modern Law Review*, Vol. 65, No. 3, 2002, pp. 317-359, N. Krisch, *Beyond Constitutionalism. The Pluralist Structure of Postnational Law*, Oxford, Oxford University Press, 2011, A. Stone Sweet, 'Constitutionalism, Legal Pluralism and International Regimes', *Indiana Journal of Global Legal Studies*, No. 16, 2009, p. 631 and the following and M. Avbelj & J. Komárek (Eds.) *Constitutional Pluralism in the European Union and Beyond*, Oxford, Hart Publishing, 2012.

community by virtue of institutional design centered around national governments and parliaments is increasingly problematic and to an extent dysfunctional.

Hence, one of the challenges of our epoch is whether the courts are in a better position to address the legitimacy and coordination issues produced in the course of the clash between and eventually transition from Westphalian to post-Westphalian constitutionalism. Judicial dialogue produces politicization of courts and judicialization of politics. In times of crisis of representation, democracy and representative democracy and dismantling of sovereignty two types of actors are trying to take the torch of political leadership. These are the people using radical forms of direct, deliberative and participatory democracy and even having recourse to political disobedience and the experts – the courts and the bureaucracies.

In that context, the politicization of courts might not seem to be necessarily a typical feature of post-Westphalian constitutionalism. It might be much more a result of the weakness of the political players and their incapability to engage with the problems arising out of the need to govern under the radically changed socio-political conditions of the supranational constitutionalism, global governance and information and technology revolution. However, I believe that the challenges and changes are not only functional. They go deeper beneath the surface and produce a need for structural adjustment to the age of constitutional pluralism. In this global legal disorder the courts seem as potential institutional winners. They are better equipped to deal with the coordination issues stemming out of constitutional pluralism. In that regard, judicial dialogue is the result of the efforts of the multiple constitutional orders to rearrange themselves in a more coherent way through the mediation of the supreme courts, the constitutional courts and the international and supranational courts. However, the judicial dialogue functions also as a transformative device for the role of courts in the course of transition from Westphalian to early post-Westphalian constitutionalism.

1.3 Judicial Dialogue as Transformative Device for the Role of Courts in the Course of Transition from Westphalian to Early Post-Westphalian Constitutionalism

Westphalian constitutionalism ascribes an exclusively or predominantly non-political role for the courts. Especially in its continental European version the courts are supposed to be apolitical agents of the will of the democratic legislator – the parliament, the government and, incidentally, the people. The Montesquieu's formulas that the courts are only '*la bouche de la loi*' and that the judicial power should be '*en quelque façon, nulle*'[25] have been deeply entrenched in the constitutional ideology of most European states for centuries. According to the traditional Westphalian constitutional logic, enshrined in

25 *See* Ch. de Montesquieu, *De l'esprit des lois*, Ellipses Marketing, 2015.

both constitutional ideology as well as constitutional design, courts should not engage in domestic or international politics. The sphere of the external power of the state is reserved entirely for the political players that possess sufficient democratic legitimacy and efficiency credentials. These are the head of state, the government, the parliament and, in crucial moments, also the people.

Under Westphalian conditions the judges are allowed to enter in institutional dialogue with the political branches of power. Such institutional dialogue is accomplished in the process of control for constitutionality, legality or compliance with international and EU law. However, they are supposed to have no political discretion in the course of control for legality and law implementation. The courts should be administrators of law, but not creators of law and, thus, not politicians.

The 'political self-restraint' of the courts is logically controversial when it comes to institutional dialogue with political institutions such as the government and the parliament. When entering into dialogue with political institutions, the courts are also engaging in politics despite their presumed attempt to use only legal arguments. This is due to the fact that legally framed institutional dialogue led in legal terms and with legal arguments is still a form of political enterprise both substantially and with a view on the actors; last but not least, because it usually determines preferred outcomes and thus involves discretion. Indeed, the political potential of judicial dialogue between the supreme courts, the ordinary courts and the constitutional court was ever present also under Westphalian constitutionalism. The conceptualization of the judges as non-political domestic actors got massively questioned during the second half of the XX and the beginning of the XXI centuries.

One of the main challenges to this ideal perception of the courts stems out of the establishment of constitutional courts as central players not only on the national constitutional chess board, but also in the context of the supranational and global constitutionalism. Initially established as the Kelsenian type of 'negative legislators', they have almost immediately departed from this position which was still reconcilable with the traditional Westphalian role of the courts. Many constitutional courts have gradually but persistently transformed themselves into activist courts functioning even as 'positive legislators'. Two strands of their activism should be emphasized. The first one is the accomplishment of 'virtual amendment of the constitution' on the basis of its 'open texture'.[26] The second one is the engagement in institutional dialogue predominantly with two types of institutions. These are the national parliaments and the international, supranational and foreign supreme and constitutional courts.

---

26 For the open texture of law, *see* H.L.A. Hart, *The Concept of Law*, Oxford, Oxford University Press, 1997, pp. 124-136.

Thus, judicial dialogue was among the main precursors of politicization of the constitutional courts. It enabled the constitutional courts to become key factors in the external power of the state, main actors in the process of 'ordering of constitutional orders'[27] and ultimate players in multilevel and pluralist constitutional and constituent power games. This is particularly true for activist and powerful constitutional courts which have a long tradition of durable engagement with judicial dialogue with the Court of Justice of the EU (CJEU). Clear examples are the German Federal Constitutional Court and the Italian Constitutional Court. However, some other courts, such as the Portuguese Constitutional Court, have also promoted their constitutional standing and increased their importance using tactics for engagement with vertical judicial dialogue with the CJEU.[28]

The main precursor of the establishment of judicial dialogue as post-Westphalian phenomenon bridging constitutionalism 'within' and 'beyond' statehood is the competence of the courts to control the compliance of domestic legislation with international and EU law. This is especially true for the constitutional courts. Indeed, it should be noted that not all constitutional courts can or are willing to perform such control.

Actually, the control for compliance of domestic legislation with international law and especially with EU law was one of the 'points of no return' which enabled the courts to become guardians of international and supranational legal standards and to gradually emancipate from their presumable non-political status and institutional and ideological entrenchment in domestic legal orders. The courts have practiced policy making, determining what law is and accomplishing legal policy even under Westphalian constitutional law. However, this was predominantly domestic law and policy making. The principle of non-interference of courts in international relations persisted until the last decades of the XX century despite the gradual overcoming of the dogma of the non-political nature of the jurisprudence and the limitation of the functions of courts in administering the application of law and dispute settlement in late Westphalian modernity. Hence, the engagement of courts in international and EU related judicial or broader institutional dialogue seems to be rather late modern and early post-Westphalian phenomenon.

Thus, international and supranational judicial dialogue, related to preliminary references to the CJEU, control for compliance of domestic legislation with international and supranational law, explicit or implicit affirmative practices or 'judicial revolts' against the

27 For the concept of 'ordering of constitutional orders', *see* E. Tanchev, 'The Contemporary Supranational Constitutional Pluralism or the Ordering of Constitutional Orders', *in* P. Kirov P (Ed.) *Constitutional Studies 2012-2013*, Sofia, 'St. Kliment Ohridski' University Press, 2014 (in Bulgarian), pp. 171-198.

28 *See, e.g.*, Decisions on Case 575/2014, 15 August 2014, Case 141/2015, 25 February 2015 and Case 360/2012, 5 July of the Portuguese Constitutional Court. For more information about these decisions of the Portuguese Constitutional Court, *see* F. Pereira Coutinho and N. Piçarra N 'Portugal', *in* A. Albi, S. Bardutzky (Eds.) *National Constitutions in European and Global Governance: Democracy, Rights, the Rule of Law. National Reports*, The Hague, T.M.C. Asser Press, 2019 (forthcoming).

case law of the European Court of Human Rights (ECtHR) or the CJEU, and strategic and tactical use of judicial precedents of these courts in domestic jurisprudence have been the main reasons for the transformation of the courts from 'mouth of the law' and law application machines into masters of the emerging global networked jurisprudence in the age of constitutional pluralism.

Horizontal judicial dialogue[29] enables the courts to learn from each other,[30] but also to strengthen their position in institutional dialogue at home by referring to foreign jurisprudence as a source of legal argumentation.[31] Such referral allows the courts to promote their strategic or tactical goals and policies on the domestic constitutional and political scene.[32] Europeanization or nationalism, human rights friendly policies or defense of state interests, specific sector-based policies are more easily 'sold' on the 'domestic market of political and constitutional ideas' if they are based on arguments stemming out of the case law of powerful foreign courts or courts which are admired and followed due to historical, political or anthropological reasons. Clear case is the influence of the EU-related case law of the German Federal Constitutional Court on the jurisprudence of the courts in Central and Eastern Europe – especially the Polish and the Czech Constitutional Courts.

Vertical judicial dialogue makes the courts – especially the constitutional and supreme courts – participants in the external and the constituent power of the state.[33] Vertical judicial dialogue runs against key ideas of Westphalian constitutionalism. Judicial dialogue enables the courts to gain the position of authoritative speakers of the national community. It allows them to become ultimate players in multilevel constituent power games[34] acting on behalf of the 'official sovereign', which is usually the people or the nation. Judicial dialogue breaks the monopoly of the parliament and government over

29 *See* M. Claes & M. de Visser, M 'Are you networked yet? On Dialogues in European Judicial Networks', *Utrecht Law Review*, Vol. 8, No. 2, 2012, p. 100 and the following.

30 For the role of horizontal judicial dialogue in the establishment of a 'global community of courts' or a 'global judicial empire',*see* A.M. Slaughter Op. cit., p. 191 and the following. A different approach based on empirical criticism to this hypothesis is provided by A. Wiener and Ph. Liste Op. cit., pp. 263-296. A. M. Slaughter outlines two phenomena related to the horizontal judicial dialogue. She defines them as constitutional cross-fertilization and as a combination of judicial cooperation and conflict in transnational litigation. *See* A. M. Slaughter, Op. cit., p. 193 and the following.

31 *See, e.g.*, T. Groppi & M.-C. Ponthoreau (Eds.) The Use of Foreign Precedents by Constitutional Judges, Oxford, Hart publishing, 2013 p. 60 and the following and J. Bell, 'The Argumentative Status of Foreign Legal Arguments', *Utrecht Law Review*, Vol. 8, No. 2, 2012, p. 8 and the following.

32 *See* A.M. Slaughter Op. cit., p. 191 and the following.

33 For the distinction between horizontal and vertical judicial dialogue and for the five categories of judicial dialogue outlined by him, *see* A. Rosas, 'The European Court of Justice in Context: Forms and Patterns of Judicial Dialogue', *European Journal of Legal Studies*, Vol. 1, No 2, 2007, p. 1 and p. 5 and the following.

34 *See* M. Belov, 'Constitutional Courts as Ultimate Players in Multilevel Constituent Power Games: the Bulgarian Case', *in* M. Belov (Ed.), *Courts, Politics and Constitutional Law*, Oxford, Routledge, 2020 (forthcoming).

the external power. It triggers an unprecedented 'judicialization of international and European politics',[35] but leads also in parallel to politicization of the judiciary.[36]

Thus, the emergence and spread of judicial dialogue as an important phenomenon of contemporary constitutional law within and beyond statehood is an indicator of a structural, conceptual and paradigmatic shift towards a new form of constitutionalism – the post-Westphalian constitutionalism. This is true for both horizontal and vertical judicial dialogue.

1.4 Judicial Dialogue and Its Relationship to Key Westphalian and Post-Westphalian Concepts

An important approach for determining whether judicial dialogue is a Westphalian or a post-Westphalian concept might be its comparison with key Westphalian and post-Westphalian concepts. The conceptual allocation of judicial dialogue and its comparison with key phenomena of structural importance may well expose its conceptual parameters and its systematic relationship within the conceptual network of Westphalian or post-Westphalian constitutionalism.

It should be clarified that there are principles and elements of the institutional design which belong to the hard core of Westphalian constitutionalism and other principles and aspects of the institutional design which are of great importance for modern constitutionalism, but are not essential for its Westphalian characteristics. In other words, there are typically Westphalian features of modern constitutionalism and other characteristic elements which have emerged in the context of Westphalian statehood. They have been framed by Westphalian constitutionalism and amalgamated with Westphalian constitutional axiology and institutional design without being necessarily Westphalian – sovereigntist, hierarchical, territorially self-enclosed – themselves. The same is true for the post-Westphalian constitutionalism comprising typical post-Westphalian features that are antipodes of the core of the Westphalian constitutionalism and other features which are emerging, modifying or coexisting with the early post-Westphalian constitutionalism.

The hard core of Westphalian constitutionalism comprises sovereignty, constitutional supremacy, hierarchy and fixed territoriality of power. Westphalian constitutionalism presupposes self-sufficiency of hierarchical constitutional order framed by a fixed 'con-

35 *See* R. Hirschl, 'The Judicialization of Politics', in G. Caldeira, R.D. Kelemen & K. Whittington (Eds.) *Oxford Handbook of Law and Politics*, Oxford, Oxford University Press, 2008.

36 For the general problem of the judicialization of politics and politicization of the judiciary, *see, e.g.*, D. Weiden, 'Judicial Politicization, Ideology, and Activism at the High Courts of the United States, Canada, and Australia', *Political Research Quarterly*, Vol. 64, No. 2, 2011, pp. 335-347 and P. Domingo, 'Judicialization of politics or politicization of the judiciary? Recent trends in Latin America', *Democratization*, Vol. 11, No. 1, 2004, p. 104 and the following.

tainer-like' territoriality.[37] Democracy, especially representative party democracy, is also largely dependent on the hard core of Westphalian constitutionalism which is why it is close to its core although not belonging to it due to two main reasons. First, not all Westphalian constitutional orders have been democracies or at least sufficiently democratic in terms of the mass democracy of the XX century. Second, democracy can eventually exist also in a post-Westphalian context. Representative democracy gradually became a key constitutional principle of the late Westphalian modernity. It has emerged on an early stage, but has been more durably established on several waves during the late XIX and the XX centuries. However, it is currently exposed to multiple pressures some of which have post-Westphalian character.

Power polycentrism is not limited to Westphalian constitutionalism. In fact, long-lasting and important phases of Westphalian statehood have been marked by power monism and power corporatism as antipodes of polycentrism and separation of powers. However, the constitutional models for separation of powers have been tailored according to the shapes of XIX and XX centuries Westphalian constitutional orders. The Westphalian theories and models for separation of powers are increasingly incapable of coping with the shifts and transformations of the socio-political and power reality at the beginning of the XXI century.[38]

Rule of law is a principle which emerged in the early modernity. It played a decisive role in the transformation of Westphalian pre-constitutional statehood to Westphalian constitutionalism. It has strong chances to persist also in the context of post-Westphalian constitutionalism. This is due to the fact that it is not ontologically bound with statehood in an absolute way and its teleology is directed towards management of diversity within both hierarchical and non-hierarchical orders.

The welfare state is also constitutional principle of most of the European states, but it is not directly related to Westphalian constitutionalism, which is why it will not be discussed here although the welfare state undergoes crucial change in the context of the clash between Westphalian and post-Westphalian constitutionalism.

Judicial dialogue demonstrates a tense relationship with the pillars of Westphalian statehood. It is not at ease with both Westphalian constitutional law and with Westphalian international law. Judicial dialogue runs in parallel with traditional patterns of accomplishment of state sovereignty. Strategic and fundamental decisions with profound constitutional importance are supposed to be taken by the sovereign, usually the people, through a system of institutions of the constituent power. Key decisions related to the day-to-day implementation of state power are entrusted to all state bodies, but constitu-

37 For the state as 'territorial container', *see* N. Brenner, 'Beyond state-centrism? Space, Territoriality and Geographical Scale in Globalization Studies', *Theory and Society*, Vol. 28, No. 1, 1999, p. 55.

38 *See* M. Belov, 'Separation of Powers Reconsidered: a Proposal for a New Theoretical Model at the Beginning of the 21st Century' *in* A. Geisler A, M. Hein & S. Hummel (Eds.) *Law, Politics and the Constitution. New Perspectives from Legal and Political Theory*, Frankfurt/Main, Peter Lang, 2014, pp. 47-60.

tional and external politics is the traditional domain of the government, the head of state and the parliament. Indeed, the courts might also be defined as agents of the sovereign power of the state. Supreme and constitutional courts may be conceptualized as safeguards of sovereignty, guardians of the constitutional core, protectors of the constitutional supremacy and institutions setting the limits of the validity, primacy and direct effect of international and supranational law.

However, the practice of judicial dialogue also shows that, in the course of the accomplishment of these functions, the courts actually ascertain their own central position as key players in multilevel constituent power games.[39] The process of drawing demarcation lines between national, international and supranational law enables the courts to function as gatekeepers of the bridge between different legal and constitutional orders. Thus, safeguarding sovereignty and constitutional supremacy as pillars of Westphalian constitutionalism turns out to be frequently accomplished by using relatively novel concepts such as constitutional identity[40] and 'counter-limits'. This is done through judicial dialogue in an increasingly pluralist context.

Here it should be noted that constitutional pluralism[41] is an early post-Westphalian concept and matrix for 'ordering of constitutional orders'.[42] In that regard, it differs from multilevel constitutionalism which is concept and matrix typical also for Westphalian constitutionalism and applicable in traditional multilevel orders such as the federations and the confederations.[43]

Of course, there might be also a different view on constitutional identity and 'counter-limits' and thus also on judicial dialogue as an important device for their development. One might say that although different from sovereignty and constitutional supremacy they are anyway instruments safeguarding constitutional nationalism. Constitutional supremacy might be a bit too rigid and incapable of addressing challenges stemming out of the primacy of the EU law and the judicial activism of international and supranational courts producing virtual amendment and development of constitutional principles, val-

39 *See* D. Petric, 'On Neo-Institutionalism, the Court of Justice of the EU and General Principles', *in* M. Belov (Ed.) *Rule of Law at the Beginning of the Twenty-First Century*, The Hague, Eleven International Publishing, 2018, p. 175 and the following.

40 For some classical accounts of the concept of constitutional identity, *see* M. Rosenfeld, 'Constitutional Identity', *in* M. Rosenfeld & A. Sajo (Eds.) *The Oxford Handbook of Comparative Constitutional Law*, Oxford, Oxford University Press, 2012, C. Alcoberro Llivina & A. Saiz Arnaiz (Eds.) *National Constitutional Identity and European Integration*, Cambridge, Intersentia, 2013, pp. 1-326 and P. Faraguna, 'Constitutional Identity in the EU – A Shield or a Sword?' *German Law Journal*, Vol. 18, No. 7, 2017, p. 1617 and the following.

41 For the concept of constitutional pluralism, *see* N. MacCormick Op. cit., N. Walker, Op. cit., p. 317-359, N. Krisch, Op. cit., A. Stone Sweet op. cit., p. 631 and the following and M. Avbelj and J. Komárek Op. cit.

42 *See* E. Tanchev, Op. cit.

43 A. Rosas makes an important distinction between feudal systems based on monism, the dualist nation state systems based on a distinction between national and international law and the post-modern systems grounded on constitutional pluralism and "involving globalization, regionalization as well as localization". *See* A. Rosas, Op. cit., p. 1.

ues and human rights. Hence, constitutional identity and 'counter-limits' may be put in place not as post-Westphalian, post-nationalist and pluralist concepts but exactly as safeguards for the constitutional supremacy and state sovereignty. And this is indeed the way these concepts have been used by many of the constitutional courts, for example, by the Italian Constitutional Court in the Taricco case and by the German Constitutional Court in the OMT case. Thus, the question might arise whether they are not simply the 'new face of Westphalia'.[44]

I believe that constitutional identity is a chameleonic concept. It serves as a limitation to the primacy of EU law and as a barrier to other constitutional standards stemming out of the supranational constitutionalism of the EU and the international law. However, it might be used also as an excuse for transfer of sovereignty to international and supranational organizations and for allowing the primacy of EU law and international law over the elements of the domestic constitution which are not covered by the national constitutional identity. This controversial use of constitutional identity is the result of the judicial negotiation of its parameter, scope, contents and meaning by the courts as authoritative speakers of the socio-political community framed by the national constitution. And this jurisprudential negotiation of meaning is accomplished precisely by virtue of judicial dialogue.

To sum up, judicial dialogue may safeguard and reinforce sovereignty and its legal dimension – the constitutional supremacy. However, it may also produce shift from popular, national or parliamentary to judicial sovereignty. Moreover, it may even outsource key decisions with structural importance for the maintenance of the equilibrium between different legal orders in the context of constitutional pluralism to a 'global judicial empire'.[45] Thus, it may produce a post-Westphalian 'networked judicial sovereignty' functioning in parallel to the 'official' Westphalian version of state and popular sovereignty. This does not mean that it is the courts which are producing a post-Westphalian situation characterized by the rule of law instead of democracy. Indeed, the courts, together with the international and supranational bureaucracies, are the main institutional beneficiaries of the collapse of Westphalian sovereigntist type of democracy. However, they are not necessarily protagonists of a 'new post-democratic Westphalia' based on a mixture of elitism, globalism and regional protectionism. The courts may lean towards a supranational juristocracy. Nevertheless, they may also be the main factor for the preservation of the necessary degree of democracy in the current epoch exactly because of the fact that they are detached from populist politics.[46] The Westphalian function of

44 I am grateful to Emanuel Casterllarin for this very proper expression and generally for his arguments related to the conceptualization of constitutional identity and 'counter-limits' as Westphalian and not as post-Westphalian concepts.

45 *See* A.M. Slaughter Op. cit., p. 191 and the following.

46 For the role of courts in the context of rising populist constitutionalism and illiberalism, *see* A. Harel, 'Courts in a Populist World', available at: *Verfassungsblog.de*, 2017, p. 1-4 and M. Hailbronner & D. Landau, 'Introduction: Constitutional Courts and Populism', available at: *Verfassungsblog.de*, 2017, pp. 1-4.

judicial dialogue of safeguarding constitutional supremacy, constitutional core, constitutional identity and state sovereignty is actually supplemented by a post-Westphalian function of coordination of legal and constitutional orders and promotion of the 'open statehood'[47] and supranational constitutionalism. The protection of the domestic 'constitutional bastion' by the supreme and constitutional courts as ultimate defenders of the national constitutionally based community is paralleled and sometimes overshadowed by the building of bridges between national, international and supranational law. Negative sovereignty, emphasizing independence and autonomy, is partially transformed into positive sovereignty aiming at integration in global and supranational constitutionalism and in the international legal community.

Judicial dialogue transforms the very idea of sovereignty from an exclusive and holistic concept into an inclusive and fragmented one. Instead of denominating a coherent and holistic ultimate source of exclusive territorial domination, sovereignty is reshaped into a bargaining chip strategically and tactically used by the courts in the process of building of bridges between the legal and constitutional orders via judicial dialogue. This process is asymmetric because it concerns different aspects of sovereignty. Financial and budgetary sovereignty is the object of jurisprudential bargaining between the national constitutional and supreme courts and the CJEU. Human rights sovereignty is usually the object of jurisprudential negotiation and deliberation between the domestic constitutional and supreme courts and the ECtHR and the CJEU[48] at the core, periphery and within permissible limitations of the human rights and freedoms simultaneously provided by the European Convention on Human Rights and the constitutions of the Member States of the Council of Europe.

Thus, the discursive judicial dialogues in different constitutional law domains in fact transform sovereignty from an absolute, holistic and sacred category, defined in 'either-or' terms and as ultima ratio of the constitutional order, into a more flexible, fragmented and pragmatic phenomenon. Indeed, cases like Taricco and OMT are still framed in 'either-or' terms and look like a confirmation rather than as rejection of the 'black or white' nature of sovereignty. However, it is also true that the judicial dialogue in specific policy domains fragments the sovereignty in the sense that it allows different outcomes in different policy areas. This is exactly my point here – judicial dialogue may still produce 'sovereign-like outcomes' in a specific domain. But in general it also fosters the fragmentation of sovereignty according to the different branches of law in which it is conducted by the domestic, the international and the supranational courts.

Actually, sovereignty is starting to serve as a point of negotiation between a multitude of courts and as bargaining strategy and ultimate power asset for the national constitu-

47 For the concept of open statehood, *see* S. Hobe, 'Statehood at the End of the 20th Century – The Model of the "Open State": A German Perspective', *Austrian Review of International and European Law*, No. 12, 1996, pp. 127-154.

48 *See, e.g.*, Melloni and Taricco cases.

tional and supreme courts in the course of strategic judicial constitutional policy-making via judicial dialogue. Consequently, judicial dialogue contributes to the pragmatic and discursive use of sovereignty thus transforming it from sacred and absolute pillar of Westphalian constitutionalism into a relative, relational and flexible tool of early post-Westphalian judicial constitutional policy-making via jurisprudential networking and framing.

There is tension also between judicial dialogue and separation of powers. It also stems out of the shift from Westphalian to post-Westphalian constitutional ideology, constitutional design and constitutional pragmatics. There are two dimensions of this tension. The first one is related to the separation between constituent and constituted powers. The second one concerns the horizontal separation of powers. Again, it should be recalled that separation of powers is not a genuinely Westphalian principle but the traditional theories and institutional models for separation of powers are. This is particularly true for the theory of Montesquieu on the horizontal separation of powers especially for the theory on the separation between constituent and constituted powers which is a logical and necessary continuation of the sovereigntist type of constitutionalism – the Westphalian constitutionalism. Thus, a mismatch between them and the judicial dialogue may be indicative of its Westphalian or post-Westphalian nature.

In the Westphalian constitutional framework, the courts belong to the judicial power which is a constituted power. However, even in Westphalian constitutional theory, it is a well-established truth that judicial interpretation of the law, especially the use of teleological interpretation and analogy, allows the courts to be more than simple machines for law application. The discussion on the role of constitutional courts as 'negative' or even 'positive' legislators functioning in parallel to the parliament as 'typical' or democratically empowered legislator is central to the late Westphalian constitutionalism. This discussion is an ongoing one since the first half of the XX century.[49]

The development of fully fledged international law, especially the emergence of supranational and global constitutionalism and constitutional pluralism almost inevitably triggered the need of judicial dialogue as a device for 'ordering of constitutional and legal orders'. Thus, the courts – especially the supreme and the constitutional courts – became inevitable players in multiple powers in which they were previously prohibited to participate. The gatekeeper position of courts on the points of intersection between national, supranational and international law, their role as ultimate players in multilevel and pluralist constituent power games, their inclusion in the external and financial power of the state are simultaneously producing tendencies directed towards fundamental reconcep-

49 *See, e.g.*, A. Brewer-Carías (Ed.) *Constitutional Courts as Negative Legislators*, Cambridge, Cambridge University Press, 2011 A. Brewer-Carías (Ed.) *Constitutional Courts as Positive Legislators. A Comparative Law Study*. Cambridge, Cambridge University Press, 2017, H. Kelsen, 'Judicial Review of Legislation: A Comparative Study of the Austrian and the American Constitution', *The Journal of Politics*, No. 4, 1942, pp. 188-189 and J.J. Moreso JJ, 'Kelsen on Justifying Judicial Review', *in* G. Ramírez G (Ed.) *Ecos de Kelsen: Vidas, obras y controversias*, Bogotá, Editorial Universidad Externado de Colombia, 2012, pp. 354-378.

tualization of the theory and constitutional model of separation of powers. The most important among them are the blurring of the lines between constituent and constituted powers and between judicial, legislative and external power fostered by the expansion of the courts as key players in domestic, international and supranational legal orders.

In such a context, the judicial dialogue serves as a device for communication, coordination and connection between the nodes of the 'global judicial empire'. Judicial dialogue is reinforcing the separation of powers and the delimitation of power, authority and validity domains between the domestic, international and supranational courts in multilevel and pluralist power games. At the same time, however, it blurs traditional distinctions between constituent and constituted and between legislative and judicial power. Thus, while judicial dialogue aids the emergence of post-Westphalian power constellations and the drawing of demarcation lines between multiple constitutional and international legal orders, it is rather problematic from the viewpoint of traditional or Westphalian concepts of separation of powers, which is why the principle of separation of powers is both endangered and promoted by virtue of judicial dialogue. In any case, it is in a process of transformation from Westphalian ordering scheme limited exclusively within the confines of 'constitutionalism within statehood' into an early post-Westphalian principle applicable to the emerging supranational and global constitutionalism. In other words, separation of powers may be conceived as being adjusted to the early post-Westphalian reality through judicial dialogue. This is another argument that judicial dialogue is predominantly an early post-Westphalian phenomenon bridging Westphalian and post-Westphalian constitutionalism as well as constitutionalism 'within' and 'beyond' statehood.

The relationship between judicial dialogue and democracy is rather contradictory. It is also very much dependent on the theoretical standpoint, the concept of democracy applied in the analysis and enshrined in the constitutional model and the historical period in which it is assessed. The theory and normative model of representative democracy tried to reconcile liberalism with democracy, rule of law with democracy and sovereignty and liberty with majority rule.[50] In this context, judicial dialogue may be interpreted as an element of representative democracy, as a safeguard for the coexistence of multiple democratic orders and as a component of a complex constitutional design which has the task of facilitating the rule of law in the context of democracy.

However, we are currently witnessing the disentanglement of the liberal from the democratic trend, a component or tradition in modern constitutionalism.[51] The emer-

50 For the liberal and revolutionary traditions in constitutionalism, *see* P. Blokker, Op. cit. For the balance between representation and democracy, *see* M. Brito Vieira & D. Runciman, *Representation*, Cambridge, Polity Press, 2008.

51 *See* P. Blokker, Op. cit.

gence of illiberal democracies,[52] the rise of neo-nationalism[53] and its legal dimension – the constitutional neo-nationalism, the development of populist constitutionalism,[54] anti-global constitutionalism, global anti-constitutionalism[55] and global illiberalism are the most visible manifestations of the divorce between liberalism and democracy. They are contemporary offspring of the radical democratic or revolutionary discourse[56] in Westphalian constitutionalism.

Judicial dialogue is hardly compatible with this second, radical democratic, revolutionary, populist or illiberal trend in constitutionalism and constitutional law. It is not reconcilable with extreme majoritarianism, with sovereignism and with radical democracy. The idea that it is the courts, more precisely the constitutional and supreme courts, which should 'control the pulse' of the composite constitutional orders jointly constructed by domestic, international and supranational strands is in deep contradiction with the claims for re-establishment of majority rule pursuing the 'common good' via strong executives and reinforced parliamentary majorities and based on permanent support by the people.

In that regard, judicial dialogue may be interpreted as Westphalian constitutional concept only in the context of one of the Westphalian discourses on constitutional democracy. This is the liberal constitutionalism which puts special emphasis on counter-majoritarian safeguards for liberty, rule of law and political moderation and expertise. However, even liberal constitutionalism is not at ease with the concept of judicial dialogue. This is due to the fact that liberal constitutionalism is frequently combined with parliamentarism and even with parliamentocentrism. A clear case is the British constitutionalism providing for the principle of parliamentary sovereignty and supremacy.

Consequently, it seems that judicial dialogue is rather a post-Westphalian concept. This suggestion should be proven by analysis of the relationship between judicial dialogue and the other early post-Westphalian concepts. In my opinion, such concepts are constitutional identity, global judicial empire, global rule of law and constitutional pluralism. This is due to the fact that they go beyond holistic concepts of sovereignty, absolute constitutional supremacy and closed statehood and are enabling the maintenance and development of 'constitutionalism beyond statehood',[57] supranational and global.

In my account, rule of law is both a Westphalian and a post-Westphalian principle of organization of the legal and, later on, also of the constitutional order. It has emerged at

52 For the concept of illiberal democracy, *see* F. Zakaria, Op. cit.

53 *See, e.g.*, M. Eger & S. Valdez, 'Neo-nationalism in Western Europe', *European Sociological Review*, Vol. 31, No. 1, 2015, pp. 115-130.

54 *See* P. Blokker, Op. cit. and Corrias, Op. cit., p. 6-26.

55 *See* K. Lachmayer, Op. cit.

56 *See* P. Blokker, Op. cit.

57 For the 'constitutionalism beyond statehood', *see* P. Dobner & M. Loughlin (Eds.) *Twilight of Constitutionalism?* Oxford, Oxford University Press, 2010 and N. Walker, 'Taking Constitutionalism beyond the State', *Political Studies*, Vol. 56, No. 3, 2008, pp. 519-543.

the early dawn of modern statehood in the course of transition from absolutism to constitutionalism. Indeed, rule of law as a coherent concept and fully fledged and well-institutionalized constitutional principle has been enshrined in the constitutional systems at a later stage – during the second half of the XIX century. However, the fundamental ideas of rule of law and its institutional nucleus consisting of its main values and core elements had emerged earlier. This had happened precisely at the edge of transition from absolutism to constitutionalism. Rule of law had persisted throughout the constitutional modernity and seems to have the potential and capacity to overcome and outlive the clash between Westphalian and post-Westphalian constitutionalism. Thus, rule of law will be the most important ordering principle in the context of post-Westphalian constitutionalism, global constitutionalism and constitutional pluralism.

Rule of law and judicial dialogue intuitively seem to be mutually reinforcing phenomena. The courts are the natural protectors and promoters of rule of law. They are safeguards of the supremacy of the constitution and the primacy of the international and supranational law. They are key safeguards for human rights. The courts are promoters of legal certainty, guardians of the legitimate expectations of the citizens and are gradually becoming the masters of the legal order. The courts perform these important functions both within and beyond statehood. Thus, they are pillars of the rule of law beyond and within statehood in the context of both Westphalian and post-Westphalian constitutionalism.

Furthermore, rule of law is the key legitimation principle of the global judicial empire which is gradually emerging since the second half of the XX century. The network of international, supranational and national – especially constitutional and supreme – courts which have been established in the recent decades is structured around the principle of rule of law. In fact, rule of law is a principle which is *per se* capable of mastering the complexity of composite legal orders and of pluralist and fragmented societies. Rule of law has emerged in early modernity in order to cope with the increasing diversity of modern societies. Global rule of law will be fundamental prerequisite for 'ordering of constitutional orders' in a global constitutional pluralism.

This is why judicial dialogue plays and will continue to play an instrumental and pivotal role in the maintenance of global rule of law. It is the device promoting coordination between different constitutional and legal orders, coherence and cohesion within each of them and consistency with some fundamental basic values of civilized society. In this regard, post-Westphalian constitutionalism which should necessarily be based on recognition, pluralism and diversity, will require global rule of law promoted to a great extent by virtue of judicial dialogue.

Of course, a post-national future is not necessarily limited to post-Westphalian constitutionalism and constitutional pluralism. A neo-Westphalian regional constitutionalism, in which the world will be divided into big regional blocs with constitutional character, might also be possible. Such a model will be based on introspective constitutional model resembling Westphalian premises and constructive logic, but applied on a regional level and in a post-national situation. However, even in this case the courts will play an important role for resolving claims of validity, authority and recognition. In fact, the courts will perform the role of membranes allowing or preventing the mutual penetration of the neo-Westphalian regional constitutional orders.

Consequently, judicial dialogue is essential for the maintenance of rule of law in the context of constitutional pluralism. Constitutional pluralism requires institutionalized forms of inter-institutional dialogue on the strategic points of intersection between the different legal and constitutional orders. The international and supranational courts – especially the ECtHR and the CJEU, and the domestic courts – more precisely the supreme and the constitutional courts, are best equipped to perform such dialogue. They are expert institutions which possess the necessary knowledge and skills for rule of law based and rule of law directed at further development of national, supranational and global constitutionalism in the context of constitutional pluralism.

However, constitutional pluralism is a framework concept defining the constitutional reality as a networked and pluricentric order composed of overlapping orders, jurisdictions and claims of authority.[58] In contrast to domestic legal order or to multilevel constitutional order a pluralist constitutional order is heterarchical. Heterarchy requires networked system of intersystemic communication, coordination and governance. This is why a networked global or at least regional 'judicial empire' seems to be an institutional response which is most adequate to the challenges of constitutional pluralism. Judicial networking can be structured in different ways. It may consist of horizontal and vertical judicial dialogue (functional networking), judicial networks, organizations and conferences (informal organizational networking) or in the establishment of polycentric structure of the international and supranational judicial system (institutional networking).[59]

In this context, judicial dialogue, producing functional networking, is of crucial importance for the maintenance of the consistency of the pluralist supranational and global constitutional order. From that perspective, judicial dialogue and constitutional pluralism are mutually related phenomena belonging to the realm of the early post-Westphalian constitutionalism or at least triggered by the clash between Westphalian and post-Westphalian constitutionalism. In other words, even if judicial dialogue and constitutional pluralism are not entirely detached from their Westphalian origin and thus are not fully novel concepts they are at least leading explanatory and ordering paradigms on the edge between Westphalian and post-Westphalian constitutionalism.

Finally, judicial dialogue and constitutional identity are also deeply intertwined phenomena of the early post-Westphalian reality. This is due to the fact that constitutional identity is to a great extent shaped by virtue of judicial dialogue between the CJEU and

58 *See* N. MacCormick, Op. cit., N. Walker, Op. cit., pp. 317-359, N. Krisch, Op. cit., A. Stone Sweet, Op. cit., p. 631 and the following and M. Avbelj and J. Komárek, Op. cit.

59 *See also*, M. Claes & M. de Visser, Op. cit., p. 100 and the following.

the national constitutional courts. The constitutional identity can hardly be outlined by virtue of parliamentary deliberation, deliberative or direct democracy.

The constitutional courts have both the incentives and the capacity to determine the constitutional identity of the states serving as a permissive platform for outsourcing of constitutional competences to the EU order or, vice versa, as 'counter-limits' to the transfer of sovereignty and to the penetration of international and supranational legal standards in the domestic legal order. These processes are rather questionable from the viewpoint of popular sovereignty, separation of powers and democracy as key principles of the Westphalian constitutionalism belonging to its core or periphery. They are in fact contradictory to the concept of sovereignty as the cornerstone of both Westphalian statehood and Westphalian constitutionalism. And this is exactly a key argument that both judicial dialogue and its result – the judicial shaping of constitutional identity, are in fact early post-Westphalian phenomena.

1.5 Conclusion

It has been proven that judicial dialogue is an early post-Westphalian concept. This conclusion can be drawn on the basis of the historical evolution of the role of constitutional, supreme, international and supranational courts from administrators of law though 'negative legislators' and elements of the rule of law and checks and balances principles to ultimate players in multilevel and pluralist constitutional games. Another argument is the rather problematic legitimacy of judicial dialogue with regard to the principles of Westphalian constitutional law. Indeed, judicial dialogue is to a great extent the result of the late Westphalian institutional design, but is in permanent tension with a large part of the Westphalian constitutional axiology and constitutional ideology.

This is one of the 'constructive cracks' of the late Westphalian constitutionalism. It consists in the fact that judicial dialogue is accomplished by institutions, some of which – the ordinary, supreme and constitutional courts – are elements of the Westphalian constitutional design. However, they are entrenched in institutional dialogue not only with their 'traditional institutional partners' – the governments and the parliaments, but also with international and supranational courts the latter being pillars of the emerging supranational and global constitutionalism. Moreover, judicial dialogue is at odds with Westphalian versions of sovereignty, democracy and separation of powers. Such discrepancy between institutional design and constitutional axiology is a clear indicator of the clash between Westphalian and post-Westphalian constitutionalism at the beginning of the XXI century.

In this regard, judicial dialogue is both the symptom of a crisis and one of its possible solutions and remedies. The spread of judicial dialogue and its status as an important contemporary phenomenon demonstrates the shift of decision-making centers in constitutional politics from political and democratic institutions such as the parliaments and the governments to expert and counter-majoritarian institutions such as the courts. Frequently, judicial dialogue resembles 'dribbling of the ball in the center of the constitutional and political playground' where the courts are aiding the politicians to come at joint or unilateral decisive conclusions for the future of their constitutional communities. Sometimes, judicial dialogue produces 'three point shots' allowing the courts to take decisions with fundamental importance for the constitutional order and the socio-political community instead of the political players. Thus, the courts are becoming ultimate players in multilevel and pluralist constitutional and constituent power games.

Such effects stemming out of the judicial dialogue indicate structural problems of representative democracy, separation of powers and sovereign decision making. They raise concerns regarding 'judicialization of politics' and 'politicization of the judiciary'. However, they are also pointing at eventual solutions of democratic and sovereigntist stalemates of the late Westphalian modernity. Taking the lead, the courts are gradually molding new constitutional ideologies, constitutional axiology and constitutional design which go beyond 'closed statehood', sovereignty and territorially entrenched democracy. These tendencies may be evaluated in positive or negative ways or both. However, they are definitely beyond the intellectual, conceptual and institutional framework of Westphalian constitutionalism, which is why judicial dialogue should be defined as a post-Westphalian phenomenon

2 Constitutional Dialogue as an Expression of Trust and Distrust in Multilevel Governance

Patricia Popelier and Catherine Van De Heyning

2.1 Towards a Framework for Understanding of Constitutional Dialogue

The idea of constitutional dialogue came into vogue with the capturing of the growing interdependence of legal system under theories of legal pluralism.[1] In a network of intermingled legal systems, a growing transnational interaction of courts was observed and put under the label of constitutional dialogue. In an effort to give a common understanding of this phenomenon, Meuwese and Snel defined it as

> a sequel of implicitly or explicitly shaped communications back and forth between two or more actors characterized by the absence of a dominant actor – or at least by a bracketing of dominance – with the shared intention of improving the practice of interpreting, reviewing, writing or amending constitutions.[2]

Although the authors propose an agenda for both empirical and normative research, there is a normative dimension in the very definition they put forward: all participants should pursue the common goal of improving constitutions. Scholars identify various purposes, depending on the angle from which judicial dialogue is observed. For example, under a theory of legal pluralism,

> the aim of constitutional conversations should ideally be to help ensure the smooth operation of a system in which there is no agreement on hierarchy and on the idea of ultimate authority and to avoid conflict in those circumstances.[3]

---

1 M. Claes, M. de Visser, P. Popelier & C. Van de Heyning, 'Introduction: On Constitutional Conversations', *in* M. Claes et. al. (eds) *Constitutional Conversations. Actors, Topics and Procedures,* Antwerp, Intersentia, 2012, pp. 2-3.

2 A. Meuwese & M. Snel, 'Constitutional Dialogue: an Overview', *Utrecht Law Review,* Vol. 9, 2013, p. 126.

3 Claes et al., 2012, p. 5.

Yet, in linguistic theories, purpose is immaterial for the definition of 'dialogue', which simply refers to a sequence of utterances in which more than one speaker is engaged successively.[4] It is institutionalization that transforms the nature of dialogue into a meaningful activity: a dialogue should further the aim for which it was institutionalized in the first place. In the absence of institutionalization, participants have their own reasons for engaging in a dialogue, which may or may not coincide, but the occurrence of a shared intention is not an inherent quality nor is it a criterion to qualify a dialogue as successful.

In reality, even participants in an institutionalized dialogue can have various reasons for stepping into the conversation. Especially when they function in different contexts, the idea that all participants are driven by a common purpose becomes highly idealistic. The question, then, is how they can be driven to participating in the dialogue in such a way that its purpose is achieved. If this proves difficult, another question is whether the purpose of the institutionalized dialogue is well-chosen in the first place; perhaps the conversation should rather serve a different purpose.

To answer these questions, we need to identify the purpose of the institutionalized dialogue and understand the motives of the direct and indirect participants in the conversation. By direct participants, we refer to the actors addressed by the institutionalized mechanism. Indirect actors put the institutions into motion. To capture their motives, we turn to concepts of 'trust' and 'distrust'. Our intuition is that (1) institutional dialogue hides a much broader conversation between multiple direct and indirect actors with different purposes; and that (2) a multi-level complex of trust and distrust determines the frequency and quality of the institutional dialogue.[5]

The aim of this chapter is to develop these propositions as a theoretical model for future research on institutional dialogues. Such analysis helps to find out whether institutional engineering may further the purpose of the mechanism. As this is only an explorative chapter, we only explain the main components of the model, and then apply it to one particular case: the judicial dialogue between the Belgian Constitutional Court and the European Court of Justice (CJEU) through the mechanism of preliminary questions. Preliminary questions to the CJEU are selected because this is the most institutionalized form of transnational dialogue. We further focus on constitutional courts because, as constitutional watchdog, they have a clearly defined purpose, and they are interested in dialogues on (national) constitutional matters.[6] This distinguishes them from other courts, whose interest in preliminary references have been analyzed in terms of economic,

4 M. Dascal, 'Introduction' *in* M. Dascal (ed.) *Dialogue: an interdisciplinary approach,* Amsterdam/Philadelphia, John Benjamins Publishing Company, 1985, p. 4.

5 M. Infantino, 'The Italian Constitutional Court in the European Space. An empirical approach'. Paper presented at the workshop on 'Dialogues on Constitutional Justice' for the Italian Constitutional Justice Project in Rome, University of Notre Dame, July 2018. Forthcoming in a book project by V. Barsotti, P.G. Carozza, M. Cartabia and A. Simoncini on *A Global Dialogue as a Method.*

6 M. Claes, 'Luxembourg, Here We Come? Constitutional Courts and the Preliminary Reference Procedure', *German L. Journal,* Vol. 16, 2015, pp. 1334-1335.

political and structural factors such as judicial competition, judicial empowerment, the level of economic activity, population size, access to justice and litigation rate and compliance with EU law.[7] Finally, the Belgian Constitutional Court is selected because it was the first to refer to the CJEU and is the most active of all constitutional courts to do so,[8] and has a reputation as Europe-friendly court.[9] Our aim is not to test the propositions, but to give indications that they bring a promising frame for further research on judicial dialogue.

The propositions implied in our intuition that constitutional conversations need more differentiation and are linked with concepts of trust and distrust structures the chapter.[10] First, we identify the actors in the dialogue as well as the official and unofficial purposes (Section 2.2). Next, we explain the concepts of trust and distrust and link this with institutional dialogue (Section 2.3). While we point to various indications for our propositions in the dialogue between the Belgian Constitutional Court and the CJEU in each section, we bring both components together in one case study (Section 2.4).

2.2 The Multiple Actors and Purposes in the Institutional Dialogue through Preliminary References

2.2.1 *The Mechanisms of Preliminary References and Its Purpose*

The mechanism of preliminary references is laid down in Article 267 of the Treaty on the Functioning of the European Union (TFEU), the Statute of the CJEU and the Rules of Procedure of the Court. According to Article 267, the TFEU, the CJEU has the power to give preliminary rulings on the interpretation of EU law and on the validity of secondary EU law. Any court or tribunal of a Member State may request a preliminary ruling whenever such a question is raised; this is an obligation for those courts against whose decisions there is no judicial remedy under national law.

---

7 M. Broberg & N. Fenger, 'Are Structural Factors (Part of)) the Explanation?', *European Law Journal*, Vol. 19, 2013, pp. 488-501; G. Tridimas & T. Tridimas, 'National Courts and the European Court of Justice: a public choice analysis of the preliminary reference procedure', *International Rev of Law and Economics*, Vol. 24, 2004, pp. 125-145.

8 By 2017, the Belgian constitutional court had already sent 28 (in the meantime 32) preliminary references. By contrast, the Austrian constitutional court comes second with 5 preliminary references and the Italian constitutional court third with 3 preliminary references. The Court of Justice, Annual activity report 2017.

9 M Claes, *The National Courts' Mandate in the European Constitution*, Oxford, Hart Publishing, 2006, p. 262.

10 In this contribution, we understand constitutional conversations as the formal interaction between the ECJ and domestic constitutional actors via preliminary references rather than on the basis of the content of the conversation (*e.g.* questions on the delineation of competences granted by the constitution). As such, all preliminary questions by the Belgian constitutional court will be included. *See* Claes *et al.*, 2012.

The CJEU has clarified the purpose of the task to give preliminary rulings with great emphasis on the need to ensure uniform interpretation and application of EU law throughout the Union.[11] It sees this as

> the veritable cornerstone of the operation of the internal market, since it plays a fundamental role in ensuring that the law established by the treaties retains its Community character with a view to guaranteeing that that law has the same effect in all circumstances in all the member states of the European Union.[12]

This way, it perceives itself as a constitutional court, with a role that is similar to that of constitutional courts in national legal systems.[13]

With this purpose in mind, it is essential that all national courts participate in the system with the shared intention of achieving the objectives of the treaties, at least, according to the CJEU, *in any case which is constitutional in character or which otherwise raises a question of importance for the development of the law.*[14] The CJEU explicitly refers to the system as "a dialogue" and praises this dialogue for having developed the EU legal order by allowing the Court to identify the "essential characteristics of the Community legal order", in particular "its primacy over the laws of the Member States, the direct effect of a whole series of provisions and the right of individuals to obtain redress when their rights are infringed by a breach of Community law for which a member state is responsible".[15]

This implies that national courts become cooperative agents of the EU system and share the goal of the uniform application of the treaties in general and the furthering of the internal market in particular. It has been noted that in reality, the cooperative nature of the mechanisms is not always observed, which is why the Rules of Procedures have become more stringent over time.[16] Constitutional courts in particular have been hesitant to send preliminary references.[17] Having been assigned with the particular task of protecting the national constitution, it is difficult for them to step into a dialogue with the purpose of ensuring the uniform application of EU law where this interferes with the constitution, and to submit themselves to the authority of the CJEU.

---

11 Report of the Court of Justice on certain aspects of the application of the Treaty on European Union 1995.
12 Report, p. 5.
13 Report, p. 2.
14 Report, p. 3.
15 Report, p. 4.
16 B. Wägenbaur, *Court of Justice of the EU - Commentary on Statute and Rules of Procedure*, C.H. Beck, Hart and Nomos, 2013, p. 68.
17 *See* J. Komarek, 'The Place of Constitutional Courts in the EU', *EuConst* Vol. 9, 2013, pp. 429-443; G. Martinico, 'Preliminary References and Constitutional Courts: Are You in the Mood for Dialogue?' *in* F. Fontanelli *et al.* (eds), *Shaping Rule of Law through Dialogue*, Europa Law Publishing, 2010, pp. 221-249.

Yet, over time, nationalist counter-reactions have started to transform the identity of the European Union. With clauses such as Article 4.2 of the Treaty on the European Union (TEU), which demands respect for the national identities of Member States, and Article 5.3 on subsidiarity, the core value of the EU legal system, centered on the internal market, is put into perspective by the dynamics between integration goals and national sovereignty claims. This gives national courts an opportunity to shift the purpose of the formal dialogue by arguing for national identity considerations in order to tone down the prevalence of EU law, or by questioning EU laws in light of the subsidiarity principle. These types of arguments are more easily included in constitutional narratives developed by constitutional courts. Constitutional courts have in effect opened dialogues on constitutional matters such as fundamental rights, constitutional limits to the European mandate and constitutional identity.[18]

Forcing the CJEU in such conversation, however, would make it drift away from the mechanism's initial purpose to ensure the uniform application as a precondition for an internal market. Until now, the CJEU has been reluctant to go along wholeheartedly with such shift.[19] This does not mean that the CJEU has been tone-deaf for the calls of the constitutional courts. On several issues the CJEU has taken the concerns of constitutional courts on board, most notably when recognizing fundamental rights as an integral part of EU law.[20] However, the CJEU "Europeanized" the issue, rather than recognizing this new approach as a reply to the constitutional concerns or providing a margin for constitutional values or principles.[21] As such, it prevents open conflicts but does not mitigate the constitutional court's underlying concern for the safeguarding of its own prerogatives and constitutional identity. The narrative has not shifted since the first rulings on the relation between the EU and constitutional courts.[22]

2.2.2 *Actors in the Preliminary References Dialogue*

Article 267 TFEU addresses two direct actors that participate in the preliminary references dialogue: a national court, and the CJEU. However, where this provision states that a preliminary reference can or must be sent 'whenever a question is raised', the litigants

18 *See* C. Van De Heyning, 'The European Perspective: From Lingua Franca to a Common Language', in Claes *et al.*, 2012, pp. 181-204.

19 Van De Heyning, 2012, p. 204.

20 CJEU, C-11/70 *Internationale Handelsgesellschaft mbH v. Einfuhr- und Vorratstelle fur Getreide und Futtermittel* [1970] ECR I-1125, para. 4.

21 In this well-known case, the CJEU argued that it would not set aside a Council Regulation on grounds of a potential violation of national constitutional law as this would have an adverse effect on the uniformity and efficacy of EU law. However, the CJEU argued that such argument could be taken on board if an "analogous guarantee inherent in EU law" existed. *Ibid.*

22 In contrast to the relationship of the CJEU to the ECtHR, whereby the CJEU has elaborated on the interaction and actively nurtured a judicial dialogue in its rulings.

before the national court materialize. In fact, indirect actors are present before the national court as well as the CJEU. It is useful to identify these actors, as they may all act in the pursuit of different purposes and have different relations of trust towards one another.

Actors before the Belgian Constitutional Court

The Belgian Constitutional Court was established in the 1980s as a result of the federalization process, which called for a neutral arbiter to solve federalism competence disputes. Gradually, its powers increased to include review of Acts of Parliament against fundamental rights and, via the equality clause, other constitutional disputes. Cases can be brought before the Court through annulment requests (within six months after publication of the Act) and preliminary references (without time limit). In annulment proceedings, petitioners file a direct action against an Act of Parliament within six months after its publication.

In annulment proceedings, petitioners are either (1) a federal or subnational government; (2) the president of a legislative assembly or (3) any person with an interest. The last category covers individuals, firms, public entities, NGOs, and so on. In preliminary reference cases, national courts or tribunals refer a question on the constitutionality of an Act of Parliament to the Constitutional Court.

Whenever a case is brought before the Constitutional Court, and it is not decided in a fast procedure for being manifestly inadmissible, founded or unfounded, the registry notifies (1) the federal and subnational governments and presidents of legislative assemblies; (2) the litigants before the referring court, and, (3) by way of an announcement in the Official Gazette, the wider public.[23] The government that represents the author of the Act of Parliament becomes a direct party. The other governments, the Presidents of legislative assemblies and the litigants before the national court can interfere as intervening parties. Other persons may also intervene if they give evidence of an interest in the outcome of the case, for example, if they are involved in similar litigations.[24]

This way, and especially in the case of abstract review, the Constitutional Court becomes a forum for dialogue between the legislators and stakeholders.

Actors before the CJEU

Before the CJEU as well, several parties can participate in preliminary ruling proceedings: the parties to the main proceedings, the Member States, the European Commission, and the institution which adopted the act the validity or interpretation of which is in dispute.[25] This way, all participants in the proceedings before the Belgian Constitutional Court can also participate in the proceedings before the CJEU, where additional partici-

23 Arts. 74 and 76-78 of the Special Law on the Constitutional Court.

24 Art. 87, Special Law on the Constitutional Court.

25 Third parties can also intervene in particular cases, *see* Art. 96 Rules of Procedure.

pants may join them. In addition, the Advocate General takes on part of the conversation, assisting the CJEU in making its decision.

Parties participating in the preliminary ruling proceedings can submit observations. This is a significant procedural rule: empirical research gives evidence that the CJEU is sensitive to these observations, which are experienced as political constraints. Both national governments and the Commission can affect the outcome of the preliminary ruling.[26] Hence, national governments may tone down the Court's agenda to accelerate the integration process if this runs counter to their preferences.

The Constitutional Court itself is not a party to the proceedings. However, indirectly, through framing the issue, the Constitutional Court provides a framework of review for the CJEU similar to how national courts frame constitutional issues when they refer a preliminary question to the Constitutional Court. How the question is articulated, constitutes a means of communication between the CJEU and the Constitutional Court.

2.2.3 *Indications for a Multiple-Purpose Conversation between the Belgian Constitutional Court and the CJEU*

The decision to refer a preliminary reference to the CJEU or not, is not necessarily inspired by the need to solve a technical question of EU law. The Constitutional Court regularly refuses to send a preliminary question, even if the *acte claire* theory does not apply.[27] If we compare the set of 26 preliminary reference decisions until 2016[28] with the set of 24 refusals in the same time period,[29] two variables stand out: salience and case outcome. We discuss salience in this paragraph, and case outcome in the next section.

Salience is measured by three indicators: referral to the full bench, the number or type of participants (more than 5, or more than 2 different types) and media attention before the judgment.[30] A case is not salient if no indicator is present, low salient when one is present, medium salient if two or highly salient if all three indicators are present. Even if, in our limited samples, the difference is not overwhelming, we still observe that salient cases are more likely to lead to a preliminary reference than no or low salient cases. In the sample of 26 preliminary references to the CJEU which so far have led to a final outcome,

26 C.J. Carrubba, M. Gabel and C. Hankla, 'Judicial Behavior under Political Constraints: Evidence from the European Court of Justice', *American Pol. Science Rev*, Vol. 102, 2008, pp. 449-450.

27 P. Van Nuffel, *Het Europees recht in de rechtspraak van het Arbitragehof* (European law in the case law of the Constitutional Court), in A. Alen (ed), *20 jaar Arbitragehof*, Antwerp, Kluwer, 2005, p. 43-45.

28 The set can be found on the website of the Constitutional Court, http://www.const-court.be. The preliminary references sent to the CJEU after that date has not yet led to a final decision.

29 Const. Court Nos. 81/2000, 100/2000, 136/2000, 94/2003, 143/2003, 151/2003, 92/2006, 139/2006, 121/2008, 84/2010, 99/2010, 131/2010, 128/2011, 180/2011, 40/2012, 161/2012, 27/2014, 107/2014, 32/2015, 66/2015, 114/2015, 35/2016, 89/2016, 125/2016, 19/2017, 109/2017.

30 J De Jaegere, *Judicial Review and Strategic Behaviour*, Oxford, Intersentia, 2019 (forthcoming).

a majority of 18 cases were medium or highly salient, whereas in the sample of refusals, this was the case for only 11 out of 24.

Most cases where the Belgian constitutional court decides to refer a preliminary question are salient only within Belgium. These cases do not necessarily trigger constitutional concern in other Member States, resulting in no or only a few Member States intervening before the CJEU. Of six high salient cases out of our sample, two triggered the intervention of two other Member States, in two others, only one other Member State intervened, and in the last two, no other Member State intervened. This is an indication that the Belgian Constitutional Court does not refer because the topic affects the fundamental principles of EU law or its interaction with national law, relevant to all; instead, it refers to solve a problem that is of particular domestic importance.

By referring to the CJEU, then, the Constitutional Court may widen the internal conversation, thereby mixing a conversation on constitutional rights and principles with a conversation on the scope of EU integration. The CJEU should be careful to acknowledge this, because, a supranational court is just as likely to lose legitimacy in the relationship with individual Member States if it does not fully take into account the sensitivity of a case within a Member State.[31] This brings us to the issue of trust and distrust.

However, salience of these cases may transcend Belgian borders. Where the validity or conformity of EU law with fundamental rights is raised before the highest courts in other Member States or hotly debated in European jurisprudence, the Belgian Constitutional Court is likely to join the debate by sending a preliminary question when brought before its bench. In such cases, the Court uses a concrete case to join in and position itself in a conversation that was already ongoing at the European level.[32] Such cases will then result in several countries intervening in the proceedings before the CJEU. A clear example is the 'Advocaten voor de Wereld' case on the validity of the European Arrest Warrant.[33] The conformity of the EAW with constitutional law and European fundamental rights law was already discussed before national courts and a recurrent topic in jurisprudence at the time of the preliminary reference.[34] In the proceedings before the CJEU, nine Member States intervened before the CJEU.[35] Another example concerns the preliminary

31 E. Voeten, 'Public Opinion and the Legitimacy of the Courts', *Theoretical Inquiries in Law*, Vol. 14, 2012, p. 416.

32 One could argue that the Belgian Constitutional Court plays an interesting mitigating role within the European constitutional discourse as most constitutional courts do not send preliminary questions to the CJEU. The Belgian Court thus translates constitutional concerns to the EU level.

33 Constitutional Court, 13 July 2005, nr 124/2005 (judgment of referral). The same is true for the second preliminary question of the Belgian Constitutional Court regarding the EAW, namely Belgian Constitutional Court, 24 July 2009, nr. 128/2009 (judgment of referral), resulting in CJEU decision C-305/05 *Ordre des Barreaux Francophones et Germanophone and others v. Conseil des Ministres* [2007] ECR I-5305.

34 In most Member States the validity of the EAW in view of EU law or constitutional law has been discussed resulting in several preliminary questions, most notably the German constitutional court (BVerfG, Case 2 BvR 2236/04, 18 July 2005 and later BVerfG, Case 2 BvR 2735/14, 15 December 2015) and the Spanish constitutional court (Tribunal Constitucional, decision of 9 June 2011 (resulting in the Melloni-case).

35 CJEU, C-303/05 *Advocaten voor de Wereld v. Leden van de Ministerraad* [2007] ECR I-03633.

question on the protection of legal privilege in relation to notification duties, in this case under the money-laundering directive.[36] An interesting example is the Constitutional Court's recent preliminary reference on the validity of the national data retention legislation.[37] Following the CJEU's cases *Digital Rights Ireland*[38] and *Tele2/Watson*[39] firmly restricting the conditions for the retention of telecommunication data, many Member States were wondering how to proceed to safeguard effective criminal investigations and intelligence operations while remaining within the legal framework set by the CJEU.[40] In addition, several supreme courts and constitutional courts are again confronted with questions on balancing the protection of personal data with the public interest of fighting serious crime and public safety.[41] Given that most authors had already indicated that the Belgian law was clearly at odds with the CJEU case law,[42] the Belgian Constitutional Court could have decided the case without a referral. However, by sending a preliminary question to the CJEU, the court actively seeks participation in the European debate on this contemporary issue. In essence, this question is a critique on the outcome in the case Tele2/Watson suggesting that the CJEU should also take other interests into account.

36 Constitutional Court 13 July 2005, nr. 126/2005 (judgment of referral), CJEU, C-305/05 Ordre des barreaux francophones et germanophone and others [2007] ECR I-5305 and Belgian Constitutional Court nr. 10/2008, 23 January 2008 (final judgment). Several previous cases on the scope of legal privilege had already been dealt with by the CJEU responding to preliminary questions of mostly UK and German courts, for example, discussion in the Akzo Nobel case on the perspective on legal privilege (T-125/30 R and *T-253/03 R Akzo Nobel Chemicals and Others v. Commission* [2003] ECR II-4771) and earlier Case *155/79 AM & S v. Commission [1982] E.C.R. 1575.*

37 Constitutional Court 19 July 2018, nr. 96/18 (judgment of referral) and pending (Case C-520/18).

38 CJEU 8 April 2014, *Digital Rights Ireland Ltd v. Minister for Communications, Marine and Natural Resources and Others and Kärntner Landesregierung and Others*, Joined cases C-293/12 and C-594/12, ECLI: EU:C:2014:238.

39 CJEU 21 December 2016, Tele2 Sverige and Watson, Joined cases C-203-15 and C-698/15, ECLI:EU: C:2016:970.

40 *See, e.g.*, active requests of Member States for new data retention legislation, in C. Stupp, 'Member states ask for new EU data retention rules', available at (accessed 29 March 2019): https://www.euractiv.com/section/digital/news/member-states-ask-for-new-eu-data-retention-rules/.

41 *See* most recent information from the Estonian Supreme Court having sent a preliminary question on the compatibility of the domestic data retention legislation with EU law, Tweede Kamer, JBZ-Raad, 2 January 2019.

42 A. Gosse, 'Dans quelle mesure les autorités judiciaires belges peuvent-elles contraindre des entreprises de télécommunication étrangères à collaborer à une enquête pénale en Belgique?', *Dr. pén.entr.* No. 3, 2017, S. Royer and C. Conings, 'Ook hervormde dataretentiewet staat onder druk', *Juristenkrant*, No. 134, 2017, p. 1, C. Van de Heyning, 'Het gebruik van telecommunicatiegegevens in het strafrechtelijk onderzoek in gevaar?', *RABG*, Vol. 7, 2017, p. 533-538 and C. Forget, 'L'obligation de conservation des "métadonnées", la fin d'une longue saga juridique?', *Journal des Tribunaux*, No. 6683, 2017, p. 233.

2.3 A MULTILEVEL COMPLEX OF TRUST AND DISTRUST

2.3.1 *Trust and Distrust*

Trust is, in essence, a psychological state that defines a person's expectations that another person, on whom one depends, will act favorable to one's interests, or does at least not have the intention to harm them.[43] By contrast, distrust is the suspicion that the other will act in a hostile or harmful way, or is not interested in one's welfare.[44]

These are fundamental notions for legal systems. Trust lays the foundation for the legal system as a whole and for contractual relationships in particular. States are structured as systems of organized trust and distrust: representative democracy implements fiduciary theory, whereas the rule of law and the separation of powers are based on a general distrust in persons in power. Nonetheless, constitutional scholars have generally left the concept of organizational trust to social scientists, turning to related, more familiar concepts such as legitimacy. Yet, trust is a useful concept to explain judicial dialogue, as it enables to schematize the circles of participants, each with their own purposes. In the context of preliminary references, the concept of trust holds that a national court will be more willing to send a preliminary question to the CJEU if it expects that the CJEU will act favorably to its interests. In legal scholarship, trust in this context has been defined as 'national judges' subjective belief about whether the CJEU will follow an expected course of action under conditions of uncertainty'.[45] An essential addition is that the national court must also believe that the expected outcome will not harm the national court's interests.[46] This may be crucial when, for example, a national constitutional court expects that the CJEU, when called to apply the national identity clause, will not sufficiently value the national perspective. Or if the national supreme or constitutional court suspects that the CJEU will not be sufficiently respectful towards the national supreme or constitutional court with the risk of undermining the latter's authority within the national system.[47]

43 R.M. Kramer, 'Trust and Distrust in Organisations; Emerging Perspectives, Enduring Questions', *Annu. Rev. Psychol.*, Vol. 50, 1999, p. 571; D.M. Rousseau, S.B. Sitkin, R.S. Burt and C. Camerer, 'Not so Different after All: a Cross-Discipline View of Trust', *The Academy of Management Review*, Vol. 23, 1998, p. 395.

44 Kramer, 1999, p. 587.

45 J.A. Mayoral, 'In the CJEU Judges Trust: A New Approach in the Judicial Construction of Europe', *JCMS*, Vol. 55, 2017, pp. 552, 556.

46 In this sense also Mayoral 2017, p. 552, although it is not included in his definition.

47 We note that the rationales for lower courts might differ from higher courts within the same national system. *E.g.* a constitutional court or supreme court might be wary of restrictions to its prerogatives by the CJEU or loss of authority within the national legal order, while a lower court might be willing to send preliminary questions to circumvent the supreme or constitutional court.

2.3.2 *Mechanisms to Build Trust at the European Level*

For courts of last instance, such as constitutional courts, an obligation to refer is in place. While this is, in trust literature, labeled 'deterrence-based trust', such duty can rather be seen as a mechanism for controlling behavior inspired by the absence of trust, or even by distrust.[48] The opening up of preliminary references to lower courts has also been perceived as a sign of distrust in the Supreme Court's willingness to participate in the dialogue.[49] However, apart from the State's potential liability for breach of EU law by the refusal of a national court to refer a preliminary reference,[50] no strong enforcement mechanism is in place.[51] This means that the preliminary reference mechanisms still rely on tools to build trust. At the EU level, institutional, substantive and informal mechanisms are established to this effect.

Institutional controls. Institutional controls aim at furthering trust in the CJEU, by ensuring that the ruling will be correct and timely. To further instill confidence in the capability of the judges, independence and expertise are important selection criteria, as well as the common accord of the Member States.[52] In addition, factors that frustrate trust, such as passing a reasonable term, are addressed: the CJEU pointed to some reorganizations that were made in order to reduce the time for preliminary rulings,[53] and an accelerated procedure can be requested in urgent cases.[54] Still, the average duration of preliminary reference proceedings is 15 to 16 months,[55] whereas the Constitutional Court is expected to decide within a term of 12 months.[56]

Substantive controls. To convince national courts of its reliability, the CJEU uses self-references.[57] Also, the Court's sensitivity for political constraints by intervening national governments can be seen as an effort to keep the Member States' trust in the institution. Further, the introduction of the *acte claire* theory to relax the duty to send preliminary references, can be regarded as a sign of confidence in the national supreme courts.[58] Moreover, out of respect for the autonomy of national courts, the CJEU is not entitled to interpret national law.[59]

---

48 Rousseau *et al.*, 1998, p. 399.
49 Komarek, 2013, p. 97.
50 *Case 224/01, Köbler v. Republik österreich*, [2003] ECR I-10239.
51 T. Tridimas, 'Knocking on heaven's door: fragmentation, efficiency and defiance in the preliminary reference procedure', *CMLRev*, Vol. 40, 2003, p. 14.
52 Art. 253 TFEU.
53 Report 1995.
54 Arts. 105 and 107 Rules of Procedure.
55 Court of Justice, Annual Report Judicial Activity 2017, for the years 2013-2017.
56 Art. 109 Special Law on the Constitutional Court.
57 M. Jacob, *Precedents and Case-Based Reasoning in the European Court of Justice*, Cambridge, Cambridge University Press, 2014, p. 7.
58 *Case 283/81, CILFIT v. Ministry of Health* [1982] ECR 3415.
59 D. Sarmiento, 'Half a Case at a Time: Dealing with Judicial Minimalism at the European Court of Justice', in Claes *et al.*, 2012, p. 17.

Informal mechanisms. The CJEU tries to build relational trust by visiting Member States, mostly on the invitation of supreme courts or constitutional courts.[60] Also, it publishes yearly activity reports, where it highlights its most important judgments and gives statistical information on its activities. By pointing out which constitutional courts have sent preliminary references to the CJEU, the CJEU may encourage other constitutional courts to follow the lead. This is because, as studies have shown, third parties may play an important role in the diffusion of trust.[61] This, however, was not an explanatory factor in the case of Belgium, as the Belgian Constitutional Court, being the first to send a preliminary reference, was rather the pioneer that paved the way for other constitutional courts to turn to the CJEU.[62]

2.3.3 *Incentives for the Constitutional Court to Trust*

In turn, the Constitutional Court may be inclined to refer a preliminary question if it relies on the CJEU to give clear guidance for the interpretation of complex or obscure EU law.[63] In addition, it may be more willing to send a preliminary reference when it relies on the CJEU to solve a salient case as a way to depoliticize its decision. In this case, the trust it puts in the CJEU is calculus-based:[64] it serves the Constitutional Court's own interests, instead of the shared purpose identified above.

We have already pointed out that the Belgian Constitutional Court is more likely to refer to the CJEU in salient cases. More generally, there is statistical evidence that the Belgian Constitutional Court uses EU law and the European Convention of human rights significantly more often in salient cases.[65] This implies that the Constitutional Court doubts that governments or the wider public has enough trust in the Court itself to accept a decision in sensitive cases but trusts upon the CJEU to depoliticize the matter. A precondition is that the wider public confides in the CJEU. If not, reference to the CJEU will not help the national court to protect itself against criticism. Confidence in a supranational court is dependent on the trust placed in the organization of which it forms a part.[66] According to the Eurobarometer, the Belgians' trust in the EU is above average.[67]

When comparing the sample of preliminary references with the sample of refusals, case outcome also comes to the fore as an important variable. In the set of preliminary

---

60 A. Rosas, 'The European Court of Justice in Context: Forms and Patterns of Judicial Dialogue', *Eu. J. Legal Studies*, Vol. 1, 2007, p. 132.
61 Kramer, 1999, pp. 576-577.
62 Martinico, 2010, pp. 225, 232.
63 Mayoral, 2017, pp. 557-558.
64 For this notion, *see* Rousseau *et al.*, 1998, pp. 399-400.
65 De Jaegere, 2019.
66 Voeten, 2012, p. 416.
67 *See*, apart from the country reports, also European Commission, Standard Eurobarometer 90 – Autumn 2018.

reference decisions, the challenged law was (at least partially) invalidated in a majority of 15 out of 26 judgments. In the set of refusals, only 6 out of 24 decisions led to invalidation in the final judgment. In other words: the Constitutional Court is more likely to send a preliminary reference, if it envisages the invalidation of the Act of Parliament. This indicates that the Court has strategic reasons for sending a preliminary reference: since the invalidation of an Act exposes the Court to criticism because of the counter-majoritarian difficulty, it is more inclined to put the blame on an external body if it contemplates invalidation. This way, it safeguards its neutrality and therefore its trustworthiness. This is especially important in salient cases, as is reflected in the sample: the difference becomes even more apparent when we combine salience and case outcome. If we compare medium and high salient cases in both sets, we find that when a preliminary reference is sent, this mostly leads to invalidation (14 out of 18 cases). By contrast, when the Court refuses to send a preliminary reference, the final case outcome is more likely a rejection (8 out of 11 cases).

The Constitutional Court may spontaneously decide to refer a preliminary question to the CJEU, or it may be pressured to do so by the parties before it. These parties may have different reasons for requesting a preliminary reference. The parties that challenge a parliamentary act may put more trust in the CJEU than in the Constitutional Court to interpret EU law, especially in technical matters. Distrust in the Constitutional Court may be expertise-based, as judges and clerks are mostly selected on the basis of their knowledge of constitutional, administrative or international law (or, for half of the judges, on the basis of their former mandate in a federal or subnational Parliament). For this reason, they accept the costs of procedural delays. They may be more inclined to accepts delay costs in abstract review cases, when they are not entangled in a concrete litigation, and especially if they act in a general interest, for example, as an NGO. The petitioner or the defending government may distrust the outcome of the case on the basis of the Constitutional Court's earlier judgments, and demand a preliminary reference to turn that case law. Or the petitioner or defending government may challenge the EU act, in which case they have no choice than to trust in the CJEU's capability and willingness to critically review EU acts, considering its monopoly for invalidating secondary EU acts.

In turn, the Constitutional Court may refuse to send a preliminary reference if it does not trust upon the CJEU to give a timely ruling, which in turn delays the proceedings before the Constitutional Court and may harm its own credibility. This is especially the case if the Constitutional Court itself is seized by a preliminary reference that arose from a concrete litigation before another court. Therefore, if a new issue of EU law would arise before the Constitutional Court after a preliminary reference has already been sent[68] or the proceedings up to the Constitutional Court had already been lengthy, the Constitutional Court can be expected to refrain from sending the matter to the CJEU. Also, the Constitutional Court may not trust in the CJEU to fully comprehend what is at stake at the national level and therefore decide to keep matters in its own hands. This means that even if the CJEU proves its trustworthiness by building a consistent set of case law in line with the integrative purpose of the European project, different views on the nature of the European project and the optimal balance between EU rules and national values may cause distrust in judicial relations.[69] By contrast, if the CJEU shows respect for national constitutional structures and shares concerns for fundamental constitutional values such as fundamental rights, constitutional courts may be more inclined to step into a formal dialogue.[70]

It is important to keep in mind that trust is a dynamic concept: it can be built, and it can decline again.[71] If trust is indeed the psychological state that motivates actors to enter into a meaningful dialogue, then it is important to continuously make efforts to consolidate and strengthen trust.

2.4 TRUST AND DISTRUST IN THE FORMAL DIALOGUE BETWEEN THE BELGIAN CONSTITUTIONAL COURT AND THE CJEU: A CASE STUDY

2.4.1 *The Social Care Insurance Case: Background*

The Social Care Insurance case, like so many other cases, illustrates how different actors in the conversation have different purposes. It starts as (1) a conversation between the parties about the constitutional structure. When the EU component is brought in, it becomes (2) a conversation about constitutional integrity. Then, still other actors join in to turn it into (3) a conversation about European integration.

In this case, the Flemish Community, a state in the Belgian federation, adopted a system to address care risk by paying the costs for care services to persons with insufficient resources. It benefitted persons with residence within the jurisdiction of the Flemish

68 *E.g.* the Constitutional Court had already sent a preliminary reference on the compatibility of the money-laundering directive with Art. 6 ECHR, when it was confronted with a new issue on its compatibility with Art. 8 ECHR. The Constitutional Court decided the matter itself on the basis of its own analysis: Constitutional Court no. 10/2008, 23 January 2008. *See* C. Van de Heyning, 'What role for the constitutional judge: the money-laundering directive and human rights', *in* A. Alen *et al.* (eds), *Liberae Cogitationes: Liber Amicorum Marc Bossuyt*, Antwerp, Intersentia, 2014, pp. 769-786.

69 Mayoral, 2017, pp. 558, 561-562.

70 Martinico believes this to be one of the explanatory factors for the turn in the Italian Constitutional Court's attitude, Martinico, 2010, pp. 237-245.

71 Rousseau *et al.*, 1998, p. 396.

Community. The residence-criterion was the obvious criterion for the locus of competence, because the law established a system of solidarity between residents, funded, partially, by taxes raised on the basis of residence, not income, and therefore the benefits were also granted on the basis of residence.[72] Remarks were made by the Council of State, in its advisory position, and upon the request by Dutch Members of the European Parliament, the European Commission started infringement procedures. As a result, an exception was added to exclude persons residing in Belgium but working abroad, and to include non-Belgians residing abroad, but employed in the Flemish Community.

2.4.2 A Conversation with Multiple Actors and Purposes

In this case, several conversations overlap leading to a complex coming together of incentives, expectations and deterrents that can be categorized in terms of trust and distrust.

Conversation 1. The first conversation entails the inter-federalized conversation between the Flemish Community on the one hand and the French Community and Walloon Region on the other. The Flemish law followed upon failed attempts to introduce such an instrument at the federal level.[73] The other entities challenged the Act, although the Constitutional Court had already confirmed the Flemish Community's competence in a previous decision.[74] On the basis of the exclusivity principle,[75] the French Community was competent to provide similar benefits to its residents, but did not have equivalent means and feared internal competition for residents in view of the benefits provided by the Flemish Community. Given the established position of the Constitutional Court, the French-speaking Community requested a preliminary reference to the CJEU.[76] The argument was that the care insurance discriminated, because it included non-Belgians employed in Flanders but living abroad, but excluded Belgians employed in Flanders but, after having lived abroad, now residing elsewhere in Belgium. This way, EU law was relied upon as a strategy to judicialize a domestic political conflict.

Conversation 2. The Flemish Government argued against the preliminary reference, holding that the EU perspective was not relevant, since this was merely a consequence of the constitutional system of allocation of competences. The Constitutional Court, as guardian of the constitution, had to decide between upholding the integrity of the constitutional system or undermining it by applying EU law to particular situations, with its

72 J. Velaers, 'Social Federalism and the distribution of competences in Belgium', in B. Cantillon, P. Popelier & N. Mussche (eds), *Social Federalism: the Creation of a Layered Welfare State,* Antwerp, Intersentia, 2011, p. 150.

73 *See* B. Cantillon, 'On the possibilities and limitations of a layered social security system in Belgium' in Cantillon, Popelier & Mussche, 2011, pp. 72-73.

74 Case No. 33/2001, 13 March 2001.

75 Council of State, Advisory Opinion of 21 April 2004, Parl. Doc. Senate, Special Session 2003, No. 3-38/2.

76 Case No. 51/2006, 19 April 2006, A.5.1.1.

contrasting view of the place of employment instead of residence as the locus of competence. As a way out, it acknowledged the French Community's request for a preliminary reference, which was clearly framed to provoke a violation-decision,[77] but rephrased it to question the application and interpretation of EU law. This way, it took refuge in the CJEU to counter the Commission's position. In its judgment of referral, it pointed to the fundamentals of the Belgian constitutional system of power allocation, based on exclusivity, and to the fact that this matter was essentially located within the borders of one Member State.[78]

Or continuation of conversation 1? In another interpretation, the Court was using EU law to take a balanced position in the face of an internal political power struggle and to please all parties. The acceptance by the constitutional court that both the federal government and the Communities could be competent to regulate the matter, depending on the angle that was taken,[79] was disputed in Belgium in view of exclusivity as the basic power allocation principle in Belgian federalism.[80] The CJEU could help the Constitutional Courts to reach a balanced outcome: accept the Flemish Community's powers in the field, but partially satisfy the French Community by granting people residing in the French- (and German-) speaking part, but employed in the Flemish territory, access to this benefit. From this point of view, the referral served the de-politicization and resolution of an internal power conflict.

Conversation 3. The Advocate General quite radically argued that the locus of employment should be the key criterion including for Belgian nationals that had not previously made use of the freedom of movement. However, she did caution that the matter should be discussed more profoundly and regretted for that reason that only the Dutch government had intervened.[81] The CJEU took a middle position, imposing the employment criterion upon situations with an EU dimension,[82] but suggesting to also apply it to Belgian nationals residing in the French- or German-speaking part, in the absence of an EU dimension.[83] This was, clearly, a conversation about the integrity of EU law, and an effort to align national systems as much as possible to the European one.

---

77 The proposed question was whether the TEU and the EU Regulation opposed discrimination between national and non-national residents.

78 B.13.3.

79 For a discussion: J. Vanpraet, 'Towards a two-speed social security system in federal Belgium?' *in* Cantillon, Popelier & Mussche, 2011, pp. 159-169.

80 In Belgium: either the federal government, the Communities or the Regions. On the principles of power allocation in Belgium, *see* P. Popelier, 'Zuständigkeitsteilung in Belgien: Kompetenzverteilung als Kenzeichen Multinationalen Konfliktsmanagement', *in* A. Gamper *et al.* (eds), *Föderale Kompetenzverteilung in Europa*, Baden-Baden, Nomos, 2016, pp. 151-180.

81 Conclusion of the Advocate General Sharpston in Case C-212/06, of 28 June 2007.

82 Case *C-212/6, Government of the French Community and Walloon Government v. Flemish Government*, 1 April 2008.

83 *Ibid.*, para. 40: "It may nevertheless be remarked that interpretation of provisions of Community law might possibly be of use to the national court, having regard too to situations classed as purely internal."

Conclusion of the conversation. As a result, the Belgian Constitutional Court upheld the Flemish law, with this exception.[84] Hence, the place of employment is the determining factor for inclusion in the care insurance system as soon as there is an EU dimension, but not in purely internal situations. The end of the conversations, then, was that (1) the constitutional structure based on exclusive powers was partially broken to empower both the states and the federal level, to satisfy all parties before the Court; (2) the integrity of the constitutional system of power allocation based on residence was partially undermined to conform with EU law and (3) integrity of the EU law system was secured but not in the most maximalist way.

One conclusion, then, is that constitutional conversations may lead to compromises, but also that the CJEU needs a sufficient number of participants to support radical moves. Another conclusion is that while judicial dialogue between Constitutional Courts and the CJEU is a tale about power relations between the EU and the Member States, the EU may, in fact, only play a side role in a conversation that mainly revolves around internal power relations.

2.4.3 *Trust and Distrust as Driving Factors*

The Care Insurance case shows that considerations of trust and distrust can be drivers for preliminary references, and that this is not merely a one-on-one relationship between the referring court and the CJEU.

French Community versus the Flemish Community: Remarkably, the federal government did not take action against the Flemish law in order to protect federal powers. The conversation concerned a conflict of powers, but the petitioners' powers were unaffected. This can be seen as a sign of distrust to be understood in the specific Belgian context: a dyadic federation opposing a Dutch- and a French speaking group, with differential appreciation of autonomy and (con-)federalism as well as different economic resources. Possibly, the French Community suspected the Flemish Community of using the social care insurance law as a test case to expand its powers to affect the centralized social security system.

French Community versus the Constitutional Court and the CJEU: In principle, an annulment request can be seen as a sign of trust in the Constitutional Court to deliver a judgment in the petitioner's favor. In this case, however, the French Community had no reason to trust the Constitutional Court. As mentioned, in an earlier decision, the Constitutional Court had already confirmed the Flemish Community's competence to establish a social care system. Instead, it put trust in the CJEU to take a European perspective and to not bother too much about the Belgian constitutional structure. Worst-case scenario was that the CJEU, from this European perspective, would force an exception to the

84 Belgian Constitutional Court No. 11/2009, 21 January 2009.

basic regulation. The French-speaking Community could then use this to plead for a coherent solution. Best-case scenario was that the CJEU would command the application of the employment criterion overall. As such, there was a substantial incentive in terms of trust for the French community to seek guidance from the CJEU.

Flemish Community versus the Constitutional Court and the CJEU: The Flemish Community had every reason to ward off the request for a preliminary reference. It put trust in the Constitutional Court, given its previous decision, but not in the CJEU, considering its reputation.

Constitutional Court versus the CJEU, the French-speaking Community, the Flemish Community, and the public. The Constitutional Court is concerned about its trustworthiness towards all relevant actors: the federal government and the states (Communities and Regions), but also the public at large. Earlier research gave evidence that the Court takes a balanced position in federal competence disputes, and that this position is often based upon strategic considerations.[85] Institutional guarantees secure its trustworthiness in this respect, for example, the language parity in its composition. In this case, consistency was important. It risked losing the Flemish Community's trust if it would now turn its previous decision in favor of the Community's competence. Moreover, it was concerned about the integrity of the constitutional structure. The CJEU could be trusted to guard compliance with the free movement principles, but it does not have a reputation to take domestic concerns into account if they affect the effectiveness of European integration.

By referring a preliminary reference, however, the Constitutional Court could 'outsource' the issue and protect its own trustworthiness to all federal entities as it did not take the position while taking into account all perspectives in its decision of referral. The Constitutional Court has accepted the superiority of EU law and often turns to EU law to solve a domestic dispute. Therefore, it would be inconsistent to set aside EU law to protect the integrity of the constitutional structure – unless the CJEU itself would allow this. Worst-case scenario, but the most expected outcome, was that the CJEU would secure free movement in all situations with an EU dimension. Best-case scenario was that the CJEU would positively reply to the Constitutional Court's invitation to widen the purpose of the conversation to include domestic values and concerns. The only situation in which the CJEU risked to lose the Constitutional Court's trust, was if the CJEU would have followed the Advocate General's view, and command the employment criterion even to Belgians in purely internal situations.

Hence, a complex set of trust and distrust relations may explain the behavior of the relevant actors in preliminary reference proceedings. Moreover, a specific decision (EU rules of free movement also apply in internal situations) may be applauded by one actor (the French Community) but distort the trust of other actors (the Constitutional Court and the Flemish Community). The key question for the trustees, then, is whose trust is

85 P. Popelier and S. Bielen, 'How Courts Decide Federalism Disputes', *Publius: the Journal of Federalism*, 2019, pp. 23-24.

most important to win or to keep. This, clearly, is a question that surpasses the interests of the particular parties in the case at hand. Consistency is the best option to gain trust. If the Court wishes to push for a more radical path without losing trustworthiness, it needs to include more participants in the conversation to cover all sides. Hence, the Advocate General's reservation to her own proposal to apply EU law to internal situations, considering the limited number of intervening Member States and the Constitutional Court's referral to the CJEU before excluding EU law in favor of the integrity of the constitutional structure. This is where the trust perspective and the judicial conversation perspective meet.

2.5 Conclusion

In this chapter, we argued that concepts of trust and distrust are helpful to understand the complexity of institutionalized constitutional conversations. Even if we focus on a clear-cut mechanism for dialogue, such as preliminary references to the CJEU, this cannot simply be regarded as a dialogue between two courts. Instead, circles of participants in the conversation are included at both levels, each with their own interests, with varying relationships of trust and distrust, and with different purposes for joining the conversation. In this regard, it is especially useful to examine conversations with constitutional courts: because of their specific mandate as guardian of the national constitution, the scope and nature of these conversations are likely to differ from those with ordinary courts.

Our conclusion is that it is utopian to expect constitutional courts to enter into a conversation with the CJEU with the sole purpose of furthering the uniform application of the treaties in general and of the internal market in particular. Clinging on to this can be counter-effective, as non-responsiveness to the domestic concerns and values raised by constitutional courts may frustrate trust. As a result, constitutional courts may return to a position of distrust and decline from sending further preliminary references.[86] Ideally, then, the conversation should be aimed at finding an optimal balance between European integration and national constitutional principles.

As mentioned in the introduction, the CJEU so far has been reluctant to go along with such shift, showing willingness to respect constitutional concerns mainly if these can be 'Europeanized'. The question, then, is how the CJEU can be driven to participate in the dialogue with a different mind-set. In a study to explain centralization tendencies in the CJEU, Vaubel concluded that an important explanatory factor is 'self-selection'.[87] Judges in the CJEU are trained in EU law and have a bias in favor of the EU. The solution to this

86 Claes, 2015, p. 1342.

87 R. Vaubel, 'Constitutional courts as promoters of political centralization: Lessons for the Court of Justice', *European Journal of Law and Economics*, Vol. 28, 2009, p. 218.

is to promote informal conversations between constitutional courts and the CJEU, not merely through informal visits, but also by exchanging judges. Vaubel adds that the combination of two tasks reinforces the tendency to centralize: the task of allocating powers between the Member States and the Union, and the task of interpreting Union law within the Union's powers. He therefore suggests creating a 'Subsidiarity Court' consisting of judges of the Member States' apex courts for limited terms, with the sole task of adjudicating cases concerning the division of powers between the Member States and the Union.[88] For a balanced conversation, and to enhance institutional trust, we propose to also add judges from the CJEU. Institutional engineering, then, may turn a dialogue of the deaf into a constructive conversation.

88 He refers to a suggestion proposed on several occasions by himself and other members of the 'European Constitutional Group', *e.g.* P. Bernholz, F. Schneider, R. Vaubel & F. Vibert, 'An Alternative Constitutional Treaty for the European Union' (2004) 118 *Public Choice* Vol. 118, 2004, pp. 451-468.

3 The Court of Justice of the EU as an EU Constitutional Court: Is It Lawful (and Desirable)?

Ivan Ingravallo

3.1 Introductory Remarks

The author discusses the topic of the judicial dialogue with the main point being the fact that the Court of Justice of the EU (CJEU or the Court) has progressively acquired the role of a Constitutional Court in the EEC/EC/EU legal system. At times this led to some controversy between the CJEU and the national Constitutional Courts of EU Member States. The author refers to mechanisms that are well-known in national legal systems possessing a written Constitution and a Constitutional Court entrusted with the power to adjudicate on contradictions between the national constitutional rules and other legal rules. The author's legal analysis can also be helpful in relation to those national legal systems that do not have a Constitution and/or a Constitutional Court.

The author is aware that it is risky to apply theoretical notions of a specific branch of law – in this case, the constitutional law – to an institution (the CJEU) that belongs to another branch of law (the EU law). However, he chooses to follow the approach promoted by the CJEU in its own case law instead of following a more doctrinal approach.[1] For that reason, the author prefers to abstain from making references to specific authors or national legal doctrines.

It is well-known that the CJEU has had a formidable role in shaping the process of progressive integration of the European States. To put it simply, in the course of time the Member States negotiated and acceded to the EEC/EC/EU Treaties, the EU institutions discussed and adopted the secondary EU law, but it was the CJEU that was in the position

---

1 The topic of the legal reasoning of the CJEU is hotly debated. *See* J. Bengoetxea, *The Legal Reasoning of the European Court of Justice*, Oxford, Claredon Press, 1993; U. Everling, 'Reflections on the Reasoning in the Judgments of the Court of Justice of European Communities', *in Festskrift til Ole Due*, København, G.E.C. Gads Forlag, 1994, pp. 55-74; N. Fennelly, 'Legal Interpretation at the European Court of Justice', *Fordham International Law Journal*, Vol. 20, No. 3, 1997, pp. 656-679; O. Pollicino, 'Legal Reasoning of the Court of Justice in the Context of the Principle of Equality between Judicial Activism and Self-restraint', *German Law Journal*, Vol. 5, No. 3, 2004, pp. 283-317; G. Beck, *The Legal Reasoning of the Court of Justice of the EU*, Oxford, Hart, 2012; G. Conway, *The Limits of Legal Reasoning and the European Court of Justice*, Cambridge, CUP, 2012; K. Lenaerts, 'How the ECJ Thinks: A Study on Judicial Legitimacy', *Fordham International Law Journal*, Vol. 36, No. 5, 2013, pp. 1302-1371.

of key interpreter of the EU law. That is why it is impossible to properly understand the EU legal system without recognizing the 60-year long contribution of the CJEU for the EU integration.[2]

It was predominantly during the first three decades of the European integration, when the Treaties remained largely unchanged, that the jurisprudence of the CJEU, together with a proactive attitude of the European Commission, reinforced the newly established legal system, its autonomy and primacy over the national legal systems.

The CJEU has progressively created a 'web' (or a 'net') of jurisprudence. This way its judgments should not be seen in isolation, but should be included in a 'flux' of jurisprudence.[3] As a consequence they gradually became difficult to be challenged. In addition the CJEU has defined its own jurisdiction as part of 'the very foundations of the Community'.[4]

Here, the author is considering the constitutional attitude of the Court in relation to two different legal systems: the national and the international. In both cases the 'constitutional' approach is visible from and stems out of the case law of the CJEU. On the one hand, this approach is based on the supremacy of the EU law over the national legal systems.[5] It has been produced by virtue of an approach similar to the one used in federal states with regard to the relationship between the 'central' government and the federal units. On the other hand, the constitutional approach is also founded on the autonomy of the EU legal order with regard to the international law.

3.2 The Main Features of the CJEU and the Evolution of Its Role

The founding Member States of the EU decided to set up a Court since the very beginning of the integration process. In the Treaty of 1951 establishing the European Coal and Steel

2 *See, ex multis*, R. Lecourt, *L'Europe des juges*, Bruxelles, Bruylant, 1976; A. Arnull, *The European Union and Its Court of Justice*, 2nd ed., Oxford, OUP, 2006.

3 F. Capotorti, 'Le sentenze della Corte di giustizia delle Comunità europee', *in La sentenza in Europa. Metodo, tecnica e stile*, Padova, CEDAM, 1988, pp. 230-247; A. Arnull, 'Interpretation and Precedent in European Community Law', *in* M. Andenas & F. Jacobs (Eds), *European Community Law in the English Courts*, Oxford, Claredon Press, 1998, pp. 115-136; E. Sharpston, 'Transparency and Clear Legal Language in the European Union: Ambiguous Legislative Texts, Laconic Pronouncements and the Credibility of the Judicial System', *Cambridge Yearbook of European Legal Studies*, Vol. 12, 2009-2010, pp. 409-423.

4 Court of Justice, opinion of 14 December 1991 in Case 1/91, para. 71.

5 G.F. Mancini, 'The Making of a Constitution for Europe', *Common Market Law Review*, Vol. 26, No. 4, 1989, pp. 595-614; T.C. Hartley, 'The European Court, Judicial Objectivity and the Constitution of the European Union', *Law Quarterly Review*, Vol. 112, January 1996, pp. 95-109; M. Poiares Maduro, 'Interpreting European Law: Judicial Adjudication in the Context of Constitutional Pluralism', *in Estudos em homenagem ao Professor Doutor Paulo de Pitta e Cunha*, Coimbra, Almedina, vol. I, 2010, pp. 833-850; G. Itzcovich, 'The European Court of Justice as a Constitutional Court. Legal Reasoning in a Comparative Perspective', 2014, www.stals.sssup.it/files/itzcovich%204%202014.pdf (Accessed 14 April 2019).

Community (TECSC) the newly established Court was entrusted with the task to 'ensure that in the interpretation and application of the Treaties the law is observed' (Art. 31 TECSC).[6] This has been confirmed in the reform Treaties and it is now stated by Article 19 of the Treaty on the European Union (TEU).

The main tool used by the Court in order to shape and to strengthen the supranational legal system was the preliminary ruling procedure provided by Article 177 of the Treaty of 1957 establishing the European Economic Community (TEEC) and presently regulated by Article 267 of the Treaty on the Functioning of the European Union (TFEU). The Court gives preliminary rulings concerning the interpretation of the Treaties and the validity and interpretation of acts adopted by the institutions.

The Member States, by virtue of the same article, imposed upon their national jurisdictions 'against whose decisions there is no judicial remedy under national law' the duty to ask the Court to interpret the Treaties and to construe or evaluate the legislation coming from the (then) newly established organization. The Court itself clarified that

> the authority of an interpretation under Article 177 [now 267] already given by the Court may deprive the obligation of its purpose and thus empty it of its substance. Such is the case especially when the question raised is materially identical with a question which has already been the subject of a preliminary ruling in a similar case.[7]

In another judgment, the Court added:

> the same effect...may be produced where previous decisions of the Court have already dealt with the point of law in question...even though the questions at issue are not strictly identical

or

> the correct application of Community law may be so obvious as to leave no scope for any reasonable doubt as to the manner in which the question raised is to be resolved. Before it comes to the conclusion that such is the case, the national court or tribunal must be convinced that the matter is equally obvious to the courts of the other Member States and to the Court of Justice.[8]

---

6 G. Bebr, 'The Development of a Community Law by the Court of the European Coal and Steel Community', *Minnesota Law Review*, Vol. 42, No. 5, 1958, pp. 845-878.

7 Court of Justice, judgment of 27 March 1963 in Joined Cases 28 to 30/62,*Da Costa*.

8 Court of Justice, judgment of 6 October 1982 in Case 283/81, *CILFIT*, paras. 14 and 16.

In a recent judgment, the CJEU declared firmly that the EU judicial system 'has as its keystone the preliminary ruling procedure'.[9]

Moreover, the CJEU affirmed that, exceptionally, there is state's liability 'for an infringement of Community law by a decision of a national court adjudicating at last instance' when 'the court has manifestly infringed the applicable law'. This infringement 'will be sufficiently serious where the decision concerned was made in manifest breach of the case-law of the Court in the matter' and among the factors that produce liability there is the 'non-compliance by the court in question with its obligation to make a reference for a preliminary ruling'.[10] In the *Lucchini* judgment, the Court declared that 'Community law precludes the application of a provision of national law...which seeks to lay down the principle of *res judicata*...in breach of Community law'.[11] In another judgment, it affirmed that

> EU law does not require a judicial body automatically to go back on a judgment having the authority of *res judicata* in order to take into account the interpretation of a relevant provision of EU law adopted by the Court after delivery of that judgment,

although 'the principle of *res judicata* does not preclude recognition of the principle of State liability for a decision of a court adjudicating at last instance'.[12]

The hierarchical relationship between the EEC/EC/EU system, including its Court, and the national ones, including their judges, emerges from a renowned judgment, where the Court stated that national courts

> do not have the power to declare acts of the Community institutions invalid... Divergences between courts in the Member States as to the validity of Community acts would be liable to place in jeopardy the very unity of the Community legal order and detract from the fundamental requirement of legal certainty. The same conclusion is dictated by consideration of the necessary coherence of the system of judicial protection established by the Treaty...Since Article 173 [now 263 TFEU] gives the Court exclusive jurisdiction to declare void an act of a Community institution, the coherence of the system requires that where the validity of a Community act is challenged before a national court the power to declare the act invalid must also be reserved to the Court of Justice.[13]

9 Court of Justice [Grand Chamber], judgment of 24 October 2018 in Case C-234/17, *XC*, para. 176.
10 Court of Justice, judgment of 30 September 2002 in Case C-224/01, *Köbler*, paras. 53, 56 and 55.
11 Court of Justice [Grand Chamber], judgment of 18 July 2007 in Case C-119/05, *Lucchini*, para. 63.
12 Case C-234/17, *XC*, paras. 54 and 58.
13 Court of Justice, judgment of 22 October 1987 in Case 314/85, *Foto-Frost*, paras. 15-17.

During the decades the Court has accomplished the interpretative function that the Member States assigned to it. From the beginning it has applied a predominantly teleological (functional) approach to the interpretation of the Treaties and the secondary law[14] including in cases when it considered the latter's validity, combined with a dynamic and evolutive mood and with a smart use of the notion of *effet utile*.[15] From the Court's perspective these interpretative approaches appear logical[16] and can hardly be criticized. It would be quite ingenuous to expect from the Court 'of' the Community an approach against the Community or simply deferential to the will of the national governments.[17]

The Court has adopted such an interpretative approach in order to foster the autonomy of the EEC/EC/EU legal system. This autonomy refers to both the international legal system as well as that of the Member States, coining the notion of 'supranational' as different from the international and national ('the Community constitutes a new legal order of international law';[18] 'By contrast with ordinary international treaties, the EEC Treaty has created its own legal system').[19]

A decisive step further has been to combine this autonomy with the integration of the supranational legal system with the national ones and to establish its prevalence over them. In the *Costa v. ENEL* judgment, the Court declared that this legal system 'became

14 P. Pescatore, 'Les objectifs de la Communauté européenne comme principes d'interprétation dans la jurisprudence de la Cour de justice', *in Miscellanea W. J. Ganshof van der Meersch*, Bruxelles, ULB, vol. II, 1972, pp. 325-363; A. Albors Llorens, 'The European Court of Justice, More than a Teleological Court', *Cambridge Yearbook of European Legal Studies*, Vol. 2, 1999, pp. 373-398; J. Joussen, 'L'interpretazione (teleologica) del diritto comunitario', *Rivista critica del diritto privato*, Vol. 9, No. 4, 2001, pp. 491-537.

15 H. Kutscher, 'Méthodes d'interprétation vue par un juge à la Cour', *in Rencontre judiciaire et universitaire, 27-28 septembre 1976*, Luxembourg, Cour de justice, 1976, pp. I.1-I.53 ss.; A.E. Bredimas, *Methods of Interpretation and Community Law*, Amsterdam, North-Holland Publishing, 1978; J. Mertens de Wilmars, 'Réflexions sur les méthodes d'interprétation de la Cour de justice des Communautés européennes', *Cahiers de droit européen*, Vol. 22, No. 1, 1986, pp. 5-20; T. Koopmans, 'The Theory of Interpretation and the Court of Justice', *in* D. O'Keeffe (Ed.), *Judicial Review in European Union Law: Liber Amicorum in Honour of Lord Slynn of Hadley*, The Hague, Kluwer, 2000, pp. 45-58; G. Itzcovich, 'The Interpretation of Community Law by the European Court of Justice', *German Law Journal*, Vol. 10, No. 5, 2009, pp. 537-559; K. Lenaerts & J.A. Gutiérrez-Fons, 'To Say What the Law of the EU Is: Methods of Interpretation and the European Court of Justice', 2013, http://cadmus.eui.eu/handle/1814/28339 (Accessed 14 April 2019).

16 R. Ormand, 'L'utilisation particulière de la méthode d'interprétation des traités selon leur «effet utile» par la Cour de Justice des Communautés Européennes', *Revue trimestrielle de droit européen*, Vol. 12, No. 4, 1976, pp. 624-634; I. Ingravallo, *L'effetto utile nell'interpretazione del diritto dell'Unione europea*, Bari, Cacucci, 2017.

17 About the 'activism' of the CJEU, *see ex multis*, T. Tridimas, 'The Court of Justice and Judicial Activism', *European Law Review*, Vol. 21, No. 3, 1996, pp. 199-210; V. Constantinesco, 'The ECJ as a Law-maker *praeter aut contra legem*?' *in* D. O'Keeffe (Ed.), *Judicial Review in European Union Law: Liber Amicorum in Honour of Lord Slynn of Hadley*, The Hague, Kluwer, 2000, pp. 73-79; S. Weatherill, 'Activism and Restraint in the European Court of Justice', *in* P. Capps *et al.* (Eds), *Asserting Jurisdiction. International and European Legal Perspectives*, Oxford, Hart, 2003, pp. 255-281; E. Muir, M. Dawson & B. de Witte, 'Introduction: The European Court of Justice as a Political Actor', *in* M. Dawson *et al.* (Eds), *Judicial Activism at the European Court of Justice*, Cheltenham, Edward Elgar, 2013, pp. 1-10; A. Arnull, 'Judicial Activism and the European Court of Justice: How Should Academics Respond?', *ibid.*, pp. 211-232.

18 Court of Justice, judgment of 5 February 1963 in Case 26/62, *van Gend & Loos.*

19 Court of Justice, judgment of 15 July 1964 in Case 6/64, *Costa v. ENEL.*

an integral part of the legal systems of the Member States and ... their courts are bound to apply'; 'the law stemming from the Treaty, an independent source of law, could not ... be overridden by domestic legal provisions ... without being deprived of its character as Community law and without the legal basis of the Community itself being called into question.' As the Court adamantly affirmed in one of its most renowned subsequent judgments: 'the EEC Treaty has created its own legal system, which is integrated into the legal systems of the Member States and which their courts are bound to apply'.[20]

In line with this approach and with respect to fundamental rights, the Court affirmed: 'Recourse to legal rules or concepts of national law in order to judge the validity of measures adopted by the institutions of the Community would have an adverse effect on the uniformity and efficacy of Community law. ... [R]espect for fundamental rights forms an integral part of the general principles of law protected by the Court of Justice.'[21] And in a more recent judgment the CJEU confirmed that, 'by virtue of the principle of primacy of EU law, which is an essential feature of the EU legal order ... rules of national law, even of a constitutional order, cannot be allowed to undermine the effectiveness of EU law on the territory of that State.'[22]

In the renowned *Simmenthal* judgment, the Court declared firmly:

> in accordance with the principle of the precedence of Community law [these provisions] not only by their entry into force render automatically inapplicable any conflicting provision of current national law but ... also preclude the valid adoption of new national legislative measures; every national court must ... apply Community law ... and must accordingly set aside any provision of national law which may conflict; every national court is under a duty to give full effect to those provision [of Community law], if necessary refusing of its own motion to apply any conflicting provision of national legislation, even if adopted subsequently, and it is not necessary for the court to request or await the prior setting aside of such provision by legislative or other constitutional means.[23]

20 Court of Justice, judgment of 19 November 1991 in Joined Cases C-6/90 and C-9/90, *Francovich*, para. 31.

21 Court of Justice, judgment of 17 December 1970 in Case 11/70, *Internationale Handelsgesellschaft mbH*, paras. 3-4.

22 Court of Justice [Grand Chamber], judgment of 26 February 2013 in Case C-399/11, *Melloni*, para. 59.

23 Court of Justice, judgment of 9 March 1978 in Case 106/77, *Simmenthal*, paras. 17, 21 and 24. *See also* Court of Justice [Grand Chamber], judgment of 20 March 2018 in Case C-537/16, *Garlsson*, para. 67. In another judgment, the Court affirmed: 'the national court which, adjudicating as court of final instance, has complied with its obligation to make a reference to the Court for a preliminary ruling under the third paragraph of Article 267 TFEU, is bound, for the purposes of the decision to be given in the main proceedings, by the interpretation of the provisions at issue given by the Court and must, if necessary, *disregard any national case-law which it considers inconsistent with EU law*'; Court of Justice [Grand Chamber], judgment of 5 April 2016 in Case C-689/13, *Puligienica*, para. 38 (emphasis added).

This is also true for the national administrative authorities as the Court declared in the *F.lli Costanzo* judgment (1989)[24] and recently confirmed in *The Trustees of the BT Pension Scheme* judgment (2017).[25]

In several recent judgments the CJEU not only has confirmed this stance, but it has also added:

> Any provision of a national legal system and any legislative, administrative or judicial practice which might impair the effectiveness of European Union law by withholding from the national court having jurisdiction to apply such law the power to do everything necessary at the moment of its application to set aside national legislative provisions which might prevent European Union rules from having full force and effect are incompatible with these requirements, which are the very essence of European Union law.[26]

In another judgment, the CJEU added that

> the requirement to give full effect to EU law includes the obligation on a national court to alter established case-law, where necessary, if that is based on an interpretation of national law that is incompatible with EU law.[27]

3.3 The Self-Proclaimed 'Constitutional' Character of the CJEU

It is indisputable that the CJEU has been a formidable 'engine' for the establishment of 'an ever closer union among the peoples of Europe', just to recall the words contained in the preamble of the TEEC of 1957 and of the current EU Treaties. Moreover, it has repeatedly referred to national judges as 'community' judges when they are confronted with EEC/EC/EU rules, asking them to interpret and apply these rules following a coherent and uniform approach.[28]

---

24 Court of Justice, judgment of 22 June 1989 in Case 103/88, *F.lli Costanzo*, para. 31.

25 Court of Justice, judgment of 14 September 2017 in Case C-628/15, *The Trustees of the BT Pension Scheme*, para. 54. *See also* Court of Justice [Grand Chamber], judgment of 6 March 2018 in Joined Cases C-52/16 and C-113/16, *SEGRO*, para. 46.

26 Court of Justice [Grand Chamber], judgment of 26 February 2013 in *Case C-617/10, Åkerberg Fransson*, para. 46. *See also* Court of Justice, judgment of 11 September 2014 in Case C-112/13, *A*, para. 37.

27 Court of Justice [Grand Chamber], judgment of 5 July 2016 in Case C-614/14, *Ognyanov*, para. 35.

28 R. Monaco, 'Hauptreferat/Rapport Général', *in Zehn Jahre Rechtsprechung des Gerichtshofs der Europäischen Gemeinschaften/Dix ans de jurisprudence de la Cour de justice des Communautés européennes*, Köln, Carl Heymanns Verlag KG, 1965; T. Koopmans, 'The Birth of European Law at the Crossroads of Legal Traditions', *American Journal of Comparative Law*, Vol. 39, No. 3, 1991, pp. 493-507; U. Everling, 'On the Judge-made Law of the European Community's Courts', *in* D. O'Keeffe (Ed.), *Judicial Review in European Union Law: Liber Amicorum in Honour of Lord Slynn of Hadley*, The Hague, Kluwer, 2000, pp. 29-44.

> The following reasoning is indicative of the 'constitutional' mood of the EU Court:
> national courts and tribunals, in collaboration with the Court of Justice, fulfil a duty entrusted to them jointly of ensuring that in the interpretation and application of the Treaties the law is observed;

their independence is 'essential to the proper working of the judicial cooperation system embodied by the preliminary ruling mechanism under Article 267 TFEU'.[29] The same is true in relation to the mutual trust between the EU Member States as regards the execution of a European arrest warrant.[30]

The preliminary ruling procedure is essential in this respect. By means of this procedure, the CJEU has been capable not only to foster the uniform interpretation[31] and application of EU rules (via the *erga omnes* effect of its judgments), but also to 'indirectly' evaluate the conformity of national legislation with the supranational rules. Furthermore, it has elaborated and/or promoted many legal constructions, such as the direct effect of EEC/EC/EU legal rules, the principle of loyal cooperation, the relevance of human rights and democracy at supranational level, and so on.

In 1990, the Court affirmed that 'in applying national law...the national court called upon to interpret it is required to do so, as far as possible, in the light of the wording and the purpose of the directive in order to achieve the result pursued by the latter'.[32] This is also true with reference to the whole EU legal system, including the former pillars.[33] In a very recent judgment, the CJEU declared that

> although it is true that the authors of the Treaties have ascribed only limited powers to the Union in criminal matters, it is nonetheless apparent from the case-law of the Court that EU law sets certain limits to the powers of Member States in such matters.[34]

---

29 Court of Justice [Grand Chamber], judgment of 27 February 2018 in Case C-64/16, *Associação Sindacal dos Juízes Portugueses*, paras. 33 and 43.

30 *See, ex multis*, Court of Justice [Grand Chamber], judgment of 5 April 2016 in Joined Cases C-404/15 and C-659/15 PPU, *Aranyosi*, para. 78; Court of Justice [Grand Chamber], judgment of 25 July 2018 in Case C-216/18 PPU, *LM*, paras. 35, 36 and 43; and Court of Justice, judgment of 25 July 2018 in Case C-220/18 PPU, *ML*, paras. 48, 49 and 112.

31 Court of Justice [Grand Chamber], judgment of 21 December 2011 in Joined Cases C-424/10 and C-425/10, *Ziolkowski*, para. 32: 'It must be noted, first, that, according to settled case-law, the need for a uniform application of European Union law and the principle of equality require that the terms of a provision of European Union law which makes no express reference to the law of the Member States for the purpose of determining its meaning and scope must normally be given an independent and uniform interpretation throughout the European Union'.

32 Court of Justice, judgment of 13 November 1990 in Case C-106/89, *Marleasing*, para. 8.

33 Court of Justice [Grand Chamber], judgment of 16 June 2005 in Case C-105/03, *Pupino*, para. 43.

34 Court of Justice [Grand Chamber], judgment of 26 February 2019 in Joined Cases C-202/18 and C-238/18, *Rimšēvičs*, para. 57.

In the title of this chapter, a question has been posed as to whether the EU Court is a Constitutional Court. The problem is whether such a notion is in accordance with the law and if it is desirable. The answers to these two questions may not be the same because they depend on two different circumstances. The desirability relies upon one's preferences, it is intrinsically personal. The lawfulness instead is rooted within the respective legal system. From the viewpoint of the EU legal system there is no doubt that the Court is and considers itself as the Constitutional Court of the EU.

This is self-evident as it emerges from renowned judgments and opinions delivered by the CJEU. It is sufficient to recall here the *Les Verts* judgment (1986). According to it

> the European Economic Community [now the EU] is a Community based on the rule of law, inasmuch as neither its Member States nor its institutions can avoid a review of the question whether the measures adopted by them are in conformity with the basic constitutional charter, the Treaty.[35]

In the recent and very important judgment about the right to a unilateral revocation of the notification of withdrawal of the UK from the Union, the CJEU confirmed that

> it must be borne in mind that the founding Treaties, which constitute the basic constitutional charter of the European Union … established, unlike ordinary international treaties, a new legal order, possessing its own institutions, for the benefit of which the Member States thereof have limited their sovereign rights, in ever wider fields, and the subjects of which comprise not only those States but also their nationals.[36]

In a previous judgment, delivered on 29 October 1980, the Court declared that at Community level there was (and still is, of course) 'the fundamental democratic principle that the peoples should take part in the exercise of powers through the intermediary of a representative assembly'.[37] In another renowned judgment the Court confirmed

> that the Community is based on the rule of law, inasmuch as neither its Member States nor its institutions can avoid review of the conformity of their acts with the basic constitutional charter, the EC Treaty, which established a complete system of legal remedies and procedures designed to enable the Court of Justice to review the legality of acts of the institutions; the review by the Court of the validity of any Community measure in the light of fundamental rights

35 Court of Justice, judgment of 23 April 1986 in Case 294/83, *Les Verts*, para. 23.
36 Court of Justice [Full Court], judgment of 10 December 2018 in Case C-621/18, *Wightman*, para. 44.
37 Court of Justice, judgment of 29 October 1980 in Case 138/79, *Roquette Frères*, para. 33.

> must be considered to be the expression, in a community based on the rule of law, of a constitutional guarantee stemming from the EC Treaty as an autonomous legal system.[38]

In the opinion of December 2014 on the accession (to be more precise: 'against the accession') of the EU to the European Convention on Human Rights (ECHR), the CJEU declared that the EU has 'its own constitutional framework',[39] a 'basic constitutional charter: the Treaties' and a 'constitutional structure'.[40] It added:

> The autonomy enjoyed by EU law in relation to the laws of the Member States and in relation to international law requires that the interpretation of those fundamental rights be ensured within the framework of the structure and objectives of the EU. In order to ensure that the specific characteristics and the autonomy of that legal order are preserved, the Treaties have established a judicial system intended to ensure consistency and uniformity in the interpretation of EU law.[41]

The legal framework is clear and coherent: the EEC/EC/EU legal system is an autonomous legal system, which is superior to the national legal systems of its Member States; the EEC/EC/EU Treaties are its Constitutional Charter and its main Court, the CJEU, which 'shall ensure that in the interpretation and application of the Treaties the law is observed', has a constitutional nature.

3.4 The Member States Acceptance of the Approach Followed by the CJEU

The Member States have accepted that role of the CJEU by reaffirming the preliminary ruling procedure in the several reforms undertaken after the Single European Act of 1986. Furthermore, in the reform Treaties the States have included many of the novel stances developed in the Court's jurisprudence.

The Member States were not duty-bound and sometimes, albeit randomly, they have chosen not to follow the CJEU. Important example, *inter alia*, is the case law on the 'parallel competencies' elaborated by the Court in 1971 in order to determine on the

38 Court of Justice [Grand Chamber], judgment of 3 September 2008 in Joined Cases C-402/05 P and C-415/05 P, *Kadi*, paras. 281 and 316.

39 Court of Justice [Full Court], opinion of 18 December 2014 in Case 2/13, para. 157. In a later judgment the EU Court added 'that constitutional framework guarantees everyone the opportunity to obtain the effective protection of rights conferred by the EU legal order before a national decision with the force of *res judicata* even comes into existence': Case C-234/17, *XC*, para. 46.

40 Opinion 2/13, paras. 163 and 165.

41 Opinion 2/13, paras. 170 and 174.

exclusive competence to conclude an international agreement.[42] The States have accepted the so-called '*AETS* formula' only in 2007 with the Treaty of Lisbon, including in Articles 3.2 and 216.1 TFEU. Another example relates to the EU citizenship, which has not evolved notwithstanding the attempts of the CJEU to strengthen it, repeatedly affirming, since 2001, that 'Union citizenship is destined to be the fundamental status of nationals of the Member States'.[43]

I would like to refer also to the relationship between EU competencies in the Common Foreign and Security Policy (CFSP). In a judgment of 20 May 2008 the CJEU affirmed that under Article 47 TEU pre-Lisbon Treaty 'none of the provision of the EC Treaty is to be affected by a provision of the Treaty of the European Union';[44] but by the Treaty of Lisbon the Member States have modified the content of this Article, that is now Article 40 TEU, adding that 'Similarly, the implementation of the policies listed in [the TFEU] shall not affect the application of the procedures and the extent of the powers of the institutions in the field of CFSP'. It is worth mentioning that in a recent judgment the CJEU has attempted once again to broaden its competences to the CFSP, affirming that 'the principle of effective judicial protection nonetheless implies that the exclusion of [its] jurisdiction in the field of the CFSP should be interpreted strictly' and that it 'has jurisdiction to give preliminary rulings, under Article 267 TFEU, on the validity of acts adopted on the basis of provisions relating to the CFSP'.[45]

A further confirmation derives from Article 50 TEU on the withdrawal from the EU, that refutes another well-known declaration made by the CJEU in the *Costa v. ENEL* judgment:

> the transfer by the States from their domestic legal system to the Community legal system of the rights and obligations arising under the Treaty carries with it a *permanent* limitation of their sovereign rights.[46]

Indeed, the role played by the CJEU and the relevance of its jurisprudence have been accepted by all Member States that have joined the EEC/EC/EU since the early 1970s. The jurisprudence in fact is part of the *acquis communautaire* that every State acceding to the EU shall implement in its legal system as a prerequisite for the admission into the Union.

42 Court of Justice, judgment of 31 March 1971 in Case 22/70, *AETS*, paras. 17-19.

43 Court of Justice, judgment of 20 September 2001 in Case C-184/99, *Grzelczyk*, para. 31. The same statement is included in several subsequent judgments. *See, ex multis*, Court of Justice, judgment of 2 October 2003 in Case C-148/02, *Garcia Avello*, para. 22; Court of Justice [Grand Chamber], judgment of 11 November 2014 in Case C-333/13, *Dano*, para. 58; Court of Justice, judgment of 2 June 2016 in Case C-233/14, *European Commission* v. *Kingdom of the Netherlands*, para. 75.

44 Court of Justice [Grand Chamber], judgment of 20 May 2008 in Case C-91/05, *ECOWAS*, para. 32.

45 Court of Justice [Grand Chamber], judgment of 28 March 2017 in Case C-72/15, *Rosneft*, paras. 74 and 81.

46 Emphasis added.

3.5 The Conflict between the CJEU and National Courts and the Continuous Need for Dialogue

Indeed, some of the judgments of the CJEU are not convincing. Good examples are *Pringle* and *Gauweiler* judgments, devoted to economic and monetary policy.[47] Another example is the *Melloni* judgment. In *Melloni* where the CJEU declared that

> national authorities and courts remain free to apply national standards of protection of fundamental rights, if the level of protection provided for by the Charter, as interpreted by the Court, and the primacy, unity and effectiveness of EU law are not thereby compromised.[48]

Further examples are the previously mentioned Opinion 2/13 on the accession of the EU to the ECHR, which affirms the Treaties are 'an independent source of law',[49] or some judgments which limited the enjoyment of social rights. However, what really matters is the very fact that the Member States do accept and respect them. This is the case of most of the judgments of the CJEU.

Nevertheless, there are also a minimal number of cases where the decisions of the CJEU have not been accepted by some Constitutional Courts of the EU Member States. One of the main reasons for such rejections is the progressive growth of competences attributed to the EEC/EC/EU combined with the increasing number of its Member States, which has quadrupled since 1951. Moreover, while the EU Court in the 1960s and 1970s aimed at strengthening the European integration and the EEC legal system, nowadays it is more restrained because it has accomplished its task. At present, the EU is a solid organization with a strong legal system.

The above-mentioned minimal percentage of non-acceptance of CJEU decisions is of crucial importance. This is due to the fact that it relates to key issues such as the protection of fundamental human rights, which also concerns fundamental national constitutional principles. This minimal percentage of non-acceptance represents the current *hiatus* between the federalist (EU constitutional) approach of the CJEU and the national constitutional approach of Constitutional Courts of the Member States.

The Constitutional Courts of the Member States may have felt to be 'downgraded' and 'frustrated' in their relationship with the CJEU also because of the direct link between the national judges and the CJEU provided for by Article 267 TFEU. Occasionally, there is a conflict between the case law of the EU Court and judgments of the domestic Constitu-

47 Court of Justice [Full Court], judgment of 27 November 2012 in Case C-370/12, *Pringle*; Court of Justice [Grand Chamber], judgment of 16 June 2015 in Case C-62/14, *Gauweiler*. *See* Chapters 5 and 6 written by Cesare Pinelli and Gavin Barret, respectively.

48 Case C-399/11, *Melloni*, para. 60.

49 Opinion 2/13, para. 166.

tional Courts. Notwithstanding the fact that nowadays the national Constitutional Courts have accepted to be considered national courts of last instance in the context of Article 267 TFEU and have requested the EU Court to give preliminary rulings[50] they do not fully accept the constitutional standing of the CJEU.[51]

More precisely, if the CJEU supports a federalist approach to the legal systems of the EU Member States, the same approach is not always approved by some Constitutional Courts and the primacy of the EU law over national law is not completely accepted. As it is well known, the national Constitutional Courts do not accept the constitutional and federalist approach promoted by the CJEU. Some of them have developed the concept of 'counter-limits' in order to legitimately not apply EEC/EC/EU rules which are deemed contrary to 'the fundamental and mandatory constitutional principles'.

The national Constitutional Courts have progressively lost a relevant portion of their competences to the benefit of the EU Court and of their own national judges. Some of them reacted defending their role and reaffirming the duty of the national judges to refer to them the questions of conflict between national rules and national Constitutions and the EU rules.[52]

As a result the CJEU reacted reaffirming that

> a national court which, in a case concerning EU law, considers that a provision of national law is not only contrary to EU law, but also unconstitutional, does not lose the right or escape the obligation under Article 267 TFEU to refer questions to the Court of Justice on the interpretation or validity of EU law by reason of the fact that the declaration, that a rule of national law is unconstitutional, is subject to a mandatory reference to a constitutional court. The effectiveness of EU law would be in jeopardy if the existence of an obligation to refer a matter to a constitutional court could prevent a national court hearing a case governed by EU law from exercising the right conferred on it by Article 267 TFEU; According to the settled case-law of the Court in order to ensure the primacy of EU law, the functioning of that system of cooperation [between the Court of Justice and the national courts] requires the national court to be free to refer to the Court for a preliminary ruling any question that it considers necessary, at whatever stage of the proceedings it considers appropriate, even at the end of an interlocutory procedure for the review of constitutionality.[53]

50 A noteworthy exception is the Portuguese Constitutional Court.

51 See Chapter 2 written by Patricia Popelier and Catherine Van De Heyning.

52 For the relevant case law, see Chapter 4 written by Aleksandra Kustra-Rogatka and Chapter 11 by Silvia Marino.

53 Court of Justice [Grand Chamber], judgment of 22 June 2010 in Joined Cases C-188/10 and C-189/10, *Melki*, paras. 45 and 52.

In another judgment, the CJEU openly declared that

> the effectiveness of EU law would be impaired and the effectiveness of Article 267 TFEU diminished if, as a result of the fact that an interlocutory procedure for review of constitutionality is pending, the national court were precluded from referring questions to the Court for a preliminary ruling and immediately applying EU law in a manner consistent with the Court's decision or case-law.[54]

And in a more recent judgment the CJEU firmly declared:

> The fact that the [Italian] Corte Constituzionale ... gave a ruling on the compatibility of the provisions of national law ... with the provisions of the Italian Constitution ... has no bearing on the obligation, laid down in Article 267 TFEU, to refer questions concerning the interpretation of EU law to the Court of Justice.[55]

This troublesome situation has increased the need for an enhanced 'dialogue' between the EU Court and the national Constitutional Courts.

3.6 The CJEU's Approach as Constitutional Court in Relation to International Agreements Concluded by the EU

In the opinion of the CJEU, the European Treaties are not international agreements *per se* but they are actually a Constitution. This Constitution is a 'rigid' one. In fact, as the CJEU provided that 'the Treaty [TEEC; now TEU and TFEU] can only be modified by means of the amendment procedure'.[56]

The CJEU, when confronted with international law rules, in particular with international treaties concluded by the EC/EU, has followed an approach similar to that of the national Constitutional Courts. In fact, considering that Article 216.2 TFEU provides that the agreements 'concluded by the Union are binding upon the institutions of the Union and its Member States', it held that this binding force occurs only after the adoption of EC/EU acts of transposition of those agreements in the EC/EU legal systems. The same concept exists in several Member States where the international treaties are becoming binding (for national institutions as well as for the local ones) only after the process of their domestic implementation. In a subsequent judgment, the CJEU has added that 'an

54 Court of Justice, judgment of 4 June 2015 in Case C-5/14, *Kernkraftwerke*, para 36.

55 Court of Justice, judgment of 20 December 2017 in Case C-322/16, *Global Starnet Ltd*, para. 25.

56 Court of Justice, judgment of 8 April 1976 in Case 43/75, *Defrenne*, para. 58.

international agreement cannot affect the allocation of powers fixed by the Treaties or, consequently, the autonomy of the Community legal system, observance of which is ensured by the Court'.[57]

A federalist approach has been followed by the CJEU in the *Kupferberg* judgment. The Court reasoned that the relationship between the EEC and its Member States in the fulfilment of an international obligation deriving from an agreement concluded by the Community resembles the relationship between the governmental authorities of a state and its local authorities:

> In ensuring respect for commitments arising from an agreement concluded by the Community institutions the Member States fulfil an obligation not only in relation to the non-Member country concerned but also and above all in relation to the Community which has assumed responsibility for the due performance of the agreement.[58]

The primacy of the international agreements concluded by the EEC/EC/EU over provisions of secondary legislation and the duty to interpret the latter, as far as it is possible, 'in a manner that is consistent with those agreements' have also been affirmed by the Court.[59] These are two elements which usually characterize the relationship between the international treaties and the national legal system. Moreover, in the opinion of the CJEU, the international agreements can only have direct effect exceptionally and the pertinent case law elaborated with reference to the GATT has been extended to its successor, the WTO, and to many other international treaties.[60] This reasoning demonstrates the Court's willingness to 'protect' its own legal system from any automatic implementation of legal rules coming from abroad. In sum, as regards the relationship between EU law and international law, the CJEU prefers a 'dualistic' approach, similar to that followed by many national legal systems in line with its essentially constitutional nature.

The caution of the CJEU for international agreements also include those that are legally binding for all EU Member States and relates to fundamental human rights protection, such as the ECHR. Notwithstanding the clear instruction provided for by Article

57 Joined Cases C-402/05 P and C-415/05 P, *Kadi*, para. 282.

58 Court of Justice, judgment of 26 October 1982 in Case 104/81, *Kupferberg*, para. 13.

59 Court of Justice, judgment of 10 September 1996 in Case C-61/94, *Commission* v. *Germany*, para. 52.

60 *See, ex multis*, Court of Justice, judgment of 24 October 1973 in Case 9/73, *Schlüter*; Court of Justice, judgment of 23 November 1999 in Case C-149/96, *Portugal* v. *Council*; Court of Justice, judgment of 14 December 2000 in Joined Cases C-300/98 and C-392/98, *Dior*.

6.2 TEU[61] and the provisions of the EU Charter of Fundamental Rights,[62] which is now legally binding, the Court has repeatedly declared that the ECHR 'does not constitute, as long as the European Union has not acceded to it, a legal instrument which has been formally incorporated into European Union law'.[63] In the opinion 2/13, which was specifically devoted to the accession of the EU to the ECHR, it added that

> an international agreement may affect its own powers only if the indispensable conditions for safeguarding the essential character of these powers are satisfied and, consequently, there is no adverse effect on the autonomy of the EU legal order;

it added that 'accession is liable to upset the underlying balance of the EU and undermine the autonomy of EU law', as well as 'affect the autonomy and effectiveness of the preliminary ruling procedure' and 'do not ensure that the specific characteristics of the EU and EU law are preserved'; and it also stated that there would be 'a breach of the principle that the Court of Justice has exclusive jurisdiction over the definitive interpretation of EU law'.[64]

Furthermore, the CJEU has declared inconsistent with the EU legal system international rules that

> have the effect of prejudicing the constitutional principles of the EC Treaty, which include the principle that all Community acts must respect fundamental rights, that respect constituting a condition for their lawfulness which it is for the Court to review in the framework of the complete system of legal remedies established by the Treaty.[65]

---

61 Art. 6.2 TEU: 'The Union *shall accede* to the European Convention for the Protection of Human Rights and Fundamental Freedoms' (emphasis added).

62 Art. 52.3 of the Charter: 'In so far as this Charter contains rights which correspond to rights guaranteed by the Convention for the Protection of Human Rights and Fundamental Freedoms, *the meaning and scope of those rights shall be the same as those laid down by the said Convention.* This provision shall not prevent Union law providing more extensive protection' (emphasis added). Article 53 of the Charter: 'Nothing in this Charter shall be interpreted as restricting or adversely affecting human rights and fundamental freedoms as recognized, in their respective fields of application, by Union law and international law and by international agreements to which the Union or all the Member States are party, *including* the European Convention for the Protection of Human Rights and Fundamental Freedoms' (emphasis added).

63 Case C-617/10, *Åkerberg Fransson*, para. 44; Case C-537/16, *Garlsson*, para. 24.

64 Opinion 2/13, paras. 183, 194, 197, 235 and 246.

65 Joined Cases C-402/05 P and C-415/05 P, *Kadi*, para. 285.

3.7 Concluding Remarks

I would like conclude this chapter with comments on a very recent judgment triggered by the decision of the Latvian authorities to suspend from office the Governor of the Latvian Central Bank, who is also a member of the Governing Council of the ECB. The Governor was accused of bribery.

The CJEU, judging for the first time on the basis of the jurisdiction conferred to it by the second subparagraph of Article 14.2 of the Statute of the European System of Central Banks (ESCB) and The European Central Bank (ECB),[66] has directly annulled the act of a national authority (the Anti-Corruption Office). The CJEU upheld that this subparagraph

> derogates from the general distribution of powers between the national courts and the courts of the European Union as provided for by the Treaties ... However, that derogation can be explained by the particular context of the ESCB within which it operates [characterized by] a less marked distinction between the EU legal order and national legal orders'; in such a situation, 'by way of exception, a decision taken by a national authority relieving one of those governors from office may be referred to the Court.[67]

By virtue of this judgment the CJEU furthered the federalist stance on the relationship between the EU legal system and the national legal orders. Such decision may remain an exception. Or, it may become another piece of the jurisprudential network created by the EU Court for the purpose of strengthening the primacy of the EU legal system, thus reiterating once again its teleological approach to the European integration.

In this chapter, I have tried to demonstrate how the CJEU, by virtue of its jurisprudence, has shaped the main features of the EEC/EC/EU legal system. Over the decades it has progressively promoted the autonomy of this system from the national ones and from the international legal system, as well as its integration and its primacy over the national legal systems. This attitude of the Court has been widely accepted by the EU Member States, but a few relevant discrepancies remain with some national Constitutional Courts, especially in the field of human rights protection. The latter have expressed a different opinion about the relationship between the national constitutions and the supranational law, thus triggering an enhanced 'dialogue' between the CJEU and them. It is not possible

---

66 Article 14.2 of Protocol No. 4 to the European Treaties: 'A Governor may be relieved from office only if he no longer fulfils the conditions required for the performance of his duties or if he has been guilty of serious misconduct. A decision to this effect may be referred to the Court of Justice by the Governor concerned or the Governing Council on grounds of infringement of these Treaties or of any rule of law relating to their application.'

67 Joined Cases C-202/18 and C-238/18, *Rimšēvičs*, paras. 69-70.

to foresee what will happen in the future because the EU integration is a 'process' which is not easy to confine into a rigid 'scheme'. But it is undisputable that only a sincere and open-minded dialogue can produce positive results.

4 Constitutional Courts, Fundamental Rights and Judicial Dialogue with the Court of Justice of the European Union

Aleksandra Kustra-Rogatka

4.1 The Role of Constitutional Courts in the Multilevel System of Fundamental Rights Protection in Europe

The last decade has been a period marked by increasingly complicated relations between the CJEU, constitutional courts and national courts.[1] New problems have arisen (perhaps previously unnoticed), such as the question of the temporal effect of a constitutional court ruling declaring a national standard incompatible with EU law as unconstitutional, but deferring the date when it loses its binding force (*Filipiak*[2] and *Winner Wetten*[3] cases), or the priority of constitutionality control over the preliminary ruling procedure (*Melki and Abdeli*[4]).

In this context, it is worth noting the observed tendency for constitutional courts to move away from the strategy of splendid isolation, which consists in ignoring the contemporary image of the EU legal system and strictly separating constitutional problems from issues related to European integration. It turns out that this strategy does not work in the long term. This is because it often downgrades the constitutional court in the internal legal order *vis-à-vis* other judicial authorities that will actively apply the EU law and use it to undermine the role of the constitutional court as the ultimate interpreter of constitutional norms.[5]

---

1 J. Komárek, 'The Place of Constitutional Courts in the EU,' *European Constitutional Law Review*, Vol. 9, Issue 3, 2013, pp. 420-450.

2 Judgment of 19 November 2009 in Case C-314/08, *Krzysztof Filipiak v Dyrektor Izby Skarbowej w Poznaniu (Filipiak)*, ECLI:EU:C:2009:719.

3 Judgment of 8 September 2010 in Case C-409/06, *Winner Wetten GmbH v Bürgermeisterin der Stadt Bergheim (Winner Wetten)*, ECLI:EU:C:2010:503.

4 Judgment of 22 June 2010 in joined Cases C-188/10 and C-189/10, *Aziz Melki* (C-188/10), *Sélim Abdeli* (C-189/10) (*Melki Abdeli*), ECLI:EU:C:2010:363.

5 M. Bobek, 'The Impact of the European Mandate of Ordinary Courts on the Position of Constitutional Courts' *in* M. Claes, M. de Visser, P. Popelier, C. Van de Heyning (Eds.) *Constitutional Conversations in Europe*, Cambridge, Intersentia (2012) pp. 287-308.

Moving away from the strategy of isolation in favor of accepting the pluralistic nature[6] of the materially understood national constitution[7] (which is subject to significant Europeanization) also results in a growing number of constitutional courts, which use the proceduralized form of discourse[8] with the CJEU, that is, references for preliminary rulings.[9] Questions for preliminary rulings by constitutional courts are evidence that con-

6 1. *See* N. MacCormick, 'The Maastricht Urteil: Sovereignty Now,' *European Law Journal*, Vol. 1, Issue 3, 1995; N. MacCormick, *Questioning Sovereignty: Law, State and Nation in the European Commonwealth*, 1st ed., Oxford, Oxford University Press 1999.
2. *See* N. Walker, 'The Idea of Constitutional Pluralism,' *Modern Law Review* Vol. 65, Issue 3, 2002, pp. 317-359; N. Walker, 'Late Sovereignty in the European Union' in: N. Walker (Ed.) *Sovereignty in Transition*, Oxford, Portland, Hart Publishing 2003, pp. 3-32.
3. Since then, some seminal works have been published. *See* M. P. Maduro, 'Contrapunctual Law: Europe's Constitutional Pluralism in Action' in N. Walker (Ed.), 2003, pp. 501-537; N. Walker, 'Postnational Constitutionalism and the Problem of Translation' in J. Weiler, M. Wind (Eds.) *European Constitutionalism Beyond the State*, Cambridge, Cambridge University Press 2003, pp. 27-54; N. Barber, 'Legal Pluralism and the European Union', *European Law Journal* Vol. 12, Issue 3, 2006, pp. 306-329; M. P. Maduro, 'Interpreting European Law: Judicial Adjudication in a Context of Constitutional Pluralism,' *Journal of European Legal Studies* Vol. 1, Issue 2, 2007, pp. 1-21; M. Kumm, 'The Cosmopolitan Turn in Constitutionalism: On the Relationship Between Constitutionalism in and Beyond the State' in J. Dunoff, J. Trachtman (Eds.) *Ruling the World? Constitutionalism, International Law and Global Governance*, Cambridge, Cambridge University Press 2009, pp. 258-325; N. Krisch, *Beyond Constitutionalism: The Pluralist Structure of Postnational Law*, Oxford, Oxford University Press 2010; M. Avbelj, J. Komárek (Eds.) *Constitutional Pluralism in the European Union and Beyond*, Oxford, Portland, Hart Publishing 2012.

7 The term refers to Kelsen's distinction of "formal" and "material" constitution. While the "formal" constitution is the written document, the constitution in its full, the "material" sense includes the set of norms at the highest level of the legal system dictating the methods through which norms are created, interpreted, and applied. It may consist of a wide array of laws and customs, some perhaps enshrined in a constitutional document and others developed through legislation, judgment, convention, or other practices of the constituted organs of government. *See* H. Kelsen, *General Theory of Law and State*, 1st ed. Cambridge, Harvard University Press 1945.

8 The term "procedural form of discourse" refers to the distinction between an open and hidden dialogue of courts made by F. Fontanello and G. Martinico The open dialogue (here: procedural form of discourse) takes the form of preliminary references. The hidden dialogue refers to the difference in jurisprudence techniques through which a non-legally bound harmonization is pursued, and mostly achieved. *See* G. Martinico, F. Fontanelli, 'The Hidden Dialogue: When Judicial Competitors Collaborate,' *Global Jurist* Vol. 8, Issue 3, 2008, pp. 1-31.

9 M. Claes, 'Luxembourg, Here We Come? Constitutional Courts and the Preliminary Reference Procedure', *German Law Journal* Vol. 16, Issue 6, 2015, pp. 1331-1342; G. Martinico, 'Preliminary Reference and Constitutional Courts: Are You in the Mood for Dialogue?' in F. Fontanelli, G. Martinico, P. Carrozza (Eds.) *Shaping Rule of Law through Dialogue*, Groningen, Europa Law Publishing 2010, pp. 224-227.

temporary constitutionalism is perceived through its heterarchy[10] with the division of interpretative competences characteristic of legal pluralism.[11]

One of the most important factors influencing the dialogue between constitutional courts and the CJEU is currently the multilevel system of protecting fundamental rights, including the Charter of Fundamental Rights of the EU. Despite the CJEU's clearly observable ambitions to strengthen its position within the EU system of protecting fundamental rights, constitutional courts strive, at least partially, to protect the constitutional standards developed in their case law. It is worth stressing that this is a sheer paradox, since at the beginning of the process of European integration, the case law of constitutional courts was one of the main factors motivating the CJEU to recognize the protection of fundamental rights as one of the general principles of the EU (formerly the European Communities), and then to develop the Community catalogue of fundamental rights.

The aim of this chapter is to analyze two preliminary references of constitutional courts: the Constitutional Court of Spain in the *Melloni*[12] case and the Italian Constitutional Court in the *Tarrico II*[13] case, which show that constitutional courts, when initiating preliminary ruling proceedings before the CJEU, try, with varying degrees of success, to protect the constitutional standards of fundamental rights developed in their case law, if they are superior to the standard guaranteed by the Charter of Fundamental Rights. These aspirations, although they may raise controversy, are more legitimate in a situation where the CJEU avoids any real control of the compatibility of EU legislation with the rights protected by the EU. Then, the role of constitutional courts within the framework of European constitutional democracy[14] will be to enforce hierarchical compliance in this area. One example may be provided by the case of the Data Retention Directive[15] validity.

10 N. Walker, 'Late Sovereignty in the European Union' in N. Walker (Ed.) *Sovereignty in Transition*, 1st ed. Oxford, Portland, Hart Publishing 2003, pp. 3-32; Walker 2002, pp. 317-359; N. Walker, S. Tierney, 'Introduction: A Constitutional Mosaic? Exploring the New Frontiers of Europe's Constitutionalism' in N. Walker, J. Shaw, S. Tierney (Eds.) *Europe's Constitutional Mosaic*, Oxford, Portland, Hart Publishing 2011, pp. 1-18; M. Huomo-Kettunen, 'Heterarchical Constitutional Structures in the European Legal Space,' *European Journal of Legal Studies*, Vol. 6, Issue 1, 2013, pp. 47-65.

11 A. T. Pérez, 'Melloni in Three Acts: From Dialogue to Monologue,' *European Constitutional Law Review*, Vol. 10, Issue 2, 2014, pp. 308-331.

12 Judgment of 26 February 2013, Case C-399/11, *Stefano Melloni v Ministerio Fiscal*, ECLI:EU:C:2013:107.

13 Judgment of 5 December 2017, Case C-42/17, *M.A.S., M.B.*, ECLI:EU:C:2017:936.

14 J. Komárek, 'National constitutional courts in the European constitutional democracy,' *International Journal of Constitutional Law* Vol. 12, Issue 3, 2014, pp. 525-544.

15 Directive 2006/24/EC of the European Parliament and of the Council of 15 March 2006 on the retention of data generated or processed in connection with the provision of publicly available electronic communications services or of public communications networks and amending Directive 2002/58/EC; Document 32006L0024

Before the CJEU in the *Digital Rights Ireland and Seitlinger and Others Judgment*[16] annulled the directive, many national constitutional courts raised concerns about its compliance with constitutional rights.[17]

4.2 The Melloni Case – Charter of Fundamental Rights as a Maximum Standard of Protection

The *Melloni* case refers to an Italian citizen who was sentenced in Italy, *in absentia*, to ten years' imprisonment for bankruptcy fraud. During the proceedings before the Italian judicial authorities, Mr. Melloni was represented by two lawyers of his choice. Following the issue of the European arrest warrant (EAW) by an Italian court, Mr. Melloni was detained in Spain in 2008 and, on 12 December 2008, the competent Spanish judicial authority, the *Audiencia National*, decided to execute the EAW against the detainee and transfer him to the Italian Republic. This decision was taken even before the ruling by the Constitutional Court of Spain in 2009, in which, by setting a high standard of constitutional protection of the right to a fair trial, it prohibited the transfer with regard to the EAW if the sentence passed in another Member State was rendered *in absentia*, even if the accused had been properly informed of the trial.

In its decision of 12 December 2008, the *Audiencia National* considered that, although the judgment of the Italian court had been given *in absentia*, Mr. Melloni was aware of the trial and voluntarily chose not to appear in court. In addition, he himself chose two lawyers to defend him. The convict lodged a constitutional complaint (*recurso de amparo*) with the Constitutional Court of Spain, claiming infringement of his right to

16 Judgment of 8 April 2014 in Joined Cases C-293/12 and C-594/12, *Digital Rights Ireland Ltd (C-293/12) v Minister for Communications and others, Kärntner Landesregierung (C-594/12), Michael Seitlinger, Christof Tschohl and others (Digital Rights Ireland)*, ECLI:EU:C:2014:238. *See* O. Lynskey, 'The Data Retention Directive is incompatible with the rights to privacy and data retention protection and is invalid in its entirety: Digital Rights Ireland,' *Common Market Law Review* Vol. 51, Issue 6, 2014, pp. 1789-1812.

17 Ch. Jones, 'National legal challenges to the Data Retention Directive' Available at: ulawanalysis.blogspot.com/2014/04/national-legal-challenges-to-data.html (Accessed: April 2019).

a fair trial guaranteed by Article 24 (2) of the Spanish Constitution. In his view, the infringement of his right to a fair trial was the result of a conviction passed in his absence.

The Constitutional Court of Spain, faced with a difficult situation in which it had to balance the standard of protecting the right to a fair trial established by its own decision in 2009, against the obligation to comply with the rules of the EU law (which were the origin of the *Audiencia National*'s decision to transfer), decided to refer three questions to the CJEU for a preliminary ruling.[18]

The questions for a preliminary ruling by the Constitutional Court of Spain were an excellent opportunity for the CJEU to clarify the normative meaning of Article 53 of the Charter. In the judgment of 26 February 2013 in the *Melloni*[19] case, the CJEU ruled that the right of the accused to appear personally at the trial is an important element of the right to a fair trial, but that this right is not absolute. There is no violation of the right to a fair trial, even if the accused did not appear in person, as long as he was informed of the scheduled date and place of the trial or if he was defended by a counselor to whom he had given a mandate.[20]

Such interpretation is in line with the European Court of Human Rights (ECtHR) ruling as regards the interpretation of Article 6 (1) and (3) of the European Convention on Human Rights (ECHR).[21] CJEU ruled that Article 4a (1) of Framework Decision 2002/584 complies with the requirements of Articles 47 and 48 (2) of the Charter.[22] The interpretation that Article 53 of the Charter should allow a Member State to apply a standard of protecting fundamental rights guaranteed by the constitution if it is superior to the standard resulting from the Charter and to refuse to apply the provisions of EU law was considered by it as inadmissible. Such an interpretation would allow a Member State to make the execution of a European arrest warrant issued for the purpose of executing a decision rendered *in absentia*, subject to conditions aimed at avoiding limita-

---

18 *See* A. T. Pérez A, 'Spanish Constitutional Court. Constitutional Dialogue on the European Arrest Warrant: The Spanish Constitutional Court Knocking on Luxembourg's Door; Spanish Constitutional Court, Order of 9 June 2011, ATC 86/2011,' *European Constitutional Law Review* Vol. 8, Issue 1, 2012, pp. 105-127; M. González Pascual, 'Mutual Recognition and Fundamental Constitutional Rights: The First Preliminary Reference of the Constitutional Court in Spain' in M. Claes, M. de Visser, P. Popelier, C. Van de Heyning (Eds.) 2012, pp. 161-174; A. Tinsley, 'Note on the Reference in C-399/11 Melloni,' *New Journal of European Criminal Law* Vol. 3, Issue 1, 2012, pp. 19-30. It should be noted that one judge, P. Tremps, had an opinion that opposed that of the above-mentioned court decision of 9 June 2011. According to this judge, the pro-EU interpretation of the provisions of the Spanish Constitution enabled a change in the existing doctrine of indirect violation of the essence of constitutional law, and thus did not require the question for preliminary ruling. Thus, paradoxically, a dissenting opinion, although it criticizes the use of the preliminary ruling procedure, goes a step further in its "pro-European" attitude than most members of the Spanish Constitutional Court.

19 Case C-399/11 *Melloni. See* N. de Boer, 'Addressing rights divergences under the Charter: *Melloni*,' *Common Market Law Review* Vol. 50, Issue 4, 2013, pp. 1083-1103.

20 *See* Case C-399/11 *Melloni*, para. 49 of the judgment.

21 *See* Case C-399/11 *Melloni*, para. 50 of the judgment.

22 *See* Case C-399/11 *Melloni*, para. 54 of the judgment.

tion or violation of rights guaranteed by the constitution, even if the application of such conditions was not allowed by Article 4a (1) of the Framework Decision 2002/584.[23]

The adoption of such an interpretation would infringe the principle of the primacy of the EU law in so far as it would allow a Member State to create an obstacle to the application of EU laws which fully comply with the Charter in the event of failure by such acts to respect the fundamental rights guaranteed by the constitution of that state.[24] Thus, by undermining the uniformity of the standard of protecting fundamental rights set out in the Framework Decision, it would lead to a breach of the principles of mutual trust and mutual recognition which the Framework Decision seeks to strengthen and, consequently, to jeopardizing its effectiveness.[25]

On 26 February 2013, in addition to the *Melloni* case, the CJEU resolved another case in which the main problem was the interpretation of the Charter provisions: the *Åkerberg Fransson* case.[26] Both judgments must be read in conjunction, not only because of the coincident date, as it is only "in a package" that they fully define the current position of the CJEU on the impact of the Charter's provisions on national legal systems.[27] While the *Åkerberg Fransson* judgment addressed the problem of the scope of applying Charter's provisions (Art. 51 of the Charter) to national law,[28] in the *Melloni* judgment the main problem the CJEU had to deal with was the problem of how to resolve conflicts between national (constitutional) standards of protection and the standard set by the Charter, where the legal system of a Member State guarantees a superior standard of protection than the standard guaranteed by the Charter.

In the *Melloni* judgment, the CJEU assumed that Article 53 of the Charter could not be regarded as an exception to the priority rule and thus rejected the interpretation that Article 53 of the Charter has a function identical to Article 53 of the ECHR. According to the CJEU, the Charter does not always set a minimum standard. In some cases, it may be treated as a legal basis for setting a standard for the maximum protection of a given law in the EU legal order. The consequence of this position is an acknowledgement that the Constitutional Court may have to lower the standard of constitutional protection that has already been guaranteed, if – in accordance with the interpretation of Article 51 (1) of the Charter assumed in the *Åkerberg Fransson* judgment – its provisions relate to the actions of the Member States. Of course, a situation may also arise in which the constitu-

23 *See* Case C-399/11 *Melloni*, para. 56 of the judgment.

24 *See* Case C-399/11 *Melloni*, para. 58 of the judgment.

25 *See* Case C-399/11 *Melloni*, para. 63 of the judgment.

26 Judgment of 26 February 2013 in Case C-617/10, *Åklagaren v. Hans Åkerberg Fransson* (*Åkerberg Fransson*), ECLI:EU:C:2013:105.

27 X. Groussot, I. Olsson, 'Clarifying or Diluting the Application of the EU Charter of Fundamental Rights? – The Judgments in Åkerberg and Melloni,' *Lund Student EU Law Review* Vol. II, 2013, pp. 7-35.

28 B. van Bockel B, P. Wattel, 'New Wine into Old Wineskins: The Scope of the Charter of Fundamental Rights of the EU after Åkerberg Fransson,' *European Law Review* Vol. 38, Issue 6, 2013, pp. 866-883; F. Fontanelli, 'Hic Sunt Nationes: The Elusive Limits of the EU Charter and the German Constitutional Watchdog,' *European Constitutional Law Review* Vol. 9, Issue 2, 2013 pp. 315-334.

tional standard is lower than the one guaranteed by the Charter. In such a case, the constitutional court (and any national court) will be obliged to apply this higher standard. In practice, therefore, when the Charter applies to the actions of the Member States, the standard guaranteed by the Charter is a 'mandatory standard.'

According to settled case law, by virtue of the primacy of the EU law, the invocation of provisions of national law by a Member State, even of a constitutional rank, cannot affect the effectiveness of the EU law in its territory.[29] However, where an EU law act requires the adoption of national enforcement acts, national authorities and courts are empowered under Article 53 of the Charter to apply national standards for the protection of fundamental rights "in so far as the application of those standards does not undermine the level of protection afforded by the Charter as interpreted by the Court, and the primacy, unity and effectiveness of the EU law."[30]

According to N. de Boer, in the*Melloni* judgment the CJEU treated the principle of primacy as the sole point of reference in determining the normative meaning of Article 53 of the Charter. Even the confusing phrase 'in their respective fields of application' seems to be of little relevance to the CJEU.[31] It follows from the quoted passage that only if constitutional standards do not undermine, firstly, the level of protection afforded by the Charter and, secondly, the principles of primacy, uniformity and effectiveness of the EU law, can constitutional courts apply them in cases which fall within the scope of application of the Charter's standards, pursuant to Article 51 of the Charter.[32] The *Melloni* judgment has therefore proved to be a significant step towards strengthening the Charter as a legal instrument that affects national legal orders and thus the courts of the Member States.

4.3 Judgment of the Spanish Constitutional Court of 13 February 2014: How to Lower the Constitutional Standard without Full Implementation of the *Melloni* Judgment

The judgment of the Constitutional Court of Spain of 13 February 2014 in case no. STC 26/2014, in response to the decision of the CJEU in the *Melloni* case, proves that constitutional courts, even by initiating the preliminary ruling procedure (and thus renouncing isolationism *vis-à-vis* the CJEU) sometimes tries to avoid long-term consequences result-

29 *See* Case C-399/11 *Melloni*, para. 59 of the judgment.
30 *See* Case C-399/11 *Melloni*, para. 60 of the judgment.
31 *See* N. de Boer 2013, pp. 1083-1103.
32 Case C-399/11 *Melloni*, para. 60 of the judgment. It is worth noting the argument raised by N. de Boer, according to which the above proposal refers only to the first of the two classic types of situation in which the Charter applies to Member States (situation of implementing EU law norms). It does not apply to cases where the state, on the grounds of an important public interest other than the protection of fundamental rights, lays down regulations aimed at introducing a derogation from the fundamental freedoms of the market provided for in the Treaties. *See* N. de Boer 2013, pp. 1083-1103.

ing from the dialogue with the CJEU. By the same token, despite submitting questions for preliminary ruling, they wish to mark their autonomy and maintain their position as the ultimate player in multilevel constitutional games.

Until the judgment of 13 February 2014, the Constitutional Court had consistently assumed that the Spanish authorities indirectly violated the Constitution if they complied with the decision of a foreign judicial authority which infringed the essence of the fundamental right protected under the Spanish Constitution. The essence of a fundamental right is defined by the Constitutional Court as the inalienable core of a right resulting from inherent human dignity. It follows from Article 10 (2) of the Spanish Constitution that, in order to ensure the protection of the essence of fundamental rights, the Constitutional Court is obliged to take into account international agreements on the protection of fundamental rights.

Since 2000, the Constitutional Court had also assumed that one of the elements of the 'core' of the right to a fair trial provided by Article 24 (2) of the Spanish Constitution was the right to be present at the trial in criminal proceedings concerning serious crimes. In the case of an extradition of persons convicted *in absentia*, this meant that the person concerned had the right to challenge the decision to being surrendered to the authorities of another State, even if that person had been properly notified of the trial and was represented at the trial by an agent of his or her choice. This position was confirmed by the Constitutional Court in subsequent judgments (STC 177/2006 and STC 199/2009), including cases of transfer within the EAW. However, the standard of protection adopted by the Constitutional Court of Spain appeared to be contrary to the current Article 4a (1) of the Framework Decision related to the EAW, as confirmed by the CJEU in the *Melloni* case judgment.

In the judgment of 13 February 2014, the Constitutional Court modified its previous jurisprudence according to which the essence of the right to a fair trial does not require that a person convicted*in absentia* should be able to apply for a retrial if he or she was duly informed of the trial, voluntarily and unequivocally waived the right to be present at the trial and was at the same time represented by an attorney at the trial.[33] Applying the amended standard of protection, the Constitutional Court rejected the constitutional complaint (*recurso de amparo*) brought by *Mr. Melloni*, pointing out that the applicant had been properly informed of the trial, appointed two lawyers of his choice to represent him at different stages of the criminal proceedings and voluntarily decided to waive the right to be present at the trial. However, a change in the jurisprudence regarding the core of the right to a fair trial took place through reinterpretation of Article 24 (2) of the

33 It should be stressed, however, that this argument refers explicitly only to the situation of the so-called indirect violation of the Constitution through the execution of the decision of a foreign judicial body by the Spanish authorities. It is therefore not clear whether this reduced standard of protection also applies to Spanish criminal proceedings without a foreign element if the amendment of criminal law in Spain would make it possible to pass judgments *in absentia* in cases of serious crimes.

Constitution (which guarantees this right at the constitutional level). On the basis of Article 10 of the Constitution, the Constitutional Court referred to international law (ECHR) as an interpretative basis for constitutionally guaranteed fundamental rights. Therefore, it did not consider – which was an alternative – that the lowering of the constitutional standard of protection was a consequence of implementing the Framework Decision with regard to the EAW and was an exception to the generally guaranteed standard of protection, which was constitutionally legitimized by the Spanish merger clause (Art. 93 of the Spanish Constitution).[34] The adoption of such a competitive way of implementing the *Melloni* judgment (opted for by the authors of dissenting opinions) would, however, require a significant modification of the existing case law of the Constitutional Court concerning the relationship between EU law and the Spanish constitution. The Constitutional Court clearly wanted to avoid this.[35]

The Constitutional Court maintains that Article 93 of the Constitution does not provide a legal basis for the recognition of the EU law as an element of the 'constitutional canon,' and thus acceptable benchmarks of control before the Constitutional Court (*see* judgments STC 28/1991 or 41/2002). The application of Article 93 in the judgment of 13 February 2014 would fully integrate constitutional rules into the EU law. The Constitutional Court of Spain, along the same lines, would also prevent future conflicts between the EU law and the Constitution. On the other hand, it would also mean that the level of protecting the constitutional rights would vary depending on whether a legal situation would fall within the scope of the EU law. In this case, the Constitutional Court of Spain would have no control over the level of protection standards applied in practice. The choice of the majority could therefore be dictated by the desire to protect the position

34 The judges Asua, Roca and Ollero were the authors of dissenting opinions. Judge Adela Asua stressed in her *votum separatum* that the Constitutional Court did not sufficiently address the importance of Art. 53 of the Charter for the protection of fundamental rights in the national legal order. She pointed out that the legal basis for the decision of the Constitutional Court should be Art. 93 of the Spanish Constitution (which is the constitutional basis for Spain's integration into the EU) and not Art. 24(2), which guarantees the right to a fair trial in conjunction with Art. 10(2) of the Constitution, which sets out the principles for the interpretation of fundamental rights in accordance with international agreements. In cases similar to the case being settled, where the case refers to issues that are fully harmonized at the level of the EU law, the EU law cannot be merely a criterion for interpreting constitutional norms, but should be the sole legal basis for the decision of the Constitutional Court. In addition, it stressed the particularly flagrant, from its point of view, lack of reference by the Constitutional Court to the*Åkerberg Fransson* judgment, which complements the doctrine of *Melloni*. Judge Encarnación Roca took a similar position in her *votum separatum*, while Judge Andrés Ollero, on the other hand, took the view that the argumentation which involved recalling the theses set out in the 2004 Declaration was justified. However, like the other authors of dissenting opinions, he stated that the Constitutional Court need not have lowered the generally binding constitutional standard of protecting the right to a fair trial. In his opinion, a change in the existing case law of the Constitutional Court should have been limited to the execution of the EAW, and thus considered an exception resulting from Art. 93 of the Constitution.

35 A.T. Pérez, 'Melloni in Three Acts: From Dialogue to Monologue,' *European Constitutional Law Review*, Vol. 10, Issue 2, 2014, pp. 308-331.

of the Constitutional Court as the court of the last word, which determines the content of constitutional norms, including fundamental rights.

Of course, this is a kind of 'Pyrrhic victory' of the constitutional supremacy and the constitutional court. In practice, this decision means a significant lowering of the level of protection guaranteed so far. As a result of this judgment, the Constitutional Court has retained the basic principles of the constitutional significance of the EU law, which have been shaped in the case law to date. The price to be paid is the need to change the interpretation of the inalienable core of the right to a fair trial. The way in which the judgment of the CJEU has been enforced, accepted by the ruling majority, has a much broader impact on the constitutional standard of protecting the right to a fair trial with regard to extradition on the basis of judgments passed *in absentia*. As a result, it makes the generally lowered standard of protection apply both to surrender proceedings between Member States under the EAW procedure and to extradition procedures resulting from agreements concluded with non-EU countries.

It should be stressed that the rationale for the judgment which lowers the existing standard of protection of the right to a fair trial is characterized by a lack of consistency. It follows from the judgment of the Constitutional Court of Spain that this change was a result of an interpretation of Article 24 (2) of the Constitution, which, through the systemic context (Art. 10 of the Constitution), took into account the case-law interpretation of Article 6 of the ECHR and Articles 47 and 48 of the Charter. However, these norms in themselves do not prohibit the application of a higher standard.

Indeed, the ECHR is always considered to be an act that lays down a minimum standard of protection (Art. 53 of ECHR), while Articles 47 and 48 of the Charter, without their connection with the *Melloni* judgment, do not prescribe that national standards are to be lowered to the level guaranteed by the Charter. Moreover, by taking the ECtHR's judgment in *Sejdovic v. Italy* as the main argument (the ECtHR adopted a lower standard of protection than the Spanish one),[36] the Constitutional Court of Spain also turned out to be inconsistent, since after the ECtHR's judgment in 2009, it upheld the existing standard of protection against extradition on the basis of a judgment passed*in absentia.*[37]

The lack of consistency is also noticeable further on in the reasoning, where, on the one hand, the Constitutional Court stressed the importance of the CJEU judgment in the

36 In the judgment of the ECtHR in *Sejdovic v. Italy* (§ 82 *et seq.*) The Grand Chamber of the ECtHR concluded that there is no violation of Art. 6 of the ECHR if the person voluntarily and unequivocally renounces the right to physical presence at the trial and is represented at the trial by a counselor.

37 This inconsistency may be due to the fact that the Judge-Rapporteur in the case was Judge Encarnación Roca, the authoress of one of the dissenting opinions, a person who did not identify with the content of the statement of reasons.

Melloni case for modifying the concept of the constitutional right to a fair trial,[38] but on the other hand, it pointed out that the judgment of the CJEU must be read in accordance with the general concept of relations between the Spanish Constitution and the EU law adopted by the ECtHR, which is set out in Declaration 1/2004. This declaration constitutes the jurisprudential foundation for defining the constitutional conditions for Spain's participation in the integration process.[39] By referring to the ECtHR judgment in *Sejdovic v. Italy*, the Constitutional Court avoided the necessity to respond to the interpretation of Article 53 of the Charter adopted in the *Melloni* judgment and underlined its jurisprudential autonomy in relation to the position of the CJEU. This is due to the fact that, although the Constitutional Court of Spain referred extensively to the ruling of the CJEU, it was only to the extent that the CJEU considered that restrictions of the right to a retrial do not interfere with Articles 47 and 48(2) of the Charter. At the same time, the Constitutional Court stressed that a similar approach had been adopted by the ECtHR even earlier. On the basis of these findings, the Constitutional Court modified the interpretation of Article 24 of the Constitution adopted so far in its case law, lowering the general standard of protection of the right to a fair trial.

In its judgment of 13 February 2014, the Constitutional Court of Spain did not consider the impact of Article 53 of the Charter on the revision of the current standard of constitutional protection. This is a particularly important remark in the context of deliberations on the relationship between constitutional courts and the interpretation of Article 53 of the Charter adopted by the CJEU. In the judgment of the Constitutional Court, the change in the jurisprudence is presented as a result of the reinterpretation of Article 24 (2) of the Spanish Constitution, which, in accordance with Article 10 (2) of the Constitution, takes into account international standards for the protection of fundamental rights. This means that constitutional courts in their jurisprudence, even if they accept

---

38 The Constitutional Court referred to para. 49 of the *Melloni* judgment, in which the CJEU stated that: "Regarding the scope of the right to an effective judicial remedy and to a fair trial provided for in Art. 47 of the Charter, and the rights of the defence guaranteed by Art. 48(2) thereof, it should be observed that, although the right of the accused to appear in person at his trial is an essential component of the right to a fair trial, that right is not absolute (*see, inter alia*, Case C-619/10, *Trade Agency* [2012] ECR, paras. 52 and 55). The accused may waive that right of his free will, either expressly or tacitly, provided that the waiver is established in an unequivocal manner, is attended by minimum safeguards commensurate to its importance and does not run counter to any important public interest. In particular, violation of the right to a fair trial has not been established, even where the accused did not appear in person, if he was informed of the date and place of the trial or was defended by a legal counsellor to whom he had given a mandate to do so." It should be noted, however, that the CJEU also appealed to the ECtHR rulings and stated in Section 50 of the reasoning that "his interpretation of Articles 47 and 48(2) of the Charter is in keeping with the scope that has been recognised for the rights guaranteed by Article 6(1) and (3) of the ECHR by the case-law of the European Court of Human Rights (*see, inter alia*, ECtHR, *Medenica v. Switzerland*, no. 20491/92, § 56 to 59, ECHR 2001VI; *Sejdovic v. Italy* [GC], no. 56581/00, § 84, 86 and 98, ECHR 2006II; and *Haralampiev v. Bulgaria*, no. 29648/03, § 32 and 33, 24 April 2012)".

39 For more on the topic, *see* R. A. García R, 'The Spanish Constitution and the European Constitution: The Script for a Virtual Collision and Other Observations on the Principle of Primacy,' *German Law Journal* Vol. 6, Issue 6, 2005, pp. 1001-1024.

the consequences of the theses formulated in the *Åkerberg Fransson* and *Melloni* judgments, may try to maintain their status of 'supreme interpreter of fundamental rights' in the national legal order.

4.4 The *Taricco II* Case (*M.A.S. & M.B.*) – Constitutional Traditions of the Member States versus the Fiscal Interests of the EU

The *Taricco II* case was initiated by referral for a preliminary ruling by the Italian Constitutional Court. The term *Taricco II*[40] adopted by the commentators (official designation of the case: *M.A.S. & M.B.*) follows from the close link between the preliminary ruling of the Constitutional Court and the *Taricco* case previously decided by the CJEU (judgment of the CJEU of 8 September 2015 in case C-105/14). Both cases referred to the application of the provisions of the Italian Penal Code to govern the limitation period, to persons accused of cross-border VAT fraud. Italian legislation is characterized by short limitation periods for the prosecution of this type of crime. The reference for a preliminary ruling in the *Taricco* case, followed by the judgment of the CJEU in 2015, was initiated by the Court in Cuneo.[41] It was resolving a criminal case in which several Italian taxpayers (including Mr. Ivo Taricco) were charged with creating and orchestrating a criminal organization in the tax years 2005-2009 to form fraudulent legal structures, the so-called *VAT carousel*. It saw a conflict between Italian legislation and the EU law. On the one hand, the provisions of the EU law, Article 325 TFEU, require Member States to effectively combat fraud that poses a threat to the financial interests of the EU, while on the other hand the provisions of the Italian Criminal Law have led in practice to the lack of possibility of interrupting the statute of limitations and discontinuing criminal proceedings in cross-border VAT-related organized crime cases.[42]

In its judgment of 8 September 2015 in Case C-105/14, the CJEU confirmed the arguments set out in the order for reference. The CJEU concluded that the disputable provisions of the Italian criminal law may jeopardize the obligations imposed on the Member States by Article 325 (1) and (2) TFEU, in a situation where they prevent the imposition of effective and dissuasive criminal penalties in a significant number of cases of serious fraud which poses a threat to the financial interests of the EU or provides for longer

40 *See, inter alia*, D. Burchardt, 'Belittling the Primacy of EU Law in Taricco II,' VerfBlog, 2017/12/07 Available at https://verfassungsblog.de/belittling-the-primacy-of-eu-law-in-taricco-ii/ (Accessed: March 2019); G. Zaccaroni, F. Rossi, 'Settling the Dust? An Analysis of Taricco II from an EU Constitutional and Criminal Law Perspective' Available at https://europeanlawblog.eu/2018/04/12/settling-the-dust-an-analysis-of-taricco-ii-from-an-eu-constitutional-and-criminal-law-perspective/ (Accessed: April 2019), Rossi 2018; Ch. Amalfitano, O. Pollicino, 'Two Courts, two Languages? The Taricco Saga Ends on a Worrying Note,' VerfBlog, 2018/6/05 Available at https://verfassungsblog.de/two-courts-two-languages-the-taricco-saga-ends-on-a-worrying-note/ (Accessed: March 2019).

41 Reference for a preliminary ruling of 5 March 2014.

42 *See* Case C-105/14, *Taricco* paras. 23-24.

limitation periods for fraud which poses a threat to the financial interests of the Member State concerned than for fraud that poses a threat to the financial interests of the European Union. Unexpectedly, the CJEU also added that national courts should verify whether this is the case and, if necessary, waive the application of national provisions governing the maximum extension of the limitation period in order to enable the effective prosecution of the alleged offences. According to the CJEU, such non-application of national provisions would be without prejudice to Article 49 of the Charter of Fundamental Rights of the European Union (principles of legality and proportionality of offences and penalties) (ECHR) and Article 7 of ECHR (prohibition of punishment without legal basis) in relation to ongoing criminal proceedings.[43]

The judgment of the CJEU in the *Taricco* case caused divergent jurisprudence in Italian courts, which started to interpret the consequences of the judgment of the CJEU in different ways. The interpretation of the part of the judgment in which the CJEU applied the accumulation of several vague terms such as "serious fraud" or "a significant number of cases" raised major doubts. Divergences were discernible even in cases decided by the Court of Cassation.

Doubts of interpretation were finally resolved in the procedure of legal questions to the Italian Constitutional Court. Two courts, independent of each other, the Court of Cassation and the Court of Appeal in Milan, submitted questions to the Constitutional Court for a preliminary ruling. They sought to establish whether or not the application of the so-called *Taricco* test in the Italian legal order, based on vague criteria, leads to a breach of the constitutional principle of the statutory definition of conditions for criminal liability, as expressed in Article 25 of the Italian Constitution, and *ex post* determination of the scope of criminality. Both the referring courts emphasized that according to well-established Italian legal tradition, the limitation period is an integral part of substantive criminal law (constituting a temporal dimension of criminal liability).

The Constitutional Court decided to initiate a preliminary ruling procedure before deciding on the case. In the order for reference of 26 January 2017 No 24/2017, it submitted three questions to the CJEU for a preliminary ruling, alleging that the *Taricco* test was not sufficiently precise, and since prescription periods were recognized as an element of substantive criminal law within the Italian legal order, the *Taricco* ruling was contrary to the Italian Constitution.[44]

The order for reference of the Constitutional Court No 24/2017, on the one hand, when initiating the preliminary ruling procedure, should be regarded as an instrument of a dialogue between national constitutional courts and the CJEU in order to resolve na-

43 A critical analysis of the judgment of the CJEU in the *Taricco* case in the context of political relations between the CJEU and national criminal courts – *see* E. Billis, 'The European Court of Justice: a "quasi-constitutional Court" in Criminal Matters? The Taricco Judgment and Its Shortcomings', *New Journal of European Criminal Law*, Vol. 7, Issue 1, 2016, pp. 20-38.

44 The text of the decision is available at www.cortecostituzionale.it/actionSchedaPronuncia.do?anno=2017&numero=24.

tional constitutional problems within the framework of the EU legal categories. In this context, it is worth noting the Italian Constitutional Court's reference to Article 4 TEU and Articles 49 and 53 of the Charter.[45]

On the other hand, this order for reference is undoubtedly an example of a new category of questions referred for a preliminary ruling by the constitutional courts, which, like the German Federal Constitutional Court (FCC) reference in the *Gauweiler* case,[46] are named in literature as threatening references of appeal.[47] Just as the FCC in the *Gauweiler* case "threatened" the CJEU with the initiation of constitutional control of EU law through the prism of constitutional identity of the Federal Republic of Germany,[48] the Constitutional Court suggested in its referral an activation of constitutional control of the *Taricco* test from the perspective of permissible restrictions on sovereignty in connection with the Italian Republic's membership in the EU, the so-called *controlimiti*. Contrary to the FCC's order for reference in the *Gauweiler* case, the Constitutional Court's decision to initiate the preliminary ruling procedure in the so-called *Taricco II* case should, however, be seen as an expression of common sense, compromise and willingness to cooperate, as the Constitutional Court rejected two extreme alternatives: (1) the application of the *controlimiti* doctrine without initiating the preliminary ruling procedure, and (2) the full acceptance of the application of the *Taricco* test in the Italian legal system.[49]

The *Taricco II* case was dealt with under the accelerated preliminary ruling procedure. The Advocate General presented his opinion on 18 July 2017 and the judgment of the CJEU in the Grand Chamber was delivered on 5 December 2017.[50] The fact that the CJEU resolved the case within less than one year proves the importance of the problem presented by the Constitutional Court.

The Advocate General's opinion and the Grand Chamber's judgment were based on contradictory assumptions and put forward totally different arguments. Advocate Gen-

45 *See, inter alia*, G. Rugge, 'The Italian Constitutional Court on Taricco: Unleashing the normative potential of 'national identity'?' *Questions of International Law* Vol. 37, 2017, pp. 21-39.

46 Decision of the Second Senate of German FCC of 14 January 2014, ref. 2 BvR 2728/13, English translation of the decision available at: www.bverfg.de/e/rs20140114_2bvr272813en.html.

47 *See* D. Paris, 'Carrot and Stick. The Italian Constitutional Court's Preliminary Reference in the Case Taricco', *Questions of International Law* Vol. 37, 2017, pp. 5-6.

48 For more on the topic, *see* M. Claes, H.-J. Reestman, 'The Protection of National Constitutional Identity and the Limits of European Integration at the Occasion of the Gauweiler Case', *German Law Journal* Vol. 4, Issue 4, 2015, pp. 917-970.

49 *See* M. Bassini, 'Taricco and sons: a 'dangerous' exercise of judicial cooperation?' Available at www.academia.edu/34064874/Taricco_and_sons_a_dangerous_exercise_of_judicial_cooperation Accessed: March 2019; M. Bassini, O. Pollicino, 'The Taricco Decision: A Last Attempt to Avoid a Clash between EU Law and the Italian Constitution', VerfBlog, 2017/1/28 Available at: https://verfassungsblog.de/the-taricco-decision-a-last-attempt-to-avoid-a-clash-between-eu-law-and-the-italian-constitution/ Accessed March 2019

50 Judgment of 5 December 2017 in Case C-42/17 *M.A.S., M.B. v. Presidente del Consiglio dei Ministri* (*M.A.S., M.B*), ECLI:EU:C:2017:936.

eral Bot, who also prepared an opinion in the *Melloni* case, in both cases, took the view that the absolute principle of the primacy of the EU law over national law must be protected. Marco Bassini and Oreste Pollicino rightly described Bot's opinion in *Taricco II* as probably the most conservative and radical view of the primacy of the EU law.[51] While in the *Melloni* case the CJEU took Bot's point of view, in *Taricco II* it followed a different path. Instead of adapting to the difficult task of determining the scope of Italy's constitutional identity, it decided to vest the national court with the possibility of exceptionally rejecting the EU law. First, it assumed that Article 325 of TFEU is an area of shared competence, which was not harmonized at the time of the dispute and, as a consequence, Member States had a certain margin of manoeuver as regards fraud in the EU's financial interest.[52] In the next stage of legal reasoning, it resolved that the principle of legality in criminal matters is protected by Article 49 of the Charter and is part of the "constitutional traditions" shared by EU Member States. For this reason, the CJEU concluded that it is the national judge who determines whether the application of Article 325 of TFEU is contrary to the constitutional identity of the Member State concerned.[53]

This allowed the CJEU to formulate a sentence that constitutes a much more liberal view of the principle of primacy than it adopted in the *Melloni* case. In the judgment of 5 December 2017, the CJEU ruled that:

> Article 325(1) and (2) TFEU must be interpreted as requiring the national court, in criminal proceedings for infringements relating to value added tax, to disapply national provisions on limitation, forming part of national substantive law, which prevent the application of effective and deterrent criminal penalties in a significant number of cases of serious fraud affecting the financial interests of the European Union, or which lay down shorter limitation periods for cases of serious fraud affecting those interests than for those affecting the financial interests of the Member State concerned, unless that disapplication entails a breach of the principle that offences and penalties must be defined by law because of the lack of precision of the applicable law or because of the retroactive application of legislation imposing conditions of criminal liability stricter than those in force at the time the infringement was committed.[54]

The CJEU judgment in the *Taricco II* case is a "light at the end of the tunnel" for the opponents of the radical concept of the primacy of the EU law. So far, discussions on

51 *Cf.* M. Bassini, O. Pollicino, 'The Opinion of Advocate General Bot in Taricco II: Seven "Deadly" Sins and a Modest Proposal', VerfBlog, 2017/8/02 Available at https://verfassungsblog.de/the-opinion-of-advocate-general-bot-in-taricco-ii-seven-deadly-sins-and-a-modest-proposal/ (Accessed March 2019).

52 *See* Case C-42/17 *M.A.S., M.B.* paras. 43-44 of the judgment.

53 *See* Case C-42/17 *M.A.S., M.B.* para. 52 of the judgment.

54 Case C-42/17 *M.A.S., M.B.* para. 64 of the judgment.

possible normative grounds for introducing an exception to the primacy principle have focused on Article 4 (2) TEU and the concept of constitutional identity. The CJEU itself relied on the adaptation of constitutional norms as a point of reference for the interpretation of the EU primary law rather than on the recognition of the constitutional values of Member States as an autonomous legal basis under the EU law for the adoption of an exception to the principle of primacy. The judgments in *Omega*[55] and *Sayn-Wittgenstein*[56] cases, among others, illustrate this jurisprudence approach. In *Taricco II*, the CJEU went one step further. It did not highlight Article 4 (2) but Article 6 (3) TEU. In so doing, it brought to the fore the universalism of common constitutional traditions, and not the localness or particularity stemming from the essence of the concepts of national and constitutional identity.

The judgment of the CJEU met with divergent opinions among lawyers. Some pointed to its main advantages: the abandonment of a radical version of the principle of primacy in such a sensitive area as the principles of criminal liability[57] and the justification of the judgment which expresses empathy in relation to national constitutional courts.[58] Others criticized, first of all, the inconsistencies in the argumentation of the solution. The critics of the resolution stressed the problems related to the establishment in its justification of appropriate relations between the key concepts: national identity under Article 4 (2) TEU, its national equivalent as adopted in the jurisprudence of national constitutional courts, that is, constitutional identity, and the common constitutional traditions under Article 6 (3) TEU.[59]

55 Judgment of 14 October 2004, Case C-36/02 *Omega Spielhallen- und Automatenaufstellungs-GmbH V Oberbürgermeisterin der Bundesstadt Bonn*, ECLI:EU:C:2004:614.

56 *See* N. de Boer 2013, pp. 1083-1103.

57 *See* M. Fichera, 'Taricco II: the Italian Constitutional Court raises its voice and the Court of Justice listens,' Available at http://eulawanalysis.blogspot.com/2017/12/criminal-law-human-rights-and.html (Accessed March 2019).

58 *See* D. Sarmiento, 'An Instruction Manual to Stop a Judicial Rebellion (before it is too late, of course)', VerfBlog, 2017/2/02. Available at https://verfassungsblog.de/an-instruction-manual-to-stop-a-judicial-rebellion-before-it-is-too-late-of-course/ (Accessed March 2019).

59 *See* D. Burchardt, 'Belittling the Primacy of EU Law in Taricco II,' VerfBlog, 2017/12/07 Available at https://verfassungsblog.de/belittling-the-primacy-of-eu-law-in-taricco-ii/ (Accessed March 2019); M. Bassini, O. Pollicino, 'Defusing the Taricco Bomb through Fostering Constitutional Tolerance: All Roads Lead to Rome,' VerfBlog, 2017/12/05. Available at https://verfassungsblog.de/defusing-the-taricco-bomb-through-fostering-constitutional-tolerance-all-roads-lead-to-rome/ (Accessed March 2019); M. Sousa Ferro, 'ECJ on Taricco II: a game changer? The primacy and effectiveness of EU law take a serious hit.' Available at www.linkedin.com/pulse/ecj-taricco-ii-game-changer-primacy-effectiveness-eu-law-sousa-ferro (Accessed: March 2019).

Apart from the undoubtedly significant deficiencies in the justification of the CJEU judgment, a fundamental modification of the arguments formulated in the *Taricco* ruling in 2015[60] is crucial for the case. The CJEU allowed national courts to apply national criminal law provisions that do not comply with the *Taricco* test if their disapplication were to result in a breach of the principle of legality of criminal offences and penalties, or in retroactive effect of provisions, laying down stricter conditions of liability than those in force at the time when the offence was committed. The CJEU's view on the *Taricco* test through the prism of the values that are a part of Europe's constitutional heritage was an unquestionable tribute to the Constitutional Court. As Marco Bassini and Oreste Pollicino state, the CJEU accepted in *Taricco II*, the Constitutional Court's suggestion to identify common constitutional traditions (but not constitutional identity) as a *lingua franca* of cooperative constitutionalism in Europe.[61]

4.5 Judgment of the Italian Constitutional Court of 31 May 2018 – Unexpected Confrontation

The conciliatory nature of the CJEU judgment in the*Taricco II* case made a confrontational reaction by the Constitutional Court unlikely.[62] Yet it became a fact. In the controversial judgment of 31 May 2018 No 115/2018,[63] the Constitutional Court considered all the questions submitted by national courts to be unfounded, as the *Taricco* test was not applicable in the cases they were considering due to temporal reasons.[64] Indeed, both judgments of the CJEU in the *Taricco* and *Taricco II* cases showed that the so-called *Taricco* test did not apply to situations that arose before the judgment of the CJEU in this case (8 September 2015). In both cases where the Italian courts (the Court of Cassation and the Court in Milan) decided to submit legal questions to the Constitutional Court, the facts did indeed relate to events that took place on that date. The courts could

60 A separate question is how to treat this modification. Whether it is an abandonment of earlier arguments or just their development, the key to answering this question lies with the interpretation of para. 53 of the reasoning of the *Taricco* ruling of 2015, where, in the form of *obiter dictum*, the CJEU pointed out that "if the national court decides to disapply the national provisions at issue, it must also ensure that the fundamental rights of the persons concerned are respected." Indeed, in that case penalties may be imposed on those persons who, in all likelihood, would not have had penalties imposed on them if those provisions of national law had been applied.

61 *See* M. Bassini, O. Pollicino, 2017 'Defusing…' Similarly, M. Bonelli, 'The Taricco saga and the consolidation of judicial dialogue in the European Union', *Maastricht Journal of European and Comparative Law* Vol. 25, Issue 3, pp. 357–373, available at http://journals.sagepub.com/doi/pdf/10.1177/1023263X18773046.

62 *See* Ch. Amalfitano, O. Pollicino, 'Two Courts, Two Languages? The Taricco Saga Ends on a Worrying Note,' VerfBlog, 2018/6/05. Available at https://verfassungsblog.de/two-courts-two-languages-the-taricco-saga-ends-on-a-worrying-note/ (Accessed: March 2019).

63 The text of the decision is available at https://www.cortecostituzionale.it/actionSchedaPronuncia.do?anno=2018&numero=115.

64 The main theses of the decision in English is available at https://www.cortecostituzionale.it/documenti/comunicatistampa/CC_CS_20180607121930.pdf.

therefore apply the controversial provisions of the Italian Penal Code (Arts. 160 (3) and 161 (2)) and established the statute of limitations.

The Constitutional Court, however, went one step further. In its judgment it stated that even if the facts of one of the cases referred to acts committed after 8 September 2015, the requesting courts could not apply the *Taricco* test anyway, as it is incompatible with the principle of legal certainty of criminal law enshrined in Article 25 (2) of the Italian Constitution.[65] The Constitutional Court pointed out that in civil law countries such as Italy, the principle of legal certainty of criminal law requires that the legislator designs the law in such a way that individuals are able to predict the consequences of their behavior. The principles of criminal liability of an individual must derive directly from legal provisions,[66] and Article 325 TFEU, on which the CJEU based the entire *Taricco* test, does not meet the criterion of legal certainty of the criminal provisions thus established.[67]

The most controversial element of the reasoning for the judgment of the Constitutional Court of 31 May 2018 is the argument that Article 325 TFEU cannot be directly applied. Although the Constitutional Court formally admitted that only the CJEU has the competence to interpret EU law provisions uniformly and to determine whether they are directly effective (para. 12 of the judgment), in fact it openly opposed both rulings of the CJEU (*Taricco* and *Taricco II*), stating that Article 325 (1) and (2) TFEU and the *Taricco* test do not respect the (national) requirement to precisely define criminal law principles (para. 11 of the judgment). According to Chiara Amalfitano and Oreste Pollicino, even if, contrary to the arguments formulated by the CJEU in *Taricco* (para. 51) and *Taricco II* (para. 38) judgments, Article 325 (1) and (2) TFEU cannot be considered sufficiently clear, precise and unconditional, the Constitutional Court seems to go beyond its competence. It is not for the Constitutional Court (or any national court) to determine whether and, if so, which EU rules have a direct effect.[68]

In this judgment, the Constitutional Court's lack of willingness to enter into a real dialogue with the CJEU, contrary to the declarations resulting from the reasons for the decision and its official discussion, is somewhat astounding. In its reasoning, the Constitutional Court completely ignored the CJEU's emphasis in *Taricco II* on the concept of common constitutional traditions under Article 6 (3) TEU. In several places of its reasoning, it smoothly combined its current jurisprudence on *controlimiti* with the now increasingly popular notion of constitutional identity. Thus, it stressed the importance of local constitutional values (paras. 5 and 11 of the ruling).[69]

65 Ch. Amalfitano, O. Pollicino, 2018.
66 Case No 115/2018, para. 11 of the judgment.
67 *See* Case No 115/2018, para. 12 of the judgment.
68 Ch. Amalfitano, O. Pollicino 2018.
69 Ch. Amalfitano, O. Pollicino 2018.

4.6 Final Comments

The modern system of protecting fundamental rights in the European legal area, which is constitutionalized under the Charter, means that constitutional courts are forced to re-evaluate their role as national guardians of respecting human rights. They have been transformed from entities that demanded the development of the EU system for the protection of fundamental rights, to courts whose current position may be, at least in part, called into question. The jurisprudential expansionism of the CJEU, as seen in the judgments of *Åkerberg Fransson* and*Melloni* as well as, indirectly, in the opinion of the CJEU of 18 December 2014[70] on the draft accession of the EU to the ECHR, makes the application of the Charter's standards one of the most serious challenges facing constitutional courts today. The extent to which a constitutional court engages in dialogue with the CJEU depends on a number of factors, including the position of the constitutional court within the national judicial system, the general position of the court in relation to the European integration process, as well as the system of sources of law in force in the Member State concerned.

The *Melloni* and *Tarrico II* cases point to a wide range of problems that arise in connection with the attempts by constitutional courts that find themselves in a multilevel but closely integrated[71] European system of protecting fundamental rights. Trying to maintain at least partial autonomy in setting constitutional standards of protection, constitutional courts may also implement the judgments of the CJEU by reinterpreting the previously guaranteed standard of protection on their own. However, such a method of implementing the CJEU jurisprudence may in practice, paradoxically, result in a wider impact of the EU standard and a general lowering of the current level of constitutional protection, even in the face of legal situations which have no connection with EU law. The constitutional court's autonomous reasoning for a decision to lower (*Melloni*) or maintain (*Taricco II*) the constitutional standard of human rights protection also broadens the spectrum of possible reactions on the part of national courts. There is a risk of discrepancies in jurisprudence, as individual national courts may refer in their rulings either to a judgment of the CJEU or to an autonomous decision of a constitutional court. In a sense, national courts will thus determine their relationship to the so-called Community mandate given to them by the *Simmenthal* judgment and the limits of being bound by the constitutional court's jurisprudence.

70 Case 2/13 opinion of the CJEU of 18 December 2014, ECLI:EU:C:2014:2454.

71 P. Eeckhout, 'Human Rights and the Autonomy of EU Law: Pluralism or Integration,' *Current Legal Problems* Vol. 66, Issue 1, 2013, pp. 169-202.

Part II
Judicial Dialogue in Financial Matters

5 Are Courts Engaged in a 'Dialogue' on Financial Matters?

Cesare Pinelli

5.1 On Whether and How Courts Interact on Financial Matters

In the aftermath of the 2008 Eurozone's crisis European and constitutional courts were increasingly involved in financial matters. The legality of measures with which the Eurozone Member States reacted to the crisis was then at stake, no less than alleged infringements of citizens' fundamental rights caused by austerity programs. Cases were brought for these reasons before constitutional courts, some of which made preliminary references to the Court of Justice of the EU (CJEU) and before the European Court of Human Rights.

Scholars have extensively treated the question of whether this case law changed the relationship between courts and the political branches, while minor attention was devoted to the issue whether courts continued to interact among themselves when it comes to financial matters, and eventually to the problem of how such interaction may take place. However, some argued that the German Constitutional Court's preliminary reference to the CJEU in the *Gauweiler* case would signal 'the end of constitutional pluralism', to the extent that Europe's two most powerful courts were finally forced to confront the incompatibility of their positions on the issue of *Kompetenz-Kompetenz*.[1] For others, on the contrary, such issue was irrelevant for both courts, with the effect that the enduring vigor of constitutional pluralism was not denied.[2] At any rate, the question needs to be examined after having explored the 'special relationships' arising between courts with respect to financial matters.

1 D. Kelemen (2016), 'On the Unsustainability of Constitutional Pluralism: European Supremacy and the Survival of the Eurozone', *Maastricht Journal of European and Comparative Law*, Vol. 23, No. 1, p. 23, and D. Sarmiento (2015), 'The OMT Case and the Demise of the Pluralist Movement', https//despiteourdifferencesblog.wordpress.com/2015/09/21.

2 A. Bobić (2017), 'Constitutional Pluralism Is Not Dead: An Analysis of Interactions between Constitutional Courts of Member States and the European Court of Justice', *German Law Journal*, Vol. 18, No. 6, p. 1427.

5.2 THE DEBATE ON THE COURTS' REACTION TO THE FINANCIAL CRISIS

Opinions regarding the courts' reaction to the financial crisis differ strikingly. For some, the latter has "dramatically increased the powers of the judiciary vis-a-vis the political branches, making economic and monetary affairs in Europe more judicialized than even in a hyper-judicialized system like the US".[3] Others observe instead that the fairly large number of cases dealing with the crisis measures can be explained by the uncertain legal nature of some of those measures and should not veil the fact that "the overall attitude of those courts has been to respect the choices made either by the political institutions (national governments or Eurogroup), or by the European Central Bank".[4] Finally, the attitude of courts such as the CJEU and the German Federal Constitutional Court (FCC) reveals the risk of a 'de-judicialization' of the EU institutional assessment, to the extent that "it accepts the primacy of discretionary politics in the management of the crisis and fails to develop any criteria against which the legitimacy of these practices might be assessed".[5]

Going from the 'dramatic increase' of the judicial power to the system's 'de-judicialization', these assumptions cover the whole spectrum of possibilities regarding the well-known dichotomy between judicial activism and judicial self-restraint. The very use of such dichotomy presupposes, however, that courts are able to express a common attitude toward legislatures, be it of deference or of interventionism. This happens typically within states. Even within the EU, the longstanding interactions between European and domestic courts for the protection of citizens' fundamental rights are reputed to ensure common positions vis-à-vis the political branches. The very formation of a judicial 'dialogue', to use the celebrated formula that was coined decades ago by Bruno Genevois,[6] presupposes the mutual recognition of the same function, irrespective of the legal order to which each court pertains.[7] However, such dialogue appears prima facie more difficult when it comes to financial matters, given their highly political implications. Hence, there is a need for inquiring into how European and domestic courts managed the issue and the related changes affecting their role.

---

3 F. Fabbrini (2016), *Economic Governance in Europe: Comparative Paradoxes, Constitutional Challenges*, Oxford University Press, Oxford, p. 63.

4 B. De Witte (2018), 'Judicialization of the Euro Crisis? A Critical Evaluation', F. Allen, E. Carletti and M. Gulati (eds.), *Institutions and the Crisis*, EUI, p. 108.

5 M. Emerson & C. Joerges (2013), *Who Is the Guardian for Constitutionalism in Europe after the Financial Crisis?* LSE Europe in Question Discussion Papers, p. 23.

6 J.-P. Costa (2017), *La Cour européenne des droits de l'homme. Des juges pour la liberté*, Paris, Dalloz, p. 123.

7 *See* already J.H.H. Weiler (1995), 'Fundamental Rights and Fundamental Boundaries: On Standards and Values in the Protection of Human Rights', N.A. Newhal & A. Rosas (eds.), *The European Union and Human Rights*, Dordrecht, Kluwer, p. 73.

5.3 Responses to Alleged Breaches of Fundamental Rights and to the Legality of Measures Adopted During the Eurozone Crisis

While responding to alleged breaches of fundamental rights due to austerity measures taken at the EU level, courts were already accustomed with such a challenge, and as it has been demonstrated in a comparative overview concerning the Italian, the Portuguese, and the Spanish jurisprudence,

> Euro-crisis law has confirmed or strengthened trends in constitutional jurisprudence that were already present before the financial crisis or that could be detected through a close look at constitutional judgments delivered before the most acute phase of the crisis, i.e. the one leading to a request for financial support or assistance.[8]

Things are different for the CJEU, being frequently criticized for its non-interventionist stance with regard to judicial actions challenging the compatibility of austerity measures with the protection of fundamental rights. And yet, it is admitted, this attitude reflects the usual judicial refrain from constraining the capacity of political bodies to react in the face of an emergency.[9]

A different and more interesting approach was instead necessitated by the adoption of international agreements or of soft law instruments with which the EU Member States and the European Central Bank (ECB) reacted to the financial crisis. These are the introduction of mechanisms of financial assistance, the possibility for Member States facing financial difficulties to receive aid from the EU and its Member States, the conditionality rule, and the ECB's Outright Monetary Transaction (OMT) program. These measures posed the issue of their compatibility both with EU law and with national constitutions in abstract terms, without direct implication on the concrete protection of citizens' fundamental rights. Courts were thus confronted with a paradigm shift involving a closer connection of their decisions with those of political and technical authorities.

5.4 Procedural Limits to Judicial Review: The Conseil Constitutionnel's Ruling and the Irish Supreme Court's Preliminary Reference to CJEU

A procedural aspect deserves particular attention. Not all constitutional courts of the EU Member States possess the competence of reviewing in abstract terms the compatibility of

---

8 C. Fasone (2014), *Constitutional Courts Facing the Euro Crisis. Italy, Portugal and Spain in Comparative Perspective*, EUI Working Papers, p. 3.

9 F. Costamagna (2016), 'The Court of Justice and the Demise of the Rule of Law in the EU Economic Governance: The Case of Social Rights', *Carlo Alberto Notebooks*, No. 487, p. 22.

legal acts either before or after their adoption with the respective constitutions. With respect to the already-mentioned measures such task was exerted by the courts of Slovenia, Estonia, Ireland, Germany, Austria, Hungary, France and Belgium. These elements suffice to demonstrate that the usual interactions between courts, particularly those concerning the protection of fundamental rights, are strongly reduced when it comes to the abstract or objective control.

While examining the compatibility of the Eurozone crisis measures with the respective constitutions most courts, with the exception of the FCC, avoided to engage in a constitutional identity review, nor did they deploy a strategy in their relation with the CJEU. Overall, despite the number of complaints invoking a violation of parliamentary prerogatives by Euro-crisis measures, these courts appeared reluctant in ensuring a judicial safeguard to the budgetary authority of the legislature.[10] They rather

> found their own way of performing a credible constitutional analysis, dismantling the potentially explosive constitutional implications of some treaty provisions, and taking the edge off arguments that the ESM or Fiscal Compact undermined national parliamentary democracy. Their judgments have helped to legitimize the ratification of those treaties, and have thus contributed to a major shift in the functioning of EMU.[11]

Some, such as the French *Conseil Constitutionnel*, were called to decide on whether the *Fiscal Compact* required a constitutional reform to the extent that it provides the balanced budget clause. The *Conseil* denied that this was the case, relying on the 'principle of budgetary sincerity' and on the assertion that an organic law would adequately comply with the *Fiscal Compact*'s obligations.[12]

The Irish Supreme Court had instead to deal with a challenge by a member of the Irish parliament, Mr. Pringle, against the ratification of the European Stability Mechanism (ESM) Treaty by Ireland. Mr. Pringle firstly argued that ratification by the Irish parliament without a prior referendum would be unconstitutional, but that argument was rejected by the court. Mr. Pringle also argued that the conclusion of the ESM Treaty breached various provisions of EU law, and this challenge was referred by the Irish Supreme Court to the CJEU, on the ground that the ESM Treaty infringed inter alia the no-bail-out rule contained in Article 125 of the Treaty on the Functioning of the European Union (TFEU).[13] Interestingly, the Irish Supreme Court's preliminary reference did not

---

10 C. Fasone (2018), 'Do Constitutional Courts Care about Parliaments in the Euro-Crisis? On the Precedence of the "Constitutional Identity Review"', *Italian Journal of Public Law*, No. 10, p. 388.

11 B. De Witte, 'Judicialization of the Euro crisis?', p. 104.

12 Conseil Constitutionnel, Décision n° 2012-653 DC, 9 August 2012.

13 Supreme Court of Ireland, No. 339/2012, 31 July 2012.

concern the sovereignty claim, which was rejected, but the sole compatibility under EU law of the mentioned EU Member States' international obligations.

5.5 The Bundesverfassungsgericht's Case Law

The FCC's approach appears strikingly different from that of the other courts. First, in some of the below-mentioned cases, the FCC exerted its abstract control through a creative move on procedural grounds, declaring the admissibility of individual constitutional complaints that required a wide interpretation of the right to vote enshrined in Article 38, Paragraph 1, of the German Basic Law. Such interpretation had already been experimented in the *Lisbon* decision, where Members of the Bundestag were entitled to lodge a constitutional complaint as 'any person' within the meaning of § 90.1 of the FCC Act. According to the FCC,

> they do not invoke their status under constitutional law *vis-à-vis* a body entitled to be a party in *Organstreit* proceedings but allege a violation of their fundamental rights by public authority (see BVerfGE 64, 301 <312>; 99, 19 <29>; 108, 251 <267>) (§ 170).

For this reason, scholars asked themselves whether

> if it is up to a judicial body to create such a procedure if is not foreseen by the constitution or when the procedural conditions for an objective review of constitutionality are not met in the particular case.[14]

Some of them depicted the *Lisbon* decision as 'a political manifesto from the judges'.[15]

Furthermore, the FCC interpreted the right to vote in a way that would be irremediably impaired if the powers of the chamber where the people are represented were severely limited. This interpretation was connected in the *Lisbon* decision with Article 20 of the Basic Law which identifies the source of the state authority in the people and the elections and with Article 79(3) of the Basic Law according to which the democratic principle is an unamendable part of the German constitutional identity. This has been made with a view of launching a constitutional identity review focused on the ability of the national parliament to perform its representative function toward the citizens when EU decision-making is at stake.

---

14 M. Wendel (2011), 'Lisbon before the Courts: Comparative Perspectives', in *EuConst*, p. 114.

15 C. Tomuschat (2009), 'The Ruling of the German Constitutional Court on the Treaty of Lisbon', *German Law Journal*, Vol. 10, No. 8, p. 1259.

In this respect, the *Lisbon* decision creates the premises for the case law on the Eurozone crisis measures to the extent that these might encroach upon the *Bundestag*'s budgetary powers which the FCC was ready to protect. Such approach affected all the rulings on financial matters ranging from the decision on the loan agreement between Greece and the European Financial Stability Facility,[16] to the judgements on the European Stability Mechanism,[17] the preliminary references to the CJEU regarding, respectively, the OMT decision of the ECB[18] and the ECB's 'quantitative easing',[19] and the final response to the CJEU.[20] In such case law, the *Bundesverfassungsgericht* insists in ensuring the preliminary *Bundestag*'s consent, or at least its right of information, on governmental decisions concerning the adoption of Eurozone's measures, irrespective of whether these are taken under EU law or under international law. Leaving aside a series of questions, I will draw attention on how the FCC structured its approach on cases concerning these measures and on its own relationship with the CJEU in particular.

To that end, a first step consisted in consolidating the *Lisbon* decision's creation of a constitutional identity review based on procedural arrangements such as that of admitting individual complaints by an MP as 'any person'. This occurred, in particular, in the OMT case, originated from a complaint brought inter alia by Peter Gauweiler, who was a member of the *Bundestag*. Scholars continued to debate on whether the FCC had unduly forged such arrangement, or whether the *Bundestag*'s unwillingness to raise a claim pertaining to the compatibility of legislation with the Basic Law under Article 93(1) no. 2 justified the FCC's approach in invoking the citizens' right to elect the Parliament to reassess compliance with the principle of parliamentary budget.[21] At any rate, these considerations concern solely the German constitutional order, while such procedural arrangement should also be viewed in the perspective of the FCC's relationship with the CJEU.

It is difficult to deny that, by reinforcing the chances of preventive scrutiny over the Eurozone crisis measures, the *Bundesverfassungsgericht* aimed at ensuring a prompt maintenance of the constitutional system vis-à-vis EU law as interpreted and partially forged by the CJEU. As it has been observed, the need of pronouncing the 'first word' is often perceived by courts as more important than that of having the 'final word'.[22] This is particularly true for what concerns abstract review including cases that concern the legal ascertainment of the boundaries between the EU and its Member States on financial

---

16 BVerfG, 2 BvR 987/10, 7 September 2011.

17 BVerfG, 2 BvE 8/11, 28 February 2012, and BverfG, 2 BvE 4/11, 19 June 2012.

18 BVerfG, 2 BvR 2278/13, 14 January 2014.

19 BVerfG, 2 BvR 859/15, 2 BvR 980/16, 2 BvR 2006/15, 2 BvR 1651/15, Order of 18 July 2017.

20 BVerfG, 2 BvR 2728/13, 2 BvR 2729/13, 2 BvR 2730/13, 2 BvR 2731/13, 2 BvE 13/13, 21 June 2016.

21 S. Recker (2011), '*Casenote – Euro Rescue Package Case*: The German Federal Constitutional Court Protects the Principle of Parliamentary Budget', *German Law Journal*, Vol. 12, No. 11, p. 2074.

22 N. Lupo (2018), 'The Advantage of Having the "First Word" in the Composite European Constitution', *Italian Journal of Public Law*, Vol. 10, p. 193.

matters. Even the FCC's choice of making for the first time a preliminary reference to the CJEU should be viewed against such background.

In the OMT case, the "seemingly high barrier to assume an *ultra vires* act (the transgression of competences being 'blatant' and 'structurally important', in the words of the *BVerfG*)" was for the first time overstepped.[23] While asking the CJEU to assess the validity of the decisions of the ECB's Governing Council of 6 September 2012 in light of the TFEU's relevant provisions and of Protocol No. 4 on the Statute of the European System of Central Banks and of the ECB, the FCC linked *ultra vires* review to the use of the principle of conferred powers, on the ground that "there are important reasons to assume that [the OMT program] exceeds the European Central Bank's monetary policy mandate and thus infringes the powers of the Member States, and that it violates the prohibition of monetary financing of the budget". The 'unusual tone' of this assertion gave the impression of a 'pre-judgement' of invalidity of the act,[24] providing the CJEU "with the (sole?) interpretation of EU primary law that, according to the FCC, is consistent with the German Basic Law".[25]

And yet, was the choice of making a preliminary reference to the CJEU incoherent with such assertion and with the scope of the FCC's 'undivided and final jurisdiction'?[26] In *Honeywell*, the *Bundesverfassungsgericht* had already announced that before declaring an EU act to be *ultra vires* it would afford the CJEU

> the opportunity to interpret the Treaties, as well as to rule on the validity and interpretation of the acts in question, in the context of preliminary ruling proceedings according to Article 267 TFEU, insofar as it has not yet clarified the questions which have arisen.[27]

On the other hand, the FCC's refusal to make preliminary references to the CJEU was considered a crucial symptom of the fact that

---

23 E.J. Lohse (2015), 'The German Constitutional Court and Preliminary References – Still a Match Not Made in Heaven?' *German Law Journal*, Vol. 16, No. 6, p. 1506.

24 J. Snell (2015), 'Gauweiler: Some Institutional Aspects', *European Law Review*, p. 133.

25 J. Alberti (2018), 'Challenging the Evolution of the EMU: The Justiciability of Soft Law Measures Enacted by the ECB against the Financial Crisis before the European Courts? *Yearbook of European Law*, Vol. 37, No. 1, p. 637.

26 As affirmed by G. Beck (2014), 'The Court of Justice, the Bundesverfassungsgericht and the Legal Reasoning during the Euro Crisis: The Rule of Law as a Far-Weather Phenomenon', *European Public Law*, Vol. 20, No. 3, p. 558.

27 BverfG, 2 BvR 2661/06, 6 July 2010.

> constitutional guardianship within the Union cannot yet be regarded as having been entrusted to one single body. It has both national and European masters: masters who may be in disagreement with one another.[28]

Finally, the message sent to the CJEU in the OMT case was far from excluding a final say from the FCC itself.

Although deprived of a dialogic attitude, the preliminary reference aimed at structuring a relationship with the CJEU which the FCC reputed of the utmost importance in light of the specific issue at stake, that of drawing, possibly once and for all, the boundaries between monetary and economic policy in the EMU.

As it has been noted, the FCC's judgement represented "a structural answer to the functional interpretation of the monetary policy, which belongs to what has been defined as the economic constitution of the European Union" and, at the same time, "decided to detail an explanation of the theoretical differences between the two concepts".[29]

The CJEU's response, as we will see, escaped the 'final' dilemma proposed by the FCC. But the latter, although accepting such response, in *Weiss* issued a second preliminary reference to the CJEU on the question of whether the ECB's Public Sector Purchase Program (PSPP), as part of the 'quantitative easing', complied with the letter of the Treaties, in particular with the principle of conferral (Art. 5 TEU), and with the prohibition of monetary financing (Art. 123 TFEU), with the effect of infringing the principle of democracy laid down in the Basic Law and thereby of undermining German constitutional identity. This judgement reinforced as such the FCC's relationship with the CJEU without withdrawing however from the identity review, requiring a clear description of the conditions under which the ECB can operate.[30] In addition, the FCC

> voiced its concerns much more cautiously in tone than in the OMT case and based them exclusively on the restrictions on this type of activity that, in the FCC's reading, the ECJ itself enunciated in its OMT judgement.[31]

28 M. Emerson & C. Joerges, *Who Is the Guardian for Constitutionalism in Europe after the Financial Crisis?*, p. 7.

29 G. Zaccaroni (2018), 'The Good, the Bad and the Ugly: National Constitutional Judges and the EU Constitutional Identity', *Italian Journal of Public Law*, Vol. 10, p. 434.

30 G. Zaccaroni, 'The Good, the Bad and the Ugly', p. 438.

31 G. Lübbe-Wolf (2019), 'Transnational Judicial Interactions and the Diplomatization of Judicial Decision-Making', in C. Landfried (ed.), *Judicial Power. How Constitutional Courts Affect Political Transformations*, Cambridge University Press, Cambridge, p. 247.

5.6 The CJEU's Responses

In *Pringle*, the CJEU held that the ESM treaty was compatible with EU law, in particular with the no-bail-out clause of Article 125 of the TFEU, because it created a financial rescue mechanism for Eurozone states facing major sovereign debt problems without directly assuming their debts, but rather granting loans to those countries. While adopting a literal reading of Article 125 TFEU the Court of Justice added that the reason why the grant of financial assistance by the stability mechanism is subject to strict conditionality under Paragraph 3 of Article 136 TFEU

> is in order to ensure that that mechanism will operate in a way that will comply with European Union law, including the measures adopted by the Union in the context of the coordination of the Member States' economic policies (para. 69).

On the other hand, the CJEU stated that the conditionality prescribed

> does not constitute an instrument for the coordination of the economic policies of the Member States, but is intended to ensure that the activities of the ESM are compatible with, inter alia, Article 125 TFEU and the coordinating measures adopted by the Union (para. 111).[32]

However, the Court's admission that the additional paragraph to Article 136 TFEU was introduced with the aim of legitimizing a mechanism whose legal basis was strongly disputed under EU law proves that it consisted in establishing an emergency rule, such as that of making financial support dependent on loan agreements specifying not only the *level* of cuts to be made but also *in what areas* they are to be made by a Member State.[33] Stipulating that the mentioned provision renders 'strict conditionality' compatible with the coordination of national economic policies obliterates a crucial point. As it has been observed,

> the *Pringle* judgment endorses a shift in the EU's monetary constitution from crisis prevention to crisis management, when bailout funds are only granted in conjunction with the imposition of strict conditionality on beneficiary states. By making the imposition of strict conditionality a constitutional requirement, the Court has imported a concept with controversial reputation into EU law. This constitutional shift in the narrow sense also has constitutional implications in a broader sense; the imposition of strict conditionality is sure to change

32 ECJ, C:2012:756, 11. 2012 – Case C-370/12 *Pringle*.
33 J. White (2015), 'Authority after Emergency Rule', *The Modern Law Review*, p. 590.

> the constraints within which the political bargaining of the beneficiary states take place.[34]

Furthermore, the CJEU denied that the ESM was in breach of the general principle of effective judicial protection as enshrined in Article 47 of the Charter of Fundamental Rights since

> the Member States are not implementing Union law within the meaning of Article 51 (1) of the Charter, when they establish a stability mechanism such as the ESM where, as it is clear from paragraph 105 of this judgment, the EU and TFEU Treaties do not confer any specific competence on the Union to establish such a mechanism (para. 180).

The Court's approach to the interplay between EU law and an international instrument as the ESM Treaty was thus clearly formal and led to a contradiction. While confining its scrutiny to the mere ascertainment of the Member States' purpose of legitimizing emergency measures through an amendment to the TFEU, the Court admitted the irrelevance of EU primary law (such as the Charter's provisions) vis-à-vis those measures being enacted by international instruments. Alternatively, it had to admit that the amendment was not reconcilable with foundational principles of the European project such as equality, mutual respect, and co-operation transformed 'into command-and-control relationships'.[35] Such admission would amount to challenging the European Council, which the Court did not dare to do.

In *Gauweiler and others*, the CJEU responded to the first FCC's preliminary reference. The judgement has appeared

> complaisant with respect to admissibility. What might have been read as a sharp threat to disobey, was benevolently and correctly, as it turned out, interpreted as provisional hypotheses. The answers given on the merits, however, were not quite as accommodating.[36]

The CJEU affirmed that the OMT program "is intended to rectify the disruption to the monetary policy transmission mechanism caused by the specific situation of government bonds issued by certain Member States" (para. 55) and that it could not be "treated as equivalent to an economic policy measure" to the extent that it interfered only indirectly

34 P.-A. Van Malleghem (2013), '*Pringle*: A Paradigm Shift in the European Union Monetary Constitution', *German Law Journal*, Vol. 14, No. 1, pp. 163-4.

35 C. Joerges (2017), 'The Overburdening of Law by Ordoliberalism and the Integration Project', in J. Hien & C. Joerges (eds.), *Ordoliberalism, Law and the Rule of Economics*, Hart, Oxford, p. 196.

36 G. Lübbe-Wolf, 'Transnational Judicial Interactions', p. 246.

in the field of economic policy (para. 59). The fact that the ECB made the implementation of the program conditional upon full compliance with the European Financial Stability Facility (EFSF) or ESM macroeconomic adjustment programs did not bring the Court to a different conclusion. The purchase of government bonds on the secondary market subject to a condition of compliance with a macroeconomic adjustment program could indeed be regarded as falling within economic policy when the purchase is undertaken by the ESM, with the difference, however, that the latter "is intended to safeguard the stability of the euro area, that objective not falling within monetary policy", while the ECB may use that instrument "only in so far as is necessary for the maintenance of price stability" (para. 64), and "is not intended to take the place of that of the ESM in order to achieve the latter's objectives but must, on the contrary, be implemented independently on the basis of the objectives particular to monetary policy" (para. 65).

On the other hand, the Court held that, when it makes choices of a technical nature and undertakes forecasts and complex assessments, the ECB "must be allowed ... a broad discretion", subject to a proportionality test only for the obligation "to examine carefully and impartially all the relevant elements of the situation in question and to give an adequate statement of the reasons for its decisions" (para. 69). Unsurprisingly, the conclusion was that the ECB's analysis of the economic situation of the euro area was not 'vitiated by a manifest error of assessment' (para. 74).

Finally, in *Weiss* the CJEU responded to the second FCC's preliminary reference.[37] Relying both on *Pringle* and on *Gauweiler*, it asserted that

> a monetary policy measure cannot be treated as equivalent to an economic policy measure for the sole reason that it may have indirect effects that can also be sought in the context of economic policy.

Resorting to the proportionality test it added that

> the PSPP programme, in its underlying principle, does not manifestly go beyond what is necessary to raise inflation rates. It is clear, inter alia, that it was not possible to counter the risk of deflation by means of the other instruments available to the ESCB. Key interest rates were at their lower bound and the ESCB had, for several months, already been implementing a programme of large-scale purchases of private sector assets.

As for the alleged infringement of the prohibition of monetary financing, the CJEU replied that implementation of the PSPP program "is not equivalent to a purchase of bonds

37 CJEU, Case C-493/17, 11 December 2018.

on the primary markets and does not reduce the impetus of the Member States to follow a sound budgetary policy" due to two reasons. The first one is that

> safeguards are built into the PSPP which ensure that a private operator cannot be certain, when it purchases bonds issued by a Member State, that those bonds will actually be bought by the ESCB in the foreseeable future.

The second reason is that

> the PSPP programme does not enable the Member States to determine their budgetary policy without taking account of the fact that, in the medium term, continuity in the implementation of the PSPP is in no way guaranteed and that they will thus be led, in the event of a deficit, to seek financing on the markets without being able to take advantage of the easing of financing conditions that implementation of the PSPP may entail.

5.7 The Key CJEU's Rulings: A Comparison

It is time to compare the key decisions adopted by the Luxembourg Court on financial matters. *Pringle* and *Gauweiler* differ with regard to their origins, the issues at stake, and the consequences of the following decisions. The Irish Supreme Court had rejected the 'sovereignty claim', while the FCC maintained that its assumption of an EU *ultra vires* act was intrinsically connected with an identity review. Moreover, the ESM's compatibility with EU law raised the general issue of whether and to which extent EU institutions could participate in an agreement with states outside the confines of the EU.[38] The OMT's compatibility with EU law was regarded instead as a single soft-law measure,[39] although posing the general question of the definition of the boundaries between monetary and economic policy under EU primary law.

Finally, the already-mentioned differences were not without consequences for the related decisions. *Pringle* said the final word on the possibility for the CJEU of checking the legal constraints issued by the ESM Treaty, because, according to the Irish Supreme Court's ruling, it would have no effect on the Irish constitutional order and also because of the scope of the decision. *Gauweiler*, to the contrary, left entirely open the possibility of further judicial scrutiny, due not only to the interaction which the FCC sought to establish with the CJEU but also due to the fact that the ECB might take other decisions affecting the monetary/economic policy divide, as *Weiss* has clearly demonstrated.

---

38 P. Craig (2013), 'Pringle and Use of EU Institutions outside the EU Legal Framework: Foundations, Procedure and Substance', *EuConst* 9, p. 263.

39 J. Alberti, 'Challenging the Evolution of the EMU', p. 627.

It might be argued that *Pringle* and *Gauweiler* differ in regards to the CJEU's approach as well. While in *Pringle* the CJEU resorted to a formalistic approach in distinguishing the ESM treaty from EU law more than required from the former's nature of international treaty; *Gauweiler* reflected, on the contrary, a substantial approach with the aim of putting under the label of 'monetary policy' all the tasks that the ECB had decided to acquire beyond the TFEU's letter.

However, such contradiction clearly reflects the CJEU's maintenance of the measures adopted in the Eurozone as institutional responses to the crisis. It is these measures that reveal a contradiction, namely that between the pretention of national governments to create a system based on automatisms, through the *Fiscal Compact* in particular, whose effects appeared to influence the common currency's stability, and the discretionary powers acquired by the ECB beyond the maintenance of price stability due to the failure of the measures taken by the political branches. In this respect, we should not only ask ourselves what is left of the powers of the Member States in the sphere of economic policy, on the presumption that *Gauweiler* legitimized the ECB as "an extremely powerful actor, albeit one which needs the support of the machinery ensuring the targeted conditionality of financial assistance" and with the implication that "Europe's 'economic constitution' and its entire constitutional configuration has been replaced by the discretionary decision-making powers of an unaccountable technocracy".[40] This is just one side of the coin. The other one consists of the imposition of structural convergence of the southern with the northern economies of the Eurozone as created by the ESM and the Fiscal Compact and

> command-and-control interventions, which are guided by the presumption that one size will fits all, are accompanied by the risk of destructive effects. The imposition of changes with disintegrative impact is not only unwise it is also illegitimate.[41]

It is against this uncomfortable background that we should evaluate the CJEU's approach. Its deference toward the Member States and the EU institutions on the one hand, and towards the ECB on the other, simply adhered to the contradictory developments that took place in the EMU in the aftermath of the financial crisis. Given the fact that such crisis precipitated the Euro crisis, *Pringle*'s rule that the EU institutions can participate in an agreement with states outside the EU confines, provided that such involvement is compatible with the Lisbon Treaty and does not alter the essential character of the powers conferred on the institutions by that Treaty, was

---

40 C. Joerges (2018), 'Comments on the Draft Treaty on the Democratisation of the Governance of the Euro Area', *European Papers*, Vol. 3, p. 78.

41 C. Joerges, 'Comments on the Fraft Treaty', p. 80.

> premised on the need to legitimate whatever action was required by EU institutions within whatever institutional forum to stave off the impending collapse of Greece, Portugal and Ireland, with devastating effects for the entire EU. The very fact that the ESM held out the promise of some permanent stability mechanism, and was integrally related to the aim of repairing the economic limb of EMU, made it all important to legitimate institutional involvement and the controls they were given under the ESM Treaty.[42]

Gauweiler's relying on the technical nature of the ECB choices with a view to justify 'a broad discretion' regarding the use of the PSPP reveals as well the CJEU's need to legitimate the action of EU institutions vis-à-vis the euro crisis.

In both cases, the CJEU went beyond the deference toward the institutional actors that were involved in the respective decisions. It reflected awareness of a financial emergency and, at the same time, a pragmatic approach in reacting to it.

5.8 The Bundesverfassungsgericht's Approach Compared with That of the CJEU

Nothing similar can be said of the FCC. Significantly, the preliminary reference highlighted the fact that neither the legal nor the economic doctrine agreed on OMT as the appropriate monetary policy transmission mechanism for safeguarding the singleness of monetary policy. The CJEU replied that

> the fact, mentioned by the referring court, that that reasoned analysis has been subject to challenge does not, in itself, suffice to call into question, since, given that questions of monetary policy are usually of controversial nature and in view of the ESCB's broad discretion, nothing more can be required from the ESCB apart from that it use its economic expertise and the necessary technical means at its disposal to carry out that analysis with all care and accuracy.[43]

While relying on the ECB's expertise, the CJEU rejected the FCC's invitation to define the OMT's appropriateness for safeguarding the euro. Even on this point, it proved thus its pragmatism in dealing with the ECB's responses to an emergency due to the biggest challenge which the euro had ever met.

The FCC's point of departure was radically different. It presupposed the conviction that rather than being merely contingent on the need to counteract an emergency the measures taken by the EU Member States during the Euro crisis were part of the Euro-

42 P. Craig, 'Pringle and the Use of EU institutions', p. 268.
43 Case C-62/14 *Gauweiler*, EU: C: 2915: 400, para. 75.

pean economic constitution and that the courts' mission consisted in checking the validity of whatever act of the EU institutions in light of that constitution. After having strengthened in its previous case law on the Eurozone financial measures 'the link between the *Bundestag*'s budgetary responsibility and a distinctly German philosophy of stability (*i.e.*, price stability and the independence of the ECB above all)' the nature of the EMU as a stability community (*Stabilitätsgemeinschaft*) becomes 'the core of a refurbished European economic constitution.'[44]

Against such background what the CJEU called the 'broad discretion' of the ECB appeared simply unacceptable to the FCC. It is true that, in the OMT case, the FCC's political role was unprecedented as demonstrated inter alia by the two dissenting judges one of whom claimed that the Court increasingly appeared to overstep the limits and boundaries of its powers and expertise.[45] However, even the acquisition by the FCC of that political role appears less relevant than the objective that guided the Court, namely to become the guardian of the continent's constitutional orthodoxy, or, more precisely, of 'a refurbished European economic constitution'.

5.9 CONCLUDING REMARKS

It is difficult to deny that 'the ping-pong game' between the FCC and the CJEU[46] ended with the prevalence of the latter's orientation. However, such conclusion would not be adequate to the purposes of this inquiry. The question does not consist in ascertaining 'who won', but rather in exploring how courts interacted with one another on financial matters during the Eurozone crisis in the exertion of abstract review.

Apart from the Irish Supreme Court's preliminary ruling to the CJEU, the sole interaction was that between the FCC and the CJEU. The other constitutional courts confined themselves to check the compatibility of the measures adopted in the Eurozone with the respective constitutions. Some scholars urged national courts such as the Czech Constitutional Court and the Danish Supreme Court, who had declared CJEU judgements *ultra vires* in the past, to "follow the FCC's example and grant the ECJ a right 'to tolerance of error' when exercising *ultra vires* review, which would facilitate the cooperation between national courts and the ECJ significantly".[47] But nothing of that sort happened, with the

44 M. Emerson & C. Joerges, *Who Is the Guardian for Constitutionalism in Europe after the Financial Crisis?*, p. 17.

45 BverfGE 134, 366, 419, dissenting opinion of Judge Lübbe-Wolf, para. 2 (14 January 2014). On this *see* F.C. Maier (2019), 'Judicial Power and European Integration. The Case of Germany', in C. Landfried (ed.), *Judicial Power. How Constitutional Courts Affect Political Transformations*, Cambridge University Press, Cambridge, 2019, pp. 196-7.

46 G. Lübbe-Wolf, 'Transnational Judicial Interactions', p. 246.

47 A. Edenharter (2018), 'Fundamental Rights Protection in the EU: The ECJ's Difficult Mission to Strike a Balance between Uniformity and Diversity', *Italian Journal of Public Law*, Vol. 10, p. 419.

effect of delegitimizing the role of guardian of the European constitutional orthodoxy which the FCC had sought to acquire in its confrontations with the CJEU.

While drawing some tentative conclusion, acquiescence of constitutional courts different from the FCC to the constitutional challenges posed by the previously mentioned measures should not be underestimated, revealing concern for the financial consequences of their decisions.[48] But this attitude, though marking a clear difference from the 'dialogues' occurring between courts, particularly on the protection of fundamental rights, is far from surprising and not likely per se to impede further dialogical approaches on other issues.

What is even more important is whether the fact that the controversy ended with the prevalence of the CJEU's orientation might lead to the conclusion that a *kompetenz-kompetenz* issue was thus settled. In light of the aforementioned considerations my answer is negative. Not only both courts exhibited a self-restraint attitude in their mutual responses, the CJEU having avoided to provoke the FCC on constitutional identity, and the latter being most prudent when reaching its final decision and upholding the OMT mechanism as interpreted by the CJEU.[49] A CJEU's move was no less crucial. The FCC's preliminary reference, as we have seen, was provided with theoretical implications concerning Europe's economic constitution that would risk a confrontation in terms of a final say. While ignoring these, the CJEU centered on the function performed by the OMT mechanism in securing the Eurozone's stability. This shifting to pragmatic considerations put the premises for giving an asymmetrical response to the FCC and for proposing to continue the ping-pong as if it was a zero-sum game: exactly what was required for the sake of constitutional pluralism.

---

48 D. Sarmiento (2015), 'The OMT Case and the Demise of the Pluralist Movement', https//despiteourdifferencesblog.wordpress.com/2015/09/21.

49 Bobić, 2017, p. 1428.

6 The Role of Courts in the Eurozone

Gavin Barrett

6.1 Introduction

The Eurozone has been at the epicenter of much of the European Union's constitutional evolution in recent times. In the form in which the Economic and Monetary Union (EMU) was created by the 1992 Maastricht Treaty, it has been well described as in reality having been a mere monetary union rather than an economic and monetary one, with only imperfect agreement having been possible in crucial areas such as fiscal rules and banking supervision.[1] Consequently, when successive banking and sovereign debt crises struck from 2007 onwards, rapid constitutional development became inescapable if the single currency zone was to survive. In this heavily contested period involving rewriting and reinterpreting EMU *Grundnormen* and the simultaneous rescue of several Eurozone states from insolvency by means which involved rigorous austerity and considerable public hardship, it is scarcely surprising that the judicial branch found itself called into play at both EU and national levels. The intention of this chapter is to attempt to make some general observations about how courts have gone about their role in the two decades since currency union became a reality and to identify characteristics and trends in European Court of Justice and national court rulings alike relating to the functioning and evolution of the Eurozone. It seems important to reflect both on the findings of courts regarding the Eurozone and on the appropriate role for courts of law, as opposed to, for example, European-level institutions such as the European Central Bank or the EU legislative organs or, indeed, national-level executives and legislatures.

From an early stage,[2] the European Court of Justice showed reluctance to play an activist role in the political minefield of economic coordination, perhaps seeing that enough explosive political potential adhered to such issues to risk entirely derailing the still-evolving Eurozone, if insensitively handled. Such early restraint proved enduring. Called upon to adjudicate in several kinds of case in the Eurozone crisis era, the Court showed both considerable dexterity and a notable degree of deference to the political process throughout. Some cases concerned general constitutional developments in the Eurozone. In *Pringle*, the Court (in plenary session) upheld the establishment of the European Stability Mechanism, enabling the European Union's political masters sufficient flexibility to keep a vital plank in the Eurozone raft and provided en route a teleological, if somewhat

1 *See* H. James, *Making the European* Union, Cambridge Massachusetts, Belknap Harvard, 2012, p. 2.
2 *See* Case C-27/04 *Commission v. Council* ECLI:EU:C:2004:436.

controversial, interpretation to the no-bailout clause. Similarly, in *Gauweiler*, the legality of the European Central Bank's (ECB) transformational Outright Monetary Transactions program was confirmed by the Court in the teeth of a threatening-sounding reference by Germany's *Bundesverfassungsgericht*. Restraint was also seen in cases in which the Court received preliminary references concerning memoranda of understanding. The Court – with at times less-than-convincing reasoning – kept itself well clear of politically toxic pronouncements concerning austerity measures.

The Court of Justice has not been the only judicial body called into play when it comes to adjudicating on the Eurozone. National courts too have had a role. Facilitated in particular by the considerable recourse by policy-makers to international law instruments rather than EU law measures in developing the Eurozone,[3] national courts across the Eurozone have also found themselves called upon to deal with general challenges to EMU measures. In general – with the partial exception of the *Bundesverfassungsgericht* – they too have acted with very considerable restraint. A range of national courts have also had to deal with challenges related to memoranda of understanding. Better placed than the Court of Justice of the European Union (CJEU) to deal with such challenges, their response to their role has varied. Most showed notable deference. The Portuguese Constitutional Court, for one, showed willingness to inflict a bloody nose on its national administration, thereby triggering in effect a process of dialogue with government and troika alike.

The remainder of this chapter is divided into two parts, one looking at the European Court of Justice and the other looking at the role of national courts, and seeks to discuss the contribution and approach of both courts to the development of the Eurozone over time, insofar as this is possible in a chapter of this length.

6.2 EUROPEAN COURT OF JUSTICE

The case law of the European Court of Justice relating to the Eurozone is not of course exclusively the product of the banking and sovereign debt crises. Rather, the Court's jurisprudence can be divided between pre-crisis-era case law, crisis-era rulings, and, increasingly now also, in the light of more recent rulings, post-crisis-era jurisprudence.

3 *See* on this topic *e.g.*, F. Fabbrini, 'The Euro-Crisis and the Courts: Judicial Review and the Political Process in Comparative Perspective', *Berkeley Journal of International Law*, 32, 2014, p. 64.

6.2.1 Pre-Crisis-Era Case Law of the European Court of Justice

The original role of the Court in the design of the constitution of what is now the European Union is too well known to require any repetition here. In cases like *Van Gend en Loos*,[4] *Costa v. ENEL*,[5] *Internationale Handelsgesellchaft*,[6] *Simmenthal*,[7] *Van Duyn*,[8] *Marleasing*,[9] *Francovich*,[10] and *Brasserie du pêcheur*,[11] the European Court of Justice has played a major role in fashioning the very structure of the Union.

As regards the structure of EMU, however, designed at a much later stage and in far more detail than the text concerning the institutional structure of the original treaties (which left far more unstated[12]), the European Court of Justice has always played a more modest role and, indeed, initially, incomparably more so. And yet rulings of some importance were arrived at by the Court even at an early stage. Hence, the relative rights of the 'ins' and 'outs' of economic and monetary union were elucidated in the 2015 judgment of the General Court in *United Kingdom v. European Central Bank (ECB)*,[13] a judgment which would have proved to be of greater permanent significance if the UK had not opted to leave the European Union in the wake of the 2016 Brexit referendum.

Far less impressive (although politically, perhaps the only decision they could have reached) was the decision of the plenary session of the European Court of Justice in the 2004 case of *Commission v. Council*[14] in which the Court declined to annul the Council's failure to adopt the formal instruments contained in the Commission's recommendations under the excessive deficit procedure. This was a decision in line with earlier jurisprudence of the Court. However, it left the Commission without power to compel the Council to impose sanctions on Eurozone states which violated the Stability and Growth Pact. In effect, it involved the Court of Justice standing back and effectively allowing Member States to proceed with budgetary misbehavior that subsequently reached its apotheosis in the case of Greece and the triggering of a crisis that almost led to the destruction of the economic and monetary union. It has been argued that the Court could have done more: It is not without reason that Hinarejos has described *Commission v. Council* as "the

---

4 Case 26-62 *NV Algemene Transport- en Expeditie Onderneming van Gend & Loos v. Netherlands Inland Revenue Administration* ECLI:EU:C:1963:1.

5 Case 6-64 *Costa v. ENEL* ECLI:EU:C:1964:66.

6 Case 11/70 *Internationale Handelsgesellschaft mbH v. Einfuhr- und Vorratsstelle für Getreide und Futtermittel* ECLI:EU:C:1970:114.

7 Case 106/77 *Amministrazione delle Finanze dello Stato v. Simmenthal SpA* ECLI:EU:C:1978:49.

8 Case 41/74 *Van Duyn v. Home Office* ECLI:EU:C:1974:133.

9 C-106/89 *Marleasing v. Comercial Internacional de Alimentación* ECLI:EU:C:1990:395.

10 Cases C-6/90 and C-9/90 *Francovich and Bonifaci v. Italy* ECLI:EU:C:1991:428.

11 C-46/93 and C-48/93 *Brasserie du pêcheur v. Bundesrepublik Deutschland* and*The Queen v. Secretary of State for Transport, ex parte Factortame and others* ECLI:EU:C:1996:79.

12 Much of the expansion in the size of what became the EC Treaty at Maastricht was accounted for by the insertion of voluminous rules relating to economic and monetary union.

13 Case T-496/11 ECLI:EU:T:2015:133.

14 Case C-27/04 ECLI:EU:C:2004:436.

Court's most notorious pronouncement" concerning EMU.[15] It is nonetheless also true, however, that budgetary discipline is often an area of massive potential political controversy and that political problems cannot always be solved with legal decisions.

There were other decisions of note in the pre-crisis era, such as the July 2003 ruling of the Court in *Commission v. European Central Bank*[16] where the Court usefully reined in the ECB, rapping it across the knuckles with a stinging reminder that recognition of ECB independence did not have the consequence of separating it entirely from the European Union and exempting it from every rule of EU law.[17] The Court[18] annulled an ECB decision on fraud prevention which had established the ECB's own anti-fraud investigation framework without any reference to the powers of the European Anti-Fraud Office, OLAF.[19] The ECB's argument that the OLAF regulation was itself void as the ECB should have been consulted before its adoption[20] failed to impress the Court, which noted that the ECB had not been assigned any specific tasks regarding the prevention of fraud detrimental to the financial interests of the Community.[21]

This was thus a useful case on the scope of the extent to consult the ECB in adopting legislation. However, it pales into relative insignificance compared to the crisis-era case law of the Court and to which it is now proposed to turn.

6.2.2 *Crisis-Era Case Law of the European Court of Justice*

Following the outbreak of an economic crisis in 2007, the emergence of a trend toward increased involvement on the part of the Courts in monetary and fiscal issues became visible. Fabbrini has argued that

> the Euro-crisis and the legal and institutional responses to it have dramatically increased the powers of the judiciary *vis-à-vis* the political branches, making

15 *See* A. Hinarejos, *The Euro Area Crisis in Constitutional* Perspective, Oxford, Oxford University Press, 2015, p. 121.
16 Case C-11/00 ECLI:EU:C:2003:395 Analyzed in S. Lambrinoc, *The Legal Duty to Consult the European Central Bank: National and EU Consultations* (ECB Legal Working Paper Series No. 9/November 2009).
17 Para. 135 of the ruling of the Court.
18 At the behest of the Commission (supported by the Council and Parliament and the Netherlands).
19 Decision ECB/1999/5 of 7 October 1999.
20 Regulation (EC) No. 1073/1999.
21 Para. 111 of the ruling of the Court.

economic and monetary affairs in Europe more judicialized that even in a hyper-judicialized system like the US.[22]

It is true that the role of the Court of Justice in the process of navigation toward an exit from the crisis can scarcely be overemphasized. Nonetheless, a certain degree of balance is also required here. As will be seen, in its key decisions, the Court of Justice in reality exercised considerable circumspection. It is thus also absolutely correct to say (as Hinarejos does) that the Court ultimately "tended to take a back seat to the political, often intergovernmental, process".[23] On the other hand, it also needs to be borne in mind that such judicial circumspection was deliberate and was not always the legally obvious interpretation for the Court to take cognizance of the Treaty provisions concerned. And it was ultimately arguably key to the survival of the Eurozone. What it is perhaps key to recall is that *Van Gend en Loos, Costa,* and the like were decided at a time when judicial activism was needed to advance the cause of European integration. In contrast, the major euro-crisis cases were decided when the safeguarding of European integration needed something quite different, namely, that the law not become an obstacle. Thanks to the case law of the Court of Justice, this need was met.

Overall, the jurisprudence of the Court of Justice on the economic crisis has been well summarized as falling into three different categories of case:[24] first, rulings concerning the legality of general developments or reforms altering the structure or underpinnings of EMU (cases like *Pringle*[25] and *Gauweiler,*[26] to which we can now add cases like *Weiss*[27]); second, rulings linked to the fallout of rescue packages and the conditionality imposed on Member States as a result (most of which, however, have been declared inadmissible by the Court[28]); and third, there are what Fabbrini terms cases "reviewing regulatory or

22 F. Fabbrini, *Economic Governance in Europe – Comparative Paradoxes and Constitutional Challenges*, Oxford, Oxford University Press, 2016, p. 64, where he also observes "the legal and institutional measures enacted by the political branches of government to respond to the crisis have increasingly fallen prey to the scrutiny of the courts, both at the national and at the supranational level" (*Ibid.*, p. 63.) Elsewhere, the same author refers to the judiciary as having acquired "an extensive and pervasive influence in the fiscal and economic domain ... reflected in the great preoccupation with which policy-makers and financial markets alike have awaited most of the judgments considered above" (*Loc cit.*, n. 4, p. 109).

23 Hinarejos, *op. cit.*, n. 16, p. 121. A point which has also had to be acknowledged by Fabbrini himself (*Loc. cit.*, n. 4 at 99-100).

24 *Ibid.*, p. 122.

25 Case C-370/12 *Pringle v. Government of Ireland, Ireland and the Attorney General* ECLI:EU:C:2012:756. This was a judgment of the full Court of Justice.

26 Case C-62/14 *Gauweiler and others v. Deutscher Bundestag* ECLI:EU:C:2015:400. This was a hearing of the Grand Chamber of the Court of Justice.

27 Case C-493/17 *Weiss and others* ECLI:EU:C:2018:1000.

28 Case T-541/10 *ADEDY and others v. Council* ECLI:EU:T:2012:626; Case T-327/13 *Mallis and Malli v. European Commission and European Central Bank* ECLI:EU:T:2014:909. Note also the action dismissed by the General Court in Case T-289/13 *Ledra Advertising Ltd v. European Commission and European Central Bank* ECLI:EU:T:2014:981. *See* on the latter two cases, R. Repasi, 'Judicial Protection against Austerity Measures in the Euro Area: Ledra and Mallis' (2017) 54 CMLRev 1123.

legislative measures pushing for greater financial integration against the opposition of a single member state".[29] Most of these rulings however concern initiatives which seek to build on single market law in the financial field, such as the debates over the possible introduction of a financial transaction tax and the short-selling regulation and bankers' bonuses, rather than areas of law focused on the Eurozone. As such, they are not dealt with further in this chapter.[30]

The first category of cases – those on general reforms – are of the most concern, although in a chapter of this length, it is possible only to make some brief observations about them.

6.2.2.1 Pringle[31]

The *Pringle* case may be described as the case in which the European Court of Justice cautiously deferred to a revolution which had been effected by the Member States in order to save the Eurozone: a revolution, in effect to save the status quo.[32] At, as well as subsequent to, Maastricht,[33] the Member States (circumscribed, in fairness to them, by the bounds of what was then politically possible) had created a Eurozone with measures aimed at preventing crises, but almost entirely lacking in structures or mechanisms designed to cope with a crisis, once one actually happened. Dramatic measures – first temporary (in the form of the creation of the European Financial Stability Facility [EFSF] and the European Financial Stability Mechanism [EFSM]), then permanent (in the shape of the creation of the European Stability Mechanism – a permanent rescue mechanism created to lend to states experiencing a sovereign debt crisis and therefore in danger of default) – were therefore needed urgently to save the euro when crisis struck.[34]

In *Pringle*, decided at this time, the Court declined to stand in the way of the construction of the European Stability Mechanism (ESM), the most important such undertaking. This necessitated, however, a dynamic and purposive approach to the relevant Treaty provisions and, more particularly, precisely this approach to the interpretation

29 F. Fabbrini, *op. cit.*, n. 23, p. 89.

30 *See* further in this regard, Hinarejos, *op. cit.*, n. 16, p. 136 *et seq.*

31 Case C-370/12 *Pringle v. Government of Ireland, Ireland and the Attorney General* ECLI:EU:C:2012:756. This was a judgment of the full Court of Justice. *See* further B. de Witte and T. Beukers, 'The Court of Justice Approves the Creation of the European Stability Mechanism Outside the EU Legal Order: Pringle', *Common Market Law Review*, Vol. 50, No. 3, 2013, p. 805; P. Craig, 'Pringle: Legal Reasoning, Text, Purpose and Teleology', *Articles by Maurer Faculty*, Paper 2123, 2013, p. 1; and S. Adam, 'The European Stability Mechanism through the Legal Meanderings of the Union's Constitutionalism: Comment on Pringle', *European Law Review*, Vol. 6, 2013, p. 848.

32 A revolution then in which everything had to change in order to stay the same, to adapt the words of Tancredi in Giuseppe Tomasi di Lampedusa, *Il Gattopardo* (Feltrinelli, Milan 2013) "se vogliamo che tutto rimanga com'è bisogna che tutto cambi".

33 The German-inspired notion of the Stability and Growth Pact dates from after the signature by the member states of the Treaty of Maastricht.

34 *See* generally A. de Gregorio Merino, 'Legal Developments in the Economic and Monetary Union during the Debt Crisis: The Mechanisms of Financial Assistance', *Common Market Law Review*, Vol. 49, 2012, p. 1613.

of the no-bailout clause in Article 125 of the Treaty on the Functioning of the European Union (TFEU).[35] According to the Court, that clause had the aim of ensuring that Member States remained subject to market discipline, thereby encouraging prudent fiscal policy. That much of the Court's ruling was uncontroversial. The next part was not. Article 125's broader aim, according to the Court, was ensuring the financial stability of the Eurozone as a whole – a rationale which did not preclude a mechanism such as the ESM, which, it noted, was only triggered in order to safeguard the financial stability of the Eurozone as a whole – was subject to strict conditionality and maintained the responsibility of an assisted Member State *vis-à-vis* its creditors. Hinarejos has described the Court as having "adopted a teleological/*ultima ratio* interpretation of the clause" and argued that

> in doing so, it 'discovered' an ultimate objective for EMU (safeguarding the financial stability of the euro area) that had no basis in the Treaties and that supersedes the Treaty-sanctioned objectives of budgetary discipline and price stability.[36]

One way or another, the outcome of the case in *Pringle* was of great importance, and, indeed, because it confirmed the legality of the European Stability Mechanism, the case may be regarded as having been critical to the survival of the Eurozone as a whole. For that reason, the ruling is scarcely surprising.[37] The Court's teleological approach is reminiscent of its approach to questions like supremacy and direct effect in earlier cases like *Costa v. ENEL* and *Van Gend en Loos* in which the aims and the spirit of the Treaty played a pivotal role in the Court's reasoning. However, it also continued a stance of deference to the political decision-making apparatus in a highly politically controversial area which is also reminiscent of its approach in *Commission v. Council*[38] – a case that effectively ushered in the economic crisis by allowing the Council to paralyze the operation of the original Stability and Growth Pact. The 2004 case involved judicial deference in the face of political misbehavior. The 2012 case involved deference in the face of political action necessary to safeguard the Eurozone's very existence.

35 There is more to the Court's ruling than this, of course. For a good overview, *see* Hinarejos, *op. cit.*, n. 16, pp. 123-129.

36 *Ibid.*, pp. 125-126.

37 *Ibid.*, p. 127.

38 Case C-27/04 ECLI:EU:C:2004:436.

6.2.2.2 Gauweiler[39]

Gauweiler v. Deutscher Bundestag involved a challenge to the Outright Monetary Transactions (OMT) program announced by the European Central Bank in 2012.[40] OMT was never actually implemented but was nonetheless an indisputably significant initiative both because (a) its mere announcement by Mario Draghi played a key role in ending the sovereign debt crisis at that time and because (b) the threat of it being deployed remains a potent deterrent to the markets from seeking to profit from any similar such crisis in the future. (Almost incidentally, the case also involved a significant landmark in the history of interactions between national courts and the European Court of Justice for it was, rather remarkably, the first ever Article 267 reference by the European Court of Justice by the German Federal Constitutional Court, the *Bundesverfassungsgericht.*[41])

Notable features of the Court of Justice ruling in the case include (a) its restrictive interpretation of the Article 123 TFEU prohibition of monetary financing – strongly reminiscent of the similarly restrictive approach it had taken to the Article 125 TFEU no-bailout rule in the *Pringle* case, and (b) its broad interpretation of the treaty provisions on the conduct of monetary policy. As regards Article 123, here again (as in *Pringle* regarding Art. 125), the Court considered the logic of the Article at issue. It held that this logic was to encourage the Member States to follow a sound budgetary policy and further found that the various restrictions, guarantees, and conditions (including the need for compliance with a structural adjustment program) with which the OMT program was hedged would exclude any lessening of the impetus of the Member States to follow such a sound policy.[42]

As regards its interpretation of what constituted monetary policy, the Court was perhaps less convincing. The Court noted approvingly that the express aims of the OMT program were "an appropriate monetary policy transmission and the singleness of the monetary policy".[43] According to the Court, the fact that a program like the OMT program might *also* be capable of contributing to the stability of the euro area, an issue which

39 Case C-62/14 *Gauweiler and others v. Deutscher Bundestag* ECLI:EU:C:2015:400. This was a hearing of the Grand Chamber of the Court of Justice. *See* more generally V. Borger, 'Outright Monetary Transactions and the Stability Mandate of the ECB: Gauweiler', *Common Market Law Review*, Vol. 53, 2016, p. 139. *See also* the several articles published on the *Gauweiler* ruling in F. Fabbrini (ed.), 'The European Court of Justice, the European Central Bank and the Supremacy of EU Law', *Maastricht Journal of European and Comparative Law*, Vol. 23, No. 1, 2016, p.1 *et seq.*

40 For a brief summary of the *Gauweiler* ruling, *see* Fabbrini, *op. cit.*, n. 23, p. 93-97.

41 The reference may well have been an attempt to escape with dignity from the potentially disastrous trajectory the Court's own reasoning threatened to set: Brunnermeier *et al.* have described what the *Bundesverfassungsgericht* itself termed a "pronouncement of the judgment and referral for a preliminary ruling to the Court of Justice of the European Union" as "calculatedly not a ruling" and have argued that "the Court's Second Senate ... almost certainly felt that it did not want to be directly responsible for setting off a financial panic that might jeopardise the euro and the European Union" (*see* M. Brunnermeier, H. James and J. Landau, *The Euro and the Battle of* Ideas, Princeton, Princeton University Press, 2016, p. 358).

42 *See* para. 100 *et seq.*

43 *See* paras. 47 to 50 of the Court's ruling.

(as per *Pringle*) was a matter of economic policy did not call the assessment of OMT as monetary policy into question.[44] A monetary policy measure could not be treated as equivalent to an economic policy measure merely because it might have "*indirect* effects" on the stability of the euro area.[45] The Court also noted that the ECB Statute granted the ECB the power to engage in transactions on secondary sovereign bond markets.[46]

Furthermore, the mere fact that the OMT program was specifically limited to certain States' government bonds was not of a nature, of itself, to bring OMT outside the realm of monetary policy, as the program was "intended to rectify the disruption to the monetary policy transmission mechanism caused by the specific situation of government bonds issued by certain Member States".[47]

Beyond this, OMT's being conditional upon full compliance with EFSF or ESM macroeconomic adjustment programs did not alter matters. The Court acknowledged that such a government bond-buying program "may, *indirectly*, increase the impetus to comply with those adjustment programs and thus, *to some extent*, further the economic-policy objectives of those programs". However, such indirect effects did not make OMT equivalent to an economic policy measure, since the European System of Central Banks (ESCB; without prejudice to the objective of price stability) was obliged to support the general economic policies in the Union.[48]

There seems a certain sense of protesting too much to this.[49] However, regardless of this, in any case, *Gauweiler* marks another step along the route first traced by *Pringle* away from the original rule-based EMU to a more policy-based approach.[50] Put another way, EMU seems to have been moving away from what might be termed its original 'blind watchmaker' [51] form of governance (in which simple adherence to rules is expected to produce by itself the necessary elements of a functioning economic and monetary union) toward a model involving a much more discretionary and interventionist role for institutions like the ECB and for the European Stability Mechanism. Ultimately, what is most significant about *Pringle* and*Gauweiler* is that both are permissive judgments allowing the putting in place and operation of what Fabbrini terms "key components of the new architecture of EMU".[52]

---

44 Para. 51 of the judgment of the Court.

45 Para. 52 of the judgment of the Court. Emphasis added.

46 Para. 54 of the judgment of the Court, citing Art. 18.1 of the Protocol on the ESCB and the ECB.

47 Para. 55 of the judgment of the Court.

48 The Court cited Arts. 119(2) TFEU, 127(1) TFEU, and 282(2) TFEU in this regard. *See* generally, paras. 57 to 59 of the Court's judgment. Emphasis added.

49 *See* for a good account of the origins of – and controversies surrounding – the OMT program, M. Brunnermeier, H. James and J. Landau, *op. cit.*, n. 42, pp. 352-359.

50 *See* Hinarejos on OMT before the European Court of Justice (written after the *Gauweiler* reference but prior to the ruling), *op. cit.*, n. 16, pp. 129-131.

51 *See* R. Dawkins, *The Blind Watchmaker*, London, Norton, 1986, where the author uses this metaphor to describe the process of evolution.

52 Fabbrini, *op. cit.*, n. 23, p. 97.

6.2.2.3 Weiss[53]

A further contribution to this permissive process was made in the 2018 case of *Weiss and others.*[54] Like *Gauweiler*, this was a reference by the *Bundesverfassungsgericht*, which now appears to be engaging in Article 267 TFEU references with some gusto (albeit a full half-century after this Article's adoption).[55] The case can be regarded as *Gauweiler II*, since again it was brought by Gauweiler and fellow sceptics about economic and monetary union. The challenge this time was, inter alia,[56] to a decision made as part of the ECB's quantitative easing program. More specifically, it was a challenge brought before the German Courts to what is called the 'Public Sector Purchase Program (PSPP)', which in turn is the main element of the ECB's framework program, the 'Expanded Asset Purchase Program' (EAPP). Unlike the OMT program at issue in *Gauweiler*, which has never been implemented (and is therefore more a market-restraining threat than an actual program), the EAPP *has* been implemented – and the figures involved are enormous. Hofmann refers to figures cited by the *Bundesverfassunsgericht* according to which

> the EAPP has, since its instigation, had a volume between 60 and 80 billion Euros a month and an overall volume of 1,8 trillion Euros by May 2017. Of these 1,8 trillion, 1,5 trillion Euros was due to purchases under the PSPP.[57]

Thus, what was at issue before the Court in *Weiss* (a Grand Chamber of 15 judges, rather than a full Court as in *Gauweiler* and *Pringle*) was the main element of the quantitative easing program. As in the two other cases, the grounds of challenge were many and cannot all be repeated here.

Some particularly significant findings may be adverted to here however. The Court expressly confirmed its *Pringle–Gauweiler* approach that

> in order to determine whether a measure falls within the area of monetary policy it is appropriate to refer principally to the objectives of that measure. The instruments which the measure employs in order to attain those objectives are also relevant.[58]

---

53 Case C-493/17 *Weiss and others* ECLI:EU:C:2018:1000.

54 *See* for a consideration of this, H. Hofmann, 'Controlling the Powers of the ECB: Delegation, Discretion, Reasoning and Care – What Gauweiler, Weiss and Others Can Teach Us', *Ademu Working Paper Series*, WP 2018/107, Barcelona, 2018.

55 *I.e.*, in its initial form of Art. EEC.

56 The case involved various constitutional challenges before the ECB involving not only decisions of the ECB but also the participation of the German Central Bank (the *Bundesbank*) in those decisions and the alleged failures of the *Bundesbank*, German Federal Government and Parliament regarding those decisions (*see* para. 13 of the ruling of the Court of Justice.)

57 Hofmann, *op. cit.*, n. 55, pp. 2-3.

58 Para. 53 of the ruling of the Court.

The Court confirmed that the PSPP program involved monetary policy, noting that it was apparent from the decision's recital that its purpose

> is to contribute to a return of inflation rates to levels below, but close to, 2% over the medium term. In that regard, it is important to point out that the authors of the Treaties chose to define the primary objective of the Union's monetary policy – namely the maintenance of price stability – in a general and abstract manner, but did not spell out precisely how that objective was to be given concrete expression in quantitative terms.[59]

The Court reaffirmed its *Gauweiler* view that monetary policy measure cannot be treated as equivalent to an economic policy measure for the sole reason that it may have indirect effects that can also be sought in the context of economic policy.[60] It also expressly declined to concur in the *Bundesverfassungsgericht*'s view that

> that any effects of an open market operations program that were knowingly accepted and definitely foreseeable by the ESCB when the program was set up should not be regarded as 'indirect effects' of the program.[61]

The Court maintained control over the crucial borderline between monetary and economic policy, although the program of purchases at issue in *Weiss* was clearly easier territory to defend as monetary policy than the OMT program at issue in *Gauweiler* had been. The Court also retained control of the other crucial battle line regarding the legality of the PSPP: once more, a limited view was taken of the monetary financing prohibition by the Court, just as it had been in *Gauweiler*, and just as a limited view had been taken of the no-bailout rule in *Pringle*. According to the Court, the decision in *Weiss* did not violate the Article 123 monetary financing prohibition. The Court conceded that the ESCB's intervention would have been incompatible with Article 123 only if potential purchasers of government bonds on the primary markets knew *for certain* that the ESCB was going to purchase those bonds within a certain period and under conditions allowing them to act, de facto, as intermediaries for the ESCB for the direct purchase of those bonds from public authorities and bodies.[62] But it denied that such certainty existed here, although it admitted that private operators had been enabled "to foresee, to some extent, significant aspects of the ESCB's future actions on the secondary markets".[63] *Certainty* was avoided by various safeguards (such as blackout periods of

59 Paras. 54-55 of the ruling of the Court.
60 Para. 61 of the ruling of the Court citing para. 52 of *Gauweiler* and para. 56 of *Pringle*.
61 Para. 62 of the ruling of the Court.
62 Para. 110 of the ruling of the Court.
63 Para. 112 of the ruling of the Court.

uncertain duration when no bonds would be purchased) and avoidance of advance specification of purchase volumes.[64] The Court further refused to consider arguments relating to the decision's provisions on the sharing of losses, arguing that this would involve "an advisory opinion on a problem which is, at this stage, hypothetical".[65]

Overall, *Gauweiler and Weiss* have all seen the Court of Justice decline to see the law frustrate what, if it is not a revolution in economic and monetary union is at least a major evolution, a shift away from the original rule-based EMU to a more policy-based approach involving a much more discretionary and interventionist role for institutions like the ECB and for the European Stability Mechanism and less trust in the efficacy of a rigidly literal approach to rules to safeguard the continued existence of the Eurozone; as Hinarejos terms it, "a different EMU with a new overarching objective (the safeguarding of the stability of the euro area) that demands managerialism and policy-making".[66] The Court has not been the source of the great changes which have been made in EMU's structures and functioning. These have been decided upon by the Member States both inside the political structures of the European Union and outside them. But the permissive approach adopted by the Court has been key in allowing this evolutionary/revolutionary approach to continue and for things to change in order that they may remain the same. Since the alternative approach might well have marked the end of EMU, it is perhaps not surprising that the Court has adopted the approach it has. However, it has a certain level of form here – its policy of noninterventionism in a politically highly controversial area has a long history dating back to before the time of crisis. Nonetheless, it has had to work hard in order to avoid rules from an earlier phase of EMU frustrating the construction and functioning of initiatives only latterly revealed to be needed to

64 *See* para. 113 *et seq.* of the ruling of the Court.

65 *Cf.* however the Court's ruling in Case C-621/18 *Wightman and others* ECLI:EU:C:2018:999 regarding the prospect of the UK withdrawing its Art. 50 Brexit notice. At the time that case was decided, this was a hypothetical prospect, but one in relation to which the Court was content to make a ruling. Note also that the Court rejected (as it had in *Gauweiler*) any contention that the policy at issue in *Weiss* was disproportionate (*see* paras. 71-100 of the ruling of the Court).

66 Hinarejos, *op. cit.*, n. 16, p. 143. Note also Fabbrini, *loc. cit.*, n. 4, pp. 70-71, and in particular his entirely accurate observation that the "mechanisms of financial stabilization represent an entirely new addition to the architecture of the EMU constitution" constructed in the wake of the discovery "that it was actually much easier on paper than in reality to let a country of the Eurozone default without this producing a systemic effect on the stability of the Eurozone as a whole".

buttress and prevent the collapse of the EMU edifice, constructed as this was in that earlier era.[67]

Turning to the Hinarejos' second category of cases, those reviewing the legality of rescue packages provided for Member States, and the conditionality attached thereto, as already noted, most of these have been declared inadmissible by the Court or have otherwise been unsuccessful and need not detain us here. In one of the most recent (decided in July 2018), *Bourdouvali and Others v. Council of the European Union and Others,*[68] the Court dismissed on a variety of grounds the applicant bondholders' shareholders' and deposit holders' claim for damages on foot of losses allegedly suffered by them under the Cypriot bailout and which they had attributed variously to acts which they contended obliged the Republic of Cyprus to adopt measures harmful to them, in order to receive assistance which was indispensable for it.

The ruling is an interesting one, acknowledging as it does, for example, that the Euro Group is a body of the Union formally established by the Treaties and intended to contribute to achieving the objectives of the Union. The acts and conduct of the Euro Group in the exercise of its powers under EU law are therefore attributable to the European Union although the Court disagreed with the assertion that the European Union had made Cyprus adopt the measures it had.[69]

6.2.3 *Post-Crisis-Era Case Law of the European Court of Justice*

Decisions of the major importance of the *Pringle,Gauweiler*, and even *Weiss* rulings are the exception rather than the rule. The great lines of constitutional authority having now been established, we have probably moved into an era of what (for the time being at least) may be referred to as post-crisis-era jurisprudence on the part of the Court of Justice. And yet even now, rulings of major constitutional significance are possible. What may be described as a remarkable and adventurous judgment on the part of the Court of Justice occurred in the joined cases of *Rimšēvičs and European Central Bank v. Latvia*[70] where a Grand Chamber of the Court went beyond the advice offered to it by Advocate General Kokott, beyond its usual approach in judicial review cases and beyond what had been

---

67 The giving of the Court's *imprimatur* to the crisis-era evolution of the economic and monetary union has not of course been entirely uncontroversial. *See* for a critical perspective, M. Everson and C. Joerges, 'Who Is the Guardian for Constitutionalism in Europe After the Financial Crisis?', *in* S. Kröger (ed.), *Political Representation in the European Union: Still Democratic in Times of Crisis?*, Abingdon, Routledge, 2014, p. 400. *See* generally for some valuable reflections concerning the restrained approach of the Court regarding all three categories of case to come before it in the crisis era, Hinarejos, *op. cit.*, n. 16, pp. 140-144 and 152-153. Among the challenges here, as she points out, "is to elucidate those cases where the Court may be asked to review changes to the constitutional underpinnings of EMU that are not the result of the appropriate political process and that are too significant to be 'ratified' by a court" (*Ibid.*, p. 152).

68 Case T-786/14 ECLI:EU:T:2018:487.

69 *See, e.g.*, para. 129 of the Court's ruling.

70 Joined Cases C-202/18 and C-238/18 ECLI:EU:C:2019:139.

sought by the European Central Bank in this case, annulling a national measure (which had taken the shape of a decision of the Anti-Corruption Office, Latvia prohibiting Rimšēvičs from performing his duties as Governor of the Central Bank of Latvia). The Court explained its remarkable decision by reference to the wording of Article 14.2.2 of the ESCB Statute, which it viewed as expressly entrusting it with a power of review.[71] The Court acknowledged that this derogated from the general distribution of powers between the national courts and the courts of the European Union and held that

> that derogation can be explained by the particular institutional context of the ESCB within which it operates. The ESCB represents a novel legal construct in EU law which brings together national institutions, namely the national central banks, and an EU institution, namely the ECB, and causes them to cooperate closely with each other, and within which a different structure and a less marked distinction between the EU legal order and national legal orders prevails.

Article 14.2 of the Statute of the ESCB and of the ECB reflects the logic of this highly integrated system which the authors of the Treaties envisaged for the ESCB and, in particular, of the dual professional role of the governor of a national central bank, who is certainly a national authority but who acts within the framework of the ESCB and sits, where he is the governor of a national central bank of a Member State whose currency is the euro, on the main decision-making body of the ECB. It is because of this hybrid status and in order to guarantee the functional independence of the governors of the national central banks within the ESCB that, by way of exception, a decision taken by a national authority relieving one of those governors from office may be referred to the Court.

Article 14.2 of the Statute (of the ESCB and of the ECB) thus adds a legal remedy to the system of legal remedies laid down by the Treaties which is very specific, as is apparent from the very small number of persons to whom it is available, the unique subject matter of the decisions against which it may be used, and the exceptional circumstances in which it may be exercised.[72]

The decision was clearly intended to be an exceptional one. Nevertheless, it is striking that the highly integrated system envisaged by the Treaties for the ESCB, the hybrid professional role of national central bank governors, and the need to guarantee their functional independence within the ESCB played a key role in the Court arriving at its

71 This provides: "a Governor may be relieved from office only if he no longer fulfils the conditions required for the performance of his duties or if he has been guilty of serious misconduct. A decision to this effect may be referred to the Court of Justice by the Governor concerned or the Governing Council on grounds of infringement of these Treaties or of any rule of law relating to their application."

72 *See* paras. 69-71 of the ruling of the Court.

decision. This was very much a decision which could only have been arrived at in the context of economic and monetary union.[73]

Apart from rather dramatic judgments like *Rimšēvičs*, there are also many less spectacular but nonetheless significant cases being decided on areas that are centrally relevant to an economic and monetary union, such as banking union law, for example, in such areas as deposit guarantee schemes.[74] In a chapter of this length, however, they cannot delay us beyond adverting to their existence.

6.3 National Courts

6.3.1 *Why National Courts Have Been Involved in Adjudicating on the Eurozone*

National courts have played a major role on Eurozone issues in several countries, including Germany, Portugal, Estonia, Ireland, and Greece. An obvious initial question is why national courts have been involved in adjudicating on EMU-related issues in the first place, given the European nature of the issues involved, which would seem to make adjudication by a European-level jurisdiction the more natural place to which to have recourse.

A key element of the answer is that, although the issues may be European, the law is far from universally that of the European Union. Eurozone law is now broader than merely the law of European Union; hence, Kilpatrick correctly points out "the unusual and multiple legal pedigree of euro-crisis law" which encompasses

> EU law relevant to the crisis as well as international agreements entered into by subsets of EU states and administered by EU institutions (such as some of the sovereign debt loan arrangements).[75]

---

73 *See* for some reflections on the ruling, R. Smits, 'ECJ Annuls a National Measure against an Independent Central Banker', *European Law Blog*, 5 March 2019 (available online at http://europeanlawblog.eu/2019/03/05/ecj-annuls-a-national-measure-against-an-independent-central-banker/).

74 Case C-571/16 *Kantarev v. Balgarska Narodna Banka* ECLI:EU:C:2018:807; Joined Cases C-688/15 and C-109/16 *Anisimovienė and Others v. bankas 'Snoras' AB, in liquidation and others* ECLI:EU:C:2018:209; Case C-76/15 *Vervloet and Others v. Ministerraad* ECLI:EU:C:2016:975; Case C-127/14 *Surmačs v. Finanšu un kapitāla tirgus komisija* ECLI:EU:C:2015:522; Case C-671/13 *Proceedings brought by VĮ „Indėlių ir investicijų draudimas" and Nemaniūnas* ECLI:EU:C:2015:418; Case C-222/02 *Paul and others v. Federal Republic of Germany* ECLI:EU:C:2004:606; Case C-233/94 *Federal Republic of Germany v. European Parliament and Council of the European Union* ECLI:EU:C:1997:231.

75 C. Kilpatrick, 'Constitutions, Social Rights and Sovereign Debt States in Europe: A Challenging New Area of Constitutional Inquiry', *in* T. Beukers, B de Witte & C. Kilpatrick (eds.), *Constitutional Change through Euro-Crisis Law*, Cambridge, Cambridge University Press, 2017, p. 282.

The fairly extensive use made of intergovernmental treaties to rescue the European Union from its difficulties has been driven in turn at least in part by the cumbersome nature of amendment of EU treaties (which requires the unanimous agreement of all the EU Member States) and ratification or incorporation processes which in some cases can involve constitutional referendums.[76] Whatever the reasons for the phenomenon of the increased use of international law instruments, however, one consequence of it has been an increased role for national courts (*i.e.*, rather than the European Court of Justice).[77] As Fabbrini has observed, the outcome of intergovernmental management of the euro crisis has been an increased involvement of the courts in a way that could not have happened had the Community method been deployed.[78]

Moreover, in implementing such international agreements, national laws and executive action have often been given a major role to play. One example of this can be seen in the fact that the Fiscal Stability Treaty requires Member States to increase domestic controls over fiscal behavior.[79] Such substantive requirements have also led to a correspondingly increased role for domestic courts.

In contrast, a much lesser role for national courts was always to be expected in those particular areas of Eurozone law which are governed by EU law, such as those involving the application of the so-called 'six pack' of 2011 and 'two pack' of 2013, which consist of EU secondary legislation concerning budgetary discipline and processes, since the validity of EU legislation is not capable of being reviewed by national courts under the *Foto-frost* doctrine.[80]

Even if it is understood why national courts have ended up playing the role they have, the question poses itself of course as to whether it is desirable to have national courts adjudicating extensively on Eurozone issues.

Among the factors militating against national courts having such a role are the following:

i. a strong role for national courts may lead to several different legal approaches being applied to legal challenges concerning the Eurozone – and yet it seems unrealistic to expect the European Union to draft rules accommodating 19 or even 27 different constitutional and legal systems;
ii. national courts, particularly constitutional courts, are not necessarily expert in economic, financial, or banking issues, yet most of the rules of the Eurozone concern these very issues;
iii. the intervention of the courts of law lacks the same level of democratic legitimacy as that of other organs of state: courts are not elected. The lack of legitimacy may

76 Note *e.g.*, Fabbrini, *op. cit.*, n. 23, p. 65.
77 *Cf.* however, the ESM Treaty. This is an intergovernmental treaty, yet Art. 37(3) thereof nonetheless confers jurisdiction on the European Court of Justice in disputes concerning its interpretation and application.
78 *Loc. cit.*, n. 4, p. 65.
79 Fabbrini, *loc. cit.*, n. 4, pp. 69-70.
80 Case 314/85 *Foto-Frost v. Hauptzollamt Lübeck-Ost* ECLI:EU:C:1987:452.

said to be particularly telling when the courts of one country seek to adjudicate on the validity of a policy which has consequences for other states;

iv. there is also a question mark over the substantive economic benefits of strong judicial review. Notably, Ireland, with weak judicial review, exited its bailout program with extraordinary rapidity. However, so many other factors are present that it is difficult to ascribe such success to the weakness of judicial interventions or to otherwise quantify the effect of judicial review in any given case. Moreover, any claimed benefits of an absence of strong judicial review may be countered with the argument that there may be a cost in social justice terms of weak judicial review. Indeed, one's view of the benefits of judicial review may depend to some extent on where one's views lie on the political spectrum;

v. it may lead to results which are unfair and fail to strike an appropriate balance between the interests of the various Member States. National courts can, after all, be expected to favor national interests above those of other states or the European Union as a whole and, moreover, to favor the application of national constitutional doctrines above European rules. As Hinarejos has observed, "inescapably, the most assertive national courts will end up delineating the scope of the political debate for the whole of the Union." [81]

vi. a major role for national courts may store up efficiency problems for the European Union in the future, since national courts that have been accommodating during periods of (in particular, national) crisis may become more demanding in their approach once the difficult times have passed;

vii. it may lead to judicial overreach. In this regard, one should consider the particular case of the German Federal Constitutional Court, the *Bundesverfassungsgericht*, which has leveraged its own role, through its application of the *ultra vires* doctrine, effectively giving it the last word on laws passed by EU institutions.[82] (Indeed, the extent to which it has done this has not stopped short of effectively requiring the renegotiation of international law instruments.[83]) In doing so, it has also leveraged Germany's role (the economic size of which already ensures

81 *Op. cit.*, n. 16, p. 151.

82 *See, e.g.*, T. Tuominen, 'Aspects of Constitutional Pluralism in Light of the Gauweiler Saga', *European Law Review*, Vol. 43, No. 2, 2018, p. 190 *et seq.*; M. Payandeh, 'The OMT Judgment of the German Federal Constitutional Court: Repositioning the Court within the European Constitutional Architecture', *European Constitutional Law Review*, Vol. 13, 2017, p. 400, esp. pp. 411-416. *See also* the critical observations by Fabbrini regarding the approach of the French *Conseil Constitutionnel* on being asked by the President of the Republic to consider whether ratification of the Fiscal Stability Treaty was compatible with the French Constitution. (Fabbrini, *loc cit.*, n. 4, pp. 82-86 and esp. p. 86 where he observes that "the Constitutional Council seized the opportunity offered by the new European fiscal architecture and readily welcomed these institutional changes to expand its domestic powers of review".)

83 *See* the *Bundesverfassungsgericht's ESM* ruling of 12 September 2012 2 BvR 1390/12. A brief explanation of this is to be found in Bundesverfassungsgericht, *Applications for the issue of temporary injunctions to prevent the ratification of the ESM Treaty and the Fiscal Compact unsuccessful for the most part* (Press Release No. 67/2012 of 12 September 2012).

> that its withdrawal from any Eurozone initiative can fatally wound it), deploying this power in an uncompromising manner which might not have been adopted by other branches of German government, and not always impressing with its expertise or the suitability of some of its approaches to determining the legitimacy of European initiatives. (Thus, its *Lisbon* ruling sought to impose a model of democracy that was arguably not a good fit for the European Union,[84] and its *Gauweiler* reference arguably evidenced little understanding of the operation of financial markets.[85])

Fabbrini (relying in turn on Halberstam) has stressed the appropriate limits of a dynamic of judicialization regarding EMU,[86] observing

> in separation-of-powers systems three main considerations should guide the allocation of competences among alternative institutions: expertise, voice and rights. The first consideration asks which actor has the better claim of knowledge or instrumental capacity to make a decision in a given field. The second asks which actor has the better claim of representing the relevant political will. And the third asks which actor is better placed to protect rights. In the fiscal domain, the first and second considerations (expertise and voice) strongly plead in favor of letting the political branches, rather than the courts, make decisions. At the same time, the third consideration (rights) does not play a fundamental enough role in the economic domain so as to change the balance of institutional capacities in favor of greater judicial involvement.[87]

Such considerations have resonance at both European and national levels, but there are at least some counter-arguments militating in favor of a strong role for national courts:

i. It may be argued that the intervention of national courts has been necessary in relation to Eurozone affairs in order to provide legitimacy for measures which would otherwise have lacked legitimacy because they were introduced by intergovernmental measures with little consequent parliamentary control at either national or European levels.

---

84 *See* the *Bundesverfassungsgericht's Lisbon* judgment of 30 June 2009 – 2 BvE 2/08 particularly at paras. 251 *et seq.*

85 *See* Case C-62/14 *Gauweiler and others v. Deutscher Bundestag* ECLI:EU:C:2015:400 at para. 88) and the preliminary reference of the *Bundesverfassungsgericht* (Case No. 2 BvR 2728/13) (summarized in P. Craig and M. Markakis, 'Gauweiler and the Legality of Outright Monetary Transactions', *European Law Review*, Vol. 41, 2016, pp. 6-8).

86 Fabbrini, *op. cit.*, n. 23, p. 113.

87 Fabbrini, *loc. cit.*, n. 4, p. 116 *et seq.*, citing in this regard D. Halberstam, 'Constitutional Heterarchy: The Centrality of Conflict in the European Union and the United States', *in* J. Dunoff and J. Trachtman (eds.), *Ruling the World*, Cambridge, Cambridge University Press, 2009, pp. 326-327.

ii. Further in this regard, a role for national courts may facilitate acceptance of measures that would otherwise meet with greater political opposition. Thus, at one level, the intervention of national courts interferes with the smooth operation of policies which have been decided upon at European level. At another level, however, it facilitates European integration by adding a level of legitimacy which would otherwise be absent. Hence, the legitimacy added by national courts may be particularly desirable in bailout situations in which the normal conditions of democracy are often curbed: where democratic controls have been moved aside, the legitimizing function of the law and the courts takes on a particular importance.[88] Both of these advantages of national judicial intervention have been adverted to by Reestman, who has noted that the diverse harvest of judgments of the national courts has "legitimized and furthered the public and political acceptance of the treaties and thereby also a fundamental change in the functioning of the EMU: they provided a legitimacy that the political process was unable to provide on its own".[89] While admitting that this legitimacy that the judgments came at a certain price, the same writer notes unapologetically, "the judgments all somehow indicate that there is a point at which further EMU integration requires recourse to, and legitimation by, the constitutional authorities of the Member States. That is an expression of the very basic principles upon which also the European Union is built: democracy and the rule of law."[90]
iii. National courts, as Hinarejos puts it, may also be better placed than the European Courts "to choose the level at which social rights ought to be protected in a situation of financial instability".[91]

As already noted, space for a strong role for national courts in particular has been made by the non-EU law nature of memorandums of understanding, itself painfully illustrated by the lack of success claimants have had litigating rescue packages before the EU courts in Luxembourg in cases such as *Bourdouvali*[92] and by the refusal of the European Court of Justice to hear Article 267 references from Romania and Portugal concerning the

88 *Cf.* the light review applied by the Irish courts described in S. Coutts, 'Ireland: Traditional Procedures Adapted for Economic Emergency', *in* Beukers *et al., op. cit.*, n. 76, p. 230.

89 *See* J.-H. Reestman, 'Legitimacy through Adjudication: The ESM Treaty and the Fiscal Compact before the National Courts',*in* Beukers *et al., op. cit.*, n. 76, p. 243, esp. pp. 276-277 and 243.

90 *Ibid.*, p. 277.

91 *Op. cit.*, n. 16, p. 153. According to the same author,
"the defence of the national constitutional settlement [in cases on austerity], comes down to setting the minimum of social rights that needs to be protected when making hard economic policy choices in times of financial instability. The array of [decisions by national courts] portray a wide variety of approaches to this question ... the argument can be made that the CJEU should accept jurisdiction and exercise a light-touch review, leaving the possibility open for national courts to apply more stringent standards, if this is appropriate within their national judicial tradition and political context."

92 *Bourdouvali and Others v. Council of the European Union and Others* Case T-786/14 ECLI:EU:T:2018:487.

legality of national measures adopted pursuant to memoranda of understanding because it lacks jurisdiction to do so.

The nature of the issues upon which national courts have been called upon to adjudicate has varied. Some national cases have concerned challenges (either procedural or substantive) regarding the architecture of the solutions used to rescue the Eurozone from its economic crisis (often involving claims that the measures violate national constitutional identity, constitutional sovereignty clauses, or constitutional guarantees of democratic legitimacy). Cases concerning such issues have been seen, for example, in Germany, Estonia, Ireland, Slovenia, France, Poland, and Austria.[93]

Others have involved challenges to the legality of bailouts or the memoranda of understanding used to put them in place, or (more usually) the compatibility with the national constitution of measures used to implement bailout agreements. For, as Fabbrini points out,

> Eurozone member states that obtain financial aid to address a situation of quasi-default are ... subject to specific economic adjustment programs designed to reform the fundamentals of their economy and address structural weaknesses in their domestic systems in areas as far ranging as the flexibility of the labor market, the effectiveness of tax collection, the size and organization of the public administration, the nature and degree of social entitlements, and the characteristics of the banking sector.[94]

Many national-level constitutional challenges thus focus on cuts to pay, to social welfare benefits, and to pensions – giving rise to "a constitutional jurisprudence of crisis-driven [budgetary cuts]".[95] Challenges of this nature have been seen in Ireland, Portugal, Greece, Romania, Hungary, Latvia, Cyprus, and Spain.[96]

Given the economic context, it is perhaps unsurprising that considerable national judicial deference to the political process tends to be displayed in both 'architecture' and 'bailout' cases. Such deference has nonetheless been observed to be generally higher in the former variety of case, in which of course the implications of a negative ruling may be enormous.[97]

The issues decided by national courts can be categorized along lines other than the 'architecture vs. bailout-related cases' axis, however. Another possible division is that

93 *See* Reestman, *loc. cit.*, n. 90, p. 245 *et seq.*
94 *Loc. cit.*, n. 4, pp. 72-73.
95 Kilpatrick *loc. cit.*, n. 76, p. 289. The same writer points out that missing from this jurisprudence, however, is case law on health, education, and housing (*Ibid.*, p. 290).
96 *See* further Hinarejos, *op. cit.*, n. 16, p. 145 *et seq.* Since economic difficulties are scarcely to be avoided at some point in the future by any country, these seem likely to be of enduring value in terms of the guidance they offer, even once the bailouts they relate to come to an end.
97 *Ibid.*, pp. 145 and 153.

between *ex ante* challenges like that in *Pringle*,[98] in which it is sought to prevent the adoption of an instrument creating a particular institution or establishing a particular policy, and *ex post* challenges, whether these be to national legislation or executive action (such as the challenges seen to austerity measures in Portugal) or indirect challenges to European norms by reference to European standards.[99] Yet another distinction which can be drawn is that between challenges to the substance of measures and alleged procedural infringements (*e.g.*, of the role of a national parliament). The same case may of course raise both kinds of issue: The distinctions relate to the issues raised rather than to the cases themselves.

6.3.2 *What – If Any – Generalizable Lessons Can Be Learnt from Such National Cases?*

With such a large number of jurisdictions, it can be challenging to determine what (if anything) of general value may be learned from the various national rulings. Comparison is difficult. The rulings of the various national courts are filtered through different constitutional contexts. Portugal (which saw a number of high-profile constitutional challenges regarding its bailout) is a particularly obvious example of this, given the uniquely extensive social provisions made in its constitution.[100] At the other end of the scale lie Cyprus and Ireland, whose constitutions contain only limited provisions concerning social rights.[101] Even where broadly similar constitutional provisions exist, the precise formulations may also differ. The same is even more true of the detailed statutory provisions that implement directives or bailout agreements. This will of course have a bearing on differing rulings by the various national courts.

Rulings are also filtered through different constitutional structures. Some countries have specialized constitutional courts. Others do not – something, which has been argued to have had a negative effect on the robustness of judicial review in the case of Greece, for

98 *Pringle v. Government of Ireland and Others* [2012] IESC 47, [2013] 3 IR 1. *Ex ante* challenges to the ratification of international treaties are also possible in several other countries. (*See, e.g.*, Art. 54 of the French Constitution.)

99 *See* Fabbrini, *op. cit.*, n. 23, p. 66, where he also points out the pursuant to the Fiscal Stability Treaty obligation to incorporate balanced budget rules, national courts can also be asked to review whether governments are in compliance with the relevant budgetary constraints. (The question of whether such challenges will be constitutional or sub-constitutional will vary from state to state, however.)

100 Portugal's Constitution (the Preamble of which refers to "the Portuguese people's decision to … open up a path towards a socialist society") lists among the "fundamental tasks" of the State, "[promoting] the people's well-being and quality of life and real equality between the Portuguese, as well as the effective implementation of economic, social, cultural and environmental rights by means of the transformation and modernisation of economic and social structures" (Art. 9). Among rights protected under its Title II are job security, and under Title III, a very broad range of economic rights (including workers' rights such as the right to work, remuneration rights, equality and social dignity) as well as social and cultural rights.

101 Neither of these latter countries saw their respective bailouts challenged by reference to the social provisions of their respective constitutions. *See* generally on this topic, Kilpatrick *loc. cit.*, n. 76, p. 284.

example (where constitutional challenges have been decided by a number of different courts). Some states allow specially designated persons or institutions to ask for *ex ante* or *ex post* review. Others, such as Greece, do not.[102]

The constitutional bases on which challenges have been brought have also varied considerably. Kilpatrick has pointed out a broad East-West axis in this regard: In Eastern Europe, challenges have been brought on the basis of constitutional social provisions. Thus, for example, pay cuts were challenged on the constitutional right to work in Romania and pension cuts challenged there (and also in Latvia) by reference to constitutional guarantees to social security. In contrast, challenges to pay cuts and pension cuts were dealt with on the basis of other (nonsocial) constitutional provisions and bases in Portugal and Greece.[103] Not alone the rights invoked, but the broad approach taken to fending off excessive limitations on such rights in a time of economic crisis have varied, some states using, for example, a 'minimum core' approach, others focusing on proportionality, among other approaches.[104]

Constitutional challenges are also filtered through different policy assumptions. Baroncelli has highlighted that German economic policy has a stability-promoting culture that prioritizes a long-term perspective, whereas Italy looks to more short-term solutions, emphasizing liquidity. Correspondingly, and perhaps unsurprisingly, the German Constitutional Court has recognized prioritizing long-term stability as a principle with constitutional force, whereas the Italian Court in contrast has balanced the aim of debt reduction with the need to avoid damage to the welfare state.[105]

In part because of such considerations, in practice even similar constitutional provisions have received very different interpretations in different jurisdictions.[106] Nevertheless, there are also clear similarities to many of the issues faced, particularly in bailout states, with European-level assistance in coping with out-of-control sovereign debts being made conditional on austerity taking the form of cutbacks to working conditions and pay,

102 *See* further *ibid.*, p. 289 and *see* regarding the court structures in Greece, the authors cited by her there.

103 In the former case, by reference to the rule of law and the principle of equality, in the case of Greece by reference to a panoply of constitutional provisions including those guaranteeing equal participation in public burdens, the right to property, and the principles of proportionality and respect for human dignity (*Ibid.*, p. 294).

104 *See* regarding these D. Landau, 'The Promise of a Minimum Core Approach: The Colombian Model for Judicial Review of Austerity Measures', in A. Nolan (ed.), *Economic and Social Rights after the Global Financial Crisis*, Cambridge, Cambridge University Press, 2014, p. 267 and X. Contiades and A. Fotiadou, 'Social Rights in the Age of Proportionality: Global Economic Crisis and Constitutional Litigation', *International Journal of Constitutional Law*, Vol. 10, 2012, p. 660. *See* here and generally regarding the various approaches taken by national constitutional courts, Kilpatrick *loc. cit.*, n. 76, pp. 292-300.

105 S. Baroncelli, 'Long-term vs Short-Term Perspectives: Adaptation, Stability and the Roles of the Constitutional Courts in the Management of the Eurozone Crisis in Germany and Italy', *Contemporary Italian Politics*, Vol. 10, 2018, p. 36. Of course, critical analysis of such rulings may suffer from its own assumptions – Kilpatrick has pointed out "the neo-liberal default assumptions underpinning much of the analysis of euro-crisis constitutional judgments" (*Loc. cit.*, n. 76, p. 292).

106 *Ibid.*, instancing the approaches of Portugal and Greece.

social welfare, health and education, as well as a deregulatory agenda regarding worker protections and collective bargaining.[107]

Notwithstanding different approaches, some lessons of varying levels of significance have emerged. The first is that national rulings on Eurozone issues can be matters of deep national controversy within national legal systems. The archetypal demonstration of this is the ruling of the Estonian Supreme Court, the *Riigikohus*, on the compatibility of the ESM Treaty with the Estonian Constitution,[108] an issue which was decided in favor of constitutionality only on the basis of a 10-9 split among the judges after a Court hearing which was of sufficient public interest to merit being televised nationally. An example of a different kind of controversy is provided by the Portuguese Constitutional Court's rulings condemning certain austerity measures designed to secure Portuguese compliance with the terms of that country's bailout, which attracted criticism of the severest kind in some subsequent national academic commentary.[109]

A second lesson is that such rulings can be the occasion of considerable development in national constitutional jurisprudence. This has been particularly true of the seven bailout states. Examples of this abound. The Irish Supreme Court ruling in *Pringle* involved a considerable advance on the approach of the Irish Courts to the sovereignty clause in the Irish Constitution. Valuable discussion and evolving thinking regarding the concept of sovereignty was also seen in the Estonian Supreme Court's ESM ruling. Evolution of another kind was seen in the approach of the *Bundesverfassungsgericht* concerning OMT policy of the European Central Bank, which involved an arguably unwisely tigerishly worded reference being followed by a more measured response once the European Court of Justice had provided its preliminary ruling.[110]

Third, even where a legal concept is nominally the same, the interpretation given to it by different national courts may be different. The demands of concepts like equality, sovereignty, proportionality, and the various fundamental rights have been differently interpreted in different jurisdictions.[111]

Fourth, in practice, by and large, national courts have tended to react well to budgetary rules (which by their nature tend to involve consequences which lie in the future and may still be in the realms of the theoretical by the time they reach the courts), but not so

107 The preference of EU states and institutions for austerity of this nature inspired Lütz and Kranke's humorous reference to 'the European rescue of the Washington consensus'. *See* S. Lütz and M. Kranke, 'The European Rescue of the Washington consensus? EU and IMF Lending to Central and Eastern European Countries', *Review of International Political Economy*, Vol. 21, 2014, p. 310, cited in Kilpatrick, *loc. cit.*, n. 76, p. 281.

108 *See* Case 3-4-1-6-12, judgment of 12 July 2012.

109 *See* the literature cited by Kilpatrick, *loc. cit.*, n. 76, p. 291.

110 A case of a court "*wie ein Tiger gesprungen aber wie ein Bettvorleger gelandet*," without, however, in this instance meaning to give tigers unmerited praise or criticize the entirely appropriate post-reference change of approach of the *Bundesverfassungsgericht*. *See* further n. 42, above.

111 *See* for some reflections in this regard, Kilpatrick, *loc. cit.*, n. 76, pp. 296-300.

positively to bailouts and measures implementing them (which of course will tend to have had very immediate costs for individuals).

Fifth, notwithstanding the similarity of issues raised before the national courts and the extent of commonalities (including a harsh context of austerity and often severe cutbacks in social welfare provision), there has been very little cross-referencing by national courts to the reasoning of courts of other jurisdictions. There have been some (limited) Eastern European exceptions to this: In adjudicating on the legality of pension cuts, the Romanian Constitutional Court referred to the German *Bundesverfassungsgericht*.[112] In other rulings concerning the Eurozone crisis, the same Court referred to the rulings of the Hungarian, Latvian, Czech, and Lithuanian Constitutional Courts.[113] Curiously, however, such "transnational judicial communication",[114] involving reference to other national supreme courts, has only ever been a feature of Central European jurisprudence. Western European Courts in contrast had no regard for what had already happened in central European jurisdictions.[115] Two rather separate geographic zones of comparative constitutional influence (involving respectively, little such influence and none) have thus ensued within the Eurozone.[116]

Sixth, the EU law context of these situations has been largely ignored in national courts – there has been an unexplained insularity on the part of national courts.[117] Very few preliminary references have been made.[118] This may seem surprising in the light of the long-established Court of Justice approach (seen in *Internationale Handelsgesellschaft*[119]) that even technical EU rules rank higher than the most elevated national constitutional norms – which might have been expected to release a flood of challenges (by reference to EU law norms) to technical EU bailout rules by national courts called upon to prioritize the requirements of those norms over national constitutional provisions.[120] Yet this did not happen. It may have been significant that, as Kilpatrick has observed, that national bailout measures have never been "fully articulated in national constitutional challenges as either an implementation of EU law or as acts of EU institutions".[121] Nor has the "complex and variegated legal nature of the bailouts"[122] assisted the cause of recognition of their European aspect. Bailouts have had both a contractual aspect

112 Decision 1533/2011.
113 *See* Kilpatrick, *loc. cit.*, n. 76, pp. 318-319.
114 *Ibid.*, p. 318.
115 *Ibid.*, p. 319.
116 *Ibid.*
117 Thus, Kilpatrick refers to "an insular response taken by every single constitutional review court in the EU faced with euro-crisis constitutional challenges" (*Ibid.*, p. 317).
118 *See* Hinarejos, *op. cit.*, n. 16, p. 146, who points out that in most cases the national courts have adopted a purely national perspective and not made use of the Art. 267 TFEU procedure.
119 Case C-11/70 *Internationale Handelsgesellschaft mbH v. Einfuhr – und Vorratsstelle für Getreide und Futtermittel* ECLI:EU:C:1970:114.
120 *See* Kilpatrick, *loc. cit.*, n. 76, pp. 311-312.
121 *Ibid.*, pp. 314-315, citing in particular the examples of Portugal and Latvia.
122 *Ibid.*, p. 316.

(seen in the existence of memoranda of understanding) and an international law aspect (including a role for the International Monetary Fund). In the light of this, it is perhaps unsurprising that they have not been seen as classical EU measures, even if most bailouts have contained strong EU elements.[123]

This refusal to acknowledge an EU law aspect to these cases may sometimes indicate a lack of grasp of EU law on the part of national courts.[124] An alternative interpretation, however, is that it reflects a broad wish shared among national constitutional courts to keep EU courts from adjudicating on what amounts to an EU-wide social constitutional crisis.[125] Hinarejos has argued, for example, that the Greek Council of State "explicitly sought to 'sever' a possible link to EU law by labelling memoranda of understanding as declaratory political plans, rather than legally binding instruments".[126] It is noticeable, however, that in those few Article 267 references which were made (from Romania and Portugal), the Court of Justice itself held that it had no jurisdiction to hear the case,[127] finding there to be no link between EU law and reforms pursued by national governments. It is worth observing in passing that it is not clear that the drafters of bailouts have ever been that interested in having the European Court of Justice – or indeed any court – adjudicate upon them.

Seventh, although use has been made of international human rights norms, there has been very little invocation of international norms specifically focused on social rights such as International Labour Organization (ILO) norms or the text of the European Social Charter.[128]

Eighth, and perhaps depressingly, for better or for worse national courts have for the most part stood aside in the face of an economic onslaught. In the face of economic arms, the law has been largely silent.[129] Although there have been occasional significant individual judicial interventions, the role of the courts at national level has generally been limited.[130] This has a negative side in that it exposes weakness in protecting the most vulnerable. It may be argued to have a positive side, in that it leaves the economic decision-making to democratically elected and indeed more expert branches of government –

123 C. Kilpatrick, 'On the Rule of Law and Economic Emergency: The Degradation of Basic Legal Values in Europe's Bailouts', *Oxford Journal of Legal Studies*, Vol. 35, No. 2, 2015, pp. 333-334, where she observes that the initial (non-Eurozone) bailouts of Hungary, Latvia, and Romania were based on EU law (more specifically on Art. 143 TFEU, which permits the grant of mutual assistance to assist non-Eurozone states with balance of payments difficulties). The bailouts of Ireland and Portugal (both Eurozone states) were based in part on EU law, whereas the bailouts of Greece and Cyprus (also Eurozone states) were based on international agreements made by the Eurozone states.

124 Kilpatrick, *loc. cit.*, n. 76, p. 316.

125 *Ibid.*, pp. 316-317.

126 Hinarejos, *op. cit.*, n. 16, p. 146, referring to Decision of the Greek Council of State, Full Chambers, 668/2012 [28].

127 *Ibid.*, p. 133 *et seq.*

128 *See* further Kilpatrick, *loc. cit.*, n. 76, p. 319.

129 *Cf.* "*Pro Tito Annio Milone ad iudicem oratio*" ('*Pro Milone*'), speech delivered by M. Cicero in 52 BC.

130 Kilpatrick, *loc. cit.*, n. 76, pp. 325-326.

although the uncomfortable reality is that a variety of means were used to short-circuit normal parliamentary procedures and debates during the crisis, often effectively preventing the legislature from providing effective opposition to bailout terms set by international lenders.[131] One way or another, what may be said is that what could be construed as so-called juristocracy, that is, an excessive degree of judicial activism, was largely avoided during the Eurozone crisis. What occurred instead were a series of dialogues. National courts effectively engaged in an indirect dialogue with troikas,[132] and, less indirectly, with national governments and legislatures[133] (with Portugal illustrating this most graphically with what amounted to a multilevel dialogue with both). Occasionally, national constitutional court case law put some limits on the freedom of national executives and legislatures and, more indirectly, troikas of international institutions to maneuver freely as they chose in response to the economic crisis. Hence, Fabbrini has described the Portuguese Constitutional Court as having signaled

> that the future of at least one of the central features of the legal responses to the Euro-crisis, that concerning the economic adjustment measures that debtor countries shall adopt as a condition to obtain financial support, may be standing on shaky ground.[134]

More often than not, the impact of such dialogue has been quite limited, however. (Furthermore, the drastic reforms effected by Hungarian government to the role of the courts in that jurisdiction in particular showed that the dialogue between courts and executives can be far from one between equals. In that country, admittedly an extreme case, the government's reaction led to particularly dire implications for the national constitutional court itself.[135])

Ironically, speaking generally, one of the most prominent features of judicial approach to the Eurozone at both national and supranational levels has been to stand aside to let the other branches of government or governance forge ahead, in particular in the search for solutions to the sovereign debt and banking crises that ravaged the continent in recent years.[136] Such multilevel forbearance has been greeted by some with mixed feelings. Hinarejos has described the degree of restraint shown by EU and national courts as "both

131 *Ibid.*, p. 310, and *see* generally Beukers *et al.*, *op. cit.*, Part II (chapters 6-9).

132 Kilpatrick, *loc. cit.*, n. 76, pp. 307-308.

133 *Ibid.*, pp. 305-306.

134 *Loc. cit.*, n. 4, p. 103.

135 *See* further Kilpatrick, *loc. cit.*, n. 76, p. 320 *et seq.*

136 This approach has parallels: Comparison can be drawn with the position of the US Courts here. As Fabbrini observes, "although the United States is endowed with one of the most powerful and pervasive systems of judicial review worldwide, since at least the 1930s courts have widely deferred to the political branches in the economic domain, on the understanding that the political process is better placed than the judicial one to answer fundamental budgetary, financial, and economic questions" (*Loc. cit.*, n. 4, p. 120).

problematic and hardly surprising".[137] Yet it also seems justifiable to feel at least some appreciation for judicial decisions that avoided interpretations of the law so strict that international organizations, states, and institutions (both supranational and national) alike would have found it impossible to save Europe's economic and monetary union.

137 Hinarejos, *op. cit.*, n. 16, p. 121.

7 What Goes Up Must Go Up: Raising Judicial Scrutiny over the European Central Bank through Judicial Dialogue

Joan Solanes Mullor

7.1 Introduction

The European Central Bank (ECB) has always been conceived as a key actor in the institutional framework of the Economic and Monetary Union (EMU).[1] Successfully achieving monetary integration of the Member States seemed unlikely to happen without a coordinating institution at the heart of the European Union's (EU) institutional framework. Entrusted with competences on monetary policy, particularly the task of stabilizing prices,[2] from 1998 until the 2008 economic crisis, the ECB was able to go about its work without much controversy.[3] This peaceful development of the ECB took advantage of the wave of agency creation, commonly referred to as agencification, in the EU, a process that started in the 1990s and has now largely been consolidated.[4] In fact, at the outset, the ECB

---

1 At the outset of the EMU, the ECB together with the national central banks represented pivotal institutions for enabling monetary integration of the Member States. *See* the first conceptualization of the EMU in the Werner Report, calling for the creation of a so-called center of decision for economic policy and a Community system for central banks (Werner Committee, 'Report to the Council and the Commission on the Realization by Stages of Economic and Monetary Union in the Community', *Bulletin Supplement 11/1970 of the European Communities*, 1970, pp. 12-14) and, finally, the influential and starting point of EMU in the Delors Report, identifying the need to create a 'new monetary institution' as a backbone of the new European System of Central Banks (ESCB) (Committee for the Study of Economic and Monetary Union, 'Report on Economic and Monetary Union in the European Community', Luxembourg, *Office of the Official Publications of the European Communities*, 1989, pp. 21-25).

2 The ECB regulation is found in a triad of EU treaties: Art. 13 of the Treaty on European Union (TEU), Arts. 282-284 of the Treaty on the Functioning of the European Union (TFEU) and Protocol nº 4 on the Statute of the European System of Central Banks and the European Central Bank.

3 The nature of EMU and the role of the ECB were transformed by the economic and financial crisis, the latter of which grew much more active and influential within the EU institutional framework. This increased activity jeopardized the ECB's pre-crisis high reputation as a disciplined stabilizer of prices in the euro zone (*see* C. Papasavvas, 'Responsibility of the ECB in Managing the European Debt Crisis: Towards a European Banking Union?', *Law, Social Justice & Global Development (LGD)*, Vol. 2015, No. 1, 2015, pp. 4-7).

4 E. Chiti, 'The Emergence of a Community Administration: The Case of European agencies', *Common Market Law Review*, Vol. 37, No. 2, 2000, pp. 309-311.

was the only 'agency' enshrined in EU treaties. The intense debates that occurred were over the reach of the EU agencies being created and the legitimacy of sectoral executive or independent agencies within the EU system of governance.[5] Perhaps the Member States' previous experience with national central banks had conferred implicit trust in the new ECB while the other EU agencies had to fight to justify their role in the EU institutional framework.

With the 2008 economic and financial crisis, however, that trust dissipated as the ECB's decisions became decisive for national economies. The Outright Monetary Transactions (OMT) and Secondary Markets Public Sector Purchase Program (PSPP) are cornerstones of ECB activity that signal its willingness to manage actively the economic crisis.[6] These and other moves by the ECB increased the bank's visibility within the EU institutions and the Member States, and, in the end, the ECB drew fire. Its active role in economic governance, which stretched its EU mandate to protect the value of the euro and stabilize prices, led to national resistance against the institution, especially by Germany. The ECB, after all, had been conceived at the outset of the EU agencification process, and, therefore, it eventually had to confront the debate over the legitimacy and accountability of these institutions that had begun in the 1990s.

The advent of attention on the ECB in the EU agency debate entails an opportunity for new arguments and lines of action. A key shift can be seen in how national governments have now become interested in the debate that hitherto had been almost purely carried on at the EU level. The lack of communication between those two levels was constant during the EU agencification process.[7] Now, with the national institutions scrutinizing the behavior of an EU agency, the path of the EU agencification process may well be altered. Accordingly, this chapter will explore how the national interest in the ECB may bring new insights to the debate over EU agencies, especially in terms of accountability. In particular, the chapter will explore the rise of a new standard for judicial review of ECB decisions, one that is stricter than that developed by the Court of Justice of the European Union (CJEU) for EU agencies. Indeed, the judicial dialogue between national courts and the CJEU has produced a new judicial perspective, one that uses judicial dialogue itself as a crucial tool for improved legitimacy and accountability.

The chapter begins with an overview of the traditional debate on EU agencies and the ECB as an inseparable part of them, especially since the challenge of the German judiciary (7.2). It then examines the reaction of the CJEU in *Gauwelier* and *Weiss*, qualifying the standard of judicial review used by the CJEU in those cases as mixed, in that both pro-

5 The ECB was created by the Treaty of Maastricht in 1992 and was subsequently further entrenched at the treaty level, making it the only 'EU agency' secured by EU primary law.

6 The OMT program was approved at the 340th meeting of the Governing Council of the ECB on 5 and 6 September 2012. It was announced in a press release but never implemented. The PSPP was established and regulated by Decisions 2015/774, 2015/2464 and 2017/100 of the ECB.

7 J. Solanes Mullor, 'Institutional Balance, EU and National Agencification Processes: The Need for Dialogue', *Revista Española de Derecho Europeo*, Vol. 68, 2018, pp. 105-106.

cedural and substantive grounds are involved (7.3). Afterward, the chapter confronts this new standard with the traditional approach to EU agencies and illustrates how the new criteria result from a dialogical approach in which the national level has been determinant (7.4). Finally, the chapter closes with conclusions that point toward the advantages of adopting a pluralistic, dialogic perspective in the EU agencification process (7.5).

7.2 The ECB and the Wave of the EU Agencification: National Interests Waken

The ECB was created in the 1990s at the outset of the wave of the EU agencification process and benefitted from it. During the 1990s and 2000s, many EU agencies were created in a wide range of fields, and one of the first was the ECB.[8] The historical context at the time on the continent could be, without too much exaggeration, described as a 'fever' for this kind of public bodies.[9] It grew in the wake of the general trend in Europe toward the 'regulatory state' that from the 1970s and 1980s had progressively gained currency as confidence in the post-World War II Keynesian model waned.[10] The regulatory state resisted public intervention in the economy,[11] wealth redistribution as a central exercise of state action[12] and turned from politics as a reference for policy-making to a reliance on free market and expertise-oriented state intervention.[13] Agencies, with their mandated autonomy or independence from political institutions and fully staffed with experts, represented the natural institutional choice for ensuring credible regulation of private economic agents because of their expertise and isolation from politics.[14] Moreover, the specific nature and evolution of the EU also facilitated the creation of agencies. On the one hand, the EU barely had any budgetary power and was therefore forced to

---

8 For a current map of EU agencies, *see* the official website of the EU: https://europa.eu/european-union/about-eu/agencies_en (accessed 5 March 2019).

9 C. Pollit, K. Bathgate, J. Caulfield, A. Smulen & C. Talbot, 'Agency Fever? Analysis of an International Policy Fashion', *Journal of Comparative Policy Analysis: Research and Practice*, Vol. 3, No. 3, 2001, pp. 271-273.

10 G. Majone, 'The Rise of Statutory Regulation in Europe', *in* G. Majone (ed.), *Regulating Europe*, London and New York, Routledge, 1996, pp. 54-59.

11 G. Majone, 'Regulation and its modes', *in* G. Majone (ed.), *Regulating Europe*, London and New York, Routledge, 1996, p. 12.

12 G. Majone, 'Regulatory Legitimacy', *in* G. Majone (ed.), *Regulating Europe*, London and New York, Routledge, 1996, pp. 294-296.

13 G. Majone, 'The Regulatory State and Its Legitimacy Problems', *West European Politics*, Vol. 22, No. 1, 1999, p. 21.

14 S. Krapohl, 'Credible Commitment in Non-Independent Regulatory Agencies: A Comparative Analysis of the European Agencies for Pharmaceuticals and Foodstuffs', *European Law Journal*, Vol. 10, No. 5, 2004, pp. 523-525; P. Magnette, 'The Politics of Regulation in the European Union', *in* D. Geradin, R. Muñoz & N. Petit (eds.), *Regulation through Agencies in the EU: A New Paradigm of European Governance*, Cheltenham and Northampton, Edward Elgar Publishing, 2005, pp. 5-6; M. Flinders and J. Buller, 'Depoliticization, Democracy and Arena Shifting', *in* T. Christensen and P. Laegrid (eds.), *Autonomy and Regulation. Coping with Agencies in the Modern State*, Cheltenham and Northampton, Edward Elgar Publishing, 2006, pp. 58-62.

devote itself to regulatory-harmonizing policies rather than spearheading redistributive efforts. On the other, as EU competences grew in number and scope, a significant institutional deficit became evident early in the 1990s.[15] In short, these factors combined to give the new agencies a soft landing in the ongoing debates over the proper scope and power of the EU, especially within the Commission which, supported by an intense scholarly debate,[16] endorsed agencies as the proper expression of the momentum pushing for increased EU governance.[17]

Despite this momentum, the EU agencification process also attracted rich debate concerning accountability, if not legitimacy. In fact, the legitimacy of the new agencies was considered secondary and was generally questioned under the same criticism directed toward the regulatory state. Their nonrepresentative democratic deficit and tendency toward technocracy and consequent shortfalls were typical examples.[18] However, at the core of the theory of the regulatory state with agencies as its institutional arm, the idea was always to keep electoral democratic processes and politics as far as possible from the policy-making arena.[19] In other words, the agencies' advocates were well-prepared to deal with such critiques.

The accountability debate, in contrast, was much more intense. Agency advocates recognized the need to hold agencies accountable and centered their attention on developing adequate accountability mechanisms. On one side, the creation of EU agencies was

15 G. Majone, 'The European Commission as Regulator', *in* G. Majone (ed.), *Regulation Europe*, London and New York, Routledge, 1996, pp. 63-66; E. Vos, 'Reforming the European Commission: What the Role to Play for EU Agencies?', *Common Market Law Review*, Vol. 37, No. 5, 2000, pp. 113-116.

16 A. Kreher, 'Introduction', *in* A. Kreher (ed.), *The New European Agencies. Conference Report RSC 96/40*, Florence, European University Institute, 1996, pp. 1-4.

17 The first explicit endorsement of the Commission came with *European Governance. A White Paper*, Brussels, 25 July 2001 COM (2001)428 final. During the 2000s, besides creating specific EU agencies, the Commission endorsed their creation as a general practice in several strategic and negotiation documents: *Communication from the Commission COM* (2002)718 final, of 11 December 2002, on the operating framework for the European regulatory agencies; *Draft Interinstitutional Agreement* presented by the Commission COM(2005)59 final, of 22 February 2005, the operating framework for the European regulatory agencies; or the *Communication from the Commission COM*(2008)135 final, of 11 March 2008, on European agencies – the way forward.

18 A. Follesdal and S. Hix, 'Why There Is a Democratic Deficit in the EU: A Response to Majone and Moravcsik', *Journal of Common Market Studies*, Vol. 44, No. 3, 2006, pp. 542-544; M. Everson and E. Vos, (2008) 'European Risk Governance in a Global Context', *in* E. Vos (ed.), *European Risk Governance. Its Science, Its Inclusiveness and Its Effectiveness, Connex Report Series*, Vol. 6, 2008, pp. 10-16; S. De Somer, 'International and European Impulse with Regard to the Creation of Autonomous Public Bodies: An Emerging Trend', *UCL Journal of Law and Jurisprudence*, Vol. 3, No. 1, 2014, pp. 85-86.

19 G. Majone, 'Europe's "Democratic Deficit": The Question of Standards', *European Law Journal*, Vol. 4, No. 1, 1998, p. 28.

framed and limited by the well-developed principle of 'institutional balance' which operated as a check and balance mechanism in order to safeguard by cabining the powers of the EU institutions.[20] On the other hand, once agencies were created, a multiple accountability scheme was in place such that "no one controls an independent agency, yet the agency is 'under control'".[21] This multiple scheme includes establishing clear mandates for the agency,[22] an administrative process for decision-making,[23] oversight by EU institutions as principals of the agency,[24] and, finally judicial review of the agency's actions.[25] However, the strong emphasis on expertise and the isolation from politics of the EU agencification process pushed judicial review and EU institutions oversight into the shadows – because of the courts' lack of expertise and the political nature of the EU institutions charged with oversight as principals, especially the EU Parliament. Instead, the agency advocates promoted procedural forms of accountability, especially administrative processes.[26]

The ECB shares the above-mentioned theoretical framework of the EU agencification process, and its institutional design responds to the perceived need for isolation from politics and for expertise in the field of the monetary policy.[27] There are long-standing arguments to justify the autonomy or independence of central banks and, hence, assure credible, stable monetary policy.[28] The CJEU has conceptualized the ECB accordingly,

20 With regard to EU agencies, the institutional balance doctrine has been framed under the following three decisions: Judgment of 13 June 1958 in Case 9/56, *Meroni & Co., Industrie Metallurgiche, SpA v High Authority of the European Coal and Steel Community*, ECLI:EU:C:1958:7; Judgment of 14 May 1981 in Case 98/80, *Giuseppe Romano v Institut national d'assurance maladie-invalidité*, ECLI:EU:C:1981:104; and Judgment of 22 January 2014 in Case 270/12, *United Kingdom of Great Britain and Northern Ireland v European Parliament and Council of the European Union*, ECLI:EU:C:2014:18.

21 G. Majone, 'The Agency Model: The Growth of Regulation and Regulatory Institutions in the European Union', *EIPASCOPE*, Vol. 3, 1997, pp. 4-6.

22 D. Coen and M. Thatcher, 'The New Governance of Markets and Non-Majoritarian Regulators', *Governance: An International Journal of Policy Administration and Institutions*, Vol. 18, No. 3, 2005, p. 340; M. Busuioc, 'Accountability, Control and Independence: The Case of European Agencies', *European Law Journal*, Vol. 15, No. 5, 2009, p. 607.

23 Majone, 1999, pp. 9-11; Chiti, 2000, pp. 331-341; Magnette, 2005, pp. 10-15.

24 M. Pollack, 'Delegation, Agency and Agenda Setting in the European Community', *International Organization*, Vol. 51, No. 1, 1997, pp. 110-121; S. Andoura and P. Timmerman, 'Governance of the EU: The Reform of Debate of European Agencies Reignited', *European Policy Institute Network*, Working Paper No. 19, 2008, pp. 18-19.

25 Krapohl, 2004, pp. 525-527; T. Gehring and S. Krapohl, 'Supranational Regulatory Agencies between Independence and Control: The EMEA and the Authorization of Pharmaceuticals in the European Single Market', *Journal of European Public Policy*, Vol. 14, No. 2, 2007, pp. 218-220.

26 S. Borrás, C. Koutalakis & F. Wendler, 'European Agencies and Input Legitimacy: EFSA, EMEA and EPO in the Post-Delegation Phase', *Journal of European Integration*, Vol. 29, No. 5, 2007, p. 587; R. Dehousse, 'European Institutional Architecture after Amsterdam: Parliamentary System or Regulatory Structure?', *Common Market Law Review*, Vol. 35, No. 3, 1998, p. 617.

27 K. McNamara, 'Rational Fictions: Central Bank Independence and the Social Logic of Delegation', *West European Politics*, Vol. 25, No. 1. 2002, p. 52.

28 S. Lohmann, 'Optimal Commitment in Monetary Policy: Credibility versus Flexibility', *American Economic Review*, Vol. 82, 1992, p. 282; A. Alesina and G. Tabellini, 'Credibility and Politics', *European Economic Review*, Vol. 32, No. 2-3, 1988, pp. 543-546.

and the bank's independence is therefore seen as a safeguard from political interference in a field, monetary policy that requires sophisticated technical management. In this context, the CJEU has understood the independence granted by ex-Article 108 of the Treaty Establishing the European Community (TEC) and Article 130 of the Treaty on the Functioning of the European Union (TFEU) as a tool "to shield the ECB from political pressure" and,[29] at the same time, the Court has reaffirmed the expertise of the ECB.[30]

The legitimacy and accountability debates around the ECB have also been framed under the same parameters as the EU agencification process. The question of legitimacy was relegated even further because Member States had previous experience establishing independent competition and financial authorities.[31] Indeed, the EMU was originally formulated to strengthen the national central banks network at the supranational level (the European System of Central Banks [ESCB], which remains part of the institutional scheme of the EMU), and, in the end, the ECB grew naturally out of this previously established network. However, there have been always concerns over, in particular, the electoral democratic deficit of the ECB and the legitimacy of its technocratic decisions.[32]

As regards accountability, the debate has focused on oversight mechanisms rather than on the circumstances surrounding the creation of the ECB. The ECB was directly created and enshrined in the EU treaties, and, therefore, using institutional balance as a legal argument for limiting the creation of EU agencies was unavailable in the case of the ECB. This is precisely because the ECB is directly, by virtue of primary EU law, an EU institution and exercises the functions directly mandated by treaty. The ECB could never be considered as one of the new EU agencies created by secondary EU law, whose creation may infringe on the powers of the existing EU institutions and, in the end, the institutional balance of the EU established by treaties. Setting aside the constitution of the ECB, accountability in practice follows a similar approach to the general EU agencification process where the stress on technocracy led to an emphasis on procedural forms of accountability, especially focusing on the policy-making process and transparency.[33] Here again, judicial review has been marginalized as a form of accountability.

---

29 Judgment of 10 July 2003 in Case C-11/00, *Commission of the European Communities v European Central Bank*, EU:C:2003:395, para. 134; Judgment of 16 June 2015 in Case C-62/14, *Gauwelier and others v Deutscher Bundestag*, EU:C:2015:400, para. 40.

30 Case C-11/00, *Commission v European Central Bank*, para. 110; Case C-62/14, *Gauwelier*, para. 75; Judgment of 11 December 2018 in Case C-493/17, *Weiss and others*, EU:C:2018:1000, para. 91.

31 M. Thatcher, 'Regulation after Delegation: Independent Regulatory Agencies in Europe', *Journal of European Public Policy*, Vol. 9, No. 6, 2002, pp. 955-956.

32 T. Tohidipur, 'The Emperor's New Clothes: The ECB and the New Institutional Concept', *in* P. Dann and M. Rynkowski (eds.), *The Unity of the European Constitution, Beiträge zum ausländischen öffentlichen Recht und Völkerrecht*, Vol. 186, 2006, p. 175.

33 L. Bini-Smaghi and D. Gros (2001) 'Is the ECB Sufficiently Accountable and Transparent?' *European Network of Economic and Policy Research Institutes*, Working Paper Series No. 7, 2001, pp. 4-7; J. De Haan, F. Amtenbrink & S. Waller, 'The Transparency and Credibility of the European Central Bank', *Journal of Common Market Studies*, Vol. 42, No. 4, 2004, pp. 782-786.

It seems, from the narrative above, that debates over the ECB do not depart significantly from the mainstream discussions over EU agencification. However, this may change in the following years. Until the economic crisis, the EU agencification process was treated as a purely internal affair of the EU, with scant involvement of national organs.[34] The phenomenon was considered a question of internal organization for the EU system of governance to which national governments had not paid much attention. A powerful reason for this lack of interest is the nature of most EU agencies. The institutional balance argument, still relevant for the CJEU and taken seriously by the Commission,[35] has limited the creation of EU agencies but much more relevant is that the new agencies were born powerless. Most EU agencies remain consultative in nature. Very few have executive/adjudicative, much less normative, powers.[36] On the contrary, the ECB possessed strong and real powers from the very beginning, with all monetary policy under its purview. The economic crisis, when the ECB took an even more active role, highlighted its weight as an actor in the EU institutional framework and drew the attention of national governments.

It was in the context of the ECB response to the economic crisis that the Federal Constitutional Court of Germany (BVerfG) turned its eyes to the ECB. The *Gauwelier* and *Weiss* cases are the result of two preliminary references submitted by the BVerfG. In both cases, the ECB's decisions were scrutinized and national organs forced the CJEU to respond. Beyond the CJEU's subsequent scrutiny of the specific policy-making decisions of the ECB, what is extremely relevant is that, for the first time, national judges raised doubts over the legitimacy of an EU agency and the appropriate scheme of accountability for it. Indeed, the doubts raised by the BVerfG seem to land in the heart of the EU agencification process, pointing out, as a premise, the electoral democratic deficit of the ECB to the CJEU.[37] At the same time, the BVerfG does not challenge the theoretical framework of the agencification process, conceding justification for this deficit because it "takes the tested and scientifically documented special character of monetary policy into account that an independent central bank is more likely to safeguard monetary stability".[38] Its claim, rather, is that it is crucial, to safeguard democratic values, that the ECB be confined to its mandate, monetary stability. To address the legitimacy issues, the BVerfG esteems strict judicial scrutiny of the mandate of the ECB as an appropriate mechanism.[39] In short, the BVerfG is concerned with the institutional nature of the

34 Solanes Mullor, 2018, pp. 105-106.

35 M. Flinders, 'Distributed Public Governance in the European Union', *Journal of European Public Policy*, Vol. 11, No. 3, 2004, p. 527; M. Simoncini, *Administrative Regulation Beyond the Non-Delegation Doctrine*, Oxford, London, New York, New Delhi and Sydney, Hart Publishing, 2018, pp. 14-48.

36 J. Solanes Mullor, *Administraciones independientes y Estado regulador. El impacto de la Unión Europea en el Derecho Público español*, Madrid, Congreso de los Diputados, 2016, pp. 152-160.

37 BVerfG, Order of the Second Senate of 14 January 2014 – 2 BvR 2728/13, para. 59.

38 *Ibid.*

39 *Ibid.* at para. 60.

ECB – its independent status that insulates it from politics and, by consequence, the accountability mechanism of electoral democracy, and thus calls for strict judicial oversight to ensure the ECB stays within its mandate and the strict terms of the treaties. This is the gist of the demand made to the CJEU.

7.3 The ECB before the CJEU: A New Mixed Standard of Judicial Review with Procedural and Substantive Components

The preliminary reference, however, was restrained. The BVerfG focused on the interpretation of the mandate of the ECB and requested the CJEU to scrutinize its actions through the lens of its original conceptualization and boundaries. Such is typical of procedural-oriented review, in which a court examines the peripheral factors that frame a given policy-making decision.[40] In this case, the court makes sure the decision-maker has followed the mandate or acted within their competence, thus exercising *ultra vires* control over the public action. As is well known, a key dispute in the *Gauwelier* and *Weiss* cases was whether the actions of the ECB should qualify as pertaining to monetary policy assessments or, instead, served economic aims outside the boundaries of its treaty mandate.[41] Despite this limited process-oriented review, the BVerfG ultimately seems to engage in more substantive criticism of the ECB's decisions, appearing to call for the CJEU to assess the conformity of the ECB actions with EU law. It implied that a correct interpretation of the ECB's mandate called for enforcing strict limits to the ECB's policy-making power, welcoming a more substantive review attitude from the CJEU.[42]

The BVerfG's primary concern regarding the limits of the ECB's mandate was in the end related to the possible breach of the principle of conferral. This principle governs the distribution of powers between Member States and the EU. Just as the preliminary request for procedural review by the BVerfG pointed to deeper issues regarding the legitimacy of the ECB's decision-making,*ultra vires* control of the ECB would provide, at a deeper level, a means for *ultra vires* control of the general powers of the EU. The claim of lack of competence of the EU is brought when the ECB abuses its power by encroaching Member State power and thus compromises the legitimacy of EU integration from the perspective of national constitutional law. This encroachment provides the justification for the intervention of the BVerfG as a guardian of German constitutional law.[43] In this context, oversight of ECB's actions is instrumental to the primary objective of the BVerfG, which is not concerned about establishing the specific standard of judicial review of policy-making decisions of the ECB per se. Although defining the standard is an inter-

40 'Lack of competence', in which the interpretation of the limits or scope of the mandate of EU institutions is verified, is explicitly recognized as grounds for judicial review in Art. 263 TFEU.

41 BVerfG, Order of the Second Senate of 14 January 2014 – 2 BvR 2728/13, paras. 36-40.

42 *Ibid.* at para. 100.

43 *Ibid.* at paras. 44-54.

nal affair of the EU, the repercussions the standard has on the relationship between Member States and the EU essentially transforms the question into a challenge of the legitimacy of EU integration from the national perspective.

The CJEU, however, avoids this line of argumentation, and, in *Gauwelier* and *Weiss*, the court framed the controversy in terms of ordinary oversight of the ECB as an EU institution. There are no references to the conclusions that can be derived from the reasoning of the BVerfG regarding EU integration and the role of national courts as final guardians of its limits. The CJEU conceived its task as controlling the public action of an EU institution – the ECB – a task that is clearly mandated to its jurisdiction by EU law. This allows the CJEU to focus its attention on the specific action of the ECB and establish the standard of judicial review according to the parameters of EU law. The CJEU kept the debate under the strict terms of EU law, refraining from taking an uncertain path toward the national arena and the relationship between national and supranational authorities.

Still, despite the restraint of the CJEU, *Gauwelier* and *Weiss* led to a new standard of judicial review for EU agencies. I characterize this new standard as a mixed standard in that it contains both procedural and substantive components. The procedural component involves the review of the mandate of the ECB in direct response to the preliminary reference of the BVerfG. The CJEU took up the question raised by the German court by what distinguishes monetary policy from economic policy from a legal perspective.[44] It labeled and categorized the action of the ECB in terms of the treaty wording. The procedural component is also found in*Gauwelier* in the instance of another unclear legal interpretation. In this case, the issue is the possible infringement of Article 123(1) TFEU (which prohibits monetary financing of the budget).[45] In both cases, the debate is circumscribed by the mandate and competences of the ECB according to EU treaties' peripheral limits on the ECB's decision-making powers.

The substantive component involves the use of the proportionality principle. In its preliminary reference, the BVerfG proposed an interpretation in conformity with EU law that entailed substantial limits on the ECB's policy-making power. The BVerfG, however, framed its substantive conclusion under the same debate on the limits of the mandate of the ECB. In other words, the limits it set on the policy-making decision of the ECB were framed purely as a consequence of the mandate review. More clearly, the CJEU drew a line between the debate over the scope of the ECB's mandate and analyzing the specific limits of its policy-making power. With regard to the latter, the CJEU held up the proportionality principle, which was not mentioned by the BVerfG, as a tool for scrutinizing ECB's actions.

The proportionality principle is a very well-known and commonly used method for exercising judicial scrutiny under EU law. EU scholars have devoted intense study to the use of this open-ended principle that allows the CJEU to heighten or reduce the level of

44 Case C-62/14, *Gauwelier*, paras. 34-65; Case C-493/17, *Weiss*, paras. 46-70.
45 Case C-62/14, *Gauwelier*, paras. 93-127.

its deference to EU institutions or Member States when implementing decisions subject to EU law.[46] Indeed, depending on which step of the proportionality test is emphasized, the test takes on more of a procedural or substantial character with regard to its scrutiny of the public action. If the court focuses on the test of whether or not the public action pursues a legitimate aim, or whether the public action is assessed as likely to achieve that aim, the analysis tends to focus more on the parameters of the debate as well as the language and argumentative consistency. In contrast, if the step emphasized concerns the necessity of the public action, which entails review following the criteria of strict proportionality, the court may undertake either a procedural stance or a more substantial review. In the former case, the proportionality test becomes something similar to what in the U.S. administrative law is called a hard-look doctrine, in which the court analyses whether all the relevant arguments, actors and alternative policies have been accounted for in the public decision.[47] In its substantial dimension, the necessity step and strict proportionality may lead the court to proffer an opinion on the soundness of the policy and its limits.

In recent years, certain EU scholars have argued that the CJEU is turning toward a more process-oriented proportionality test.[48] The *Gauwelier* case would qualify as a case where proportionality is used in that way and, therefore, the standard should be highly deferential to the ECB.[49] Indeed, the language used in *Gauwelier* and *Weiss* does show deference and a procedural focus on the part of the CJEU in applying the proportionality test, especially in the legitimate aim and appropriateness steps. The CJEU begins by recognizing a broad degree of discretion to the ECB because of the technical expertise needed in the field,[50] discretion that only allows for procedural review to ensure all the "elements of the situation in question" are accounted for and that the ECB did "give an adequate statement of the reasons for its decisions".[51] Also regarding those two steps, the CJEU referred to the standard of review as limited to identifying any "manifest error of

---

46 J. Schwarze, *European Administrative Law*, 1st ed., London and Luxembourg, Sweet & Maxwell, 1992, pp. 296-497; H. Hofmann, G. Rowe & A. Türk, *Administrative Law and Policy of the European Union*, Oxford and New York, Oxford University Press, 2011, pp. 491-505; P. Craig, *EU Administrative Law*, 2nd ed., Oxford and New York, Oxford University Press, 2012, pp. 592-604.

47 C. Sunstein, 'Deregulation and the Hard-Look Doctrine', *The Supreme Court Review*, Vol. 1983, 1983, pp. 181-184.

48 K. Lenaerts, 'The European Court of Justice and Process-Oriented Review', *Yearbook of European Law*, Vol. 31, No. 1, 2012, pp. 2-4; H. Hofmann, 'Gauwelier and OMT: Lessons for Public Law and the European Economic Monetary Union', SSRN, https://papers.ssrn.com/sol3/papers.cfm?abstract_id=2621933, 2015. p. 16; D. Harvey, 'Towards Process-Oriented Proportionality Review in the European Union', *European Public Law*, Vol. 23, No. 1, 2017, pp. 121.

49 T. Tridimas and N. Xanthoulis, 'A Legal Analysis of the Gauwelier Case. Between Monetary Policy and Constitutional Conflict', *Maastricht Journal of European and Comparative Law*, Vol. 23, No. 1, 2016, p. 31; Harvey, 2017, pp. 109-111; M. Goldoni, 'The Limits of Legal Accountability of the European Central Bank', *George Mason Law Review*, Vol. 24, 2017, p. 614; J. Mendes, 'Bounded Discretion in EU Law: A Limited Judicial Paradigm in a Changing EU', *Modern Law Review*, Vol. 80, No. 3, 2017, pp. 470-471.

50 Case C-62/14, *Gauwelier*, para. 68; Case C-493/17, *Weiss*, para. 73.

51 Case C-62/14, *Gauwelier*, para. 69; Case C-493/17, *Weiss*, para. 30.

assessment", or, in other words, a light, highly deferential substantial review, before stating that the ECB's analysis of the economic situation and the objectives and the appropriateness of the measures taken by the CJEU satisfy this minimum standard.[52]

The substantive dimension of the proportionality test, however, is brought in at the necessity step of the proportionality test. In this phase, the CJEU engaged in a deep analysis over the nature and limits of the policy-making decisions of the ECB. In *Gauwelier*, the CJEU considered the OMT program proportional because it was limited to the purchase of government bonds (i) of Member States that were undergoing a macroeconomic adjustment program and (ii) whose maturity was limited to three years.[53] The CJEU also discussed the selective nature of purchases, a controversial factor identified by the BVerfG, and assessed the soundness of this option.[54] Regarding the compatibility of the OMT program with Article 123(1) TFEU, again the CJEU established clear judicial limits with respects the purview of the ECB.[55] Accordingly, the CJEU only accepted the OMT program under those circumscribed limits and affirmed that varying the coordinates of the program could result in a breach of the proportionality principle. In short, the policy-making power of the ECB was substantially limited by the CJEU's decision in *Gauwelier*. In addition, the CJEU also left the door open for further review of the implementation of the program in practice, for at the time of the decision the program had only been announced in the press.[56]

The limits imposed on the OMT program had already been previously publicly assumed by the ECB, and, therefore, it seems that the CJEU reaffirmed the validity of the program under the conditions established by the ECB. From this perspective, the review seems deferential. Notwithstanding, the CJEU had responded directly to the preliminary reference requested by the BVerfG and judicially established those limits. This factor radically changes the scenario from one in which the agency itself unilaterally establishes policy to one in which the policy has been analyzed by a court from the standpoint of proportionality and given approval after passing judicial scrutiny. The latter scenario, with its declaration of proportionality under the necessity test and under certain limits subject to variation, means further judicial assessment may come that could bring a different outcome.

52 Case C-62/14, *Gauwelier*, para. 74; Case, C-493/17 *Weiss*, para. 78.

53 Case C-62/14, *Gauwelier*, para. 86.

54 *Ibid.* at para. 89.

55 Case C-62/14, *Gauwelier*, paras. 93-127. The limits imposed by the CJEU are very well summarized by the BVerfG in the following way: "(i) purchases may not be announced; (ii) the volume of the purchases must be limited; (iii) there must be a minimum period between the issue of the government bonds and their purchase by the ESCB; (iv) the ESCB may purchase only government bonds of Member States that have bond market access enabling the funding of such bonds; (v) purchased bonds may only in exceptional cases be held until maturity; purchases must be restricted or ceased and purchased bonds must be remarketed should continuing the intervention of further holding of the bonds become unnecessary for achieving the monetary policy aims". BVerfG, Judgment of the Second Senate of 21 June 2016 - 2 BvR 2728/13, para. 199.

56 Case C-62/14, *Gauwelier*, para. 83.

Gauwelier would remain a merely procedural judicial review if the ECB received deferential treatment from the CJEU after deciding to deviate from the announced judicially established limits in the implementation phase because on the basis of its own assessment of the evolving conditions of the economic situation. This appears precisely to be the case in *Weiss*, where the CJEU validated the implementation decisions of the PSPP, constantly referring to the broad margin of discretion of the ECB.[57] Yet it seems that, in *Weiss*, the CJEU also opened the door to procedural-oriented review of the necessity step of the proportionality test, whereas in *Gauwelier* the references to deference were limited to the legitimate aim and appropriateness of the measure steps. We do not know what would have been CJEU's response had the ECB changed the parameters of the OMT program in a hypothetical implementation phase or, in other words, had the parameters of the initial proportionality assessment changed. If either had occurred, the proportionality principle, even in its substantive dimension, would be open-ended and ambiguous, yet would still ultimately depend on the result of the case-by-case analytical method inherent to the proportionality assessment.

In any case, the standard of judicial review that comes out of these cases combines the procedural and substantive scrutiny, and for this reason it is qualified as a mixed standard of judicial review in this chapter. The process-oriented proportionality test is pivotal in the legitimate aim and appropriateness steps, where the manifest error criteria and the expertise of the decision-maker grant a broad margin of discretion to the ECB. In contrast, the margin of discretion is reduced in the substantive component of the proportionality test that is performed in the necessity step. Without doubt, the CJEU stops short of constraining all the powers of the ECB; the BVerfG had in fact asked for greater limitations,[58] but it still imposed on some limits the OMT program in *Gauwelier* that now have the force of law. Symptomatically, the ECB has seen its powers somewhat limited following the BVerfG's acceptance of the legality of the OMT program in the wake of the CJEU's intervention.[59]

7.4 The ECB as Special Case: Strong Judicial Review Triggered by National Courts

Furthermore, this mixed standard of judicial review is stricter than those traditionally applied to EU agencies. In general, EU scholars have accepted judicial review as one of the multiple accountability mechanisms of EU agencies, yet, at the same time, they have conceived of judicial review as at most a secondary tool in the general accountability

57 Case C-493/17, *Weiss*, para. 91.

58 Tridimas and Xanthoulis, 2016, pp. 30-32.

59 BVerfG, Judgment of the Second Senate of 21 June 2016 – 2 BvR 2728/13, paras. 174-220.

framework.[60] Scholars who have specifically addressed judicial review of EU agencies have argued in favor of judicial review as an accountability mechanism,[61] as long as it is, or ought to be, deferential.[62] In the end, scholars' little attention has been devoted to judicial review as an appropriate tool for EU agency oversight, for they have generally emphasized instead the pre-eminence of the administrative process and transparency as the proper cornerstones of the accountability scheme for EU agencies.[63]

The CJEU has followed a similar path and, over the years, has held agency action judicially reviewable despite the lack of treaty provisions to that effect, or even previsions for judicial review in the secondary EU legislation that created subsequent EU agencies.[64] The CJEU has affirmed judicial review as an indispensable tool in controlling EU agencies, yet its threshold for review has been procedural and highly deferential.[65] Simply referring to the technical discretion of EU agencies when deciding the case at hand is common,[66] and, when the court does apply the proportionality principle, the application is heavily deferential to the expertise of EU agencies and, therefore, does not take up a substantive analysis of the agency action.[67] Moreover, another common occurrence in the

60 Majone, 1997, p. 6.

61 S. Griller and A. Orator, 'Meroni Revisited - Empowering European Agencies between Efficiency and Legitimacy', Newgov-04-D40-WPMMeroniRevisited.doc, 2007, accessed 5 March 2019, pp. 17-18; M. Busuioc, *The Accountability of European Agencies. Legal Provisions and Ongoing Practices*, Delft, Eburon, 2010, pp. 164-167.

62 X. Yatanagas, 'Delegation of Regulatory Authority in the European Union. The Relevance of the American Model of Independent Agencies', *Jean Monnet Working Paper 3/01*, New York University School of Law, 2001, pp. 49-52; Busuioc, 2010, pp. 190-191.

63 Majone, 1998, pp. 20-22; Dehousse, 1998, p. 617; Borrás et al., 2007, p. 587; Chiti, 2000, pp. 331-341; Magnette, 2005, pp. 10-15; A. Meuwese, Y. Schuurmans & W. Voermans, 'Towards a European Administrative Act', *Review of European Administrative Law*, Vol. 2, No. 2, 2009, pp. 16-22.

64 Judicial review of EU agencies may be directly provided for in the constituent regulations of the agency. This is the case of decision-making agencies whose adjudicatory powers are legally binding on third parties (*see*, for instance, the European Union Aviation Safety Agency, EASA, in Art. 50 Regulation (EC) 216/2008, or the European Union Intellectual Property Office, EUIPO, Art. 149.3 Regulation (EU) 2017/1001). However, even in the case of non-decision-making agencies whose actions are determinant for other EU actors, especially the Commission, whose constituent provisions do not provide for judicial review, the CJEU has indirectly declared agencies' actions reviewable through the final act of the competent EU actor (*see* Judgment of the Court of First Instance of 26 November 2002 in Case T-74/00, *Artegodan GmbH and others v Commission*, EU:T:2002:283, paras. 198-199; Judgment of the Court of First Instance of 18 December 2003 in Case T-326/99, *Nancy Fern Olivieri v Commission and European Agency for the Evaluation of Medicinal Products*, EU:T:2003:351, paras. 51-55). Finally, after the Treaty of Lisbon, Art. 263 TFEU explicitly provided for judicial review of EU agencies. This reform ended the debate over the possibility of judicial review of EU agency actions, regardless whether the latter are enshrined or not in constituent regulations.

65 M. Busuioc, *European Agencies: Law and Practices of Accountability*, Oxford, Oxford University Press, 2013, p. 220; M. Chamon, *EU Agencies: Legal and Political Limits to the Transformation of the EU Administration*, Oxford, Oxford University Press, 2016, pp. 206 and 367.

66 Judgment of the Court of First Instance of 19 November 2008 in Case T-187/06, *Ralf Schräder v Community Plant Variety Office (CPVO)*, EU:T:2008:511, paras. 59-60; Judgment of the General Court of 11 December 2014 in Case T-102/13, *Heli-Flight GmbH & Co. KG v European Aviation Safety (EASA)*, EU:T:2014:1064, paras. 74 and 90-91.

67 Judgment of the General Court of 7 March 2013 in Case T-96/10, *Rütgers Germany GmbH and others v European Chemicals Agency (ECHA)*, EU:T:2013:109, paras. 134-150.

CJEU case law reviewing EU agency actions is that the court limits its discussion to the legal interpretation of the constituent act of the agency or the meaning of the wording and scope of the sectoral legislation establishing or regulating the EU agency in question.[68] Only in *Artegodan*, considered an exception because of the stricter approach taken,[69] did the CJEU apparently move beyond mere legal analysis and engage in a sort of procedural-oriented review closer in nature to the hard-look doctrine in U.S. administrative law.[70]

The context out of which this deferential standard has been framed includes two particularly relevant factors. On the one hand, the main avenue to CJEU review of EU agency actions had been the action for annulment (Art. 263 TFEU), rather than via request for preliminary ruling (Art. 267 TFEU). The former is a procedure with little national involvement; that is, EU institutions themselves are the leading actors in triggering it. At the same time, the wording of the treaty and the CJEU's restrictive standing doctrine for individuals in this type of procedure makes it very difficult for citizens to challenge EU agency actions.[71] On the other hand, powerless EU agencies have been conceptualized as unimportant at the national level and the few preliminary rulings in the field have received little attention. In short, the EU agencification process and the questions over the role and boundaries of judicial review had largely remained an internal affair of EU institutions with minimal involvement of national organs.

The CJEU's approach in *Gauwelier* and *Weiss* substantially breaks with this longstanding pattern regarding the judicial standard of review developed during the EU agencification process, especially with regard to the substantive review introduced under the proportionality test. In this new approach, the initiative at the national level has been determinant, and the raising of a stricter standard of judicial review resulted from dialo-

68 *See*, as a relevant cases, *Thomae*, in which the discussion focused on whether the granting single community market authorization under the centralized procedure required one single name for the medicinal product being authorized or, on the contrary, whether it was possible to propose several trade names within one marketing authorization (Judgment of the Court of First Instance of 10 December 2002 in Case T-123/00, *Dr Karl Thomae GmbH v Commission*, ECLI:EU:T:2002:307); *Schering-Plough*, in which the main issue was the legitimate interest of the parties to proceed with the action for annulment because of the withdrawal of the marketing authorizations (Order of the Court of First Instance of 5 December 2007 in Case T-133/03, *Schering-Plough Ltd v Commission and European Agency for the Evaluation of Medicinal Products (EMEA)*, EU:T:2007:365), or *Behring*, in which the parties and the court discussed the correct interpretation of Art. 5 (1) Regulation 141/2000, in essence concerning whether it must be interpreted as meaning that an application for designation of a medicinal product as an orphan medicinal product may also be submitted after the marketing authorization of that medicinal product for the same therapeutic indication (Judgment of the General Court of 9 September 2010 in Case T-264/07, *CSL Behring GmbH v Commission and European Medicines Agency (EMA)*, EU:T:2010:371).

69 Chamon, 2016, p. 351.

70 *See* Case T-74/00, *Artegodan*, para. 200.

71 The 'direct and individual concern' established by Art. 263 TFEU has been strictly applied by the CJEU, and the *Plaumann* test in particular, currently good law, has severely blocked challenges by individuals against EU institutions' actions and legislation through the action for annulment procedure (*see* the Judgment of 15 July 1963 in Case C-25/62, *Plaumann & Co. v Commission of the European Community*, EU:C:1963:17).

gical interaction between the national and EU levels. Hence, the two contextual factors identified above have changed. In the ECB cases, the procedural avenue to trigger review became the preliminary ruling, meaning that the challenge to the ECB's actions was triggered by the national judiciary that submitted the request to the CJEU. In addition to the recourse to preliminary reference, the debate over the legitimacy of EU agency power has shifted. The broad margin of discretion granted to the ECB and its visibility in the management of the financial crisis drew attention at the national level, which not only framed the cases in terms of initiating review of the appropriateness of ECB's actions but also the entire legitimacy of European integration. A powerful EU agency whose actions from the perspective of national constitutional law brought the German Constitutional Court to activate the preliminary ruling mechanism in order to question the legitimacy of the ECB as an independent actor, its status as a EU agency, and request stronger accountability measures, specifically calling for strict judicial scrutiny of the ECB's mandate. The interaction of the two courts led, for the first time, to discussions over the legitimacy of the EU agencification process at the EU judicial level and reformulated the hitherto limited proportionality test into a more powerful judicial tool for EU agency oversight.

The successful recourse to the preliminary ruling not only bolsters the involvement of national organs because it was activated by a national court. Citizens now have an easier avenue to challenge EU agency actions by going through their national courts rather than being forced to follow the path of the action for annulment procedure with its restrictive standing doctrine for individuals. As cases in point, the preliminary rulings in *Gauwelier* and *Weiss* were the result of the broad and flexible standing doctrine enjoyed by German citizens for access to national constitutional justice.[72] A direct and individual concern is easier to identify in some EU agency decisions, such as, for example, *Artegodan*, where a direct legal person was involved in the granting process of marketing authorizations for medical products, but these are much more difficult to prove in the nonindividual-oriented monetary context of macroeconomic policy. Spain, in its allegations in *Gauwelier*, argued that deciding the case on the merits and not rejecting it in the admissibility phase in such preliminary ruling as the one requested by the BVerfG would entail opening a back door and therefore breaching the standing doctrine that required an action for annulment.[73] However, the CJEU disregarded this allegation, recognizing the possibility that citizens might indirectly challenge EU institution action through the preliminary ruling mechanism, as long as the national court "is seized of a genuine dispute in which the question of validity of such an act is raised on indirect grounds".[74]

72 In *Gauwelier*, the constitutional complaints were filed by more than 11,692 plaintiffs, including university professors, parliamentary groups and common citizens.

73 Case C-62/14, *Gauwelier*, para. 23.

74 *Ibid.* at para. 29.

Gauwelier and *Weiss* have thus brought new elements into the debate over the accountability of EU agencies. Taking as reference the ECB, the CJEU, together with the crucial intervention of the BVerfG, has opened the path toward stronger judicial review in the EU's multiple accountability framework of agencies. Stricter scrutiny exercised using the proportionality test now represents an actual tool at the disposal of judges questioning EU agency actions. There are other signs that point toward a trend of more substantive judicial review of expert decisions as well, for instance, the affirmation that violations of fundamental rights constitute a ground for review of agency action. In the *Laedra* case, both the Commission and ECB's actions in the Cyprus bailout and bank levy were scrutinized by the CJEU through the lens of the right to property enshrined in Article 17(1) of the Charter of Fundamental Rights of the European Union.[75] Moreover, in another recent judgment, the Commission's decision framed under its powers as an antitrust authority, in which cases the Commission brings in expertise so its actions resemble that of an agency, was subjected to strict scrutiny on the grounds of its impact on due process and the right to legal defense.[76]

Substantive and strict scrutiny based on fundamental rights represents an unexplored avenue for oversight of the EU agencification process. Here again, judicial dialogue may prove determinant as a trigger mechanism. The CJEU had been reluctant to use the proportionality principle in the EU agencification process before *Gauwelier* and *Weiss*, even though the Court was very familiar with the principle that it had commonly used in other decisions. Now, responding to national pressure, the proportionality principle has been deployed. Impact on fundamental rights represents another criteria that may now also be used by national organs to trigger substantive judicial review; national organs whose experience in dealing with fundamental rights is much greater than that of the much younger newcomer to this field, the CJEU.

7.5 Conclusions

The EU agencification process has been thoroughly discussed behind closed doors, but primarily as a purely EU internal affair without space for input from the national level. Scholars and EU institutions have pushed for the creation and gradual empowerment of EU agencies without taking into account the experience of the process at the national level. The CJEU has also mainly addressed the EU agencification process in isolation. Most of EU agency cases calling for judicial scrutiny have been addressed through the action for annulment (Art. 263 TFUE), a process in which the involvement of national

75 Judgment of the Court of 20 September 2016 in Case C-8/15 P, *Laedra Advertising Ltd and others v Commission and European Central Bank (ECB)*, EU:C:2016:701, paras. 67-76.

76 Judgment of the Court of 16 January 2019 in Case C-265/17 P, *European Commission v United Parcel Services*, Inc., EU:C:2019:23, paras. 53-58.

courts is scant. Moreover, the access of citizens to the CJEU is restricted by the standing doctrine for such procedures. As a result of this isolation over the years, the standard of judicial review of EU agency actions has been highly deferential and procedural in nature.

Judicial scrutiny of the ECB, an institution which represents an intrinsic element of the EU agencification process, may break open the debate over the standard of judicial review of EU agencies. The heightened visibility of the ECB during the crisis, together with the realization of how powerful the ECB is in comparison with other EU agencies, drew the attention of national governments. As a structural case on the legitimacy of the European integration, the BVerfG, through the preliminary ruling procedure (Art. 267 TFUE), brought legitimacy and accountability concerns over the ECB as independent agency to the fore. The BVerfG shone a spotlight of the need for stricter judicial scrutiny of the ECB's actions. Under its pressure in a high-level profile case, the CJEU strengthened the judicial control over the ECB. This chapter argues that *Gauwelier* and *Weiss* add a substantive component to the proportionality test which, combined with the already well-known procedural elements, establishes clear limits on the policy-making power of the ECB. This mixed standard of judicial review is stricter than the long-standing and highly deferential standard that had been developed over the last decades by the CJEU to review EU agency actions.

Only time will tell whether this new stricter judicial scrutiny will be consolidated for the ECB and become a reference in the entire EU agencification process. The use of the proportionality principle with both procedural and substantive components could potentially intensify judicial scrutiny of EU agencies. In addition, the increasing use of fundamental rights as grounds for review of EU agencies' actions represents another interesting path for stricter judicial scrutiny. The ECB case is one example where the CJEU took a close look at the action of an EU institution at the behest of a national court, and the outcome of the judicial dialogue at the national and supranational levels appears positive. It is conceivable that, as other EU agencies gain power and start to resemble the ECB, national courts may turn their eyes to them and call for similar scrutiny by the CJEU.

8 Taxpayer Protection in the European Legal Context: A Dialogue of the Deaf between National and Supranational Courts?

Stefano Dorigo

8.1 The Difficult Recognition of Taxpayers' Rights in National Tax Systems

The issue of taxpayers' rights is undoubtedly one of the most common in the debate concerning tax law.[1] However, the debate takes on a paradoxical character. On the one hand, scholars try to extend the scope of these rights stating that the individual remains 'relevant' even as a taxpayer.[2] On the other hand, the judicial and administrative practice within the national legal systems partially moves in a different direction.

According to the latter trend, individuals would not be afforded rights when confronted with the tax administration. The thesis that emerges is that the tax relation naturally implies a difference in positions between the taxpayer and the tax administration. Since the payment of taxes aims at financing the public expenditure of the state, there would be an imbalance between the public interest regarding the correct application and collection of taxes and the interest of the individual called to fulfill the duties required by tax laws: the first would be destined to prevail because it fulfills functions of collective interest.[3]

---

1 With regard to the relation between international charters on human rights and taxation, *see* Ph. Baker, "Taxation and the European Convention of Human Rights", *European Taxation*, Vol. 40, 2000, pp. 298-306, p. 298; D. Bentley, *Taxpayers' Rights: Theory, Origin and Implementation*, Amsterdam. Kluwer Law International, 2007, *passim*; L. Del Federico, *Tutela del contribuente ed integrazione giuridica europea. Contributo allo studio della prospettiva italiana*, Milano, Giuffré, 2010, *passim*; G. Kofler, M. Maduro, P. Pistone, *Taxation and Human Rights in Europe and the World*, Amsterdam, IBFD, 2011, *passim*; J. Malherbe, *Protection des droits fondamentaux du contribuable*, Bruxelles, Bruylant, 1993, *passim*; Y. Martinez Muñoz, *La aplicación del Convenio Europeo de Derechos Humanos en materia tributaria: un anàlisis jurisprudencial*, Cizur Menor, Editorial Aranzadi, 2002, *passim*; H. Van den Broek, "Taxation and the European Convention on Human Rights", *European Taxation*, Vol. 38, 1998, pp. 235-251, p. 235.

2 S. Dorigo, "Taxpayers' Rights: the Growing Recognition of the Right to a Fair Trial in Tax Controversies in the European Union", *Tax Notes International*, Vol. 92, 2017, pp. 1079-1085, p. 795.

3 That interpretative trend – strongly advocated by the tax administration – is criticized by those authors who assert the need for a different foundation of the relation between taxpayers and the State. *See* G. Falsitta, *Giustizia tributaria e tirannia fiscale*, Milano, Giuffré, 2008, *passim*.

There is therefore, within national law, an unresolved tension between the pragmatism of the administration and the aspirations of scholars. The resistance of the public authorities to acknowledging effective rights to taxpayers is the consequence of their will to protect the power to tax. This is perceived, in fact, as one of the most significant manifestations of sovereignty. It is therefore well protected because from its correct implementation stem those financial resources which are necessary for the government to fulfill its policies of collective interest. In short, the taxing power is still widely perceived as the 'hard core' of a state prerogative, to quote the famous expression of the European Court of Human Rights in *Ferrazzini.*[4]

Such a concept is, however, firmly based in the constitutional tradition of many states. Here the duty to pay taxes puts the taxpayer in a situation of subjection, being functional to the satisfaction of interests of a collective nature and, therefore, more valuable than those of the taxpayer himself.[5] The global economic crisis, which exploded in 2008 and is not yet overtaken, has undoubtedly strengthened this attitude: in front of the urgent need of states to increase their revenues in order to feed the public coffers, the rights of the tax administration have been emphasized to the detriment of taxpayer protection. The latter are therefore often deprived of effective rights in front of the tax administration; at most their legal position can be qualified as a mere legitimate interest, therefore completely weakened compared to that of any individual not acting as a taxpayer.

Despite the solicitations coming from academics, who advocate that it is not reasonable to think of human rights as subjective situations that can be differently afforded depending on the role played by the individual, the situation remains unbalanced in favor of the public part. In national jurisdictions, in particular those of continental legal tradition, the rights expressly recognized to the taxpayer in the course of the tax relation are rare. Moreover, even in cases where some of them are expressly provided for in legislation, procedural obstacles arise for their effective protection: many times there are no specific remedies to assert their violation in the courts, the protection in these cases being entrusted with administrative procedures that do not guarantee full equality of arms between taxpayer and financial administration.

---

4 Judgment of 12 July 2001 in case no. 44759/98 *Ferrazzini v. Italy.*

5 A thorough analysis of the main constitutional theories with regard the power to tax can be found in L. Antonini, *Dovere tributario, interesse fiscale e diritti costituzionali,* Milano, Giuffrè, 1996, *passim.* More recently, the new features of sovereignty in tax matters have been explored by a large number of scholars. Limiting to the contributions of the Italian doctrine, *see* F. Gallo, "Giustizia sociale e giustizia fiscale tra decentramento e globalizzazione", *Rivista di diritto tributario,* Vol. 14, 2004, pp. 1069-1082, p. 1069; and G. Tremonti, "La fiscalità nel terzo millennio", *Rivista di diritto finanziario e scienza delle finanze,* Vol. 57, 1998, pp. 69-83, p. 69.

This ambiguous situation is confirmed by the diffusion of 'taxpayer's bills of rights'. They are regulatory instruments listing the rights that must be recognized to the taxpayer and the correlated duties imposed on the tax administration.[6] Even in cases where they have the force of law – and, therefore, place themselves at the top of the hierarchy of sources – there are no adequate remedies that can be activated for the case of non-compliance by the financial administration. The taxpayer's protection is often entrusted to an informal body, called the taxpayer's ombudsman, which, however, does not have truly effective powers of censorship against non-compliant offices.[7]

It is therefore confirmed that even in cases where a catalog of taxpayer's rights exists and is binding according to the law, the observance of these rights is not guaranteed effectively. Again, the public tax interest prevails over the taxpayer's subjective position.

8.2 The Expanding Function of Taxpayer's Rights in the Context of the 'European' Legal Order

A heavy contribution toward the acknowledgment of taxpayer's rights comes from supranational sources. In the European context, in particular, there has been a gradual but inexorable expansion of human rights even when individual acts as taxpayer.

This process shows characters of absolute originality. Neither EU law nor the European Convention of Human Rights provide rules specifically devoted to protecting the subjective positions involved in the tax relation. On the contrary, the silence in this regard has long been interpreted as a confirmation of the irrelevance of human rights in tax matters. However, an extensive reading of the rights provided both by the EU law (in particular the Charter of Fundamental Rights of the EU) and the ECHR has been given by the international jurisprudence. In other words, supranational courts afford the taxpayers rights well beyond the strictly textual interpretation of the international norms in which they are embodied.

Hence, the EU Court of Justice repeatedly stated that, when Member States exercise their taxation powers, they must do so consistently with EU law.[8] This means that neither

6 G. Tieghi, "Taxpayer Rights: A Constitutional Perspective", www.federalismi.it/ApplOpenFilePDF.cfm?artid=38025&dpath=document&dfile=04022019234653.pdf&content=Taxpayer%2BRights%3A%2Ba%2Bconstitutional%2Bperspective%2B%2D%2Bstato%2B%2D%2Bdottrina%2B%2D%2B, 2015 (Accessed 29 March 2019), *passim.*

7 Sometimes, the influence of the ombudsman lies in the particular personality of the person in charge: one can mention, as an example, the case of Nina Olson, U.S. National Taxpayer Advocate, who has strongly affirmed the need to adequately recognize and guarantee the taxpayer rights during the tax relation. *See* N. Olson, "A Brave New World: The Taxpayer Experience in a Post-Sequester IRS", *Tax Notes*, Vol. 87, 2013, pp. 1190-1195, p. 1190.

8 The EUCJ approach to the relation between sovereignty and taxation has been qualified as "anti-sovereign": according to this view, the European jurisprudence is eroding the taxing power of the Member States in the name of the correct functioning of the common market (P. Boria, *Taxation in European Union*, Torino/Cham, Giappichelli/Springer, 2017, p. 189).

the national legislator nor the tax administration can interfere with the individual sphere of the taxpayer in order to limit or deny his rights under the Charter of Fundamental Rights of the EU or other European sources.

An example of this attitude can be found with respect to the right to a hearing before the issuance of a notice of assessment: a right that the Court of Justice has stated in general terms in *Sopropé*.[9] In the same sense, one can recall the jurisprudence according to which the prohibition of *ne bis in idem* –consecrated by Article 50 of the EU Charter of fundamental rights – also applies with regard to those tax sanctions formally referred to as administrative, but having in substance an afflictive and punitive function able to assimilate them to criminal penalties.[10]

Even clearer is the path taken by the European Court of Human Rights. Its decisions show the clear intention of not penalizing the taxpayer only because he is confronted with the tax administration. There are at least three cases that are worth recalling here.

The first concerns the invocability of the principle of due process, interpreted as applicable in tax disputes. This is perhaps the most significant example because it shows the ongoing evolution of the approach taken by the ECtHR. Differently from the American Convention,[11] the ECHR makes no evident reference to tax trials. Article 6, outlining the characteristics of the so-called *fair trial*, exclusively refers to two categories of litigations: those whose object are 'civil rights and obligations', on the one hand, and those concerning 'any criminal charge,' on the other hand. Therefore, for a long time the tax procedures have been considered outside the protection afforded by Article 6.

In a first stage, the ECtHR itself supported this interpretation. In *Ferrazzini v. Italy*,[12] the judges of Strasbourg clearly acknowledged that "tax matters still form part of the hard core of public-authority prerogatives, with the public nature of the relationship between the taxpayer and the community remaining predominant".[13] In short, according to this

---

9 About the right to be heard in fiscal matters, *see* A. Ferrari Zumbini, "La (mancata) tutela del diritto di essere sentiti nei procedimenti di *adjudication* in materia fiscal", in G. Della Cananea et al (eds), *I procedimenti amministrativi di adjudication dell'Unione europea: principi generali e discipline di settore*, Torino, Giappichelli, 2017, pp. 233-256, p. 233.

10 Judgment of 26 February 2013 in case C-617/10 *Åklagaren c. Hans Åkerberg Fransson*. On this judgment, *see* S. Dorigo, "Il rapporto tra sanzione tributaria e sanzione penale secondo la Corte di Giustizia e i possibili effetti sull'ordinamento italiano", *Rivista di Diritto Tributario*, Vol. 23, 2013, pp. 204-237, p. 204.

11 The *American Convention on Human Rights* was adopted at the Inter-American Specialized Conference on Human Rights, held at San José (Costa Rica) on 22 November 1969. Art. 8, para. 1, of this multilateral convention establishes the right for any individual to have at one's disposal an independent and impartial structure to address to "in the substantiation of any accusation of a criminal nature made against him or for the determination of his rights and obligations of a civil, labour, fiscal, or any other nature." It seems important that the tax issue is mentioned, with no ambiguity, among those where you must comply with legal guarantees. Therefore, those who wrote the Inter-American Convention were aware that there was no substantial obstacle to acknowledge to the taxpayers, who are involved in a tax proceedings, the same rights typical of the criminal law or of any other proceeding according to the law.

12 *Ferrazzini v. Italy*, cit.

13 *Ibid.*, para. 29.

view, the sovereign nature of taxation would prevent that even the trial taking place in front of the Tax Courts benefits from the procedural protection of Article 6.

Recently, however, the ECtHR, although still in a cautious and prudent way, seems willing to open some space in the conceptual foundation, apparently so rock-hard, of the interpretation followed so far. To this end, the Court frequently made reference to the *criminal head* of Article 6, para. 1, that is, where the norm recalls the hearings concerning any 'criminal charge'. In particular, the ECtHR acknowledged that those tax litigations having as their object not only the amount of tax due but also the legitimacy of tax penalties resulting from the latter should be included in the regulation provided by Article 6.[14] This achievement can be clearly inferred in the judgment concerning the *Jussila* case.[15] The ECtHR stated that

> it is ([...]) not uncommon for procedures to combine the varying elements and it may not be possible to separate those parts of the proceedings which determine a 'criminal charge' from those parts which do not.[16]

Therefore, and this is the main innovation of the judgment under consideration, the Strasbourg Court suggested that all the tax proceedings, which involve the assessment of the legitimacy of penalties stemming from a tax recovery, fall within the scope of Article 6 of ECHR. As a consequence, the so-called *hard core* of State sovereignty, not being denied, can be however seen through a rights perspective: the exercise of it, in fact, cannot exclude the compliance with some minimum procedural guarantees in favor of the taxpayer.

There is a second trend which deserves to be mentioned here. In *Ravon*,[17] the Strasbourg Court acknowledged that Article 6 does not apply exclusively to the trial; rather, it shall be respected during a tax audit as well. In that specific case, the taxpayer's right of defense during a tax inspection had been put in danger by means of a home access and the consequent document seizure aimed at checking his tax liability. The Court, though referring once again to the principles expressed in *Ferrazzini*, nevertheless stated that the case did not entirely regarded a tax issue, since "in its essence it includes the issue for the authorities to acknowledge or not the right to domicile". Consequently, the civil character of this right was 'evident.'

Finally, in *Chambaz v. Switzerland*,[18] the Court censored the behavior of the Swiss Tax Authorities which, at the time of the audit, imposed severe penalties on the taxpayer

14 ECtHR, First Chamber, 23 July 2002, appeal no. 34619/97 *Janosevic v. Sweden* and ECtHR, First Chamber, 23 July 2002, appeal no. 36985/97 *Västberga Taxi Aktiebolag and Vulic v. Sweden.*

15 ECtHR, Grand Chamber, 23 November 2006, appeal no. 73053/01, *Jussila v. Finland.*

16 ECtHR, Grand Chamber, 23 November 2006, appeal no. 73053/01, *Jussila v. Finland*, par. 45.

17 ECtHR, Third Chamber, 2 February 2008, case no. 18497/03 *Ravon and Others v. France.*

18 ECtHR, Fifth Chamber, 5 April 2012, case no. 11663/04 *Chambaz v. Switzerland.*

because of his choice not to submit the documents the officers in charge asked for, in order to prevent from being subject to a penal incrimination. In particular, the judges acknowledged that such a penalty infringed Article 6, para. 1, of ECHR being in contrast with the taxpayer's right to remain silent during the preliminary investigation; the principle *nemo tenetur se detegere* (which can be translated with the right not to self-incriminate) represents therefore an addition to the basket of rights connected with the fair trial principle; a right which can cross over the limits of the *stricto sensu* criminal proceeding and to be acknowledged in all those audits involving the fiscal authorities.[19]

Some useful indications come from the jurisprudence concerning, once again, the *ne bis in idem* principle. In its recent case law, the ECtHR acknowledged that the principle – which prohibits that a person be tried or punished twice for the same *facts* – can be invoked in disputes involving tax sanctions. Thus, the Court noticed that such a prohibition (established by Art. 4, para. 1, of the Fourth Additional Protocol to the ECHR), although literally referred only to criminal penalties, can be invoked also in case of tax proceedings, when the Tax Administration – once the criminal trial has finished and the penalty applied – claims to impose an additional administrative sanction on the taxpayer for the same fact.[20]

The European (*lato sensu*, thus comprising the EU law and the ECHR system) context – especially in its dynamic role (the jurisprudence) – seems therefore willing to afford the taxpayer rights with an approach which is largely unknown to national legal systems. The revenue concerns that characterize the latter, and somehow also influence the interpretations by the courts, are indeed unknown to supranational judicial institutions: their purpose seems to be to clearly outline the boundaries of the norms protecting human rights, avoiding those discriminations that do not find justification in urgent needs of public nature.[21]

---

19 Ph. Baker, "Recent tax cases of the European Court of Human Rights", *European Taxation*. Vol. 52, 2002, pp. 585-597, p. 585, points out that "it was clear that forcing a taxpayer to answer questions or create new documents giving information interfered with the right of silence."

20 ECtHR, Fourth Chamber, 20 May 2014, appeal no. 11828/11 *Nykänen v. Finland*. As for the position of the doctrine concerning the ECtHR case-law in relation to *ne bis in idem*, we refer to G. Cesari, "Illecito penale e tributario. Il principio del ne bis in idem alla luce della più recente giurisprudenza della Corte Europea dei Diritti dell'Uomo e di Cassazione", *Rivista di Diritto Tributario*, Vol. 24, 2014, pp. 74-92, p. 74; A. Giovannini, "La Corte EDU ribadisce il divieto di doppia sanzione e la Cassazione rinvia alla Consulta", *Corriere Tributario*, Vol. 38, 2015, pp. 905-913, p. 905; Poelmann, "Some fiscal issues of the Charter of Fundamental Rights of the European Union", *Intertax*, Vol. 43, 2015, pp. 173-178, p. 173.

21 It has been noted that "*tax is no longer purely a matter of raising revenues.*" Therefore, this is "*gradually leading to complete safeguarding of individuals rights in the field of tax law*" (T. Fortsakis, "The Role of Individuals Rights in the Europeanization of Tax Law", in G. Kofler et al (eds), *Human Rights and Taxation in Europe and the World*, Amsterdam, IBFD, 2011, pp. 95-103, p. 95).

8.3 The Problematic Transposition of Supranational Interpretations within National Systems: The Case of Taxpayer's Right to Be Heard

Faced with such an expansive trend, the national jurisprudence appears to be particularly conservative. In most cases, a restrictive attitude, functional to limit the scope of the rights affirmed in favor of the taxpayer, prevails. Such an approach shows a sort of contradiction: the national courts often make explicit reference to the European judicial guidelines declaring that they are correct and showing their willingness to implement them internally. However, sometimes, the outcome of this implementation is very different from that advocated by the supranational court. This happens when the domestic courts do not follow those guidelines because they find a difference between the concrete case which is the object of the judgment and the abstract subject matter regulated by the European rule. In other words, there is a clear mismatch between the affirmation of a principle – usually carried out by the national judge recalling the jurisprudence of supranational courts – and its application to concrete cases.

The Italian jurisprudential practice is rich of examples in this sense. A first rather relevant case is that of the taxpayer's right to be heard during the investigations of the tax administration. It has already been said that the Court of Justice – in C-349/07 *Sopropé* case – has dealt with the issue concerning the protection of taxpayer's rights in case of a tax procedure. It stated that (a) the right of defense is a fundamental right, (b) it should be protected when the tax administration is going to issue an act which could produce significant consequences on the taxpayer's sphere, and (c) in order for the right to be effectively guaranteed, the taxpayer must be allowed to interact with the administration, expressing his views, before the conclusion of the procedure and the notification of the act of assessment.

It is evident that this judgment – through the affirmation of a taxpayer's right – identifies specific and positive procedural obligations for the tax administration, whose observance is guaranteed directly by the EU basic rules. However, the Italian tax administration usually denied the relevance of that right on the basis of internal rules that did not expressly provide for it in general terms. The tax courts, for their part, offered fluctuating solutions, someone in the sense of the full acknowledgment of the taxpayer's right to be heard,[22] others in the opposite sense of the irrelevance of the supranational discipline because the Italian legal system is founded on the prevalence of the public interest to a rapid and effective revenue collection.[23]

At the end, the Joint Sections of the Italian Supreme Court – after some not irrelevant hesitations that cannot be analyzed here – in a recent judgment has created a rather imaginative solution.[24] According to this view, the right to be heard is not general, but

22 *See* Italian Court of Cassation, order no. 15905 of 6 July 2010.

23 Italian Court of Cassation, order no. 17612 of 5 September 2016.

24 Italian Court of Cassation, Joint Sections, decision no. 24823 of 9 December 2015.

can be asserted only in very definite situations and in a narrow sense. In sum, if the claim concerns VAT, then the preventive contradictory must be guaranteed under the EU rules. On the contrary, if the claims concerns direct taxes, the EU rules do not apply and, therefore, the right cannot be invoked in the absence of a national explicit provision. So far, it would seem a restrictive interpretation, but no scandal could be raised: this arrangement reflects the limits of the EU competence with regard direct taxation.

However, the Supreme Court has gone beyond and added that in case the mandatory preventive contradictory (for VAT claims) has not been realized due to the failure of the tax officers to call the taxpayer, then the validity of the assessment can be disputed only if the latter proves that in the course of the missed contradictory he would have provided decisive elements in his own favor.

It is evident that this creative interpretation goes far away from the limits that can be deduced from the jurisprudence of the CJEU, and it ends up denying the essence of the right to be heard, given the fact that also for VAT disputes that right can be ignored by the tax administration without relevant consequences: the proof that the taxpayer has to provide in order to invalidate the assessment seems in fact to be diabolical.[25]

8.4 Follows: The ne bis in idem Concerning Tax Claims

A similar attitude on the part of the national jurisprudence appears also with regard to the principle prohibiting double sanctions and its applicability to tax matters. The jurisprudence of the Italian tax courts is not at all in line with the ECtHR. The latter looks at the fact in its historical concreteness and states that double penalty is not allowed when both the criminal and the tax rule refer the sanction to the same historical fact.[26] On the contrary, in the Italian legal system, the principle of specialty,[27] not so much in its formulation as in the way it is interpreted and applied, turns out to be indifferent to the concrete characteristics of the conduct, but rather looks at the way in which the abstract subject matter is described and regulated by the norm.

25 *See*, on this issue, the critical analysis of A. Renda, "Il contraddittorio preventivo tra speranze (deluse), rassegnazione e prospettive", *Diritto e pratica tributaria*, Vol. 87, 2016, pp. 732-761, p. 732.

26 It has been recently stated that the Italian Supreme Court has gone its own way and, in so doing, has denied the influence of the supranational jurisprudence (F. Gallo, "Il *ne bis in idem* in campo tributario: un esempio per riflettere sul "ruolo" delle Alte Corti e sugli effetti delle loro pronunzie", *Rassegna tributaria*, Vol. 60, 2017, pp. 915-928, p. 917).

27 The principle of specialty, as disciplined by Art. 19 of Legislative Decree no. 74 of 2000, establishes that the same unlawful fact – even if punished by two distinct norms – shall be subjected only to the sanction provided for by the special norm. However, a definition of what is the 'special' sanction lacks, therefore a wide margin of appreciation is reserved to interpreters. *See* A. Carinci, "Il principio di specialità nelle sanzioni tributarie: tra crisi del principio e crisi del Sistema", *Rassegna tributaria*, Vol. 58, 2015, pp. 499-515, p. 499.

Such a different approach is not without consequences. The insistence on the abstract features of the case as provided for by the law leads to the conclusion that two separate sanctions are legitimate even if the illicit conduct is unique: for this purpose, it is sufficient a difference, even imperceptible, in the abstract description of the subject matter by the norms providing the two sanctions.

Following that approach, a certain national jurisprudential trend supports the correctness of multiple sanctions even in the presence of the same material violation. The Joint Sections of the Italian Supreme Court held that the principle of specialty is not invocable (and therefore, criminal penalties and tax sanctions can be combined) in the event that the fact leading to the administrative offense is only 'a part' of the fact provided for by the criminal norm, "which requires further elements and is characterized by a different time of realization".[28] Such an interpretation plainly admits the concurrent application of the two sanctions where there is a common core of material facts and a factual surplus of just one of the two offenses.

A more recent jurisprudential address, although apparently recalling the jurisprudence of the ECtHR, in fact produces an incorrect application of the principles elaborated by the latter. In its judgment no. 6993/2017, the Court of Cassation – while invoking the jurisprudence in *A and B* as a necessary point of reference for the solution of domestic cases of double sanction – specifically looks only at one of the connection criteria between the procedures provided therein, that of temporal proximity between them, and on this basis excludes the violation of the *ne bis in idem* principle in case a tax sanction and a criminal penalty are applied to the same fact of issuing and using invoices for non-existent transactions.

That interpretation thus reveals the resistance of the domestic legal system to give substance to those principles, developed by the jurisprudence of the Strasbourg Court, which are in principle considered to be completely sharable and binding.

---

28 Reference goes to the decisions no. 37424 and no. 37425 filed on 12 September 2013. In this case, the Italian Court of Cassation was asked to judge the possible concurrent application of the crimes of failure to pay VAT and withholding taxes (articles 10 bis and ter of Legislative Decree No. 74/2000) and of the corresponding administrative sanctions (Art. 13 of Legislative Decree No. 471/1997). According to the rulings referred to, the relation between the two offenses is "not of specialty, but of progression: the criminal case ([...]) essentially constitutes a violation much more serious than the administrative one and, although it necessarily contains the latter ([...]), it enriches it with essential elements (annual declaration, threshold, extended term) that are not altogether attributable to the paradigm of the specialty (which, if operating, would obviously involve the application of the criminal offense only), since they carry decisive behavioral segments ([...]) that are temporally located at a time subsequent to the administrative offense" (translation by the author. The Italian text reads as follows: "non di specialità, ma di progressione: la fattispecie penale ([...]) costituisce in sostanza una violazione molto più grave di quella amministrativa e, pur contenendo necessariamente quest'ultima ([...]), la arricchisce di elementi essenziali (dichiarazione annuale, soglia, termine allungato) che non sono complessivamente riconducibili al paradigma della specialità (che, ove operante, comporterebbe ovviamente l'applicazione del solo illecito penale), in quanto recano decisivi segmenti comportamentali ([...]) che si collocano temporalmente in un momento successivo al compimento dell'illecito amministrativo.".

8.5 FOLLOWS: THE CASE OF THE RIGHT NOT TO INCRIMINATE ONESELF

According to Italian law, during a tax audit the taxpayer does not appear to be free to stay silent. Article 52 of Presidential Decree 633/1972, concerning VAT, states that "the books, registers, records and documents whose exhibition is refused cannot be taken into consideration in favor of the taxpayer for the purposes of assessment during the administrative phase or the trial". It emerges that not only the mere refusal produces such unfavorable procedural consequence, but also the mere declaration of not owning such registers and documents as well as the 'removal of them from the inspection'. With regard to direct taxes, although Article 32, Paragraph 4 of Presidential Decree 600/1973 originally presented a similar formulation, there is a significant extension of the penalizing regime toward noncollaborative taxpayers, introduced by law 28/1999. In the current version, the prohibition of use in the administrative procedure and the trial also affects "the news and data not submitted" by the taxpayer "in response to the invitations by the Tax Officers".[29]

These tax provisions impose an immediate and complete disclosure of the defensive strategy on the taxpayer, with evident consequences also with regard to his position in the possible future criminal trial. And, in fact, in order not to incur the serious consequences provided for by the law, the taxpayer could be induced to offer documents and explanations to the auditors about the object of the investigation, thereby involuntarily fueling the circulation of the same outside the administrative circuit.[30] The risk is that, on the base of such documents, a tax evasion of an amount above a certain threshold emerges, therefore realizing the conditions for a criminal charge. At the same time, the taxpayer exposes himself to the risk of a different and more unfavorable reading of the same elements by a different authority.

It seems, in other words, that the right to remain silent, according to the brocardo *nemo tenetur se detegere* (which expresses a part of the right of defense under Art. 24 of the Italian Constitution, Art. 48, para. 2, of the EU Charter of fundamental rights and Art. 6 of the ECHR), may be circumvented in the context of a criminal trial that draws on the results of a tax audit. The national jurisprudence follows that interpretation in quite strict terms.[31]

It is evident how far this approach is to that advocated by the ECtHR in *Chambaz*. Beyond the moment in which it becomes evident, during the audit, that one goes toward

---

29 One can refer to A. Marcheselli, "Il principio di buona fede e le preclusioni per i documenti sottratti alla verifica", *Corriere tributario*, Vol. 33, 2010, pp. 53-57, p. 53.

30 The only case in which the taxpayer can escape the serious consequences of the rule occurs in the event that he proves that the failure to exhibit is the result of a non-fraudulent situation. On this aspect, *see* F. Tundo, "Solo il dolo specifico del contribuente rende inutilizzabili i documenti non esibiti durante gli accessi", *Corriere tributario*, Vol. 40, 2017, pp. 1967-1973, p. 1967.

31 The thesis exposed in the text is supported by the Italian Court of Cassation, decision no. 43552 of 20 October 2014.

a evasion over threshold and, therefore, criminally relevant, the taxpayer's right to remain in silence should in any case be protected even where there is only the risk, considering the characterizing elements of its activity or the verification method chosen by the proceeding officials, that such a situation occurs.[32]

It therefore appears to be contrary to the fundamental right of defense to impose on the taxpayer, under the threat of severe procedural preclusions, to reveal elements capable of leading to the application of sanctions of afflictive nature, regardless of the risk that a criminal procedure is initiated.[33]

8.6 The Reasons for a Dialogue between the Deaf

The picture I have quickly painted so far is somehow ambiguous. I don't refer to the content of the international instruments on the protection of human rights or the evolutive (and worthy of appreciation) jurisprudence of the supranational courts. The international and EU human rights law provides very important rules and instruments for the protection of individuals, even of those facing the tax administration. The ambiguity arises when one comes down from the international or European level to the national one: that is, when the rights embodied in the ECHR or in the EU Charter have to be guaranteed in single, specific cases that occur in the domestic context.

The impression – based on the analysis of the practice in Italy – is that there is an evident misalignment between what is imposed at the international level and what the national legal systems are ready (and willing) to do.

In my opinion, this misalignment comes from two concurring factors:

1. the literal formulation of the norms in the international instruments on human rights is often generic. This is particularly true with regard to the ECHR, and, in fact in this field, a relevant role is played, as we have seen, by the ECtHR. Consequently, the influence of those rights on the national legal systems remains uncertain as it mainly depends on an interpretative activity;
2. the constitutions – especially those introduced in the past – do not guarantee the role of the taxpayers in the course of the tax procedure; rather, they presuppose the traditional theory centered on the prevalence 'almost at any cost' of the tax interest.

---

32 The need to safeguard the taxpayer's right against self-incrimination is strongly advocated by F. Amatucci, "Le preclusioni probatorie in fase di contraddittorio e il diritto al silenzio del contribuente", in L. Del Federico et al (eds), *Convenzione europea dei diritti dell'uomo e giustizia tributaria italiana*, Torino, Giappichelli, 2014, pp. 164-180, p. 164.

33 C. Palao Taboada, *El derecho a no autoinculparse en el ámbito tributario*, Navarra, Thomson Reuters, 2008, *passim*.

As a consequence, in many cases the rights affirmed at the international level are not able to enter as such in the national legal systems or at least they can be afforded in a weakened form.

The interpretation followed by the tax administrations – and shared by the national jurisprudence – can be understood in its theoretical foundations. There is the need not to limit the power of the state to apply and collect taxes, especially in times of crisis. In this sense, the attribution of rights to the taxpayer is perceived as an instrument to weaken the fiscal sovereignty and, therefore, to hinder a crucial function like that of financing the state apparatus.

The theory about the prevalence of fiscal interests is particularly alive in some continental legal orders. In Italy, it derives from the traditional conception according to which the tax duty presupposes the subjection of the taxpayer and is as such inconsistent with the attribution of rights to the latter. Albeit this theory has been overcome with the advent of the constitution and the affirmation of the tendential equality between public and private interests, some residues of the original approach have remained in many institutes of tax law.[34]

As a consequence, part of the jurisprudence is still sensitive to the reasons of the public administration. Hence, while the courts of merit – more closely related to the concreteness of the subject matters and to the social and political needs behind them – often appear to uphold the taxpayer's reasons, the upper courts in most cases show a more conservative approach. Certainly, this attitude is the consequence of a context still influenced by traditional conceptions that are difficult to overcome. However, the apparent closure of the internal jurisprudence could be explained otherwise: its features express the fear that external influences, based on concepts and principles stemming from historical, philosophical and economic contexts so far from the internal ones, can alter the essential characteristics of the national legal system. Again, the defense of tax sovereignty, which implies impermeability with respect to interpretative position perceived as alien, comes to the fore.[35]

There is no doubt that the attitude of supranational jurisprudence with respect to tax issues is inspired by a very different logic from that typical of national courts, a logic free from the concerns of protecting the tax revenue (neither the European Union nor the ECHR system have their own tax system) and, therefore, aimed at a serene evaluation of human rights also in the context of the tax relation. In short, the jurisprudential approach

34 For example, the Italian fiscal system is full of presumptions in favor of the tax administration. Moreover, some norms impose that the taxpayer pays a part of the tax requested through a tax assessment even when the latter is under judgment before the competent tax court.

35 It has been noted, with regard the EU legal system, that "Member States are worried about the wide impact of EU rules on their sovereign power to tax; and, for the same reasons, they fear the far-reaching effects of the Union's fundamental rights regime in their domestic area" (L. Azoulai, "EU Human Rights and the Reserved Powers of the Member States", in G. Kofler et al (eds), *Human Rights and Taxation in Europe and the World*, Amsterdam, IBFD, 2011, pp. 75-82, p. 75).

of the CJEU and of the ECtHR does not know the contrast between the public fiscal interest and the protection of the taxpayers' rights. Hence, this situation facilitates the interpretation of these positions as two sides of the same coin, therefore tendentially of equal importance.

This feature feeds what has been called the dialogue between the deaf. On the one hand, supranational courts conceive human rights, also in the tax sphere, as subjective situations which must be coordinated with the public interest to apply tax laws without being submitted *a priori* to it. On the other hand, national judges, often worried that an overly rigorous application of the taxpayer's rights may lead to damage the financial balance of the state, prefer to limit the extent of those rights in the light of essential features of the legal system and its basic needs. Therefore, the balance is broken in favor of the fiscal interest.

It is interesting to note that both the European and the national jurisprudence move from the same basic assumption, namely the importance of individual rights. The divergent outcome derives from the different way in which the supranational and national courts place these rights in the context of the tax relation. For the Court of Justice and the ECtHR, the taxpayer's rights are suitable to delineate the position of one of the subjects involved in the tax relation and to give him a position of equality compared to the public part; instead, for internal judges those rights come later than public interests and, therefore, must cede to the latter in case of conflict. The different institutional paths and the conflicting interests around them justify such a divergent approach, fueling a dialogue that is only apparent.

However, it is not just a question of lack of communication. In fact, some recent cases show that the European courts tend to retrace their steps, pandering the interpretative trends of the national courts. The regression of the ECtHR (but also, in some way, of the CJEU) about the application of the *ne bis in idem* in the tax area is emblematic. The ECtHR and the CJEU have moved from judgments which stated the full applicability of the rule to cases of tax violations, to others affirming the opposite rule (the *ne bis in idem* does not concern in principle fiscal cases), unless some strict conditions are met.[36] Here the retreat of the international and supranational protection of taxpayer's rights is very much visible. It is probably induced by political considerations, namely those of not displeasing the states with interpretations perceived as too invasive of their sovereign sphere.

This outcome – luckily still limited to few cases – represents a further confirmation of the dialogue between the deaf: a dialogue so unsuccessful that one of the two parties prefers to change its positions in order not to alter the relations with the other. In doing so, the most fruitful part of the dialogue, which arises from the persistence of opposing

---

36 *See* in that sense B. Peeters, "The Ne Bis in Idem Rule: Do the EUCJ and the ECtHR Follow the Same Track?", *EC Tax Review*, Vol. 27, 2018, pp. 182-185, p. 182.

positions and aims at their synthesis, is denied. Starting from such an unsatisfactory situation, the time has come to suggest some possible solutions.

8.7 THE NECESSARY RETHINKING OF THE ROLE OF THE TAXPAYER AND HIS RIGHTS...

A first aspect that needs to be rethought concerns the role of the taxpayer and the relevance of his fundamental rights. The prevailing conception after the rising of the global economic crisis, according to which the taxpayer's rights may yield in the event that the state's interest prevail in the application and collection of taxes, is unsatisfactory. It reverts tax law with decades and denies the evolution that has taken place in the sense of the tendential parification between public interest and individual rights.

Beyond contingent reasons, the foundation of the tax power has changed. Consequently, there is no room for interpretations weakening the individual's position vis-à-vis the tax administration. In fact, taxation can no longer be understood in a neutral manner as a mere instrument for procuring the financial resources necessary for the functioning of the public organization. There is now, in almost all Western constitutions and especially in the European states, the assumption that the tax is an instrument for the redistribution of wealth among the members of the community. The social (and solidaristic) function of taxation and taxes allocates the fiscal relation outside the strict borders of sovereignty.[37] On the contrary, that function emphasizes the aim of promoting the enjoyment of rights in accordance with the principle of substantial equality.

In short, the evolution of modern constitutionalism – without doubt influenced by the supranational jurisprudence – allows us to believe that the duty to pay taxes no longer has a connotation of subjection. The payment of a tax does not serve only (or predominantly) to provide the public apparatus with operational resources. Rather, the public expenditures fulfill an equalizing function by redistributing the wealth in such a way that inequalities within an organized community are overcome. This different viewpoint makes possible to link the tax duty with the individual's fundamental rights which this redistribution aims to guarantee through the activities of the public authorities.[38]

---

37 As has been pointed out, "while some may view taxation as primarily a pragmatic task undertaken by the State to raise revenue for government functions, tax law unavoidably introduces issues of allocation and redistribution of the burdens and benefits of living in organized society" (A. Christians, "Fair Taxation as a Basic Human Right", *International Review of Constitutionalism*, Vol. 9, 2009, pp. 211-230, p. 211).

38 *See* in that sense D. Gutmann, "Taking Human Rights Seriously: Some Introductory Words on Human Rights, Taxation and the EU", in G. Kofler et al (eds), *Human Rights and Taxation in Europe and the World*, Amsterdam, IBFD, 2011, pp. 105-112, p. 105. The author correctly notes that "*the second generation of human rights*" (i.e., social human rights) "*instead of being considered as rights against the State, [...] tend to become rights to the State's intervention in social and economic matters.*" Therefore, taxation has a deep impact on them.

It follows that the taxpayer's rights must be respected as part of the tax relation. It would be contradictory to believe that a relation whose ultimate purpose is to guarantee rights can coexist with the denial of the fact that the individuals who are part of it – the taxpayers – have legally enforceable tools vis-à-vis the financial administration.

Such a thesis can find strong support precisely in the way the supranational charters of rights, as interpreted by the respective courts, intend the rights that are the object of their proclamation. Those rights in fact are proclaimed and protected in themselves, regardless of the need to defend the other interest – that of the state as an imposing entity – involved in the relation. The fact that neither the EU nor the ECHR system contemplate its own fiscal interest (as is the case for states) means that the need to preserve it is much less pressing and above all only indirect. Therefore, the typical 'fair balance' of these conventional instruments – and of the jurisprudence that applies them – is achieved denying any prevalence of the public interest over the interests of the individual.[39]

This implies that the rights proclaimed at supranational level in favor of the taxpayer should be considered by the national courts in their international dimension. Therefore, they should be in some way disconnected from the political, social and ideological context of the internal legal system and assumed instead as subjective positions which are genuinely supranational.

It is necessary to give up an interpretation of these rights conditioned by the national mode of their provision by the distinct legal systems and to consider, instead, that they should operate as they are outlined by the international instruments that proclaim them and by the jurisprudence, respectively, of the CJEU or the ECtHR. This does not mean to overturn the current conception and to suggest that the taxpayer's rights must always and in any case prevail. The same supranational jurisprudence is clear in affirming the possibility of a limitation of rights where this is required by prevailing public needs.

What is important to note, however, is that such an evaluation must take place on a case-by-case basis and with the function of realizing an effective balance between subjective positions which are opposed but have to be considered equally worthy of consideration. The idea, conveyed on a supranational level, is that in no way the recognition of a right to the taxpayer can weaken or contradict the function of the tribute, which is and

39 According to one view, "taxpayers are no longer the mere recipients of fiscal policies, but are rather to be seen as the counterparts of a legal relationship between equals, requiring cooperation with the tax authorities" (G. Menita De Flora, "A New Vision on Exercising Taxing Powers and the Right to Fair Trial in Judicial Tax Procedures under Art. 6 ECHR", in G. Kofler et al (eds), *Human Rights and Taxation in Europe and the World*, Amsterdam, IBFD, 2011, pp. 411-424, p. 411). As a consequence, a balance between their respective interests should be achieved.

remains public, particularly for its solidaristic feature. On the contrary, admitting that the implementation of the tax relation is firmly placed within a horizon of legally recognized rights can make the action of public authorities far more efficient and legitimate.[40] This is the only way to achieve a uniform and non-discriminatory application of the taxpayer's rights sanctioned at the European level and to avoid excessively 'nationalist' reactions by the national courts.

8.8 .... And the Indispensable Change of Mentality on the Part of National Judges

The proposed change of the way the fundamental rights enshrined in international and supranational law have to be conceived is undoubtedly a necessary condition to trigger a fruitful dialogue between the courts. However, in my view, it is still not sufficient. A new subjective element must be added to the objective one. It relates to the way the national judges must understand this dialogue. Let's explain this concept briefly.

It has been said that one of the reasons for the current failure of the dialogue between domestic judges and international and supranational courts lies in the tendency of the former to protect the tax authorities that would in some way be threatened by a too wide recognition of taxpayers' rights. The underlying idea is that the tax relationship is and has to remain an 'internal affair' because it is of crucial importance for the interests of the particular legal system. This conception produces an attitude which, as demonstrated by the Italian practice, does not deny the importance of supranational rights but actually produces their reassessment aiming at their adaptation to the peculiarities of the tax relation stemming out of the domestic legal order.

It seems that this is the main limitation of this conception. In a currently globalized world believing that the taxpayer's rights escape the influence of globalization and remain an exclusive 'property' of national legislators and courts is in deep contradiction with the actual trends in the development of tax law. It must be recognized that the tax relation is becoming more and more supranational.[41] This is true with regard not only to the system of sources of law but also with view to the functions and aims of taxes and taxation.

40 *See* again the author cited in the preceding footnote, who states that "the Revenue interest is no longer a supreme and untouchable legal value, but rather a legal value, whose protection may be counterbalanced by further interests that are equally important and are regulated by national constitutions and supranational law." Therefore, the principles of legality and fairness can be better guaranteed in the course of the administrative action.

41 The advent of a new way of conceiving taxation in a globalized world has been analyzed by many scholars. *See, e.g.*, R. Avi-Yonah, "A Perspective on Supra-Nationality in Tax Law", in Y. Brauner et al (eds) *Taxation and the BRICS*, Amsterdam, IBFD, 2015, pp. 33-39, p. 33; and Y. Brauner, "An International Tax Regime in Crystallization. Realities, Experiences, and Opportunities", 2002, https://papers.ssrn.com/sol3/papers.cfm?abstract_id=315685 Accessed 29 March 2019, *passim*.

It is well known that tax law is increasingly influenced not only by EU and international sources of law – especially the double taxation agreements – but also by some atypical sources of law, known as soft law, which reflect the guidelines of most states and therefore incorporates particularly authoritative guidelines for national legislators.[42] But this is not the only issue of interest. During the last decade, once again in conjunction with the global economic crisis, we are witnessing the attempt of the states to adopt common principles and rules, in the awareness that the correct conduct of the tax relation is vital not only for each legal orders, but even more for the community of states as a whole.[43]

In other words, a new conception of the tax relation is spreading beyond the boundaries of the single legal system. This is a conception that places the correct development of this relation as a condition for the well-being and the justice of the international community, attributing to this end a central relevance to a notion of transnational solidarity.[44] The correct fulfillment of the taxpayer's duty and the fair exercise of its public functions by the tax administration constitute – according to this address – tools that are interrelated and functional to pursue a fair and equitable structure in a much larger space, broader than that of each individual state. Beyond the probability of success that such a prospect will have in the future, what counts for our analysis is to note that it is now impossible to interpret the tax relation only with the parameters of domestic law.

The principles of fair taxation that are emerging at the international and supranational level (again, starting from soft law instruments, but with the novelty of their partial transposition into a binding multilateral instrument[45]), partly influenced by the interna-

42 Since many years the international practice highlights the relevance of 'guidelines' or 'code of conducts' which, although approved as mere recommendations by international bodies (mainly the OECD, but also the EU Commission), are capable of influencing the national authorities, be they the legislator or the judiciary. The increasing importance of soft law in tax matters has been highlighted by H. Gribnau, "Improving the Legitimacy of Soft Law in EU Tax Law", *Intertax*, Vol. 35, 2007, pp. 30-44, p. 30; and A. Christians, "Hard Law & Soft Law in International Taxation", 2007, https://papers.ssrn.com/sol3/papers.cfm?abstract_id=988782&download=yes Accessed 29 March 2019, *passim*.

43 The recent international practice shows the emergence of a compelling role of soft law for tax issues. One can recall the recent BEPS (base erosion and profit shifting) project elaborated by the OECD – a series of proposed actions suggested to States in order to update their national discipline concerning international taxation. These actions, although not mandatory for the States, are going to deeply influence their behavior (especially driving them to the conclusion of international agreements), so demonstrating a persuasiveness stronger than that of many formal international binding rules. About the BEPS project, *see* A. Dourado, "The Base Erosion and Profit Shifting (BEPS) Initiative under Analysis", *Intertax*, Vol. 43, 2015, pp. 2-5, p. 2.

44 The strong ties between power to tax and transnational solidarity has been put in evidence, within the EU legal system, by A. Pantazatou, "Promoting solidarity in crisis times: Building on the EU Budget and the EU Funds", *Perspectives on Federalism*, Vol. 7, 2015, pp. 50-76, *passim*.

45 I refer to the multilateral convention to implement tax treaty-related measures to prevent BEPS (so called MLI), which came into force in July 2018 with the aim to modify the double taxation conventions of the States Parties according to the new rules and principles set out in the various actions of the BEPS project. An in-depth analysis of the new multilateral convention can be found in M. Lang et al, *The OECD Multilateral Instrument for Tax Treaties. Analysis and Effects*, Alphen aan den Rijn, Wolters Kluwer, 2018, *passim*.

tional treaties on the protection of human rights, must therefore induce a change in the way national courts interpret and apply internal rules. It is no longer acceptable for the latter to remain at the center of the activity of national courts, while rights provided by international and supranational law remain confined to cases where their application is consistent with the political conditions underlying the fiscal interest of the tax administration. The circulation of models of protection, which the new international course inevitably achieves, must on the contrary encourage the recognition that these rights are not alien to the internal legal order. On the contrary, they should positively influence it in order to make it coherent with the higher standards emerging in the international fora.

This is the way in which the dialogue between supranational, international and national judges could be strengthened: while the former will be called to intercept the evolutionary lines of the international context and to translate them into 'law in action', the latter will need to engage in the difficult task of adaptation to a new context. A dialogue that – considering the premises – becomes essential, as it is only thanks to it that the internal courts can abandon a uniquely 'nationalist' vision of the tax relation and consciously open themselves to the need to adapt their own rights and principles to those conceived in the international and supranational context, freeing them from the waste of juridical ideologies that are excessively 'sovereign'.

A genuine dialogue, and not merely an apparent one (as in some of the cases that have been referred to previously), appears to be the only instrument through which projecting the national jurisprudence at the center of European (including the ECHR system) evolution toward shared principles on the role of the taxpayer both in terms of his duties and in relation to his rights.

8.9 Conclusions: Some Proposals for Strengthening the Dialogue between the Courts in the Tax Area

Finally, some reflections on the most suitable instruments for realizing an effective dialogue between national and supranational courts on the protection of taxpayers' rights have to be made. The answer to the question may seem obvious. In the legal system of the EU, there is already the instrument of the reference for a preliminary ruling, which has been used for several decades in relation to tax disputes. In fact, it has been used so frequently that today many of the most significant decisions delivered by the CJEU concern tax issues.

With regard to the ECHR, the jurisprudence of the ECtHR has always been a reference for internal judges in the interpretation of conventional rules, given the fact that the latter are perceived as living norms continuously adapted to new needs precisely by the jurisprudence of the ECtHR. Furthermore, this role should be strengthened following the recent entry into force of the additional Protocol 16 to the ECHR, which provides for the possibility for national courts 'of the highest jurisdictions' to submit to the Court a request for an opinion concerning the interpretation and the application of the provisions of the Convention in concrete cases. The mechanism that has been deliberately made similar to the reference for a preliminary ruling system existing in the EU because of the desire of its creators to promote the dialogue between the judicial authorities.[46]

In reality, the above-mentioned procedures do not seem satisfactory. The advisory instrument envisaged by Protocol 16 has a very limited subjective scope covering only the highest jurisdictions (even with the exclusion of the Constitutional Court with regard to Italy). Therefore, judges of merit are excluded from its functioning and these are the courts which are highly engaged with the substance of the concrete case and, therefore, are often more attentive to a substantialist approach in balancing the opposing interests (of the tax authorities and taxpayers). Moreover, not only the beginning of the procedure is always optional, but also the opinion eventually delivered by the chamber established within the ECtHR is never binding, even with regard to the judgment which gave rise to the question.

Some perplexities arise with regard to the suitability of a mechanism of preliminary ruling to guarantee an effective and fair exchange of interpretative messages between national and supranational courts in the field of tax law. And these problems arise apart from the above-mentioned characteristics of the referral to the ECtHR according to Protocol 16 which are themselves profoundly differentiating the instrument in question from the EU preliminary ruling and are in some way weakening its effectiveness in the context of the dialogue between the courts. In fact, the preliminary ruling gives rise to a formal and public procedure which produces the risk that the conflicting positions may become even more rigid. The publicity that the outcome of the proceedings may have (and usually has) represents, in short, the greatest inconvenience, since often the involved courts prefer to assume more 'expendable' positions in the public debate, rather than making a serious effort toward a genuine dialogue.

The experience of the *Taricco* case – which was result of a reference for a preliminary ruling and concerns, although indirectly, a tax law issue – shows precisely how the media produced clamor of some events does contribute for genuine and sincere dialogue and is pushing instead a compromise in which one of the conflicting positions prevails and the other loses.[47]

---

46 *See* in that sense the Explanatory Report to Protocol 16, which recalls that according to the Group of Wise Persons "it would be useful to introduce a system under which the national courts could apply to the Court for advisory opinions on legal questions relating to interpretation of the Convention and the protocols thereto, in order to foster dialogue between courts and enhance the Court's 'constitutional' role." The Explanatory Report can be found at www.echr.coe.int/Documents/Protocol_16_explanatory_report_ENG.pdf.

47 The critical view expressed in this article is not common. Many scholars argue that the *Taricco* case is a positive example of dialogue between national courts and the EUCJ. *See* in the latter sense M. Bonelli, "The Taricco saga and the consolidation of judicial dialogue in the European Union", *Maastricht Journal of European and Comparative Law*, Vol. 25, 2018, pp. 357-373, p. 357.

Of course, this does not diminish the usefulness of this institute, which has helped over the years for the formation of a common European spirit also on many tax issues. However, it is necessary to imagine more meaningful places and means of dialogue, far from the excessive political and media pressure that sometimes surrounds the former and, therefore, capable of achieving a more fruitful compromise between conflicting positions.

For example, one could imagine wider forms of circulation of supranational court decisions in national jurisdictions and the institutionalization of informal mechanisms of joint training between tax judges of several European states. A model could be that of the coordination meetings that take place periodically within the Eurojust project.[48] The aim is to create supranational bodies that put together tax judges from the Member States of the European Union as well as the judges of supranational courts and which promote the dialogue and the exchange of knowledge between them. The joint training tool seems to be in fact suitable to allow an effective circulation of the interpretative models, thus favoring the identification of best practices to be replicated in the national context.

This is not a particularly new idea, since for many years, especially in the context of the EU, several initiatives have been put in place to develop dialogue and joint training for judges (and more generally of legal practitioners) of the Member States. The 2011 communication of the EU Commission entitled 'Building trust in EU-wide justice in new dimension to European judicial training' states the importance of creating a genuine European legal culture and recalls that "judicial training is a crucial element of this process enhances mutual confidence between Member States, practitioners and citizens". Even before, however, the Hague Program called for "the progressive creation of a European judicial culture [...] based on training and networking".[49]

However, this process is still largely unsatisfactory. First of all, significant progress has been made so far only with regard to criminal justice, in the presence of a clear foundation of the European action in the Treaties. On the contrary, in other areas of law – such as that of civil and commercial law – the initiatives undertaken have been much less incisive. This situation is linked to the absence of equally clear justifications in the treaty norms and to the incapacity, therefore, of the European institutions to undertake direct actions that are binding for the Member States. This entailed the adoption of bottom-up training systems: starting from the initiative of private bodies representing the categories of legal operators, they go on with the subsequent support of common training actions by the Commission that recommends the adoption of the same by the Member States.[50]

48 *See* A. Weyembergh, "The Development of Eurojust: Potential and Limitations of Article 85 of the TFEU", *New Journal of European Criminal Law*, Vol. 2, 2011, pp. 75-99, p. 75.

49 G. Oberoi, "Globalisation of the judicial education discourse", *Commonwealth Law Bulletin*, Vol. 38, 2012, pp. 393-421, p. 415.

50 H. Hartnell, "EUstitia: Institutionalizing Justice in the European Union", *Northwestern Journal of International Law & Business*, Vol. 23, 2002, pp. 113-117, p. 116.

As one can see, there is no binding power for the Commission, while every responsibility remains with the Member States, both at the level of support of exponential private organizations and then at the level of transposition of the Commission's guidelines.

In such less institutionalized context, the training of tax judges suffers from further problems. The Commission documents do not deal with tax matters and – apart from some sporadic exceptions – even the exponential bodies of the judiciaries of the Member States do not attach particular importance to this matter. The European Judicial Training Network, an institution created by the Member States in 2004, identified tax law as worthy of particular attention in the context of the activity of the working groups set up within it. However, no concrete initiatives seem to have been undertaken.

An intervention by the Commission in the direction of identifying common training tools on European tax law issues now seems to be prevented by the difficulty of attributing to the EU a general competence in the matter, but also by the fears of the states that such initiatives can have a negative influence on the independence of the judiciary in such a delicate area, even from a political point of view, such as that of taxes. There is also the tendency of the European institutions to enhance the principle of subsidiarity in this field too, limiting the common intervention only to those sectors where a clear European value added can be realized.[51]

It seems to me, however, that an alternative model can still be imagined. It could refer to the experience gained within the OECD, based on the development of guidelines that are not binding for the states but whose compliance is subject to periodic revision with a consequent (public) evaluation of the greater or lesser 'virtuosity' of one state over others. The absence of a legal constraint is filled by the risk of negative publicity that the incorrect transposition of the guidelines could generate – a situation capable of pushing many states to a spontaneous adaptation.

Hence, a mechanism of this kind could perhaps also be replicated for tax matters. One could think, given the importance of fundamental rights in the action of national tax courts, to a concerted action between the EU and the Council of Europe. This could produce guidelines or models of joint training of national tax judges, including linguistic ones, whose implementation – if appropriate through the establishment of bilateral or multilateral bodies – could then be monitored at central level (by the EU Commission, for example, or by the Council of Europe itself) according to a periodic peer review procedure.

Anyhow, the proper training of judges is fundamental in every legal system, but it is even more so in a supranational context, where – as we have seen – a compromise must be reached between two different ways of conceiving the tax relation, the internal and the European one. Therefore, the development of informal but institutionalized bodies aimed at achieving a steady dialogue between national and supranational jurisdictions seems to

---

51 S. Benvenuti, "The European Judicial Training Network and Its Role in the Strategy for the Europeanization of National Judges", *International Journal for Court Administration*, Vol. 7, 2015, pp. 59-67, p. 65.

be the most suitable solution to avoid judicial approaches excessively centered on the national level and to achieve a genuinely supranational – and therefore uniform – conception of the taxpayer's rights in the context of the tax relation.

Part III
Judicial Dialogue in Private International Law and International Dispute Settlement

9 Judicial Dialogue and the Pluralist Structure of the Legal Order at the Beginning of the Twenty-First Century

Florian Heindler

9.1 Judicial Dialogue and the Application of Foreign Law[1]

This chapter addresses the application of foreign law in civil and commercial matters. It discusses the notion of foreign and domestic law both from the perspective of the legal system and from the perspective of legal practitioners. Having regard to the pluralist structure of the legal order, it questions current prevailing trends in the application of foreign law and offers solutions and new approaches triggered by current and future developments and technological progress. The chapter discusses the existing rules and practices that govern the manner in which foreign law shall be determined. It also compares the concepts of 'foreign' and 'domestic' in courts of law and in arbitral tribunals. It recalls a statement by Magister Aldricus, who stated that the choice of a judge includes a choice of law because a judge is always deemed to apply his or her own law. Finally, it links this concept with the well-known and historically tested idea of tribunals composed of judges from different jurisdictions.

9.2 The Concept of Foreign and Domestic Law

The rules in private international law refer questions about the applicable law to the law of a particular state. If the rule that has to be applied according to private international law is not a rule of the *lex fori*, the court has to apply a foreign legal rule to the case. This distinction between 'domestic' and 'foreign' is used in this chapter as well, notwithstanding that the foreign rule may not be foreign but domestic to the parties or their representatives. However, one distinction shall be made at the outset: Foreign law typically, but not necessarily, refers to two concepts of foreign law contrary to domestic law. They are: (1) foreign law is foreign from the perspective of one particular legal order, that is, from the legal order of the state in which the court is situated, and (2) foreign law is foreign

1 The author would like to thank Stella Galehr for her editorial assistance.

from the perspective of the judges, that is, from the legal order in which the judges deciding on the legal matter have been trained.

The institutional approach (1) to defining the substantive law rule as foreign offers a very clear dualistic concept. On the one hand, there is domestic law, which consists of rules that have been enacted by the lawmaker of the state in which the court is situated, and on the other hand, there is foreign law, which consists of rules that have been enacted by any other lawmaker. If we, however, recognize that the structure of legal sources and their origin is more complex, or – in order to confirm the terminology of the conference headline – pluralist, the dualist approach to foreign and domestic law has a number of weaknesses. It ignores the supranational and international dimensions of the *lex fori*, in particular, international and supranational rules that have to be directly applied by the domestic court. These are, from a private international law perspective, integral parts of the domestic legal order. If private international law rules refer to, for example, Bulgarian law, it refers to both EU regulations and to the national statutes of Bulgaria. Moreover, they determine that EU regulations are directly applicable in the case if this is provided for by the Bulgarian legal order. The dualism of domestic and foreign law furthermore ignores the efforts of harmonization that have been undertaken successfully, such as anti-money laundering rules based on the Financial Action Task Force (FATF) recommendations, rules implementing EU directives, and international model laws (e.g., the United Nations Commission on International Trade Law [UNCITRAL] Model Law on electronic commerce) or international soft law instruments.[2]

The perspective of individual judges can be similarly diverse. Lawyers are not necessarily trained in only one legal order. Pluralism in legal education includes comparative law courses at universities, studies abroad, migration of lawyers to other jurisdictions and study programs that offer conceptional legal education without references to particular legal orders. Whereas lawyers in states with national codified civil law legislations like Austria, France, Germany and Russia may find such considerations surprising, lawyers from legal orders where different rules are applicable to various territorial units, such as Canada, the United Kingdom and the United States, or from legal orders where different rules are applicable to various groups of persons (interpersonal conflicts), such as India, have to be more flexible in acknowledging different systems of substantive civil or commercial laws.

In arbitral proceedings, parties may choose the arbiter. It is seldom the case that all of the arbiters in a tribunal have been trained in the same legal system. Notwithstanding that arbitration is preferred by many parties as it is a fast-track and efficient dispute resolution mechanism, the fact that arbiters have to deal with foreign law is not taken as problematic. Whether as a result of the greater flexibility and party autonomy in arbi-

2 *See* A. Makarov, *Grundriß des internationalen Privatrechts (Fundamentals of Private International Law)*, Frankfurt, Metzner, 1970, p. 81, suggesting to apply rules stemming from comparable legal systems in case of doubt.

tral proceedings or the greater responsibilities of parties to plead the law in comparison to the continental European approach to proceedings, parties entrust their cross-border cases freely to mixed tribunals and arbiters are able to decide the cases without unreasonable delay. One exception, however, applies to the aforesaid. The parties to arbitral proceedings take account of the difference between the common law and civil law origin of the arbiters. Thus, the parties presume that a lawyer trained in a civil law jurisdiction is able to decide on a case to which the law of (another) civil law jurisdiction is applied. However, they are rather hesitant to nominate judges to whom the applicable law is completely unfamiliar. Thus, a formal distinction between foreign and domestic is not regarded as necessary in the practice of international commercial arbitration.

However, the abovementioned does not mean that the distinction between foreign and domestic law is irrelevant. This distinction leads to a discussion about the difficulties in the application of foreign law and the escape rules if foreign law cannot be properly established. If an Austrian court has to decide a question of law concerning the matrimonial property of a Chinese couple according to a rule of Chinese law, the substantive rule of Chinese law is institutionally, and from the judge's individual perspective, foreign to him or her. However, the reflections about foreign and domestic substantive law offer a new aspect to the discussion about the application of foreign law that might be relevant for many other cases.

9.3 Information about the Content of Foreign Law

Textbooks and commentaries on private international law describe the possibilities and difficulties that arise if the content of foreign law has to be established.[3] Taking account of the difficulties that stem from the application of foreign law, possible solutions often aim at reducing the complexity. Some authors propose that private international law rules more often should refer to the *lex fori* instead of referring to other legislations that might, however, be more closely connected.[4] In order to avoid the application of foreign law, lawmakers and scholars advocate rules that align *forum* and law by using parallel wording

3 *E.g.*, B. Verschraegen, '§ 3 IPRG', *in* P. Rummel & M. Lukas (eds.), *Kommentar zum Allgemeinen bürgerlichen Gesetzbuch (Commentary on the Austrian Civil Code)*, Vienna, Manz, 2019, paras. 3-7; L. Raape & F. Sturm, *Internationales Privatrecht (Private International Law)*, Munich, Vahlen, 1977, pp. 307-313.

4 *E.g.*, A. Ehrenzweig, *Private International Law: A Comparative Treatise on American International Conflicts Law, Including the Law of Admiralty*, Leyden, A.W. Sijthoff, 1967, pp. 104-110.

in the rules on international jurisdiction and the applicable law.[5] Consequently, the rules on international jurisdiction would refer the dispute to the jurisdiction of, for example, the Austrian courts, and, in parallel, the rules on the applicable law would determine the application of Austrian law.

To the extent that the distinction between foreign and domestic can be reconsidered in accordance with the above-mentioned observations, the trend toward *lex fori* and the alignment of *forum* and law can be reconsidered as well. It is per se favorable if the conflict rules in the area of jurisdiction and applicable law can be drafted in parallel. Positive examples in this respect are, for example, Article 6, Rome I Regulation and Article 19, Brussels Ibis Regulation. However, the rules on jurisdiction and applicable law cannot always be drafted in identical language. In addition, parties still have the possibility to choose any foreign law that is not the *lex fori*.[6]

In many jurisdictions, different methods are used to determine the content of foreign law. First, the question arises as to whether the court itself has to determine the content of foreign law, or whether this obligation lies with the parties. Different approaches to this question are applied. The general approach depends on whether the relevant jurisdiction applies the ideology of adversary proceedings, concedes to the parties a decisive voice on the applicable law, and requires them to plead and prove the foreign law.[7] If the legal system does not require parties to generally plead the law, the party's obligations depend on whether foreign law is treated as fact or as law in the proceedings. It can be said that in several continental European legal systems, foreign law is already treated as law in proceedings.[8] Therefore, the content of foreign law must be identified by the court *ex officio* due to the principle of *iura novit curia*.[9] Also, surprisingly, mixed systems exist. In Lithuania, courts shall only establish the content of foreign law *ex officio*, if foreign law is applied through reference by an objective connecting factor. The law chosen by the parties is applied only if a party succeeds in determining the content of the foreign law.

---

5 *E.g.*, Regulation (EU) 650/2012 recital 27; Regulation (EU) 593/2008 recital 24; E.-M. Kieninger, 'Ermittlung und Anwendung ausländischen Rechts (Determination and Application of Foreign Law)', *in* S. Leible & H. Unberath (eds.), *Brauchen wir eine Rom O-Verordnung? Überlegungen zu einem allgemeinen Teil des europäischen IPR (Do we need a Regulation 'Rome O'? Reflections on the General Part of the European PIL)*, Jena, JWV, 2013, pp. 479, 491-494; M. Brosch, *Rechtswahl und Gerichtsstandsvereinbarung im internationalen Familien- und Erbrecht der EU (Choice of Law and Choice of Court Clauses in International Family and Succession Law of the EU)*, Tübingen, Mohr Siebeck, 2019, pp. 11-12.

6 *E.g.*, Art. 3 Regulation (EU) 593/2008; Art. 14 Regulation (EU) 864/2007; Art. 15 Convention of 13 January 2000 on the International Protection of Adults.

7 Ehrenzweig, 1967, pp. 179, 190; B. Lurger and M. Melcher, *Handbuch Internationales Privatrecht (Private International Law Handbook)*, Vienna, Verlag Österreich, 2017, pp. 24-25; P. Hay, 'Berücksichtigung von Aussagen ausländischer Regierungen zum eigenen Recht im US-amerikanischen Zivilprozess (Recognition of Foreign Governments' Declarations on Their Law in US-American Civil Procedure)', *IPRax*, No. 2, 2019, p. 169.

8 Raape & Sturm, 1977, p. 306; D. Bureau & H. Watt, *Droit international privé I*, Paris, PUF, 2014, p. 512.

9 Ehrenzweig, 1967, p. 182; F. Schwind, *Internationales Privatrecht (Private International Law)*, Vienna, Manz, 1990, pp. 56-57; *cf.* A. Junker, *Internationales Privatrecht (Private International Law)*, Munich, C.H. Beck, 2017, p. 187.

Otherwise, Lithuanian law shall apply.[10] This rule, however, is incompatible with the provisions about the freedom to choose the applicable law according to the EU Private International Law (PIL) instruments.[11] Notwithstanding the application of the *iura novit curia* principle, parties, to a different extent, are required to cooperate and, thus, shall assist the court in determining the content of the foreign law. The interest of the parties is to plead foreign law so that it supports their position in the legal dispute. Therefore, legal opinions, which were ordered by the parties, and provide favorable interpretations and expert discussions about the true content of foreign law occur both in adversary and nonadversary proceedings.

Courts use different methods to determine the content of foreign law.[12] They order independent expert opinions. Experts either give written advice or answer questions as witnesses. Diplomatic or counselor authorities are consulted as well and appear in court as witnesses or give written advice about the content of the law of their state. Specialized comparative law institutes such as the Institut Suisse de Droit Comparé in Lausanne, the Max Planck-Institut für ausländisches und internationales Privatrecht in Hamburg, or the Forschungsinstitut für mittel- und osteuropäisches Wirtschaftsrecht in Vienna often provide independent advice. Judges may also consult sources directly. In particular, legal statutes are more commonly available and special information databases provide up-to-date and reliable information (e.g. the succession law website of the Notaries of Europe network). The content of foreign law is available in academic publications, which are frequently consulted by courts if the respective publication is accessible. More rarely, courts decide to make use of information provided through information exchange, which should be carried out under the rules of bilateral and multilateral treaties. More importantly, judges consult formal and informal networks. Nowadays, the European Network of Councils for the Judiciary supports judges within the European Union in an effective manner. Integration and cross-border training have the welcome side-effects such as judges building informal networks that they might consult in order to receive or verify information (provided by the parties) about the content of the applicable foreign law.

9.4 Judicial Networking

A judge's initiative to cooperate in cross-border cases has to be welcomed. Contemporary communication technology allows more effective and swifter cooperation in cross-border cases. Scholars regularly emphasize that the application of foreign law could lead to the involvement of a foreign judge in the case, but legislative measures in that domain are

10 Art 1.12. Civil Code of the Republic of Lithuania (translation), https://e-seimas.lrs.lt (accessed 9 April 2019).

11 R. Plender & M. Wilderspin, *The European Private International Law of Obligations*, London, Thomson Reuters, 2015, p. 127.

12 For an overview and analysis *see* Ehrenzweig, 1967, pp. 191-193; Verschraegen, 2019, § 4 IPRG para 3-10.

difficult to agree upon. The idea of mixed tribunals is anything but new. In medieval Serbia, King *Stefan Milutin* allowed Saxon miners to exercise their own jurisdiction. Accordingly, conflicts between Ragusian and Saxon law emerged within his territory. The king ordered that a dispute between a Ragusian and Saxon party should be decided by a Saxon and a Ragusian judge jointly. The general approach applied by Magister Aldricus to decide upon disputes that involved a conflict of law issues was that parties, by electing the judge, had also elected his statutes and customs.[13]

The examples from history show a relaxed approach to territoriality and the exclusivity of exercising power through civil and commercial jurisdiction. This relaxed approach has been a reality in the realm of commercial arbitration for several decades. Mixed tribunals that consist of judges from various jurisdictions are not the exception but the rule in international commercial arbitration. The discourse among the judges sitting on the case is cross-border, like the case itself. Commercial courts need to catch up. Currently, a number of states try to create state courts that should compete with arbitral tribunals. The most famous examples are the Singapore International Commercial Court (SICC)[14] and the Netherlands Commercial Court (NCC), which has recently held its first hearing.[15] In order to effectively compete and provide up-to-date resolution mechanisms for international disputes, specialized commercial courts require a more diverse panel of judges. A more flexible approach is thus required, in particular, when states want to establish attractive and internationally competitive state dispute resolution centers for commercial cases.

9.5 The Application of the Foreign Rule and Its Effects

Throughout all legal professions, including legal doctrine, different views exist on whether foreign law shall be treated as a law or as a fact. The question is relevant in order to decide whether a claim can be dismissed or the application of foreign law can be denied if the parties have failed to prove the content of foreign law.[16] It is also relevant with regard to the admissibility of filing an appeal.[17]

The current approach, which distinguishes and strictly separates foreign and domestic law, leads to a number of consequences. One consequence is that judgments applying foreign law do not contribute to the development of the legal system of the respective foreign jurisdiction. This means that when courts apply foreign law, the effect of that

13 Codex Chisianus E VII 218, para. 46.

14 https://www.sic.gov.sg (accessed 23 April 2019).

15 G. Antonopoulou & X. Kramer 2019, http://conflictoflaws.net/2019/the-netherlands-commercial-court-holds-its-first-hearing/ (accessed 23 April 2019).

16 *See, e.g., Cuba R. Co. v. Crosby*, 222 U.S. 473, 477 (1912); *see also, e.g., Wall Street Traders Inc. v. Sociedad Española de Construcción Naval*, 236 F. Supp. 358 (S.D.N.Y. 1963); critical Currie 1963, pp. 3-76.

17 *See, e.g.*, U.S. Supreme Court, 14 June 2018, *Animal Science Products, Inc. et al. v. Hebei Welcome Pharmaceutical Co. Ltd. et al.*, 138 S.Ct. 1865 (2018), 2018 WL 297345.

judgment is irrelevant for the legal development of the foreign legal system.[18] This holds true for a case law system as well as for a system where court rulings have a less formal or authoritative precedential effect. Whereas courts have to take into consideration domestic judgments applying the *lex fori*, foreign judgments on their *lex fori* are not regarded as court practice that has a formal standing as a source of law. However, they may take into consideration any foreign judgment, applying any comparable foreign legal rule, notwithstanding whether the comparable rule stems from the *lex fori*. However, the use of such a comparative legal method is less frequent. For example, a French court delivers a judgment, interpreting a German legal rule. If, two years later, the same or another French court has to apply a German legal rule again, it shall resort to the interpretation of the German courts instead of interpreting the relevant French ruling delivered two years earlier. This rule verifies whether the court practice established earlier is still up-to-date. However, German courts interpreting the very same rule are not required to explain whether they agree with the interpretation by the French court. There are manifold reasons to argue that the development of a legal system through the interpretation of its legal rules shall remain within the exclusive competence of domestic courts. However, approaches that are too formal raise concerns. In a case decided by the Regional Court of Munich (*Landesgericht München*), the court relied on the practice of the majority of the Austrian courts.[19] Shortly after the decision of the Regional Court of Munich was issued, the Austrian Supreme Court (*Oberster Gerichtshof*), in a landmark decision, explicitly abandoned its former case law.[20] This unambiguous shift in the Austrian court's practice, welcomed throughout legal doctrine,[21] appeared too late for the German parties. In the light of the fact that in Germany the incorrect application of foreign law is not subject to revision by the German Supreme Court (*Bundesgerichtshof*), the parties could not overturn the German decision. The shift in the Austrian court practice would have had no impact on a hypothetical appeal in Germany (German courts applying Austrian law).[22]

Major problems arise for the court that applies foreign law when the content of the foreign law is unclear in relation to its case. Courts in civil and commercial matters have to decide about the pending case. Doubts about the content of the foreign law may arise

18 Ehrenzweig, 1967, p. 193.

19 Landesgericht München, 18 April 2013, 10 O 6084/12 = IPRax 2014, 438; D. Looschelders, 'Die Rechtsstellung des gewerblichen Erbensuchers im deutsch-österreichischen Rechtsverkehr (Legal Position of Professional Searchers of Heirs in German-Austrian Cases)', *IPRax*, No. 5, 2014, p. 406.

20 Oberster Gerichtshof, 21 August 2014, 3 Ob 228/13w = IPRax 2016, 73 = EvBl 2015, 230 (annotation by Katharina Huber) = Zak 2014, 367 (annotation by Lena Kolbitsch, Dominik Prankl & David Messner).

21 F. Heindler, 'Der unbekannte Geschäftsherr: Erbensuche in Österreich (The Unknown Principal: Searching Heirs in Austria)', *IPRax*, No. 1, 2016, 79 with further references.

22 Critical in general with regard to restriction of appeal M. Wolff, *Das internationale Privatrecht Deutschlands (German Private International Law)*, Göttingen, Springer, 1954, p. 85.

easily since the foreign court is bound to statutes and court practice and cannot mobilize the mobile qualities and thrusts of principle[23] that it would discern in domestic law. It is very difficult for a court to make an argument on the content of foreign law based on reasoning by analogy, if there is no respective precedent or court practice in the foreign jurisdiction. In cases where there is insufficient case law (or a gap in the case law), similar to the situation in international law, courts should rely on the prevailing doctrine. However, according to the prevailing doctrine, applying foreign law differs from applying domestic law. A court that applies foreign law is barred from providing its own interpretation of the foreign rule. Expert witnesses and affidavits report the relevant statute and its interpretation by the courts, as well as the relevant prevailing opinion in the doctrine. However, witnesses shall not give their personal preferences on the interpretation of the rule or whether one doctrinal approach is more convincing than another. In the case of an absence of court practice and doctrinal views, or in the case of convergent views in the doctrine, the court still has to apply the foreign law but is barred from mobilizing the mobile qualities and thrusts of principle that it would discern in domestic law.

A court applying foreign law could find itself in a very different position given that it has to decide the dispute in accordance with the foreign law but does not find guidance from available sources. The retreat to domestic law contradicts the private international law regimes and ignores the legitimate expectations of the parties, in particular, in a situation where the parties have chosen the applicable law. Such application of the foreign law as domestic *ius gentium* is foreign to arbitral tribunals. State courts have to decide disputes as well. They cannot dismiss a claim, explaining that there is a lack of judicial precedent in the case law or court practice of the foreign state. Retreat to domestic rules would result in even more unexpected results than the application of foreign law. Therefore, state courts have to make use of the rules of interpretation of foreign law and try to mobilize its particular qualities and make use of its principles. Witness experts, however, should merely report about the content of foreign legislation and court practice and should not develop solutions as if they were judges in the foreign jurisdiction. However, if accordingly instructed, they could explain the rules regarding the interpretation and the way in which the decision was made by the respective foreign courts if the relevant rule of law is unclear. Nevertheless, it should be the court seized that has to decide and apply the foreign law, and if necessary, develop solutions as if it were a court in the foreign jurisdiction. Again, the distinction between foreign and domestic law must not be regarded as set in stone, leading to a lack of flexibility.

It is a given that a legal provision might be less or more foreign either to the legal system or to the judge. The concept of foreign law, therefore, is to some extent vague and

---

23 For the background of legal principles *see* F. Heindler, 'Conceptual Approaches to the Codification of International Law', *in* A. Annoni, S. Forlati & F. Salerno (eds.), *La codificazione nell'ordinamento internazionale e dell'Unione europea (XXIII Convegno – Ferrara 2018) (Codification in International and European Union Law)*, Napoli, Editoriale Scientifica, 2019, pp. 59, 62-67.

to some extent requires flexible approaches. Accordingly, courts should actively involve themselves in the discussion of foreign law to the extent that the particular circumstances of the case allow it.

9.6 Conclusions

The analysis started with a critical appraisal of the distinction between foreign and domestic in the application of a law other than the *lex loci* by a court in civil and commercial matters. It was argued that both for individual judges and for the legal system, the rule can be more foreign or less foreign. Using this observation as a starting point, a number of problems of applying foreign legal rules were discussed. A more nuanced approach to foreign and domestic law would enable a court to apply the foreign law in a more flexible manner. It would also enable the court to question the treatment of foreign law as different to the treatment of domestic law, as is the case currently in many jurisdictions. It was emphasized that a more open approach is preferable in relation to the question of how the content of foreign law can be determined. The use of contemporary communication technology and formal and informal networks coincides with a more flexible approach to the concepts of foreign and domestic. The judicial dialogue in a pluralist system of legal order affects civil courts dealing with cross-border cases as well. The application of foreign law will always be current, and an up-to-date approach should include a dialogue between lawyers who are trained and practicing in different jurisdictions.

10 The CJEU's Extensive Conception of the EU Legal Order – An Impediment to Judicial Dialogue: CJEU's Achmea Case, a Just Judicial War?

François Andia

10.1 Introduction

In *The Prince*, Nicolo Machiavelli narrated the insurgent *condottieri*'s assassination by Cesar Borgia. He had used the *bons offices* of Signor Pagolo to reconcile with them and had invited them to a banquet where he ordered their strangulation. Machiavelli also related Oliverotto da Fermo's avunculicide. Both murders had political motivations: to obtain a principality. However, Machiavelli qualified the latter as a 'wickedness' and described the former as a feat.[1] After his forfeit, Cesar Borgia sent a letter to his neighboring States, justifying his acts. His contemporaneous, notably Louis XII, King of France, applauded. Wars could be just, and so could assassinations.[2]

A lot more recently, the German Federal Court of Justice was requested by the Slovak Republic to set aside the award of an Arbitral Tribunal[3] founded on Article 8 of a bilateral investment agreement between the Kingdom of the Netherlands and the Slovak Republic (the Bilateral Investment Treaties [BIT]).[4] Under this arbitration clause, the tribunal has jurisdiction over "[a]ll disputes between one Contracting Party and an investor of the other Contracting Party concerning an investment...". The petitioning State notably argued that Articles 267 and 344 of the Treaty on the Functioning of the European Union (TFEU) preclude this arbitration clause. The German judge requested the Court of Justice of the European Union (CJEU) to issue a preliminary ruling on this matter.

---

1 Nicolo Machiavelli, *The Prince*, The Project Gutenberg Ebook, 2016, Chapter VII – Concerning New Principalities Which Are Acquired Either by the Arms of Others of by Good Fortune, and Chapter VIII – Concerning Those Who Have Obtained a Principality by Wickedness.

2 Georges Minois, *Le couteau et le poison: L'assassinat politique en Europe (1400-1800)*, Paris, Arthème Fayard, 1997, Chapitre Premier, Section Le crime élevé à la dignité d'instrument ordinaire de la politique: les Borgia.

3 Judgment of 6 March 2018 in *Case 248/16, Slovak Republic v. Achmea BV (Achmea)*, ECLI:EU:C:2018:158, para. 12.

4 *Agreement on encouragement and reciprocal protection of investments between the Kingdom of the Netherlands and the Czech and Slovak Federal Republic*, signed in Prague, 29 April 1991.

The CJEU's answer in the *Achmea* case may be compared to a political murder. Its decision has been described as a potentially fatal blow to intra-EU investment arbitration motivated by political ulterior reasons.[5]

The CJEU first highlighted the role of Articles 267 and 344 TFEU in structuring the EU legal order autonomy. They institute the preliminary ruling procedure and establish the exclusivity of dispute settlement mechanisms provided by the Treaties. As such, they create "a judicial system intended to ensure consistency and uniformity in the interpretation of EU law".[6] Then, the CJEU checked whether the arbitration clause allowed interpretation and application of EU law to 'escape' this specific judicial system. To do so, it applied a double test. First, can the Arbitral Tribunal apply or interpret EU law?[7] Second, can it request preliminary ruling to the CJEU or are its awards under a complete control of domestic judges?[8] The CJEU answered the first question positively and the second negatively. It appeared that the arbitration clause created a breach in the EU legal order, in so far as it could "prevent ... disputes from being resolved in a manner that ensures the full effectiveness of EU law",[9] and alter the unity of interpretation. The CJEU concluded that it "has an adverse effect on the autonomy of EU law" and is precluded by Articles 267 and 344 of the TFEU.[10]

Prior to this, the Arbitral Tribunal also had to decide on this matter. It first maintained that "no rule of EU law ... prohibits investor-State arbitration"[11] and that Article 344 TFEU solely applies to Member States' disputes.[12] It then recognized that although its jurisdiction is "confined to ruling upon alleged breaches of the BIT",[13] it may have to use EU law provided that it has "a bearing upon the scope of rights and obligations under the BIT".[14] The said EU law was said to contain "the EU legal doctrines, including those of supremacy, precedence, direct effect, and direct applicability".[15] However, the Arbitral Tribunal observed that "[n]either Party in the present case argued that any specific provision of EU law bore upon the case in a manner that would affect the decision or reasoning of the Tribunal under this particular BIT".[16]

Hence, the Arbitral Tribunal had seemingly taken every precaution to be respectful of the EU legal order. It limited its jurisdiction to alleged violations of the BIT, recognized

5 Hervé Guyader, 'La fin de l'arbitrage d'investissement intra-européen?', *Droit des Affaires*, No. 141, October 2018, p. 31.
6 *Case 248/16, Achmea*, paras. 32-37.
7 *Ibid.*, paras. 39-42.
8 *Ibid.*, paras. 43-53.
9 *Ibid.*, para. 56.
10 *Ibid.*, paras. 59-60.
11 PCA, Award on jurisdiction, arbitrability and suspension of 26 October 2010, *Eureko B. V. v. The Slovak Republic*, Case No. 2008-13, para. 274.
12 *Ibid.*, para. 276.
13 *Ibid.*, para. 290.
14 *Ibid.*, para. 279.
15 *Ibid.*, para. 289.
16 PCA, Final award of 7 December 2012, *Eureko B.V. v. The Slovak Republic*, Case No. 2008-13, para. 275.

the specificity of the EU legal order, stated that relevant EU law should be taken into consideration when applying the BIT provisions and, finally, controlled whether the EU law had any bearing on the current dispute. Hence, it recognized the coexistence of the two legal orders and the necessity to articulate them. In a nutshell, it established what could have been the basis for a judicial dialogue. Yet, the CJEU declared this Tribunal's arbitration clause a threat to the EU legal order's autonomy.

This contrast raises the issue of the justness of this 'assassination'. While the EU legal construction might have a greater legitimacy than the numerous intra-EU BITs, generally concluded before the adhesion to the EU and its common market, the CJEU's motivation must be analyzed. To what extent was the CJEU's decision necessary to protect the EU legal order autonomy from this 'outside' arbitrator?

This decision is based upon the possibility for an Arbitral Tribunal to interpret and apply EU law, but it does not take into consideration the fact that EU law could only be used incidentally (***10.2***). This distinction should have led the Court to moderate its answer and to prefer a more proportionate answer to the potential threat that such use could really pose to the EU legal order autonomy (***10.3***).

10.2 The Arbitral Tribunal Could Only Apply EU Law as to Ascertain Preliminary 'Legal Facts' and to Shape the BIT's Provisions

While the Arbitral Tribunal actually confined its jurisdiction to disputes related to the interpretation or application of the BIT, it also stated that EU law is part of the applicable law under Article 8(6) of the BIT.[17] The Court did not attach importance to this distinction. Instead, it merely expressed mistrust toward this Arbitral system, refusing to take for granted the Tribunal's delimitation of its jurisdiction.[18] As EU law is part of the applicable law, the Court simply concluded that an Arbitral Tribunal constituted under this arbitration clause has jurisdiction to hear disputes which "are liable to relate to the interpretation or application of EU law".[19]

There is, however, a 'cardinal' distinction between jurisdiction and applicable law.[20] The Tribunal's jurisdictional self-restrain (***6.2.1***) meant that EU law could only be applied to ascertain preliminary legal facts or to shape the BIT's provisions (***6.2.2***).

17 PCA, Award on Jurisdiction, *Eureko v. Slovak Republic*, paras. 289-290.

18 *Case 248/16, Achmea*, paras. 40-42.

19 *Ibid.*, para. 39.

20 PCA, Order No. 3 Suspension of Proceedings on Jurisdiction and Merits and Request for Further Provisional Measures of 24 June 2003, *The MOX Plant Case (Ireland v. United Kingdom)*, para. 19.

10.2.1 The Tribunal Confined Its Jurisdiction

The wording of arbitration clauses in BITs is very diverse. Some only refer to alleged breaches of part of the BIT's provisions.[21] Some refer to any breaches of the BIT.[22] And finally, others refer largely to any disputes related to an investment.[23] The BIT under scrutiny pertains to the latter. Article 8(1) is worded as follows:

> All disputes between one Contracting Party and an investor of the other Contracting Party concerning an investment of the latter....

Interpretation of such broad wording has not been unanimous. While some tribunals consider it as covering claims not based on the BIT,[24] others refuse to adopt this reading.[25] Commenting the *Vivendi v. Argentine*,[26] the *SGS v. Pakistan*,[27] and the *SGS v. Philippines*[28] cases, Yuval Shany emphasized the "discrepancies in the operative parts of the three awards – that is [notably], different holding on whether ICSID arbitral panels are competent to review contract claims".[29] In the *SGS v. Pakistan* case, for instance, the Arbitral Tribunal adopted a restrictive reading considering that the wording "while descriptive of the *factual subject matter* of the disputes, does not relate to the *legal basis* of the claims, or the *cause of action* asserted in the claims", and concluded that without these last precisions it could not consider that the clause covers non-BITs claims.[30] Yuvak Shany describes this vision as *disintegrationist* as it faces overlapping and entangling normative systems by "draw[ing] lines of separation between legal regimes and judicial

21 For instance, Art. 9(2), *Accord entre le Gouvernement de la République française et le Gouvernement de la République populaire hongroise sur l'encouragement et la protection réciproques des investissements*, Paris, 6 November 1986.

22 For instance, Art. XII(2), *Agreement between the Government of the Republic of Croatia and the Government of Canada for the Promotion and Protection of Investments*, 3 February 1997.

23 For instance, Art. 8(2), *Agreement between Bosnia and Herzegovina and the Council of Ministers of the Republic of Albania on the Reciprocal Promotion and Protection of Investments*, 17 June 2008.

24 ICSID Tribunal, Award of 11 September 2007, *Parkerings-Companiet AS v. Republic of Lithuania*, ARB/05/8, para. 261.

25 UNCITRAL, Decision on Jurisdiction of 30 April 2010, *Oostergetel v. the Slovak Republic*, para. 185.

26 ICSID Tribunal, Award of 21 November 2000, *Compañia de Aguas del Aconquija v. Argentine Republic*, ARB/97/3.

27 ICSID Tribunal, Award of 6 August 2003, *SGS Société Générale de Surveillance S.A. v. Islamic Republic of Pakistan*, ARB/01/13.

28 ICSID, Award on Jurisdiction of 29 January 2004, *SGS Société Générale de Surveillance S.A. v. Republic of the Philippines*, ARB/02/6.

29 Yuval Shany, 'Contract Claims vs. Treaty Claims: Mapping Conflicts between ICSID Decisions on Multi-sourced Investment Claims', *The American Journal of International Law*, Vol. 99, No. 4, October 2005, p. 835.

30 *SGS v. Pakistan*, para. 161.

proceedings".[31] Beyond the philosophical issue, this solution adds an unnecessary requirement to the consensual jurisdiction principle.

This solution set as a principle that a judge or arbitrator is confined to the legal order where it finds its jurisdiction. A principle that could only be overridden by an explicit clause on possible causes of action. There is, however, nothing indicating that an investment Arbitral Tribunal's function is in principle to be limited to the interpretation and application of its BIT. A judge may well 'travel' between legal orders. For instance, in the *Antoine Goetz v. Burundi* case, the arbitrator first analyzed the litigious actions under domestic law, concluding to their legality,[32] and then under international law, concluding that they are licit provided Burundi compensates the investor.[33] Moreover, States may want to establish an arbitration clause to provide investors with a neutral jurisdiction to settle every issue related to their investments, guaranteeing them impartiality whether their cause of action is related to the BIT or not. A solution that could in addition avoid the potential discrepancy between the law applicable to a situation and the law applicable by the arbitrator.[34] In any case, to determine whether this has been the choice of the contracting States, the arbitrator should only refer to their consent, principally expressed in the arbitration clause.[35] The consensual jurisdiction principle is sufficiently strict to avoid adding other restrictions.

Based on the *Vivendi v. Argentine* case, James Crawford indeed suggested an *integrationist* view. "[C]ontractual jurisdiction can be invoked under any sufficiently clear generic dispute settlement clause in a BIT ...", provided that the claim meets the arbitration clause criteria, that is, the contract is related to an investment and binds the hosting State, and is not contrary to another exclusive jurisdiction clause contained in the contract.[36]

In 2014, Christoph Schreuer reviewed arbitral jurisprudence on the interpretation of such jurisdictional clauses and concluded that despite some hesitation at the beginning, the tendency was nowadays clearly toward a broad interpretation.[37]

In the *Achmea* case, the arbitration clause was sufficiently broad to encompass disputes related to alleged EU law breaches if connected to an investment. However, the Arbitral Tribunal confined its jurisdiction to alleged violations of the BIT, thus avoiding

31 Shany, 2005, p. 844.

32 ICSID Tribunal, Award of 10 February 1999, *Antoine Goetz et consorts c. République du Burundi*, ARB/95/3, paras. 100-119.

33 *Ibid.*, paras. 120-133.

34 On this distinction *see* Mathias Forteau, 'Repenser la logique de traitements des rapports entre ordres juridiques, Changer de regard: tout ne serait-il pas affaire de droit applicable, plutôt que d'ordres juridiques?', *in* S. Bonnet (ed.), *Traité des rapports entre ordres juridiques*, Paris, LGDJ, 2016.

35 For the ICJ method on this subject, *see* Robert Kolb, *The International Court of Justice*, Oxford, Hart Publishing, 2013, pp. 400-401.

36 James Crawford, 'Treaty and Contract in Investment Arbitration', *Arbitration International*, Vol. 24, No. 3, 2008, pp. 362-363.

37 Christoph Schreuer, 'Jurisdiction and Applicable Law in Investment Treaty Arbitration', *McGill Journal of Dispute Resolution*, Vol. 1, No. 1, 2014, pp. 7-10.

the question of the exclusive jurisdiction of the EU legal system. This solution surely clarified its intent toward the EU legal order. It does not resolve, however, the question of the discrepancy between its jurisdiction and the applicable law. Indeed, "[o]ne might expect that the rules on applicable law in treaties would correspond to their rules on jurisdiction".[38]

10.2.2 *EU Law Is Indeed Applicable, but Solely as to Ascertain 'Legal Facts' and to Shape the BIT's Provisions*

There are other instances of nonmatching jurisdiction and applicable law clauses. Some BITs with narrow arbitration clauses include broader applicable law clauses[39] and vice versa.[40] The phenomenon also exists outside of the investment law field. For instance, while Article 288(1) of the United Nations Convention for the Law of the Sea (UNCLOS) provides jurisdiction over dispute "concerning the interpretation or application of this Convention", Article 293(1) contains a broader applicable law clause, including "other rules of international law not incompatible with this Convention".

This discordance in UNCLOS has caused jurisprudential divergence. On the one hand, the International Tribunal on the Law of the Sea in the *Saiga (No. 2)* case, and the Annex VII Arbitral Tribunal in the *Guyana/Surinam* case, have interpreted Article 293 UNCLOS as expanding their jurisdiction to matters related to the use of force, even though this question was not a prerequisite to the resolution of a question related to the interpretation and application of UNCLOS.[41] On the other hand, the Annex VII Arbitral Tribunal in the *MOX Plant* case has highlighted the 'cardinal' distinction between jurisdiction and applicable law clauses and concluded that the latter cannot enlarge its jurisdiction.[42]

There is no doubt that the applicable law clause can refine the judge's and the arbitrator's power when his or her jurisdiction *ratione materiae* is solely defined by a factual subject matter. In arbitration, it is common to first designate a dispute to resolve, and then a corpus of law to be applied. However, an applicable law clause should not be interpreted as to expand a jurisdiction limited by a dispute resolution clause.[43] The object

38 *Ibid.*, p. 13.

39 For instance, *Agreement on Encouragement and Reciprocal Protection of Investments between the Kingdom of the Netherlands and the Argentine Republic*, 20 October 1992; *see also* Schreuer, 2014, pp. 13-16.

40 For instance, *Agreement between Bosnia and Herzegovina and the Government of the Italian Republic on the Promotion and Protection of Investments*, 19 May 2000; *see also* Schreuer, 2014, pp. 13-16.

41 ITLOS, Judgment of 1 July 1999, *The M/V 'Saiga' (No. 2) Case (Saint Vincent and the Grenadines v. Guinea)*, para. 155; PCA, Award of 17 September 2007, *In the Matter of an Arbitration Between Guyana and Suriname*, para. 405.

42 PCA, Order No. 3 Suspension of Proceedings on Jurisdiction and Merits and Request for Further Provisional Measures of 24 June 2003, *The MOX Plant Case (Ireland v. United Kingdom)*, para. 19.

43 *See* PCA, Award of 18 March 2015, *In the matter of the Chagos Marine Protected Area Arbitration between the Republic of Mauritius and the United Kingdom of Great Britain and Northern Ireland*, para. 181.

of the applicable law clause is not to establish the judge's jurisdiction, but to define on which basis it may resolve a dispute. It is inappropriate to seek in the applicable law clause an autonomous consent to a different jurisdiction. A reading of Article 293 UNCLOS ordinary meaning gives out the same conclusion – the applicable law clause is only to be read once jurisdiction is established. Article 293 UNCLOS applies to "court and tribunal *having* jurisdiction".[44]

Lorand Bartels suggested the following articulation for the two clauses. They can both define the corpus of law, alleged breaches of which is a dispute under the arbitrator's jurisdiction.[45] However, the applicable law clause acts as *lex specialis*; when the jurisdiction provision already limits the potential causes of actions, the applicable clause cannot expand them.[46] However, it may have a complementary effect as far as it determines corpuses of law that can be used to determine incidental questions.[47] To explain this last point, Lorand Bartels introduces another distinction based on the norm's function in a case and which can be drawn between principal and incidental laws. Principal law is the basis of the claim, the corpus that has allegedly been breached, and that the judge is asked to interpret and apply in order to resolve the dispute. Incidental law covers other corpuses of law that are relevant for incidental determinations, that is, to determine the validity, applicability and interpretation of the principal norm[48] necessary to ascertain preliminary legal facts.[49] A distinction that is not to be confused with the one established by Herbert Hart between primary and secondary norms.[50]

Hence, a tribunal whose jurisdiction is limited to a given treaty may evaluate the validity of its provisions under a customary *jus cogens* norm or under another posterior treaty,[51] even though it would not have competence to resolve disputes related to this norm or that treaty as such. It could also use another corpus of law to interpret the said provisions. In the *South China Sea* arbitration, the Arbitral Tribunal recognized such a role to the Convention on Biological Diversity.[52] Finally, a tribunal could apply other corpuses of law to determine preliminary legal facts necessary for the application of the

44 *United Nations Convention on the Law of the Sea*, Montego Bay, 10 December 1982, Art. 8; *see* Peter Tzeng, 'Jurisdiction and Applicable Law Under UNCLOS', *The Yale Law Journal*, Vol. 126, No. 1, 2016, p. 246.

45 Laurent Bartels, 'Jurisdiction and Applicable Law Clauses: Where Does a Tribunal Find the Principal Norms Applicable to the Case before It?', *in* Tomer Broude and Yuval Shany (eds.), *Multi-Sourced Equivalent Norms in International Law*, Oxford, Hart Publishing, 2011, pp. 120-123.

46 *Ibid.*, pp. 123-130.

47 *Ibid.*, pp. 137-141.

48 *Ibid.*, pp. 137-140.

49 *Ibid.*, p. 140.

50 *Ibid.*, p. 120.

51 Nothing in international law practice would oppose such evaluation; it is however more likely that such issue would be studied at the preliminary phase under the judge's *competence de la competence*.

52 PCA, Award on Jurisdiction and Admissibility of 29 October 2015, *In the Matter of an Arbitration between the Republic of the Philippines and the People's Republic of China*, para. 176.

principal law. For instance, municipal law may have to be applied to establish the property of a person over shares prior to the application of a BIT.[53] And in the *Oil Platforms* case, the international law framing the use of force was relevant to determine whether a measure was 'necessary' to protect security interests, a requirement under Article XX of the 1955 Treaty of Amity between Iran and the United States.[54]

It is, however, not to be concluded that the scope of incidental law is limited by an applicable law clause. In the *Oil Platforms* case, the 1955 Treaty of Amity did not contain an applicable law clause. As Christoph Schreuer stated, "the existence and contents of a rule on applicable law appears to be of little or no consequence. A rule on choice of law that does not include domestic law is not an obstacle to its application".[55]

Finally, the distinction principal/incidental law complements the distinction principal/ancillary dispute. The former relates to the means at the judge's disposal to resolve a dispute, and the latter relates to the extent of his or her jurisdiction. In the *Chagos Marine Protected Area* case,[56] the UNCLOS was the principal law, and Mauritius asked the Tribunal to apply international law related to territorial sovereignty as to first determine whether it was the coastal State. However, the Tribunal had no jurisdiction as the sovereignty dispute was in fact the principal dispute and not just ancillary to the dispute related to the UNCLOS.[57] It is then to be concluded that a tribunal whose jurisdiction is limited to disputes related to alleged breaches of a given corpus of law may apply another corpus to ascertain legal facts as a prerequisite to the application of the principal law, only to the extent that such determination is not the principal dispute.

Hence, before the Arbitral Tribunal in the *Achmea* case, EU law was only applicable as incidental law. It could only be used to analyze the validity, applicability and interpretation of the BIT provision or to ascertain preliminary legal facts provided that the alleged breach of the BIT is a principal and not an ancillary dispute. This conclusion is partly visible in the Tribunal award, as it declared not having "jurisdiction to rule on alleged breaches of EU law as such"[58] and accepted the applicability of EU law solely to the extent that it "may have a bearing upon the scope of rights and obligations under the BIT".[59] Such use is very limited and could in fact help shaping the BIT's provision in a way that would not 'shock' the EU legal order.

---

53 ICSID, Award of 2 September 2011, *Libananco Holdings Co. Limited v. Republic of Turkey*, ARB/06/8, para. 112.

54 ICJ, Judgment of 6 November 2003, *Oil Platforms (Islamic Republic of Iran v. United States of America), I.C.J. Reports 2003*, paras. 41-42 and 78.

55 Schreuer, 2014, pp. 20.

56 PCA, Award of 18 March 2015, *Chagos Marine Protected Area*.

57 *Ibid.*, para. 221.

58 PCA, Award on Jurisdiction, *Eureko v. Slovak Republic*, para. 290.

59 *Ibid.*, para. 279.

10.3 APPLICATION OF EU LAW AS INCIDENTAL LAW DOES NOT CALL FOR THE SAME MEANS OF PROTECTION OF THE EU AUTONOMOUS LEGAL ORDER

The CJEU has concluded that the interpretation and application of EU law by an Arbitral Tribunal, in the absence of a uniform and complete control over its awards, is jeopardizing the EU legal order autonomy. As previously explained, the CJEU did not take into consideration potential differences existing between the uses of EU law as principal or incidental law. Yet, judges have in multiple instances used corpus of law coming from distinct legal orders without creating a havoc in them. It is counterintuitive to consider that the use by an Arbitral Tribunal of EU law in order to shape the BIT's provision or to determine preliminary and ancillary legal facts would endanger the EU legal order's autonomy.

For the following part, the notion of 'legal order' should be understood as a coherent aggregate of norms, structured by a set of secondary norms.[60]

In the *Achmea* case, the CJEU notably insisted on the importance of the unity of interpretation and on the preservation of the EU 'constitutional structure'.[61] These two points, the first being allowed by the specific EU judicial system and the second being composed of principles such as the direct effect or the supremacy principles, are indeed a direct cause of the existence and autonomy of the EU legal order.[62] This explains the CJEU's strict position related to its 'monopoly' of interpretation.[63] Without unity of interpretation, the aggregate of norms, the EU law, would not be a homogenous group. It would have been fragmented into several versions of the same norms, depending of the Member State applying them. A judge's dialogue could have been possible between the different States, but it would not have been as efficient as the current system. Similarly, without application of the supremacy and direct effect principles, EU law would have been, at least in part, overtaken by the architecture and hierarchy of municipal law.[64]

It should already be specified that the mere interpretation and application of EU law by an 'outside' judge is not endangering the EU legal order. There would only be a risk provided that the award is to be integrated into the EU legal order. An 'outside' judge may apply EU law, as the choice of law, to a completely 'foreign' situation without affect-

60 Georges Abi-Saab and Maryline Grange, 'Repenser la notion d'ordre juridique', *in* S. Bonnet (ed.), *Traité des rapports entre ordres juridiques*, Paris, LGDJ, 2016, pp. 483-487.

61 *Case 248/16, Achmea*, paras. 33-35.

62 Jean-Claude Gautron and Sébastien Platon, 'La naissance d'une singularité doctrinale: les européanistes', *in* S. Bonnet (ed.), *Traité des rapports entre ordres juridiques*, Paris, LGDJ, 2016, p. 111.

63 Opinion of 14 December 1991, *1/91 Draft Agreement Relating to the Creation of the European Economic Area*, ECLI:EU:C:1991:490; *see also* Opinion of 28 March 1994, *2/94 Accession to the European Convention for the Protection of Human Rights and Fundamental Freedoms*, ECLI:EU:C:1996:140; Opinion of 18 December 2014, *2/13 Agreement on the Accession of the European Union to the European Convention for the Protection of Human Rights and Fundamental Freedoms*, ECLI:EU:C:2014:2454.

64 *See* Judgement of 15 July 1964, *Case 6-64 Flaminio Costa v. E.N.E.L.*, ECLI:EU:C:1964:66.

ing the EU. Similarly, there cannot be a risk if the applied EU law is at the Parties' disposal. The Court does not consider commercial arbitration as a threat to its legal order.[65]

10.3.1 EU Law Applied to Ascertain Preliminary Legal Facts

Whether the use of EU law to ascertain preliminary and ancillary legal facts is a risk depending on the *res judicata* effect vested on this preliminary decision. If the judgement is granted *res judicata* only to the extent of its operative part, then the preliminary decision related to EU law cannot be considered as integrated inside the EU legal order. A judge of the EU can still make a definitive decision on this specific dispute. However, the *res judicata* effect is not limited to the operative part and may extend to 'decisive motivation'.

In the *Application of the Genocide Convention (Bosnia v. Serbia)* case,[66] the International Court of Justice stated that the *res judicata* effect of its judgment extended to preliminary question it had to ascertain in the course of its reasoning.

> The [ICJ] thus considers that the 1996 Judgment contained a finding, whether it be regarded as one of jurisdiction ratione personae, or as one anterior to questions of jurisdiction, *which was necessary as a matter of logical construction*, and related to the question of the FRY's capacity to appear before the Court under the Statute. The force of res judicata attaching to that judgment thus extends to that particular finding.[67]

This for instance means that the determination made by the Court in the *Oil Platforms* case regarding the violation by the United States of international law related to the use of force[68] is also vested with *res judicata* effect. This conclusion is true even though the Court's jurisdiction only existed as to alleged breaches of the 1955 Treaty of Amity.

In some Member States, the *res judicata* effect provided by decision of *exequatur* also extends to 'decisive motivation'.[69] An Arbitral Tribunal with a jurisdiction limited to a BIT could in fact take a decision on a dispute related to EU law and have this decision integrated into the EU legal order without a uniform and complete control of its award. However, this tribunal can only take such a decision provided it is preliminary to the resolution of a non-ancillary dispute related to the BIT. It is difficult to imagine in these conditions that part of the EU law interpretation and application could be *systematically*

65 *Case 248/16, Achmea*, paras. 54-55.

66 ICJ, Judgment of 26 February 2007, *Application of the Convention on the Prevention and Punishment of the Crime of Genocide (Bosnia and Herzegovina v.Serbia and Montenegro), I.C.J. Reports 2007.*

67 *Ibid.*, para. 136.

68 *See* supra.

69 French Cour de cassation, Civ. 3e, 28 October 1974, n° 73-11274.

'extracted' from the EU judicial system. There is no real risk as to the unity of interpretation that a simple control of the award under public order could not thwart.

10.3.2 EU Law Used to Shape the Principal Law

The use of EU law by an Arbitral Tribunal to analyze the applicability, validity and interpretation of a BIT's provision is normally made in order to avoid a decision that would be contrary to EU law. It is only a misinterpretation or a misapplication of EU law that could be an issue, similarly to a judgment taken without consideration of EU law. In fact, the risk does not come from the Tribunal's use of EU law, but from the existence of a decision that may contradict EU law. This risk is usually thwarted by a simple control of the Tribunal's jurisdiction and of public order.

10.4 CONCLUSION

Having confined its jurisdiction to disputes related to alleged breaches of the BIT, the Arbitral Tribunal in the *Achmea* case could only have a limited use of EU law which posed a limited risk to the EU legal order autonomy.

Considering this conclusion, one may wonder why the CJEU did not take the opportunity of Article 8's broad wording to consider that indeed such Arbitral Tribunal has jurisdiction over alleged breaches of the EU law when it comes to an investment. Even though the Arbitral Tribunal in the current case had asserted the contrary, it was not a guarantee that another tribunal under the same BIT would do the same. The CJEU surely was aware of this possibility.[70] The CJEU decided however not to follow this easy path as to be sure that its blow to intra-EU investment arbitration would be fatal. There is no doubt that the *Achmea* jurisprudence also applies to intra-EU BITs with a more restrained jurisdiction clause.[71]

Having this conclusion in mind, one may also wonder what could have been the real reason behind the CJEU's decision. A look at the Commission's opinion on the question of intra-EU BITs may provide an answer. Intra-EU BITs create protection for intra-EU investors which overlaps other protections provided by the EU single market and the EU fundamental rights.[72] Hence, the issue is not really that intra-EU BIT tribunals could limitedly use EU law but that there exists another corpus of law that is in competition

70 It notably decided not to take as granted the Tribunal decision on this point, *see Case 248/16, Achmea*, para. 40.

71 Thus, the *Achmea* jurisprudence can also apply to the Energy Charter Treaty when it comes to intra-EU investments; Art. 26 of the ECT creates a jurisdiction over alleged breaches of the ECT Part III.

72 *See* the European Commission, Press Release of 19 July 2018, *Capital Markets Union: Commission Provides Guidance on Protection of Cross-border EU investments*, IP/18/4528.

with EU law when it comes to the protection of intra-EU investment. The CJEU may have had no other choice to get rid of this corpus as it is not under a clear exclusive competence of the EU[73] and is not necessarily in contradiction with EU law.

73 The EU only having exclusive competence on extra-EU investment as part of the common commercial policy, *see* Opinion of 16 May 2017, *2/15 Free Trade Agreement between the European Union and the Republic of Singapore*, ECLI:EU:C:2017:376, paras. 35 and 80.

Part IV

The Engagement of National Courts in Judicial Dialogue – Discourses on Judicial Dialogue in Italy and Netherlands

11 The Dialogue between the Italian Constitutional Court and the Court of Justice of the European Union

Silvia Marino

11.1 The Role of the Italian Constitutional Court in Shaping the Judicial Dialogue

The Italian Constitutional Court (ICC) had been historically playing an active role in the judicial dialogue with the Court of Justice of the European Union (CJEU). The first contact between the two courts has been far from friendly. In the *Costa v. Enel* cases, the courts examined the same national rule, taking opposite approaches on the effects of EU law within the Italian legal order. The ICC applied its standard approach in the coordination between national law and international treaties, so that the founding European Economic Community's (EEC) Treaties should be recognized in Italy with the same legal value as that of an act of the Italian Parliament. Therefore, a subsequent act, approved by the Italian Parliament, could derogate from the Treaties according to the generally accepted *lex posterior* rule.[1] On the contrary, the CJEU started to draw up the principle of primacy of EU law over national law, stressing the impossibility to adopt any "unilateral act, which would be incompatible with the concept of the community".[2] The starting positions were, thus, far from being reconcilable.

The CJEU furthered the principle of primacy in the case *Internationale Handelsgesellschaft*,[3] a preliminary reference on the validity of an EEC Regulation for infringement of German constitutional fundamental rights. Here the CJEU made it clear that European Communities (EC) law could not find any limit to its implementation into national legal systems, including the fundamental rights as envisaged in the constitutions. The *strong version* of the primacy enunciated by the CJEU seemed to give preference to EC acts of secondary law over human rights granted by a constitution.

A few years later, the ICC had the opportunity to react to such clear-cut statement. In the *Frontini* case[4] it clarified the so-called controlimiti (counter limits) theory: The ICC

1 ICC 7 March 1964, n. 14.

2 Judgment of 15 July 1964 in *Case 6/64, Costa v. E.N.E.L.*, [1964] ECR 1141.

3 Judgment of 17 December 1970 in *Case 11/70, Internationale Handelsgesellschaft mbH v. Einfuhr- und Vorratsstelle für Getreide und Futtermittel* (*Internationale Handelsgesellschaft*), [1970] ECR 1125.

4 ICC 27 December 1973, n. 183.

reserved for itself the exclusive competence to scrutinize EC law in the light of the fundamental constitutional principles and values. If EC law infringed these rights, the ICC could deprive it of any effect in Italy.

Although an approximation between the two Courts seemed hard to reach, the ICC has slowly accepted the consequences of the primacy principle. In the *ICC* case,[5] it found an internal legal instrument to give prevalence to EC law over national law: the declaration of unconstitutionality of the latter for breach of Article 11 of the Italian Constitution (on limitations of sovereignty necessary to ensure peace and justice among the Nations). Still, the CJEU considered this solution as inadequate because it implied a necessary reference to the ICC and, thus, a postponement of the protection of the rights granted by EC law. In *Simmenthal*[6] the CJEU made it clear that the national judge should set aside any incompatible national law, any other internal legal remedy not being proper. With this statement, the CJEU strengthened the absolute primacy of EU law.

The final solution was the ICC accepting the principle of primacy and the subsequent inapplicability of national law. This happened in the *Granital* case,[7] with regard to EC rules with direct effect. Actually, failure to recognize the direct effect of EC law would make it impossible to set aside national law in that the judge would have no available rule to apply. Therefore, a previous evaluation of constitutionality of the incompatible national law remained necessary.[8] Notwithstanding further case law recalling these national principles, the exception of the 'controlimiti' has never been activated against EC law. Only in *Fragd*[9] the ICC examined for the first time if an EC rule infringed Italian Constitution's fundamental values, but the answer was in the negative sense, thus avoiding any strong conflict between EC law and national law.

Few years after *Internationale Handelsgesellschaft,* the German Constitutional Court (GCC) had the opportunity to take analogous positions. In the well-known *Solange I* and *Solange II* cases,[10] the GCC expressed its concerns on the absolute primacy of EC law, yet accepting it with some limitations. In the former judgment, the GCC assumed the position of the last defender of its constitution, due to the lack of any human rights-related sensitivity from the CJEU. In the latter, it takes good note of the developments within the EC, which could grant a proper level of protection of the fundamental rights. Nevertheless, the GCC kept its control against EC law gross violations of constitutional values. In the more recent *Maastricht Urteil,*[11] the GCC made it clear that it was competent to

5 ICC 30 October 1975, n. 232.

6 Judgment of 9 March 1978 in *Case 106/77, Amministrazione delle finanze dello Stato v. SpA Simmenthal (Simmenthal)*, [1978] ECR 629.

7 ICC 8 June 1984, n. 170.

8 ICC 28 March 2006, n. 129; ICC 28 January 2010, n. 28.

9 ICC 21 April 1989, n. 232.

10 BVerfGE 29 May 1974, 37, BvL 52/71; BVerfGE 22 October 1986, 73, 339 2, BvR 197/83.

11 BVerfGE 12 October 1993 – 2 BvR 2134, 2159/92; BVerfGE 6 July 2010, 126, 286; W. van Ballegooij, P. Bárd, 'Mutual Recognition and Individual Rights. Did the Court get it Right?', *New Journal of European Criminal Law*, Vol. 7, No. 4, 2016, p. 459.

examine whether measures adopted by EC institutions exceeded the sovereign powers transferred to them (*ultra vires*).

The approaches of the two constitutional courts influenced the case law of other courts that faced similar issues in the following years. While the principle of primacy was generally accepted, many courts claimed for some exceptions thereto. For example, the Polish Constitutional Court dictated a theory very similar to the 'controlimiti' doctrine in its 'Accession Treaty' judgment;[12] other tribunals as the Czech[13] and the Danish[14] Constitutional Courts implemented the *ultra vires* control.[15] The widespread acceptance of similar standards contributed to the creation of a horizontal harmonized approach to the relationships between national laws and EC law.

11.2 THE MOVE OF THE COURT OF JUSTICE TOWARD THE PROTECTION OF FUNDAMENTAL RIGHTS IN THE EUROPEAN UNION

The clear-cut declaration in *Internationale Handelsgesellschaft* could be read as an express refusal to accord protection of fundamental rights within the EC, thus jeopardizing the authority of the EC legal system. The *Nold* case reversed this idea.[16] It was an action for annulment of a Commission decision for breach of some rights granted by the German Constitution, *other national constitutions*, and *some international conventions on human rights*, such as the Convention for the Protection of Human Rights and Funda-

---

12 Wyrok Trybuna ła Konstytucyjnego K18/04 – Traktat akcesyjny, Dziennik Ustaw 2005, Nr. 86, poz. 744; K. Kowalik-Bańczyk, 'Should We Polish It Up? The Polish Constitutional Tribunal and the Idea of Supremacy of EU Law', *German Law Journal*, Vol. 6, No. 10, pp. 1355-1366. The subsequent case on the European Arrest Warrant coordinates the timing of the application of EU law with the opportunity to modify the national Constitution, without any need to activate the national limit of the protection of fundamental rights (Trybunal Konstytucyjny, 27 April 2005, n. P 1/05; A. Nußberger, 'Poland: The Constitutional Tribunal on the Implementation of the European Arrest Warrant', *International Journal of Constitutional Law*, Vol. 6, No. 1, 2008, pp. 162-170; M. Wyrzykowski, 'When Sovereignty Means Too Much: The Concept(s) of Sovereignty, European Union Membership and the Interpretation of the Constitution of the Republic of Poland', in A. Rosas et al. (eds.), *The Court of Justice and the Construction of Europe*, The Hague, Asser, 2013, p. 229.

13 Ústavní Soud, judgment of 31 January 2012, Slovak Pensions, available in English at www.usoud.cz/en/decisions/20120131-pl-us-512-slovak-pensions/ (accessed 29 May 2019); J. Komárek, 'Czech Constitutional Court Playing with Matches: The Czech Constitutional Court Declares a Judgment of the Court of Justice of the EU Ultra Vires; Judgment of 31 January 2012, Pl. ÚS 5/12, Slovak Pensions XVII', *European Constitutional Law Review*, Vol. 8, No. 2, 2012, pp. 323-337.

14 Højesteret, 6 December 2016, case 15/2014, Ajos A/S, available in English at www.supremecourt.dk/supremecourt/nyheder/pressemeddelelser/Documents/Judgment%2015-2014.pdf (accessed 29 May 2019); R. Madsen et al., 'Competing Supremacies and Clashing Institutional Rationalities: The Danish Supreme Court's Decision in the Ajos Case and the National Limits of Judicial Cooperation', *European Law Journal*, Vol. 23, Nos. 1-2, 2017, pp. 140-150.

15 Further: A. von Bogdandy & S. Schill, 'Overcoming Absolute Primacy. Respect for National Identity under the Lisbon Treaty', *Common Market Law Review*, Vol. 48, No. 5, 2011, p. 1433.

16 Judgment of 14 May 1974 in *Case 4/73, J. Nold, Kohlen- und Baustoffgroßhandlung v. Ruhrkohle Aktiengesellschaft (Nold)*, [1974] ECR 491.

mental Freedoms (or currently, the European Convention on Human Rights [ECHR]). The list of grounds demonstrated that the issue at stake was not just a 'national problem' but was also a main question for the whole EC. Therefore, the CJEU could not refuse to consider human rights at all and stated that the fundamental rights derived from the common constitutional traditions and the main international conventions had to form an integral part of EC general principles of law, which the CJEU itself was competent to protect.

The final acceptance of the role of fundamental human rights in the EC took place with the *Hauer* case,[17] a preliminary ruling from a German court. The relevance of this case rests on the comparative evaluation of the rights granted by the national constitutions of the Member States and international conventions in order to ascertain the existence and the range of the rights invoked by the applicants.

Only after this case law, the protection of fundamental rights became a crucial issue at EC level. Further developments, as the introduction of Article 6 TEU with the *Maastricht Treaty* and the draft of the Nice Charter increased the EC/EU commitment toward the protection of human rights. The further developments after the Treaty of Lisbon explain why the ICC has never applied the 'controlimiti' doctrine against EU/EC law,[18] which appeared as dead letter.[19] Indeed, the recognition of the primary legal value of the Charter of Fundamental Rights of the EU, the most modern international bill of human rights, and the duty to adhere to the ECHR could seem the happy end to the quite troubled development toward the protection of human rights within the EU. Consequently, this coordination between EU and national law has remained uncontested until quite recently.

11.3 Recent Trends within the Italian Constitutional Court

11.3.1 The References for Preliminary Rulings from the Italian Constitutional Court

This dialogue has affected the interaction between the CJEU and the ICC, too, toward a better settlement of the roles of the two courts. Since *Granital* the ICC has imposed a duty of double preliminary reference on the court seized with the dispute. First, it had to refer

17 Judgment of 13 December 1979 in *Case 44/79, Liselotte Hauer v. Land Rheinland-Pfalz* (*Hauer*), [1979] ECR 3727.

18 On the opposite, the Consiglio di Stato – State Council, the highest jurisdiction for administrative disputes – applied a sort of soft version of the 'controlimiti' doctrine in stating that there was no need to refer a preliminary question, since a previous judgment delivered by the ICC had already interpreted a national rule in accordance with fundamental rights (State Council, 8 August 2005, n. 4207).

19 The Supreme Court itself stated clearly that the 'controlimiti' doctrine was superseded due to the development of the protection of fundamental rights within the EU (Supreme Court 1 June 2012, n. 8817).

to the CJEU in order to clarify the interpretation of EU law; second, in case of further doubts, it could refer a constitutionality question to the ICC.[20] The ICC justified this sequence by the need to decide on the constitutionality of an Italian rule of law having a clear framework on EC/EU law interpretation, too.

This double burden on national judges was also due to the self-characterization of the ICC, which did not consider itself as a court or tribunal for the purposes of preliminary rulings[21] until Order No. 103/2008.[22] This was its first referral to the CJEU. The changed approach was justified by the peculiar circumstances of the case, which was a direct claim of the Presidency of the Council of Ministry against Sardinia for adopting a regional law in a subject matter allegedly falling within national competences. Therefore, in this case the ICC considered itself as performing a judicial function, according to the CJEU interpretation of Article 267 TFEU, it being the first and the last competent Court to hear the dispute.

The most meaningful step for the ICC was Order No. 207/2013, issued pending a reference on questions of constitutionality.[23] Within this competence, it was less clear whether the ICC had judicial functions to settle a litigation between parties: the real claim was pending with the court that referred the question of constitutionality, and this was the judge finally responsible for the decision. The main reasons for this overruling were not clear, because the Order did not discuss the characterization of the ICC as a national judge for the purposes of Article 267 TFEU. Furthermore, in its judgment, the CJEU did not raise any doubt on the admissibility of the request.[24] The positive key point of this case rests in the availability of direct contacts between the ICC and the CJEU.

Furthering the comparison with Germany, the GCC referred its first preliminary ruling to the CJEU in 2014,[25] and in its subsequent well-known judgment in *Gauweiler*, the CJEU took its qualification as a national judge for granted.[26]

Order No. 207/2013 was able to strengthen the cooperation between the Courts with a direct dialogue, not mediated by a double reference from the national judge. This interposition might be problematic in some peculiar circumstances, as it was clear in the case *Global Starnet*.[27] Here the CJEU stated that any previous evaluation of constitutionality did not prevent further assessments of the consistency of a national law with EU law,

---

20 ICC order 17 December 2008, n. 415; ICC order 2 April 2009, n. 100.

21 ICC 18 April 1991, n. 168; ICC order 29 December 1995, n. 536.

22 ICC order 15 April 2008, n. 103.

23 ICC order 3 July 2013, n. 207.

24 Judgment of 26 November 2014 in *Case C-418/13, Napolitano*, ECLI:EU:C:2014:2401.

25 BVerfG 14 January 2014, No. 2 BvR 2728/13.

26 Judgment of 16 June 2015 in *Case C-62/14, Peter Gauweiler a o. v. Deutscher Bundestag* (*Gauweiler*), ECLI:EU:C:2015:400; J. Nowag, 'EU Law, Constitutional Identity, and Human Dignity: A Toxic Mix?', *Common Market Law Review*, Vol. 53, No. 5, 2016, p. 1441; G. Anagnostaras, 'Solange III? Fundamental Rights Protection under National Identity Review', *European Law Review*, Vol. 42, No. 2, 2017, p. 234.

27 Judgment of 20 December 2017 in *Case C-322/16, Global Starnet Ltd v. Ministero dell'Economia e delle Finanze e Amministrazione Autonoma Monopoli di Stato* (*Global Starnet*), ECLI:EU:C:2017:985.

although the ICC expressly characterized the Italian Constitution's rules as equivalent to the Treaties rules. In these sensitive cases, a direct dialogue between the ICC and the CJEU is the best option to prevent any potential conflict of the courts' rulings.

Actually, after Order No. 207/2013, the judge seized with the dispute had two alternatives. On the one hand, it could refer to the ICC, raising doubts on the compatibility of the national rule with both the Constitution and EU law, so that the ICC could request a preliminary ruling to the CJEU. On the other hand, it could follow the path designed in *Granital*, with two consecutive references.

However, the ICC seemed to have revised its approach on the double preliminary reference with Order No. 269/2017.[28] Here, the ICC changed the chronological order of the preliminary references, stating that *first* the doubts on constitutionality had to be resolved and *then* the national court could refer to the CJEU. The ICC grounded this reversal on the ruling in the case *A v. B* of the CJEU,[29] which referred to Austria, without considering the different positions of the two national constitutional courts[30] or the conditions set by the CJEU making the priority of the constitutionality ruling lawful. Moreover, according to some scholars, this statement infringes the judgments in *Melki*[31] and in *Filipiak*,[32] where the CJEU clearly framed the limits of the admissibility of the priority of the constitutionality review. These criticisms notwithstanding, currently the various sections of the Italian Supreme Court follow different approaches: Some apply this new doctrine,[33] and others give precedence to the preliminary ruling as the best tool for the solution of the court's doubts in the case at stake.[34] According to recent ICC rulings,[35] a flexible approach seems to be preferred. The precedence of the constitutional review cannot affect the power of the ordinary judge to lodge a preliminary reference to the CJEU, it being free to decide when a preliminary ruling can be useful and necessary for

---

28 ICC 14 December 2017, n. 269; for a comment in English: R. Di Marco, 'The "Path towards European Integration" of the Italian Constitutional Court: The Primacy of EU Law in the Light of the Judgment No. 269/17', *European Papers*, Vol. 3, No. 2, pp. 843-855.

29 Judgment of 11 September 2014 in *Case C-112/13, A v. B a. o.*, ECLI:EU:C:2014:2195.

30 The Austrian Verfassungsgerichtshof, 14 March 2012, U 466/11-18; U 1836/11-13 'nationalized' the fundamental rights, stating that the ECHR has constitutional ranking and that the constitutionality control can be performed also taking as a parameter the EU Charter of fundamental rights. The outcome of this statement is a balance of the different source for the protection of fundamental rights, which have primary ranking within Austrian Constitutional order, and the prohibition to set aside national rules incompatible with the EU Charter, since the potential violation of fundamental rights must be detected by the Court itself.

31 Judgment of 22 June 2010 in *Cases C-188/10, C-189/10, Melki and Abdeli*, [2010] ECR 5667; D. Simon & A. Rigaux, 'La priorité de la QPC: harmonie(s) er dissonance(s) des monologues juridictionelles croisés', *Nouveaux Cahier du Conseil Constitutionnel*, No. 29, 2010; R. Mastroianni, 'La Corte di giustizia e il controllo di costituzionalità: *Simmenthal revisited?*', *Giurisprudenza costituzionale*, Vol. 58, No. 5, p. 4089.

32 Judgment of 19 November 2009 in *Case C-314/08, Krzysztof Filipiak v. Dyrektor Izby Skarbowej w Poznaniu (Filipiak)*, [2009] ECR 11049.

33 Supreme Court, Civil Section, order 16 February 2018, n. 3831.

34 Supreme Court, Job Section, order 30 March 2018, n. 13678.

35 ICC 23 January 2019; ICC 20 February 2019.

the dispute resolution. Therefore, national courts are not prevented to involve the CJEU, notwithstanding doubts on constitutionality.

11.3.2 *The Recent Positions of the Italian Constitutional Court toward International Instances*

Other recent ICC cases seem to have locked its position toward international obligations. In the judgment 238/14,[36] the ICC applied the 'controlimiti' doctrine for the first time.[37] The case started from some internal judgments that deprived Germany of its civil jurisdiction immunity in claims for restoration and damages caused by the gross violation of human rights during World War II.[38] Germany contested this case law, seizing the International Court of Justice (ICJ) for infringement of the rules on international immunities. The ICJ judgment made it clear that the peculiar circumstances of the case could not be accepted as an exception to Germany's jurisdictional immunity.[39] As a reaction, the ICC declared that this judgment deprived the victims of any restoration of the damages, thus breaching Articles 2 and 24 of the Italian Constitution (respectively on the recognition of the fundamental human rights, and the right to judicial action and defense). Consequently, the ICC declared the unconstitutionality of the Italian law implementing Article 94 of the UN Charter in the part where it allowed the ICJ judgment to have effects in Italy.

In the subsequent judgment 49/15, the ICC limited the effect of the European Court of Human Rights' (ECtHR) case law in Italy.[40] Accordingly, the national judge had a duty to conform its reasoning to previous judgments in two cases only, that is, if it was issued after a pilot procedure, or if it was part of a consistent jurisprudence. This ruling contradicts the 'twin judgments' delivered in 2007,[41] where the ICC recognized a peculiar legal value to the ECHR system as a privileged reference parameter for the legitimacy of national law. Although the 2007 cases denied the ECHR the same legal value as the Italian Constitution, they characterized it as one of the fundamental *Italian* sources. This would not be true anymore if the national court, seized with a case involving human rights violations, could not adapt its reasoning to a previous ECtHR decision using its natural margin of appreciation.

---

36 ICC 22 October 2014, n. 238.

37 B. Cortese, 'ECJ and National Constitutional Courts: A Collaborative Law Approach', *Diritto dell'Unione europea*, Vol. 23, No. 1, 2018, p. 69.

38 Supreme Court 11 March 2004, n. 5044, *Ferrini*.

39 ICJ 3 February 2012, Jurisdictional Immunities of the State (*Germany v. Italy*; Greece intervening).

40 ICC 26 March 2015, n. 49; V. Zagrebelsky, 'Corte cost. n. 49 del 2015, giurisprudenza della Corte europea dei diritti umani, art. 117 Cost., obblighi derivanti dalla ratifica della Convenzione', at www.osservatorioaic.it/images/rivista/pdf/Zagrebelsky%202.2015_.pdf (accessed 29 May 2019).

41 ICC 22 October 2007, nn. 348 and 349.

These cases show a recent ICC trend toward the promotion of national values, which is, however, contradictory in the perspective of human rights' protection. In the former, the refusal to accept an ICJ judgment seems justified by the wish to further the protection of fundamental rights in Italy, notwithstanding its various international obligations. In the latter, the effect risks being the opposite: The ECtHR judgment stating on a new issue, or not being adopted after a pilot judgment procedure, does not bind national judges, thus risking a gross violation of the ECHR, and the eventual enactment of a subsequent ECtHR's pilot judgment.

11.4 A NEW CHAPTER IN THE JUDICIAL DIALOGUE: JUDICIAL COOPERATION AND THE PROTECTION OF FUNDAMENTAL RIGHTS

The 'Taricco Saga' is a main chapter of this judicial dialogue. After a reference for preliminary ruling from the Court of First Instance of Cuneo, in the *Taricco* judgment,[42] the Court stated that Article 325(1) and (2) of the Treaty on the Functioning of the European Union (TFEU) had direct effect and that the Italian limitations periods for tax fraud prevented the imposition of effective penalties "in a significant number of cases of serious fraud". Consequently, national rules affected the financial interests of the EU and had to be set aside. Scholars' criticism fell on various parts of this judgment. The most striking remarks focused on the vagueness of the notions of *significant number of cases* and *serious fraud*, and the not convincingly motivated direct effect of Article 325 TFEU.[43] This notwithstanding, the Italian Supreme Court applied the '*Taricco* rule', setting aside the national rules on limitations periods.[44] However, some doubts arose on the constitutionality of this rule for breach of Article 25 of the Italian Constitution on the principle of legal certainty in criminal law. The ICC, requested to review the '*Taricco* rule' under the ICC, lodged its second preliminary reference pending a constitutionality review ever.[45] In

42 Judgment of 8 September 2015 in *Case C-105/14, Criminal proceedings against Ivo Taricco and Others* (*Taricco*), ECLI:EU:C:2015:555; M. Timmerman, 'Balancing Effective Criminal Sanctions with Effective Fundamental Rights Protection in Cases of VAT fraud: *Taricco*', *Common Market Law Review*, Vol. 53, No. 3, 2016, pp. 779-796.

43 D. Gallo, 'Controlimiti, identità nazionale e i rapporti di forza tra primato ed effetto diretto nella saga Taricco', *Diritto dell'Unione europea*, Vol. 22, No. 2, 2017, p. 258.

44 Supreme Court, III Criminal Section, 17 September 2015, n. 2210; Supreme Court, IV Criminal Section, 25 January 2016, n. 7914; Supreme Court, II Criminal Section, 7 February 2108, n. 9494.

45 ICC 26 January 2017, n. 24. This order has been largely commented by Italian scholars; for comments in English: S. Sciarra, 'Rule of Law and Mutual Trust: A Short Note on Constitutional Courts as "Institutions of Pluralism"', *Diritto dell'Unione europea*, Vol. 23, No. 3, 2018, p. 440; A. Tancredi, 'Of Direct Effect, Primacy and Constitutional Identities: Rome and Luxembourg Enmeshed in the Taricco case', at www.qil-qdi.org/direct-effect-primacy-constitutional-identities-rome-luxembourg-enmeshed-taricco-case/ (accessed 29 May 2019). D. Sarmiento, 'An Instruction Manual to Stop a Judicial Rebellion (Before It Is Too Late, Of course)', at https://verfassungsblog.de/an-instruction-manual-to-stop-a-judicial-rebellion-before-it-is-too-late-of-course/ (accessed 29 May 2019) interprets this order as a sort of rebellion of the ICC toward CJEU case law, to the same extent that the Danish Supreme Court did in the *Ajos* case.

Order 24/17, the ICC stressed the impact of any modification of limitations periods on the principles of legal certainty and of non-retroactivity in criminal law as fundamental constitutional values. Then, it characterized the two principles as part of the national constitutional identity, which the ICC must protect and the CJEU must respect according to Article 4(2) TEU. Although the ICC formally requested a clarification of the *Taricco* judgment, actually it longed for its revision, justified by the peculiar constitutional relevance of the above-mentioned principles. The ICC seemed prone to apply its 'controlimiti' doctrine, although this word does not appear in the order, if the CJEU was not ready to reverse its previous ruling.

Notwithstanding the Advocate General's opinion reinforcing the previous statement in *Taricco*,[46] the CJEU took a very cooperative approach in its final judgment *M.A.S. and M.B.*[47] The CJEU interpreted the principle of legality in criminal law as a general principle of EU law, with whom EU secondary law had to be consistent. This part of the judgment is of the utmost importance. The CJEU could have followed the path suggested in Order No. 24/17, promoting national identities, as it did in the well-known cases such as *Schmidberger, Omega* and *Sayn-Wittgenstein*.[48] Instead, it preferred a global approach, increasing the value of the principles and absorbing them as part of the general principles of EU law. This technique allowed the CJEU not to discuss either national values and peculiarities or the interpretation of Article 4(2) TEU as a sort of EU codification of the 'controlimiti' doctrine. It also allowed the Court to set aside national identity issues as not being relevant in the case. Consequently, it revisited the *Taricco* judgment[49] stating that it had no retrospective effect.

After this conciliatory position, the ICC was expected to adopt a friendly attitude, avoiding any possible conflict with the CJEU. In the opinion of the present author, this

46 L. Daniele, 'Il seguito del caso Taricco: l'Avvocato generale Bot non apre al dialogo tra Corti', *European Papers*, Vol. 2, No. 3, 2017, pp. 987-1004.

47 Judgment of 5 December 2017 in *Case C-42/17, Criminal proceedings against M.A.S. and M.B. (M.A.S. and M.B.)*, ECLI:EU:C:2017:936.

48 Judgment of 12 June 2003 in *Case C-112/00, Eugen Schmidberger, Internationale Transporte und Planzüge v. Republik Österreich (Schmidberger)*, [2003] ECR 5659; Judgment of 14 October 2004 in *Case C-36/02, Omega Spielhallen- und Automatenaufstellungs-GmbH v. Oberbürgermeisterin der Bundesstadt Bonn (Omega)*, [2004] ECR 9609; Judgment of 22 December 2010 in *Case C-208/09, Ilonka Sayn-Wittgenstein v. Landeshauptmann von Wien (Sayn-Wittgenstein)*, [2010] ECR 13693. Thus, the definition of *national identity* is far from clear and rarely can justify a departure from the general principles and freedoms of EU law (Anagnostaras, 2017, p. 234; L.S. Rossi, 'Come risolvere la "questione Taricco" … senza far leva sull'art. 4, para. 2, TUE', at www.sidiblog.org/2017/05/17/come-risolvere-la-questione-taricco-senza-far-leva-sullart-4-par-2-tue/ (accessed 29 May 2019).

49 E. Montserrat Pappalettere, 'La sentenza "Taricco bis": dalla contrapposizione degli ordinamenti al bilanciamento dei princìpi attraverso il dialogo', *Diritto dell'Unione europea*, Vol. 23, No. 1, 2018, pp. 203-221.

has not been the case. In its judgment No. 115/18,[50] the ICC declared that the references for constitutionality were groundless, since the pending criminal proceedings at issue referred to criminal offences committed before the *Taricco* judgment and thus the *Taricco* rule was not applicable according to the *M.A.S. and M.B.* clarification. This could have been the end of the case. Nevertheless, the ICC added a few considerations, which were not strictly necessary for the purposes of the pending proceedings. The ICC insisted on the lack of precision of Article 325 TFEU from which a clear rule establishing a criminal sanction could not be inferred. Insisting on constitutional guarantees, it focused on the fact that criminal liability was not established in a law, approved by the Italian Parliament, as required by Article 25 of the Italian Constitution, which could not be substituted by an authoritative judgment whose content was unpredictable from the black letter of Article 325 TFEU. Furthermore, according to the ICC, the *Taricco* case lacked precision and its statements provoked uncertainty as to the number and the seriousness of the criminal offenses even after the clarifications in the *M.A.S. and M.B.* case. Finally, referring to the national constitution and the general principles of EU law, the ICC stated that the *Taricco* rule was not applicable *without exceptions*, since it could jeopardize the national constitutional principle of legality in criminal law.

This assessment is not consistent with the *M.A.S. and M.B.* judgment, which modified the previous approach only from a retroactive perspective and confirmed the direct effects of Article 325 TFEU. The ICC deprived the statements in *Taricco* of their effects, amplifying their temporal scope of application for constitutional reasons. The 'controlimiti' doctrine was not mentioned in the judgment, but most of the ICC final evaluation depended solely on the range of Article 25 of the Italian Constitution, thus suggesting that it was indeed applying that doctrine. The quick reference to the general principles of EU at the end of the judgment does not seem solid enough in order to demonstrate that the same conclusion could be derived from EU law, notwithstanding the *M.A.S. and M.B.* ruling. Apparently, the ICC made the national peculiarities prevail over the uniform interpretation of Article 325 TFEU.

11.5 Some Final Remarks

The reasons for this turning point of the ICC are not very clear and might come as a surprise. Its strong ruling can lead us to presume that the dialogue between the courts is far from concluded, in that reactions from the CJEU are to be expected in the near future.

50 ICC 10 April 2018, n. 115; C. Amalfitano, O. Pollicino, 'Jusqu'ici tout va bien… ma non sino alla fine della storia. Luci, ombre ed atterraggio della sentenza n. 115/2018 della Corte costituzionale che chiude (?) la saga Taricco', at www.diritticomparati.it/jusquici-tout-va-bien-ma-non-sino-alla-fine-della-storia-luci-ombre-ed-atterraggio-della-sentenza-n-115-2018-della-corte-costituzionale-che-chiude-la-saga-taricco/ (accessed 29 May 2019).

There might be three intertwining explanations for this new approach.

First, the ICC might have wished to underline its exclusive and prominent role in the interpretation of the Italian Constitution and the protection of fundamental values, even against national courts that have attributed absolute primacy to the CJEU case law. In that respect, the ICC needed to stress the relevance of the Italian Constitution in the Italian legal order.

Second, the ICC might have aimed at remedying the confusion created by the interpretation and the application of the *Taricco* rule, giving final guidelines to the judges on the merits and to the Supreme Court. The ICC might have wished to emphasize that it had the last word on the impact of the judgment within the Italian legal order.

There is third and less admirable reason. Maybe the ICC is following a new wave in coordinating with international instances. On one hand, it starts to be one of the direct protagonists taking part directly in the judicial dialogue with the CJEU. On the other hand, it uses this power in order to strengthen the role of Italian Constitution values from an international perspective.

This alleged new attitude of the ICC can be subject to criticism. Indeed, the EU has so far reached a proper level of protection of fundamental rights, as the *M.A.S. and M.B.* case confirms, in the part that it underlines the European relevance of the principle of legal certainty in criminal matters. Moreover, the ECtHR is the main European jurisdiction with sole competence in the detection of human rights violations. These systems do not attack the relevance of the Italian Constitution and the national (judicial) protection of human rights, so that the ICC needs to rebel and to defend national values. The approach should rather be in the opposite sense, that is, the maximum cooperation. Indeed, the Italian Constitution is not the sole Charter of fundamental rights in force in Italy but coexists with other international and supranational sources. This coexistence is positive, because it can increase the promotion of human rights in the national, European and international contexts. Therefore, the ICC is and must remain an 'actor' of the judicial dialogue: an actor, and not the protagonist; a dialogue, and not a monologue, refraining from incautious particularisms, in order to strengthen the development of human rights within all the jurisdictions involved, including the Italian legal system.

12 Are Dutch Judges in Search of a Dialogue?

*Michiel Duchateau**

12.1 Introduction

A question that has occupied many academics and several constitutional courts at least since the *Maastricht* Judgment of the German *Bundesverfassungsgericht* (BVerfG) is to what extent EU law exists, and can be applied, independently from the Member States constitutions.[1] The Court of Justice of the European Union (CJEU) has been insistent and clear on the matter:

> EU law is characterised by the fact that it stems from an independent source of law, the Treaties, by its primacy over the laws of the Member States …, and by the direct effect of a whole series of provisions.[2]

Equally well known is the fact that most constitutional courts of the Member States, such as the German BVerfG,[3] the UK Supreme Court[4] and the Italian *Corte Costituzionale*,[5] have taken up a different position, claiming that the applicability of EU law in the Member States is still dependent on each (sovereign) Member State's constitution.[6] This in

---

* The author would like to thank professor Sofia Ranchordás for her very useful comments to an earlier version of this chapter.

1 BVerfGE 89, 155 (*Maastricht*). *See for instance* R. Barents, *De communautaire rechtsorde. Over de autonomie van het gemeenschapsrecht*, Deventer, Kluwer, 2000 and N. Walker (Ed.), *Sovereignty in Transition*, Oxford: Hart Publishing, 2003.

2 CJEU, Judgment of 6 February 2014 in *Opinion 2/13*, ECLI:EU:C:2014:48, para. 166. *Cf.* CJEU (Full Court), Judgment of 10 December 2018 in *Case C-621/18, Wightman and others*, ECLI:EU:C:2018:999.

3 2 BvE 2/08 of 30 June 2009 (*Lisbon*).

4 *R* (on the application of Miller and another) *v Secretary of State for Exiting the European Union*, UK Supreme Court 24 January 2017, [2017] UKSC 5 (*Miller*).

5 *See* S. Marino, 'The dialogue between the Italian Constitutional Court and the Court of Justice of the European Union' (Chapter 11 of this Volume).

6 Particularly the BVerfG has been very influential. T. Konstadinides, 'Dealing with Parallel Universes: Antinomies of Sovereignty and the Protection of National Identity in European Judicial Discourse', *Yearbook of European Law*, Vol. 34, No. 1, 2015, p. 150.

turn has sparked an academic debate on how to reconcile these different lines of case law that revolve around concepts such as constitutional pluralism and multilevel constitutionalism.[7]

So far, this matter has not received much attention in Dutch courts. These courts do actively engage with the CJEU, but not on this matter.[8] Like Dutch politics and the constitution itself, Dutch courts have traditionally avoided constitutional theories that are based on concepts such as democracy or sovereignty.[9] Instead, the Supreme Court (*Hoge Raad*), the government and many authors have concluded that the Dutch Constitution cannot limit the applicability of EU law in the Netherlands.[10]

However, there have been signs that the times are changing. Most visible is of course the rise of populist and strongly Euro-skeptic movements, such as the *Partij voor de Vrijheid* (Wilders) and *Forum voor Democratie* (Baudet) in the Netherlands. These right-wing political parties claim to protect national sovereignty against Europe's influence, and they put sovereignty squarely on the political agenda.[11] The rise of these parties fits into a wider European trend toward constitutional nationalism, which has also been witnessed in the UK with Brexit, and in Hungary and Poland. This seems to put the legitimacy of the EU under a lot of pressure. However, what is particularly striking is that it is not only the populists who are proposing to protect the constitution against Europe and foreign influence.

In 2007, after the Netherlands rejected the Treaty establishing a Constitution for Europe in a referendum, the Netherlands Scientific Council for Government Policy was asked to assess whether the legitimacy of the EU in the Netherlands was increasingly called into question, and to come up with solutions to this problem. This Council, whose members are scientists of renown, is an advisory body of the government that is estab-

---

7 For instance, *see* M. Poiares Maduro, 'Contrapunctual Law: Europe's Constitutional Pluralism in Action', *in* N. Walker (Ed.), *Sovereignty in Transition*, Oxford, Hart Publishing, 2003, pp. 501-537, and I. Pernice, 'Multilevel Constitutionalism and the Treaty of Amsterdam: European Constitution-making Revisited?', *Common Market Law Review*, Vol. 36, No. 4, 1999, pp. 703-750.

8 M. de Visser, 'Veranderingen in de dialoog tussen Nederlandse rechters and het Hof van Justitie? De wet prejudiciële vragen en voorstel-Halsema bezien vanuit Europees en rechtsvergelijkend perspectief', *Tijdschrift voor Constitutioneel Recht*, Vol. 3, No. 3, 2012, pp. 249, 251 and 260. J. Krommendijk, 'De hoogste Nederlandse bestuursrechters en het Hof van Justitie: geboren danspartners? Het hoe en waarom van verwijzen', *NTB*, 2017/34 and WRR (Netherlands Scientific Council for Government Policy; *Wetenschappelijke Raad voor het Regeringsbeleid*), *Europa in Nederland*, rapport to the government No. 78, Amsterdam: Amsterdam University Press, 2007, p. 12.

9 The Dutch Constitution does not refer to the people or any other constituent power. Instead, it mostly limits itself to fundamental rights and the constitutional position of the main organs. It consists of the Statute for the Kingdom of the Netherlands and the Basic Law (*Grondwet*). While the former contains the hierarchically highest norms, the latter is more elaborate.

10 *See for instance* HR 2 November 2004, ECLI:NL:HR:2004:AR1797 (*Rusttijden*). *Cf. Kamerstukken II* (Parliamentary Documents of the Lower House)*2007/08* 29 861, no. 19, p. 4 and T. Barkhuysen et al., 'Artikelen 93 en 94 Grondwet volgens Hoge Raad niet van belang voor doorwerking EG-recht', *NJB-kronieken*, Vol. 79, 2004, pp. 2289-2290, respectively.

11 On 20 March 2019, Baudet's party gained more seats than any other party in the provincial elections.

lished by law, and that reports on issues of major political and societal consequence. In its report, it proposed to introduce a 'Europe Article' in the Basic Law (*Grondwet*), like in that of many other EU Member States. This article was to set limits to Europeanization and protect certain core values of the Dutch Constitution. Contrary to the Dutch Council of State, it explicitly stated that the Netherlands should no longer rely on European law (alone) to protect its core constitutional values.[12] In addition, it claimed that the introduction of a constitutional court in the style of the German *Bundesverfassunsgericht* would help 'police' those 'borders', and enhance the legitimacy of the EU in the Netherlands.[13] This proposal has had some resonance in the literature, where authors claimed it could stimulate a judicial dialogue with the Court of Justice.[14]

Finally, in 2017, the three main Dutch administrative courts invoked the Basic Law when applying EU law and did not refer to European case law on the matter.[15] At a first glance, these three decisions confirm a long-held minority position in the Dutch literature, which claims that EU law is dependent on, and can be limited by, the constitution for its application in the Netherlands. Furthermore, they potentially are a first step toward building a line of case law that is more protective of the Dutch Constitution.[16]

As of yet, however, it remains unclear what the intent of these courts is. Like the case law of the Supreme Court, the cases do not give reasons on this rather fundamental point. The courts just choose to apply the Basic Law rather than European case law as such, with the same material result as application of the doctrine of *Costa/ENEL* would have had. Consequently, a disagreement between the Dutch main highest courts seems to have developed on the rather fundamental question of the position and applicability of EU law within the Dutch legal order. The position of the administrative courts certainly seems to have the potential to open up a judicial dialogue with the Court of Justice, but

---

12 WRR (*Wetenschappelijke Raad voor het Regeringsbeleid)*, 2007, p. 140. For the position of the Council of State (*Raad van State*), *see Kamerstukken II* 2007/08, 31 570, no. 3, para. 4.2.3. *Cf. Kamerstukken II* 1999-2000, 26 800 VI A, p. 6.

13 WRR, 2007, pp. 85-86, 98 and 141. All Dutch courts are barred from exercising constitutional review of formal legislation by Art. 120 of the Basic Law. For more information, *see* L.F.M. Besselink, 'An Open Constitution and European Integration: The Kingdom of the Netherlands', *SEW*, Vol. 44, No. 6, 1996, pp. 192-206.

14 De Visser, 2012, and V.A. van den Brink & H. van Meerten, 'Constitutionele toetsing in Nederland: de Europese dimensie', *SEW*, Vol. 55, No. 12, 2007, pp. 482-491.

15 ABRvS (*Afdeling Bestuursrechtspraak van de Raad van State)* 11 January 2017, ECLI:NL:RVS:2017:35, CRvB (*Administrative High Court*) 23 June 2017, ECLI:NL:CRVB:2017:2623 and CBb (*Administrative High Court for Trade and Industry*) 28 March 2017, ECLI:NL:CBB:2017:107.

16 On the difference between protecting constitutional identity by means of Art. 4(2) TEU and the national constitution, *see* (very elaborately) Konstadinides, 2015.

a clarification of their deviating positions is absent so far.[17] Therefore, the cases are difficult to evaluate.

This chapter analyzes the recent change in judicial behavior regarding EU law of the Dutch courts and places it in a comparative European context. It also assesses the potential of this judicial position to start a judicial dialogue on the fundamental issue of the Europeanization of core constitutional values.

The chapter is organized as follows. It starts with a brief description of the state of affairs in the Dutch literature and case law. Next, it describes the judicial doctrines on sovereignty and the applicability of EU law in the *OMT* case of the German Constitutional Court (*Bundesverfassungsgericht*) and the *Miller* case and the *HS2* case of the UK Supreme Court. It closes with an analysis of the implications of the recent behavior of Dutch courts, arguing that while it is still far from clear what the intent of the Dutch administrative courts is, the best way forward toward protecting the Dutch core constitutional values – if they were to opt for that course – would be to follow the British rather than the German example, making use of a cooperative dialogue with the Court of Justice, if needs be.

12.2 ALL QUIET ON THE DUTCH FRONT?

The question of the position and applicability of EU law within the Member States is about much more than the relation of individual norms to each other. There is a reason why Poiares Maduro has called the *Van Gend en Loos* case the '*declaration of independence* of EU law'.[18] Nothing less than the fundamental relationship between the Member States legal orders and the EU legal order is at stake.[19] More importantly, this issue is also about the constitutional loyalty of Member State judges. How should they manage the potential for conflict when both the constitution and EU law claim to take precedence over the other?[20] Given the abundance of attention these issues have drawn in both the academic literature and the case law of other courts, Dutch courts have been surprisingly

17 For a brief overview of the different meanings of 'judicial dialogue', *see* C. Zoethout, 'On the Different Meanings of "Judicial Dialogue" (book review)', *European Constitutional Law Review*, Vol. 10, No. 1, pp. 175-181 and M. Claes & M. de Visser, 'Are You Networked Yet? On Dialogues in European Judicial Networks', *Utrecht Law Review*, Vol. 8, No. 2, 2012, pp. 11-114. This chapter only deals with 'vertical' judicial dialogues between national courts and the CJEU.

18 Poiares Maduro, 2003, p. 504.

19 Abundant literature addresses this issue. *For instance, see* R. Barents, 'The Precedence of EU Law from the Perspective of Constitutional Pluralism', *European Constitutional Law Review*, Vol. 5, No. 3, 2009, pp. 421-446; G. de Búrca, 'Sovereignty and the Supremacy Doctrine of the European Court of Justice', *in* N. Walker (ed.), *Sovereignty in Transition*, Oxford, Hart Publishing, 2003, pp. 449-460 and J. Gerkrath, 'The Figure of Constitutional Law of the "Integrated State": The Case of the Grand Duchy of Luxembourg', *European Constitutional Law Review*, Vol. 10, No. 1, 2014, pp. 109-125.

20 Classic in this respect is still CJEU, Judgment of 17 December 1970 in *Case 11/70, Internationale Handelsgesellschaft*, [1970] ECR 1125, ECLI:EU:C:1970:114.

silent on them.[21] Only in 2015, the Supreme Court somewhat elaborately dealt with the matter in the case *Staat/Habing*.[22]

In essence, this case revolves around the question whether the Dutch state could be held liable for failing to correctly and timely transpose an EU directive, which ultimately resulted in a loss of vacation days by Mr. Habing. Since the 1950s, the Dutch Basic Law contains a provision (nowadays Art. 94) which (in the official translation) states that

> [s]tatutory regulations in force within the Kingdom shall not be applicable if such application is in conflict with provisions of treaties or of resolutions by international institutions that are binding on all persons.

In 1983, the constitutional legislator decided in an elaborate debate that this provision is the legal basis for the applicability of both international law and European law in the Dutch legal order. It concluded that whereas the government held that exceptions were possible for the protection of fundamental rights, EU law should be applied in the Netherlands as seamlessly as possible.[23]

However, the Supreme Court disagreed. In *Staat/Habing*, it confirmed its earlier position, which is that the applicability of EU law in the Netherlands does not rely on the Dutch Constitution, but on EU law instead. Article 94 of the Basic Law was considered of relevance only to the extent that it provides for a stricter regime of state liability than the European regime. The Court found that the EU principle of equivalence required that this stricter regime of state liability not only applied to international law but also to this particular case of nonconformity with EU law.[24]

For a long time, the main Dutch administrative courts either seemed to agree with the Supreme Court or did not take a position on the matter. First in 1995, and later in 2011, the Administrative Jurisdiction Division of the Council of State clearly accepted the autonomous applicability of EU law in the Netherlands.[25] However, in 2017, this court

---

21 There have even been special issues of scientific journals about particularly relevant cases. For instance, the second issue of the *German Law Journal* of 2014 was entirely dedicated to the *OMT* referral of the *Bundesverfassungsgericht*. This was certainly not an exceptional occurrence.

22 HR 18 September 2015, ECLI:NL:HR:2015:2722 (*Staat/Habing*). In its earlier 2003 landmark case *Rusttijden*, it simply repeated the CJEU's take on the autonomy of EU law in two short paragraphs. HR 2 November 2004, ECLI:NL:HR:2004:AR1797 (*Rusttijden*), para. 3.6.

23 *For instance, see* Besselink, 1996, p. 205, L.F.M. Besselink, 'Hoge Raad (HR), nr. C03/118HR, LJN: AO8913 (Civiel) en Hoge Raad (HR), nr. 00156/04 E, LJN: AR1797 (Strafkamer)', *SEW*, Vol. 53, No. 7/8, 2005, pp. 336-339 and L.F.M. Besselink et al., 'National Constitutional Avenues for Further EU Integration', Study, European Parliament, Directorate General for Internal Policies, Policy Department C: Citizens' Rights And Constitutional Affairs, Legal Affairs Committee, Constitutional Affairs Committee, PE 493.046 EN, Brussels, 2014, p. 159, available at: www.europarl.europa.eu/RegData/etudes/etudes/join/2014/493046/IPOL-JURI_ET%282014%29493046_EN.pdf.

24 HR 18 September 2015, ECLI:NL:HR:2015:2722 (*Staat/Habing*), paras. 3.4.2-3.4.4

25 ABRvS 7 July 1995, *AB Rechtspraak Bestuursrecht* 1997, 117 (*Metten*) and ABRvS 12 July 2011, ECLI:NL:RVS:2011:BR2048, paras. 2.3.1-2.3.2.

reversed its course when it explicitly referred to Article 94 of the Basic Law to support its judgment that national legislation should have been set aside to the extent that it contradicted a specific directive.[26] While this clearly is a different approach than in the 1995 and 2011 cases, the Court did not give any indication of this in its motivation. Article 94 was applied without any hint of this being out of the ordinary. In the months before this judgment, the two other top administrative courts had notably taken a similar approach.[27]

While these three cases are certainly dissimilar when it comes to the issues at stake, they have in common that the administrative courts choose the Basic Law over the direct application of European case law to support the setting aside of domestic legislation in favor of EU law.[28] Fundamentally, this seems to indicate that they join a minority position in the Dutch literature which argues that the position of the constitutional legislator still applies and that Article 94 of the Basic Law is the constitutional reason why EU law is to be applied in the Netherlands. The corresponding analysis is rather technical, but in essence it rests on two observations. First, the constitutional norms contained in the constitutional document called the Statute for the Kingdom of the Netherlands cannot be deviated from when concluding treaties.[29] Second, although the Basic Law does allow deviating from treaty norms, these necessitate an explicit statement of government and Parliament to that effect, something which has not occurred in the case of the European Treaties.[30] Consequently, the European Treaties cannot take precedence over the Dutch Constitution because they have not been approved in the right way to allow that.

Unfortunately, none of this reasoning was included in any of these three cases, nor did they include any reference to the other cases or scientific literature on this point. This makes the impact of these cases very challenging to assess. For instance, would the courts have taken a different approach if the material result of either approach would not have been the same? Should these cases be read as a burgeoning response to calls to protect the core values of the Dutch Constitution? Do the courts want to position themselves in a certain way vis-à-vis the Court of Justice? The lack of elaboration means that too much meaning is easily attached to the cases. For that reason, the next section does not seek to interpret the meaning of the cases as such, but assesses their *potential*, particularly in view of the 2007 proposal to follow the German example.

---

26 ABRvS 11 January 2017, ECLI:NL:RVS:2017:35, para. 3.2.

27 CRvB 23 June 2017, ECLI:NL:CRVB:2017:2623, paras. 4.9-4.11 and CBb 28 March 2017, ECLI:NL:CBB:2017:107, para. 7.2.2, respectively.

28 Interestingly, the material outcome of these cases did not depend on the position taken as to the applicability of EU law in the Netherlands.

29 H.G. Hoogers, *De normenhiërarchie van het Koninkrijk der Nederlanden. Een bijdrage aan het constitutioneel Koninkrijksrecht*, Nijmegen, Wolf Legal Publishers, 2009, pp. 51-52 and 60-61.

30 Hoogers, 2009, pp. 60-61 and C.B. Schutte, 'De stille kracht van de Nederlandse Grondwet. Beschouwingen rond het verbod aan de rechter om verdragen aan de Grondwet te toetsen', *RM Themis*, Vol. 164, No. 1, 2003, pp. 37-40. *Cf.* Besselink, 2005, p. 339.

12.3 Invoking the Constitution: What Is It Good for?

12.3.1 The Bundesverfassungsgericht

While the German Constitutional Court has a long-standing tradition of actively engaging with EU law, it was only in the relatively recent *OMT* case that it directly communicated with the CJEU.[31] The main problem it has been navigating is the potential for conflict between the 'independent' nature and applicability of EU law on the one hand, and its claim that the 'core' of the German Basic Law (*Grundgezetz*; GG) is to be protected against it on the other.[32] While the BVerfG may accept that the uniform application of EU law and its precedence over national law is of crucial importance to the EU, it still considers EU law limited by, and ultimately dependent on, the national constitutions.[33] The main reason for this is that the Basic Law contains an 'eternity clause' (Art. 79(3) GG), which protects Articles 1 and 20 of the Basic Law from amendment by any state authority.[34] On the basis of this, the Court concludes that while the German authorities were authorized to conclude the Treaties by the Basic Law, they were also necessarily limited by it. Simply put, they cannot have been able to attribute to the EU the competence to override the principles contained in Articles 1 and 20.[35] According to the BVerfG, this reading is supported by Article 23(1) GG, which confirms not only Germany's 'openness towards European integration' (in German: *Europarechtsfreundlichkeit*) but also the limitation of this integration by the eternity clause.[36]

In *OMT*, the BVerfG seems to have 'reset' this line of case law, elaborately reflecting on both the relation of the Basic Law to EU law and on its relation with the CJEU.[37] The BVerfG not only asked the CJEU for a preliminary ruling for the first time but also tried

31 BVerfG, Judgment of 21 June 2016, 2 BvR 2728/13 (hereinafter *OMT*). An English translation of almost the entire case is available here: www.bverfg.de/e/rs20160621_2bvr272813en.html. This tradition goes back to the *Solange* cases. *See* BVerfGE 37, 271 (*Solange I*) and BVerfGE 73, 339 (*Solange II*).

32 On the possibility and impact of such a conflict, *see* Barents, 2009.

33 To be precise: According to the BVerfG, the applicability and legitimacy of EU law in Germany ultimately depends on the specific attribution of competences by the Acts of Approval of the Treaties, which in turn are based on the GG. *OMT*, paras. 80-82 and 115-120.

34 The most important principles in this regard are human dignity (Art. 1) and democracy, based on popular sovereignty (Art. 20).

35 For instance, in the *Maastricht* and *Lisbon* Judgments, the BVerfG explained why and to what extent the Basic Law authorizes the German government and Parliament to conclude the Treaties of Maastricht and Lisbon. Because of the eternity clause, European law can never have precedence over the 'core' of the Basic Law. *OMT*, para. 115.

36 *OMT*, paras. 115-120.

37 For a substantive description of the *OMT* case and its relation with previous case law, *see* M. Payandeh, 'The OMT Judgment of the German Federal Constitutional Court. Repositioning the Court within the European Constitutional Architecture', *European Constitutional Law Review*, Vol. 13, No, 2, 2017, pp. 400-416. *Cf.* 2 BVerfG, Judgment of 6 July 2010, BvR 2661/06 (*Honeywell*), and BVerfG, Judgment of 30 June 2009, 2 BvE 2/08 (*Lisbon*).

to explain why it did not exercise its claimed competence of interfering with the judgment of the CJEU, even though it severely disagreed with it.[38]

Although the Constitutional Court bases the applicability of EU law in Germany on the Basic Law, it accepts the interpretative monopoly of the CJEU in principle. Even so, where agencies of the EU would "exceed their competences in a manifest (*offensichtlich*) and structurally significant (*strukturell bedeutsamm*) way", this could trigger *ultra vires* review by the BVerfG because the resulting EU law could no longer be based on a German Act of Approval, or ultimately on the will of the German people.[39] A specific type of *ultra vires* could occur should European law be contrary to the eternity clause. In such case, the constitutional identity of Germany would be threatened, which could trigger *identity review* by the Constitutional Court.[40] According to the Court, the result of both types of review can be that German public authorities are barred from applying the (interpretation of) EU law in question, while the German government and Parliament might be under an obligation to counteract it.[41]

While the *OMT* case has been analyzed as both a threat and an offer of cooperation, the Constitutional Court stresses its restraint and cooperative intent. For instance, no German court but only the Constitutional Court is allowed to exercise these kinds of review.[42] Second, the BVerfG considers itself bound to ask the CJEU for a preliminary ruling, and to interpret the EU law in line with this ruling, before finally exercising the *ultra vires* or identity review. In *OMT*, it took great pains to show that it did.[43] Third, the BVerfG even 'grants' the CJEU 'tolerance of error', which means that it goes as far as to accept the judgment of the CJEU even when it has severe objections to it as long as the CJEU uses 'accepted methods of interpretation'.[44] Reading all this, the question might even be why the Constitutional Court takes the trouble of constructing this rather complicated theory if it never intends to follow through invalidating the application of an

38 While some see this balancing act is as nothing more than a matter of saving face, it does provide an elaborate template for engaging with the CJEU. A. Pliakos & G. Anagnostaras, 'Saving Face? The German Federal Constitutional Court Decides Gauweiler', *German Law Journal*, Vol. 18, No. 1, 2017, p. 214.

39 *OMT*, paras. 115, 121, 138-154 and 157 (italics in the original, MD). Interestingly, Davies suggests that the BVerfG should not accept the CJEU's interpretative monopoly and focus on the interpretation of EU law instead. G. Davies, 'Does the Court of Justice Own the Treaties? Interpretative Pluralism as a Solution to Over-constitutionalisation', *European Law Journal*, Vol. 24, No. 6, 2018, pp. 358-375.

40 The admissibility criteria for both reviews are problematic, but beyond the scope of this contribution. *See OMT*, paras. 76-104 and Payandeh, 2017, pp. 413-415.

41 *OMT*, paras. 162-165 and 170-174.

42 *For instance, see* Payandeh, 2017, p. 404 and *OMT*, para. 150.

43 *For instance, see OMT*, paras. 170-180 and 190-209.

44 *OMT*, paras. 149-150 and 160-161.

interpretation of EU law in Germany.[45] After all, in its request for a preliminary ruling, the Court gave the impression that it would finally bite rather than just bark.[46]

One reason might be that the Constitutional Court is not all that clear on where it wants to draw the line. In *OMT*, it seems to have contradicted itself on the details of when the CJEU 'manifestly' goes too far. As Payandeh points out, it is hardly convincing that the Court claims that even the result of a 'thorough and well-reasoned interpretation', that takes the German Constitutional Court nine pages to analyze and that still is subject to fierce debate outside the courts, can be 'manifest', in the sense of 'obvious'.[47] Another reason might be that it did not want to risk a full-on conflict with the CJEU in *OMT*, or face the consequences thereof; it simply needed to save face.[48]

While that may be true, the case is still a striking attempt by one of the most influential constitutional courts to balance its task of protection of the national constitution, including the eternity clause, and the constitutional mandate of European integration. In the situation where it cannot abrogate either part of the Basic Law, it evidently intends to balance these interests through a judicial dialogue with the CJEU, even if this does not take the form of a traditional balancing test.

In *OMT*, the BVerfG seems to have reached the limits of what a constitutional court can do, short of the 'nuclear option' of nullification or secession.[49] It has tried to put absolute limits to Europeanization, explained these elaborately, directly engaged with the CJEU, and even went so far as to propose a specific interpretation of EU law rather assertively. As Davies suggests, entering into a dialogue with the CJEU on the interpretation of EU law seems to be a good way forward.[50] Setting absolute limits to Europeanization might not be, unless a court only uses these, or has to use these, an effective way of expressing genuine constitutional concerns that it is willing to balance with the genuine interests of EU law.

This also shows why the German example might not be the best example for the Netherlands to follow. Even if the legitimacy of the EU in the Netherlands may be enhanced with this style of case law, as the report of the Netherlands Scientific Council for Government Policy suggests, the constitutional legislator has not followed through on this advice. The Dutch Constitution hardly contains any provisions that clearly cannot

45 *Cf.* the Dissenting Opinion of Judge Landau in *Honeywell*, paras. 96-105.

46 BVerfG, Judgment 14. January 2014, 2 BvR 2728/13 (*OMT reference*), paras. 55-61 and 99-102 and N. Peterson, 'Karlsruhe Not Only Barks, but Finally Bites – Some Remarks on the OMT Decision of the German Constitutional Court', *German Law Journal*, Vol. 15, No. 2, 2014, pp. 321-327.

47 Payandeh, 2017, pp. 410-412 and*OMT*, paras. 149-150.

48 Pliakos & Anagnostaras, 2017, pp. 226-228.

49 For a comparison between the case law of the BVerfG and the theory of the Southern States in the American Civil War, *see for instance* R. Schütze, 'On "Federal" Ground: The European Union as an (Inter)national Phenomenon', *Common Market Law Review*, Vol. 46, No. 4, 2009, pp. 1069-1105 and M. Duchateau, *Het Europees Parlement als transnationale volksvertegenwoordiging. Een onderzoek naar volkssoevereiniteit, (con)federalisme en Europese volksvertegenwoordiging*, Deventer, Kluwer, 2014, Chapter 7.

50 Davies, 2018, p. 371.

be deviated from by EU law, and there still is no Dutch Constitutional Court. More importantly, this approach does not seem to sit well with the Dutch traditionally open approach to international law and the clear choice of the constitutional legislator in 1983 to stick to this open approach in principle.

12.3.2 The UK Supreme Court

The British example may be more helpful to the Netherlands. This example is most clearly to be found in the *Miller* case, in which the Supreme Court, like the *Bundesverfassungsgericht*, elaborately reflected on the relation between EU law and sovereignty.[51] In essence, the case revolves around the question whether the Secretary of State for Exiting the European Union needed the approval of Parliament for 'triggering' Article 50 of the Treaty on European Union (TEU). The status of EU law in the British legal order was important to this question because it is settled case law that the Crown has the prerogative power to make or unmake Treaties in the British dualist system (unless this is abrogated by Parliament), but it cannot exercise this prerogative in such a way that it changes domestic law.[52] Should EU law directly convey rights and obligations on British citizens, Parliamentary approval would be needed because exiting the EU would automatically change domestic law. An assumption the Supreme Court explicitly, yet wrongly, held was that triggering Article 50 TEU would inevitably lead to the end of Britain's EU membership, and thereby to the end of these domestically applicable European rights and obligations.[53]

Everyone involved agreed that, even though EU law is to be applied directly, without any need for a specific act of incorporation, and with precedence over even statute law, the reason why this is the case is the European Communities Act 1972, as amended.[54] Section 2(1) of that Act provides:

> All such rights, powers, liabilities, obligations and restrictions from time to time created or arising by or under the Treaties, and all such remedies and

51 *R (Miller) v Secretary of State for Exiting the European Union* [2017] UKSC 5 (24 January 2017) (hereinafter *Miller*).

52 For a thorough analysis, *see* N. Aroney, '*R (Miller) v Secretary of State for Exiting the European Union*: Three Competing Syllogisms', *The Modern Law Review*, Vol. 80, No. 4, 2017, pp. 740-745. *Cf* M.C. Elliott, 'The Supreme Court's Judgment in Miller: In Search of Constitutional Principle',*Cambridge Law Journal*, Vol. 76, No. 2, 2017, pp. 257-288.

53 *Miller*, para. 26. In *Wightman and others*, the CJEU held that, other than the EU Supreme Court assumed, the UK government could indeed withdraw its notification that it intended to withdraw from the EU. *Case C-621/18, Wightman and others*, ECLI:EU:C:2018:999.

54 *Miller*, paras. 60-68 and 87. No dissenting opinion disagreed on this point. This is in line with earlier case law. *See* P. Craig, 'Great Britain in the European Union', in J. Jowell & O. Dawn (eds.), *The Changing Constitution*, Oxford, Oxford University press, 2011, pp. 114-117 and Elliot, 2017, pp. 12-16.

> procedures from time to time provided for by or under the Treaties, as in accordance with the Treaties are without further enactment to be given legal effect or used in the United Kingdom shall be recognised and available in law, and be enforced, allowed and followed accordingly.[55]

The question that remained was how this Act related to the sovereignty of Parliament on the one hand, and the case law of the CJEU on the other.

Here, the narrative of the majority of the Supreme Court is, strictly speaking, contradictory. It held that the 1972 Act serves as a 'conduit pipe', the effect of which is to "constitute EU law [as] an independent and overriding source of domestic law".[56] As has likewise been pointed out by others, this is contradictory.[57] EU law is either an independent and overriding source of law (echoing the European case law) or dependent on a British Act for its domestic applicability. Nonetheless, the message was clear: Even though the applicability of EU Law in the UK is fully dependent on the 1972 Act, all rights, duties and rules which are derived from EU law are directly applicable in the UK.[58] In assuming that Parliament does not want to deviate from the 1972 Act, the Supreme Court has reconciled the full sovereignty of the British Parliament with the (almost) direct and independent domestic applicability of EU law. The only exception to date seems to be that British constitutional provisions that are even more fundamental to the British legal order than the European Communities Act itself are not to be deviated from. At least, that seems to be what the Supreme Court suggested in the earlier *HS2* case. In an *obiter dictum* opinion, the Court wrote that it would not readily assume that Parliament wanted to deviate from Article 9 of the Bill of Rights, which is fundamental to the relation between Parliament and the British courts.[59]

In essence then, the Court has turned the inalienability of sovereignty to the advantage of its absoluteness because, and as long as Parliament wills it so, there can be no obstacle to the applicability of EU law, including the case law of the Court of Justice. The only *caveat* that seems to apply is that some provisions of British law may be so fundamental to the British legal order that the Supreme Court will not assume that Parliament wanted to deviate from them. This clearly shows how the Court understands the relationship between the UK and the EU (however long it lasts): as an exercise of sovereignty, rather than as a limitation to it. The Court will police any limits that Parliament puts on Euro-

55 This is affirmed in Section 18 of the European Union Act 2011.

56 *Miller*, para. 65.

57 The reasons for the contradictory language seem to be mostly related to how the outcome of the case affects the balance of power between Parliament and the government. *For instance, see* Elliot 2017, pp. 12-16 and 29. *Cf.* Aroney, 2017, p. 739.

58 *Miller*, para. 62.

59 *R (HS2 Action Alliance Ltd)* v. *Secretary of State for Transport* (HS2) [2014] UKSC 3, [2014] 1 WLR 324, paras. 202-208. For a most insightful analysis of the case, *see* M.C. Elliot, 'Constitutional Legislation, European Union Law and the Nature of the United Kingdom's Contemporary Constitution', *European Constitutional Law Review*, Vol. 10, No. 3, 2014, pp. 379-392.

peanization. Parliament just happened to choose to impose (almost) none. Propitiously, the British constitution contains few, if any, formal obstacles that cannot be deviated from by Parliament.[60]

12.4 CONCLUSION

The relation between constitutional identity and Europeanization, and Member State's constitutional courts and the CJEU in particular, is as relevant today as it was directly after the German *Maastricht* Judgment. The relations between the CJEU and the German Constitutional Court were severely put to the test in the *OMT* case. This is not a unique occurrence, as is evident from the 'Taricco Saga'.[61] With these high-visibility cases, who would look for almost invisible signs that Dutch courts, with their open and cooperative tradition, are changing their stance on Europe? Certainly, there are no indications that these courts will soon be putting up the type of resistance the BVerfG and the *Corte Costituzionale* have shown. In that sense, it is understandable that there is very little international literature on recent Dutch case law on this matter. Comparative academic work generally (and rightly) reports that the 'primacy of EU law more or less goes uncontested' in the Netherlands.[62]

However, the three main Dutch administrative courts did recently change their position fundamentally, and it is hard to believe that this is a mere coincidence. It clearly shows that their acceptance of the autonomy of EU law cannot be taken for granted. This chapter has put this change of behavior in a comparative context in order to assess their potential as the start of a judicial dialogue on the fundamental issue of the Europeanization of core constitutional values. It has raised the question whether following the German example of (in)direct judicial dialogues with the CJEU, as the Netherlands Scientific Council for Government Policy (WRR) suggested in 2007, would be the best way forward.

While the Dutch Constitution does not have a 'core' that is unamendable or even a 'Europe article' that directs or limits Europeanization, there may still be a need for Dutch

---

60 For a precise explanation of this point and the requirement of a referendum that the European Union Act 2011 has introduced, *see* Besselink et al., 2014, pp. 193-195. For as discussion of the (non-)absoluteness of the sovereignty of Parliament, *see* Craig, 2011, pp. 112-113.

61 For instance, *see* Marino, this Volume, Section 4.4.4 and G. Piccirilli, 'The "*Taricco* Saga": The Italian Constitutional Court Continues Its European Journey: Italian Constitutional Court, Order of 23 November 2016 no. 24/2017; Judgment of 10 April 2018 no. 115/2018 ECJ 8 September 2015, Case C-105/14, *Ivo Taricco and Others*; 5 December 2017, Case C-42/17, *M.A.S. and M.B.*', *European Constitutional Law Review*, Vol. 14, No. 4, 2018, pp. 814-833.

62 M. Claes & J.H. Reestman, 'The Protection of National Constitutional Identity and the Limits of European Integration at the Occasion of the *Gauweiler* Case', *German Law* Journal, Vol. 16, No. 4, 2015, p. 966. *Cf.* A. Bobić, 'Constitutional Pluralism Is Not Dead: An Analysis of Interactions between Constitutional Courts of Member States and the European Court of Justice (October 10, 2016)', *German Law Journal*, Vol. 18, No. 6, 2018, p. 1411.

courts to develop a more identity-oriented narrative. Even though the Council of State believes that the core values of the Dutch Constitution are well protected at the European level, it does indeed claim that the Dutch Constitution contains core values that need protection.[63] Likewise, the advice of the WRR seems to apply even more strongly today than it did a decade ago. As in many EU Member States, a rise in strongly Euro-skeptic movements is visible in the Netherlands that put sovereignty, national identity and possibly even a 'Nexit' squarely on the political agenda. As the WRR suggested, it may enhance the legitimacy of the EU in the Netherlands to develop a clear narrative on who is responsible for the direction and limits of Europeanization. Not only could the 2017 cases of the administrative courts, which are based on Article 94 of the Basic Law, serve as a start of this, this approach would have the added benefit of conforming to a clear choice that has been made by the constitutional legislator.

If these cases would indeed be the first steps of their following the advice of the WRR, a few scenarios are plausible. Taking *Miller* as an example, they would certainly need to be much clearer and more elaborate on their understanding of the status of EU law in the Netherlands. While the practical consequences of such a new narrative are most likely to be minimal, this would make it quite visible that the reason for the dominant status of EU law is the choice of the constitutional legislator rather than that of the EU or Court of Justice.[64] Like the *Miller* case, such a line of case law could stress that Europeanization is an exercise of sovereignty rather than a limitation of it, while still assuring the unrestrained application of the EU law in the Dutch legal order. Like the European Communities Act 1972, this could serve as a good and insightful evidence of the clear choice that the Dutch constitutional legislator made in 1983.

The German example, on the other hand, seems to be less helpful for the Dutch case. While a reading is possible in which EU law is to be prevented from overriding both the statute and the Basic Law, to date the Dutch Constitution lacks any clear reference to the EU and it does not contain absolute limits. Should the Dutch courts, like the UK Supreme Court in the *HS2* case, take it upon themselves to elaborate on the Dutch core constitutional values and take a more active stance vis-à-vis the Court of Justice, an open dialogue with the Court of Justice seems to fit the Dutch cooperative tradition best. As Davies and Bobić suggest, the active stance the BVerfG took on the interpretation of EU law in *OMT*, or the UK Supreme Court in *HS2* for that matter, can serve as a good example, partic-

63 *Kamerstukken II* 2007/08, 31 570, no. 3, p. 21.

64 Irrespective of the possibility of constitutional review, a reading of the Dutch Constitution that bars courts from setting the constitution aside in favor of applying EU law, is possible. However, even in such a scenario, the content and wording of both documents generally make it easy to avoid a collision with EU law. M. Duchateau, 'Doorwerking van Europees recht en de plaats van de Nederlandse Grondwet', in S. Hardt et al. (eds.), *Bevrijdende en begrenzende soevereiniteit*, Den Haag, Bju, 2018, pp. 127-135 and L. F.M. Besselink et al., *De Nederlandse Grondwet en de Europese Unie*, Groningen, Europa Law Publishing, 2004, pp. 30-39.

ularly if it is combined with a clear explanation of these sensitivities.[65] However, Claes and Visser rightfully point out that in judicial dialogue, an exchange of *dikats* is not helpful.[66] It only seems to have turned *OMT* into a high-stakes game of 'chicken'.[67] This certainly would not fit the Dutch traditionally open approach to international law. Luckily, there are no indications that the Dutch administrative courts intend to move in such a direction.

65 Davies, 2018; Bobić, 2018, p. 1401.

66 Claes & De Visser, 2012, pp. 104-105.

67 F.C. Mayer, 'Rebels Without a Cause? A Critical Analysis of the German Constitutional Court's OMT Reference', *German Law Journal*, Vol. 15, No. 2, 2014, p. 141.

About the Editor

Dr. Martin Belov is associate professor in Constitutional and Comparative Constitutional Law at the University of Sofia 'St. Kliment Ohridski', Faculty of Law. He is also vice dean of the same law faculty. Martin Belov has been project researcher at Max-Planck Institute for European Legal History (Frankfurt am Main, Germany) and visiting researcher at the Institute for Federalism (Fribourg, Switzerland). He has specialized at the University of Oxford, Max-Planck Institute for Comparative Public Law and International Law, Heidelberg, Germany, University of Cologne, Germany and many other European academic institutions.

Martin Belov has been visiting professor and guest lecturer in European and Comparative Constitutional Law in many European universities: University of Girona (Spain), Europa-University 'Viadrina' (Frankfurt/Oder, Germany), European Law and Governance School (Athens), University of Södertorn (Stockholm, Sweden), Scuolla Superiore Sant'Anna (Pisa, Italy), University of Lisbon (Portugal), State University of Milan (Italy), University of Cologne (Germany), University of Bari 'Aldo Moro' (Italy), 'Masaryk' University (Brno, Czech Republic), Staatlichen Studienakademie (Dresden/Bautzen, Germany), University of Warsaw (Poland) etc.

Martin Belov has held public lectures at the University of Oxford, University 'Pompeu Fabra' (Barcelona), European Academy of Legal Theory, Goethe University (Frankfurt am Main), 'Sigmud Freud' University (Vienna), LUISS 'Guido Carli' (Rome), University of Lodz (Poland) and others.

Martin Belov is also member of several scientific organizations. He is member of the European Group of Public Law (EGPL), the International Association of Legislation (IAL) as well as of the Advisory Board of the CEE Forum (the Central and Eastern European Forum of Young Legal, Political and Social Theorists). He is member of the scientific board of several law journals in Italy and Serbia.

Martin Belov has published 14 books and more than 80 scientific papers.

About the Authors

François Andia (University Paris Nanterre, France)
François Andia, PhD student at Université Paris Nanterre.

Gavin Barrett (University College Dublin, Ireland)
Gavin Barrett is a professor specializing in EU Law in the Sutherland Law School, UCD and the sometime Jean Monnet Professor of European Economic and Constitutional Law there. He has written books, book chapters and articles in leading journals on Eurozone, the EU and democracy-related subjects. His latest book is *The Evolving Role of National Parliaments in the European Union: Ireland as a Case Study* (Manchester University Press, 2018).

Martin Belov (University of Sofia 'St. Kliment Ohridski', Bulgaria)
See about the editor section.

Stefano Dorigo (University of Florence, Italy)
Stefano Dorigo, PhD in International and EU Law, is a full time researcher of Tax Law at the University of Florence (Italy) and took the qualification to the functions of associate professor of Tax Law in 2013. Member of the Reviewing Board of *The Tax Law Quarterly* (Rivista trimestrale di diritto tributario) and of the *International Tax Law Review* (Rivista di diritto tributario internazionale), he has taught tax law and international and European tax law in many universities and in postgraduate courses. Author of three monographies and more than 60 essays on national, international and European tax Law published in Italian and European scientific journals.

Michiel Duchateau (University of Groningen, Netherlands)
Dr. Michiel Duchateau is Assistant Professor of Constitutional Law at the Department of Constitutional Law, Administrative Law and Public Administration at the University of Groningen. His research mainly focuses on (comparative) Europeanization of the constitutional position of EU Member State actors, sovereignty and the relation between legal orders and vertical separation of powers.

Florian Heindler ('Sigmund Freud' Private University, Vienna, Austria
Florian Heindler is an assistant professor at Sigmund Freud University in Vienna. He currently teaches private international law and Austrian private law. Florian Heindler holds a PhD degree in law from the University of Vienna as well as master degrees in

philology and law. Apart from his work in academia, Dr. Heindler is counseling for an Austrian bank and works as of counsel for an international law firm.

Catherine Van De Heyning (University of Antwerpen, Belgium)
Catherine Van de Heyning is assistant professor of European fundamental rights law at the University of Brussels and a criminal and human rights lawyer at the Brussels bar.

Ivan Ingravallo (University of Bari 'Aldo Moro', Italy)
Ivan Ingravallo is associate professor of International Law at the University of Bari Aldo Moro, where he teaches EU Law and International Institutional Law. He obtained a PhD from the University of Teramo (2003). He has published two books (Il Consiglio di sicurezza e l'amministrazione diretta di territori, Editoriale Scientifica, 2008; L'effetto utile nell'interpretazione del diritto dell'Unione europea, Cacucci, 2017), coedited another two (*Evolutions in the Law of International Organizations*, Martinus Nijhoff, 2015; *Peace Maintenance in Africa*, Springer, 2018) and is author of several articles and book chapters devoted to International Law, International Institutional Law and EU Law issues. He is editor-in-chief of the periodicals *La Comunità Internazionale* (*Editoriale Scientifica*) and *Studi sull'integrazione europea* (*Cacucci*).

Aleksandra Kustra-Rogatka (Nicolaus Copernicus University in Toruń, Poland)
The author is an assistant professor at the Nicolaus Copernicus University in Toruń. She specializes in comparative constitutional law, constitutional theory and European constitutionalism.

Silvia Marino (University of Insubria, Como/Varese, Italy)
Silvia Marino is Associate Professor of European Union Law at the University of Insubria, Cono and Varese, Italy. She has authored two monographs on civil judicial cooperation, and many articles on topics related with the area of freedom, security and justice, and with EU Competition Law.

Cesare Pinelli (University Rome 'Sapienza', Italy)
Cesare Pinelli is Full Professor of Constitutional Law at the University of Rome Sapienza. He is Director of the Doctorate in Public Law and Director of the review 'Diritto pubblico'. Prof. Pinelli is former member of the IACL's Executive Committee (2004-2010) and Member of the Venice Commission. Cesare Pinelli is author of books and essays in Italian, English, French, Portuguese and German, among which are 'The Kelsen/Schmitt controversy and the evolving relations between constitutional and international law', Ratio iuris, 2010; 'The formation of a constitutional tradition in continental Europe since World War 2', European Public Law, 22, n. 2, 2016; Constitutional Pluralism, in New

Developments in Constitutional Law. Essays in honor of Andras Sajo, eleven, 2017, 309 ss.

Patricia Popelier (University of Antwerpen, Belgium)
Patricia Popelier is full professor of constitutional law at the University of Antwerp. She is vice president of the International Association of Legislation, Member of the Jean Monnet Centre of Excellence ACTORE, Convenor of the Standing Research Group on Subnational Constitutions in Federal and Quasi-Federal Systems of the International Association of Constitutional Law, Member of the Scientific Committee of EURAC Institute for Federalism in Bolzano and Member of the Impact Assessment Observatory in Rome. She is also member of several editorial boards of journals and book series, including the journal *Theory and Practice of Legislation*. Her research covers different aspects of constitutional law, with a special interest for federalism and multilevel governance, political institutions, constitutional courts, democracy, rule of law and legislative studies.

Joan Solanes Mullor (University 'Pompeu Fabra', Spain)
Joan Solanes Mullor is a lecturer of constitutional law at Pompeu Fabra University, Barcelona. He was a postdoctoral researcher at the Faculty of Law of Trento University (2015), and he was appointed a visiting scholar at KU Leuven (2013) and a visiting researcher at Harvard Law School (2009). He received his PhD in law from Pompeu Fabra University (2014) and holds an LLM from Harvard Law School (2009) and an LLM in Public Law from Pompeu Fabra University (2008). His research focuses on institutional design, separation of powers and public regulation in national legal systems and the European Union.

Printed by Libri Plureos GmbH in Hamburg,
Germany

9 789462 369634